Sartre,
Foucault,
and Historical
Reason

Sartre, Foucault, and Historical Reason

Thomas R. Flynn

VOLUME ONE
Toward an
Existentialist
Theory
of History

The University
of Chicago Press
CHICAGO & LONDON

THOMAS R. FLYNN is the Samuel Candler Dobbs
Professor of Philosophy at Emory University. He is author
of *Sartre and Marxist Existentialism,* published by the
University of Chicago Press, and co-editor of *Dialectic and
Narrative.*

The University of Chicago Press, Chicago 60637
The University of Chicago Press, Ltd., London

© 1997 by The University of Chicago
All rights reserved. Published 1997

Printed in the United States of America

06 05 04 03 02 01 00 99 98 97   5 4 3 2 1

ISBN (cloth): 0-226-25467-4
ISBN (paper): 0-226-25468-2

Library of Congress Cataloging-in-Publication Data

Flynn, Thomas R.
     Sartre, Foucault, and historical reason / Thomas R.
Flynn.
          p.   cm.
     Includes bibliographical references and index.
     Contents: v. 1. Toward an existentialist theory of
history.
     ISBN 0-226-25467-4 — ISBN 0-226-25468-2 (pbk.)
     1. History—Philosophy.   2. Sartre, Jean Paul,
1905–   .—Contributions in philosophy of history.
3. Foucault, Michel—Contributions in philosphy of
history. I. Title.
D16.8.F628   1997
901—dc21   97-5137
                                                CIP

For Gert

Contents

Preface:
The Diary and the Map

The discipline of history has undergone considerable scrutiny in the second half of this century, chiefly at the hands of the New Historians in France and their philosophical colleagues. In particular, the rise and demise of structuralist methodologies in the 1950s and 1960s questioned the core presuppositions of traditional historiography and seemed to render the latter somehow quaint, if not thoroughly misguided.

As often happens, the extremes of the initial attacks, while serving to chasten the complacency of more traditional methodologies, revealed their own inadequacies when challenged to account for the constellation of phenomena called "human history." The humanist cast of historiography, by which individuals and peoples sought meaning and identity as well as moral guidance, had been under suspicion among specific historians of a positivist bent since the second half of the nineteenth century. The structuralists simply intensified that contrast by setting aside "total narrative" and exemplary biography in favor of microhistory and impersonal social conditioning—what Foucault calls "system." Put somewhat crudely, temporal relations, especially the linear time of traditional subject-centered narratives, were encompassed, if not subsumed, by spatial and quantitative ones. The "mapping" of historical coordinates and the comparativist charting of synchronic relationships displaced the unfolding of events along a single time line as the focus of attention, leading one major historian to insist that "time is not essential to history."[1]

But the moral and humanist aspects of the historian's enterprise die hard. Indeed, the recent concern with postmodern ethics suggests that these perennial problems have returned in different guise to haunt their poststructuralist exorcists. Still, by taking Foucault and Sartre as personifications of this conflict, it is not my intent to create a postmodern Sartre, much less a modern Foucault. Such conversions by definition are as futile in philosophy as they are in religion. The emblems of the diary and the map capture these writers' characteristic styles while underscoring their apparently irreconcilable differences in trying to "make sense" of history.

The theme of reason in history is played in many registers. To the extent that it deals with the issue of "history" as opposed to "histories," it is an ontological problem. As such, it centers on the nature and unity of the historical subject and subject matter, whose meaning/direction (*sens*) it examines. Of course, the issue is likewise epistemic in its questioning of the unity or homogeneity of historical rationality. And the broadly moral dimension of historiography, so evident in Sartre's committed history, is being questioned by less subject-oriented historical discourse. These and other aspects of the question will emerge as we pursue our comparativist study. But the decision to trace this theme in the writings of Sartre and Foucault respectively is scarcely haphazard. History is integral to the philosophical thought of each, and the various related issues arise in stark contrast throughout their works. With little exaggeration, they could be described as philosophers of temporalized and spatialized reason respectively. The significance of this characterization will emerge as we progress. But in differing over the issue of historical intelligibility, each bears the weight of an alternative and competing understanding of the nature of reason itself.

Since his death in 1980, Sartre has published more than most authors do in a lifetime. A good portion of that posthumous material, as we might expect, addresses moral concerns. But many pages of works written long before the *Critique of Dialectical Reason* are devoted to the philosophy of history, and that was not expected. With the appearance of over

450 pages of notes for the second volume of the *Critique,* subtitled by its editor "The Intelligibility of History," and the publication of over 580 pages of his *Notebooks for an Ethics,* significant portions of which grapple with the problem of relating ethics (*la morale*) and history, the time has come to reconstruct the philosophy of history that underlies Sartre's writings. Since we are dealing for the most part with fragments not intended for publication, "reconstruction" is the term that best qualifies our enterprise. The aim of the present volume is to erect an existentialist philosophy of history according to plans scattered throughout the Sartrean corpus. Like any piece of architecture, the result will have to be judged not only on its aesthetic appeal but on its ability to sustain the weight it is expected to bear.

I shall be applying these two criteria of aesthetic consistency and functionality to Sartre's reconstructed theory, for one of my chief contentions is that Sartre's entrance into theoretical history is guided by the twin and interrelated values of *moral integrity* (call it "existential authenticity with a social conscience" or what in the 1960s he termed the ideal of "integral man") and *aesthetic coherence* (the appeal of freedoms to one another in creative tension or harmony). Their interrelation, I shall argue, is mediated by the amphibious value of *unity,* which can walk on the shores of moral probity, countering the forces of division and dissolution, or swim in aesthetic waters, resisting the currents of brute facticity and the senseless. That Sartre views history from a moral perspective should come as no surprise. He has long been recognized as a philosopher with a basically moral outlook. But that his theory is heavily inspired by aesthetic considerations may raise an eyebrow or two. So I shall underscore features of what I call his "poetics" of history as we progress, leaving their summation and analysis for the conclusion of the present volume.

Sartre and Foucault were often compared in different contexts. One sensed both embarrassment and mild annoyance on the part of the younger man when the inevitable contrast was drawn. Indeed, in a moment of weakness or candor, Foucault described Sartre as the last of the nineteenth-century philosophers! The plausibility of this claim we shall appreciate once we enter what Foucault calls the "modern episteme." But my reason for studying this pair in tandem is not merely to use each as an illuminating foil for the other. There is a sense in which Foucault too is guided by a moral and an aesthetic vision of history. In his case, what may shock and perhaps even scandalize is reference to the moral, not the aesthetical, and to vision of any kind, especially if one discounts his final publications. Foucault is usually taken for (and sometimes described himself to be) a skeptic, a historical relativist, and an opponent of the hegemony of vision that Descartes and his school are credited or blamed for ushering into early modern thought. Foucault relegated talk of History with a Hegelian "H" to another discursive epoch (and its anachronistic holdouts). And yet, as I hope to show, Foucault employs a *diacritical* vision to undermine the oculocentrism of modern society, and he does so in favor of a moral ideal in his later thought, which is not unlike that of Sartrean existentialism. Indeed, he was once directly challenged with this apparent resemblance.[2]

Though it is always risky to distinguish the writer of fact from the one of intent, we shall better appreciate both thinkers if, after having followed the enterprise of each on his own terms, we assume a larger perspective to compare and contrast them. The theme of reason in history is particularly apt for this mutual study since, for both men, not only did reason enter into history but history penetrated reason. Each shared a non-Platonic view of reason and truth; both respected the practicality of reason and the politics of truth. Correspondingly, each devoted hundreds of pages to "histories," whether psychoanalytical and sociological (Sartre) or archaeological and genealogical (Foucault). In the course of our analysis, we must explain the philosophical significance of these excursions into the historian's field. For in both instances, more than mere pleasure trips, they are integral to what each takes (his kind of) philosophy to be.

A significant portion of each author's material which I shall analyze remains virtually terra incognita. This includes many of the essays and interviews gathered into the four volumes of Foucault's *Dits et écrits*[3] and several of his unpublished lectures at the Collège de France as well as the hundreds of pages of recently published Sartrean writings that I mentioned above. Although the appearance of Foucault's works caused a flurry of activity among philosophers but especially among social scientists, none of these responses, to my knowledge, has addressed the topic of reason in history at any length. And the Sartre volumes are just beginning to be appreciated.

Acknowledgments

The two volumes that constitute this project reflect the support of several foundations and institutions in addition to the many individuals from whose insights I have benefited over the years. The latter are too numerous to name, but the former include the American Council of Learned Societies, which awarded me the initial senior research fellowship that allowed me to follow Foucault's final lectures at the Collège de France just before his death in 1984. A grant from the Mellon Foundation through the National Humanities Center as well as the ideal research conditions provided by the center itself enabled me to amass sufficient material for two volumes and to write an initial draft of the first one. Emory University granted me a leave and Villanova University a visiting professorship that permitted sufficient leisure to complete the final draft of the present volume. I am deeply appreciative of the financial and moral support of the administrators, faculty, and staff of these organizations without whose assistance I could never have completed this work.

Works Frequently Cited

Also:

C   The Content of the Form (White)
HT   History and Tropology (Ankersmit)
IPH   Introduction to the Philosophy of History
           (Aron)
PS   Philosophy of Jean-Paul Sartre (ed.
           Schilpp)

Where I employ my own translations from works available
in English versions, I follow the English citation by a reference to the original, designated by "F" and the page number.

PART ONE

In the face of the royal-empiricist model, [Miche-
let] invented a republican-romantic paradigm of
history by which the latter must still conduct
itself—as long as it wishes to remain a history and
not a comparative sociology or an annex of economic or political science.
  —Jacques Rancière, *The Names of History*

Chapter One
Living History:
The Risk of Choice and the Pinch of the Real

In the notebooks that Private Jean-Paul Sartre carried with him throughout the tedious months of his mobilization in Alsace during the "Phony War" of 1939–40, amid the usual observations of a conscript ten kilometers from the front we find interspersed a series of suggestive and often brilliant philosophical reflections, many of which would find their way into *Being and Nothingness.* Here is Sartre snatching moments from the banalities of military routine to jot down thoughts on the nature of time, on authenticity, and on love, freedom, and responsibility.

It is not surprising that this intellectual diary also contains his first remarks on the meaning of history and the nature and possibility of historical knowledge. Like his companions, Sartre was shaken by the imminence of the Nazi threat and by the realization of his own powerlessness before it. But, unlike his fellow soldiers, Sartre responded with a reflective assessment of the meaning of it all, indeed, of whether one can even ask about *the* sense of it *all.* His remarks scattered throughout the six notebooks still extant constitute the beginning of what I shall be calling an "existentialist" philosophy of history. Although inchoate

To confront Sartre and Aron is to reflect on two conceptions of the relation between thought and reality, between the imaginary and the real.
—Etienne Barilier, *Les Petits Camarades*

and largely exploratory, these reflections are philosophically first-rate and in several instances serve to illuminate Sartre's observations in subsequent works. Moreover, they constitute a kind of dialogue with Sartre's friend and former schoolmate, Raymond Aron, who had distinguished himself as a philosopher of history by publishing two important works in that field the year before.[1] So let us begin our study of Sartre's emergent theory with a brief survey of Aron's position as Sartre read it in these early works.

ARON'S CHALLENGE

> Objectivity does not mean universality, but impartiality.
> —Raymond Aron, *Introduction to the Philosophy of History*

In his *Memoires,* published shortly before his death, Raymond Aron acknowledged that his doctoral dissertation, *Introduction to the Philosophy of History: An Essay on the Limits of Historical Objectivity,* was the seminal text for his subsequent thought.[2] This magisterial work constitutes his critique of historical positivism and rationalism while espousing a kind of historical relativism, namely, perspectivism, based on the priority of theory over history, the insuperable plurality of systems of interpretation, and the fact that "the preferences of the historian dictate the choice of the system."[3] Against the positivists, he asserts the futility of trying to grasp the historical event "as it was," free from decision and hence interpretation.[4] He counters historical rationalism with the aphoristic remark that "the necessity [of any historical sequence] is not real and [its] reality is not necessary" (*IPH* 223; F 279). And against both positivists and rationalists Aron argues for the priority of intuitive comprehension over lawlike explanation. He thinks his relativism follows from the denial of an absolute or ideal observer—God—presumed by positivist and rationalist alike: "The truth about the past is accessible to us if, like Hegel, we rise to an absolute point of view. It escapes us by definition if we ourselves think we are historically determined and partial" (*IPH* 99; F 123).

But Aron's is only a kind of relativism. His intention is to combat the historical relativism of Ernst Troeltsch, Wilhelm Dilthey, and others. He defends a nonabsolute objectivity that remains within the limits of ambiguous elements, on the one side, and unreachable totalities, on the other. In fact, the aim of his seminal study, as its subtitle announces, is to determine the *limits* of historical objectivity, not to deny its validity as a

concept or a working principle. Aron continues to believe in the norms
of the scholarly community, the "collective representations" shared by
a particular generation of scholars.[5] Each period "chooses" its past with
which it communicates by an ongoing reading of its documents. His
concept of collective representations, derived from Emile Durkheim but
read in a neopragmatist fashion, resembles what Richard Rorty will
later term a "community of common discourse" and Jürgen Habermas a
Kommunikationsgemeinschaft. Aron summarizes this "relativism" neatly
when he notes: "The constituent part and the totality remain elusive,
but between these two extremes objective knowledge is constructed"
(*IPH* 114; F 141). In other words, objective history must be found between indeterminable facts and ungraspable totalities. It is these limits
that Sartre will try to overcome.

In the course of his study, Aron articulates a problem that will be of
special concern for Sartre, particularly in his later years, that of the *unity*
of human history. In fact, the director of Aron's dissertation, Léon
Brunschvicg, had reproached him at its defense for turning history into
"a drama without unity."[6] On this matter, Aron is skeptical: "The unity
of human development, unintelligible if it is real, ineffective and transcendental if ideal, should be both concrete and spiritual, like that of a
person or a collectivity. It must rise above the duality of nature and
spirit, of man and his environment, for man is seeking within and by
means of history a vocation that will reconcile him with himself" (*IPH*
149; F 184). Such a quasi-Weberian task for historiography is noble but
futile, Aron assures us, because of the human's essential incompleteness
and freedom, a thesis one can easily recognize as existentialist in tone.[7]
We shall find Sartre seeking historical unity by appeal to that very freedom which Aron believes renders such unity impossible.

Yet if "ultimate" historical knowledge eludes us, if we can never
grasp atomic historical facts, first causes, or final syntheses, Aron argues
against classical historical relativism, against Troeltsch, Durkheim, and
Dilthey, for example, that a broad field of objective knowledge remains
open to us. Inspired again by Max Weber, whose thought he helped introduce into France, Aron defends the ideal of self-critical historical
(and thus philosophical) investigation. This vocation is man's ever re-
newed calling to freedom through responsible action, that is, his or her
mission to reconcile humanity and nature, essence and existence,
through participation in the collective works of the state and culture.[8]

Still, we are left to navigate according to our individual or collective lights between the simple fact and the total account, neither of which is accessible to us. And the lines of possible navigation are multiple and relative to the individual historian's interest.

SARTRE'S RESPONSE: THE ABSOLUTE EVENT

Such is Aron's challenge to his former companion, a challenge Sartre did not hesitate to take up. In one of his almost daily letters to Simone de Beauvoir from the front he observes: "Then I wrote in the notebook about history; everything in the notebook goes by problem; for a week now it has been history, and refutation of Aron, of course."[9]

Sartre could sympathize with much in Aron's theory; for example, with the claims that the lived (*le vécu*) is by nature inaccessible to reflective thought, that human freedom is essentially incomplete, and that "the theory of history is one with [*se confondre avec*] a theory of man."[10] But the basis of Aron's "skeptical moderation," namely, that "the complexity of the world of history corresponds to a pluralist anthropology" (*IPH* 276; F 349), would not sustain Sartre's philosophical leanings, whether Husserlian or (later) Marxist. Implicit in Sartre's rejection of Aron's "pluralist anthropology" is an objection to be raised by Habermas against Foucault decades later: such pluralism favors the political status quo since it provides no solid basis to legitimize social change. So Sartre undertakes this dialogue with Aron in what might be termed a series of interrupted responses, as if the cares of the day intermittently called him away from the encounter, which in fact they did.

A Nascent Ontology

I will preface Sartre's response with a brief survey of the ontology that grounds it, concepts that will form the core of his next major publication and masterwork, *Being and Nothingness,* for he always thought ontology (the question of being) was essential to philosophy properly speaking.[11] These concepts too are being worked out piecemeal in the notebooks. Sartre acknowledges three distinct, irreducible, but interrelated dimensions of being. Inspired by Hegel, he terms these "being-in-itself" or the nonconscious, "being-for-itself" or, roughly, consciousness, and "being-for-others" or the interpersonal, the public. He uses powerful metaphors to capture the difference between these three realms of being. The in-itself is inert, opaque, "sticky," and so forth. It is the sphere of brute fact, of chance, and of our facticity (the givens of our existence). The for-itself, by contrast, is spontaneous, translucent, the internal negation or "nihilation" of the in-itself, a "hole" in being. If the in-itself is thinglike in its inert self-sameness, the for-itself or consciousness is no-thingness in its spontaneity and nonself-identity. Finally, the for-others marks off the domain of other for-itselfs as Other. Irreducible to either of the other two dimensions, being-for-others depends on the contingent fact that another consciousness exists. That existence qualifies my being and makes possible a number of new relationships of which the social and the historical are paramount. Correlative to our embodiedness, the for-others denotes our liability to have the meaning of our projects "stolen" from us by the look [*le regard*] of the Other. Although Sartre does not develop these categories here as he will in *Being and Nothingness,* they are already sufficiently formulated in his mind that he can employ them with ease, as we shall now observe.

Ontological Status of the Historical Event

Aron once insisted to Sartre that his *Introduction* was a "plea for philosophical and methodological atheism" (*WD* 204). As we have just seen, he argued that both positivist and rationalist made tacit appeal to God in defense of historical objectivity. The flaw in Aron's argument, as Sartre readily observes, lies in its own idealist postulate, namely, that whatever counts as a fact must do so solely for a consciousness, and that an "absolute" fact can be so only for an absolute consciousness. Sartre had already rejected the transcendental ego.[12] In language anticipating *Being and Nothingness,* he once again resists this "degradation of the in-itself into being-for" and argues instead for the ontological status of facts as sheer "in-itself," a robustly realist position that he will never entirely abandon. But the facts in question are *historical;* it is not a case of the simple in-itself (facticity) of a single consciousness. Hence Sartre must stretch his budding ontology in a way not repeated in *Being and Nothingness* by claiming that "there is a certain in-itself, not of the for-me, but of the for-others [*pour-autrui*]" (*WD* 205; F 252). Facticity qualifies our interpersonal and public life as well. This is a decisive claim for the ontology of history he is constructing.[13] For if history is to be more than biography, it must be not just my story, it must be their story, it must be ours.

Given this analytical focus on consciousness, Sartre, the would-be realist, must escape the so-called principle of immanence, the key thesis of philosophical idealism, which entails that all reality is consciousness-referring. Epistemological idealists have traditionally argued that reality is mind-dependent and that, in George Berkeley's famous expression, "to be is to be perceived." Curiously, in the *War Diaries* Sartre does not appeal to the counterprinciple of intentionality according to which all consciousness is other-referring, a mainstay of phenomenology and basic to his own thought.[14] Rather, he points out that the existence of the "other," so graphically described by means of shame-consciousness in *Being and Nothingness,* is a fact rooted in the reality of being-in-itself. The for-others is not a luminescence that shines only while another consciousness is present, which would signify a relapse into idealism. And the reciprocity of two or more for-itselfs, he notes, is an existential modification of each. Exhibiting the kind of thinking that will continue through the *Critique,* he urges that such reciprocity, even if taken to be a mere nominalist sum of constitutive consciousnesses, presumes a prior unity. Sartre is seeking historical unity and the objectivity of historical facts and events (he fails to distinguish between them) in a realm that is ontologically prior to consciousness as such, namely, being-in-itself. He does not think this unity need be based on transcendental consciousness and ultimately on God, as Aron appears to believe. Instead, he asks whether there is not "an existence proper to the reciprocal existential modification, an existence that would be posited neither in terms of for-itself nor in terms of for-others" (*WD* 205; F 252). The answer, he implies, lies in *the special in-itself of the for-others,* which he will soon call the "event" (*WD* 299). This, we may conclude, would be the locus of historical facticity. Its temporal dimension would be what he calls "simultaneity." The only example Sartre offers confirms this view.

Consider a conversation between two people. Besides the respective facts that each happens to be talking, there is the mutuality which we call "the conversation" itself that exists beyond the being-for-itself of each participant, though not independent of the individuals involved. To borrow Sartre's metaphorical mode, "the in-itself precisely grasps afresh what escapes it in the nihilation [of the in-itself by consciousness] by giving to that very nihilation the value of a *fact* appearing in the midst of the in-itself" (*WD* 205; F 252). In other words, the occurrence of the conversation must be registered and reckoned with over and above the speech acts of the individual speakers. "This fact does not exist-for-anyone," he insists against the idealists, "it simply *is*" (*WD* 206; F 253). This is the fact or event on which his historical realism will hang.[15]

The facticity of consciousness or being-for-itself is the limit to the transparency of consciousness: "It is a fact *in-itself,* escaping any nihilation, that there exists at this very moment a *for-itself* which is nihilation of the in-itself" (*WD* 205–6; F 253). Any attempt to surmount this facticity by reflection, that is, by raising it to a second level, itself becomes a fact (a "reflective facticity") and so falls prey to the in-itself as well. In other words, there is an inescapable dimension of givenness to our every situation. We never start from absolute zero. Though he will employ terms as diverse as "being-in-itself," "simultaneity," and "the practico-inert" to express the factical dimension or givenness of any situation, this conviction will sustain Sartre's ontological "realism" throughout his career.

The inevitability of facticity, Sartre is claiming, inverts the idealist argument from immanence. If consciousness is everywhere, so too is facticity. Moreover, the latter is temporally prior; it enjoys an "already there," a "having-been" character that Karl Jaspers and Martin Heidegger had already underscored.[16] For this reason Sartre must defend his metaphysical realism with an ontology of temporality and a concept of the historical event that respect facticity while allowing for the obvious plurality of interpretations that one and the same fact permits. His study of temporality in *Being and Nothingness* expresses an individualist viewpoint and carries little immediate historical relevance. His remarks in the *War Diaries,* on the contrary, are aimed precisely at elucidating a historical realist position.

The Temporal Aspect of Historical Realism

Characterizing the fact of the conversation's having taken place, Sartre employs the odd expression "is-been" (*soit-été*) that will figure prominently in his discussion of the temporal trajectory of consciousness in *Being and Nothingness.*[17] This strange locution captures the ephemeral nature of the moment, its hard transitivity: it passes, yet its having been is irrefragable. "Time is the facticity of nihilation," Sartre urges. "Our temporality and our facticity are one and the same thing" (*WD* 210). Although an early example of what Iris Murdoch calls his penchant for "great inexact equations," this remark catches Sartre grappling with the temporal aspect of facticity (doubtless inspired by his previous study of Heidegger). As seems inevitable when reflecting on time, Sartre has recourse to metaphor, comparing this unity of temporality and facticity to the reflection we vaguely notice in the shop windows as we look at the displays, images that suddenly disappear when we change position. "However, that evanescent, iridescent, mobile reflection of the in-itself, which frolics on the surface of the for-itself and which I term facticity—that totally *inconsistent* reflection—cannot be viewed in the same way as the opaque, compact existence of *things*. The being-in-itself of the for-itself, in its ungraspable reality, is what we shall term the *event*. The event is neither an accident nor something which occurs within the framework of temporality. The event is the existential characteristic of consciousness inasmuch as the latter is recaptured by the in-itself" (*WD* 212; F 260, translation modified). This analysis of the event locates it at a level more basic than existential temporality itself. He calls that level "simultaneity," a nod toward Bergson over Heidegger. Sartre wants to account for the event uniquely in terms of his most fundamental categories, the in-itself and the for-itself, and he finds it in their mutual relation.

SARTRE'S RESPONSE: SIMULTANEITY

Sartre once acknowledged that it was his reading of Henri-Louis Bergson's *Time and Free Will* as a young man that made him want to do philosophy (*PS* 6). The full impact of Bergsonism on Sartre's philosophy, both positively and by way of reaction, has yet to be analyzed. It seems to have inspired the second prong of the younger man's defense of historical realism against Aron, simultaneity.

In Bergson's work the term serves to unify the multiplicity of temporal fluxes of agents and objects so that their relative ordered sequence can be established. The medium or "third of comparison" for any pair of fluxes is simultaneity or pure duration. Because such a medium exists, we can acknowledge the recalcitrance of past events and their sequential order without appeal to an ideal observer and without slipping into relativism or unqualified Einsteinian relativity, which became Bergson's major concern in the first quarter of the present century. As Gilles Deleuze has argued, Bergson's point in *Duration and Simultaneity* (1922) and elsewhere was not to correct Einstein but "by means of the new feature of duration (*la durée*), to give the theory of Relativity the metaphysics it lacked."[18]

After "event," the second basic concept in Sartre's initial reflections on the temporal foundation of history is "simultaneity." It is an irony to be pursued in volume 2 that this is the very term used to focus a post-modern valuing of the spatial over the temporal and of Foucauldian "histories" over Sartrean History.[19] Tellingly, however, Sartre's use of "simultaneity" is distinctively "temporal," albeit problematically so (hence the scare quotes). It is a difficult term which Sartre will subsequently abandon. But its not always univocal uses reveal his desire to achieve a living history that conveys both the risk of the possible and the pinch of the real.

We first encounter the term early in his *War Diaries*. With a blend of psychological insight and ontological acuity that will become his philosophical signature, Sartre describes the "unveiling of that terrible *simultaneity* which, fortunately, remains hidden in its full dimensions":

> I imagine if one lived that simultaneity *here* in its full dimensions, one would spend one's days with a heart that bled like Jesus's. But many things screen it from us. So I live in suspense between past and future. The events of which I learn took place long ago; and even the short-term plans about which I'm informed have already been realized (or failed) by the time I learn of them.
>
> The letters I receive are scraps of present surrounded by future; but it's a past-present surrounded by a dead future. I myself, when I write, always hesitate between two times: that in which I am, while I pen the lines for the recipient; that in which the recipient will be, when he reads my words. It doesn't make the "surrounding" unreal, merely timeless—as a result of which it's blunted and loses its harmfulness. . . . Similarly, the letters I receive no longer appear to me as worrying signs of the existence of other consciousnesses, but instead as a convenient form these consciousnesses have assumed in order to travel to me. When I read the letters . . . [these consciousnesses] are a bit petrified, a bit out of date. But if simultaneity is suddenly unveiled, then the letter is a dagger-blow. In the first place, it reveals events that are irreparable, since they are past. Secondly, it allows what is essential to escape: the present life of those consciousnesses, which have survived their letters, which have escaped from them, and which are pursuing their lives beyond those dead messages—like living beings beyond their graves. (*WD* 65–66)

"Simultaneity" in this description seems to function as the pretemporal (but not atemporal) locus of facts/events in their brute facticity and in-terrelation, conceptually and logically prior to incorporation in a narrative. But in addition to their "irreparable" character as having already occurred (as in-itself), simultaneous events enjoy that lively feature of risk and expectation that belongs to the "not yet" dimension of the human event in its present occurrence (as for-itself). This incomplete or "living" character of contemporaneous events—what we might call the *"historical present"*—is what produces the "dagger blow" effect. An apt image would be that of a film in which the voice of the deceased letter-writer utters the words as someone reads a note from a friend. In this usage, simultaneity brings us into the living presence of the agents and events "like living beings beyond their graves." We shall encounter another, related function of simultaneity when we discuss "historialization" and "comprehension" below. An existentialist approach to history will attempt to communicate this presence.

But it is the *unifying function* of "simultaneity" that is crucial for his budding theory in the *Diaries,* a function continued under other guises, namely "practico-inert" and "totality," in his later works. For Sartre, "simultaneity" denotes the "temporal" aspect of that underlying unity presumed by the reciprocity of the conversationalists, mentioned above. Again, he turns to his ontological categories to define "simultaneity" as "the connection of being which, in the unity of the in-itself, reunites from without *this* for-itself to the inner depths of the in-itself" (*WD* 212; F 260). He distinguishes this from the popular understanding of "simultaneity" as the contingent fact that several objects are found in the same present. In Sartre's technical sense, "simultaneity" is "an existential characteristic constitutive of time: the necessity for a for-itself, insofar as it is colored by the in-itself, to coexist with the totality of the in-itself whose negation it makes itself." Put more simply, "simultaneity" refers to the basic unity that obtains from a pretemporal viewpoint between a conscious occurrence and the world in its depth, that is, between a fact as registered in consciousness and all that is happening elsewhere or that has happened thus far. As he summarizes the distinction, "the in-itself of the nihilation of the in-itself is the event; the unity of the nihilated in-itself with the in-itself of the nihilation of *that* in-itself, is simultaneity" (*WD* 212; F 261). As he will later repeat in *Being and Nothingness,* "this flight of nothingness [*le néant*] before the in-itself constitutes temporality" (*WD* 212; F 261; see *BN* 123). Finally, anticipating his discussion of temporality in the later work, he designates as "the *present*" the event in simultaneity, that is, the nihilated past (*passé nié*) as such.

Although it would be misleading to translate this pretemporal and unifying role of Sartrean "simultaneity" into another idiom without qualification, one is reminded of the famous distinction between A- and B-series of events that British philosopher John M. E. McTaggert made early in this century.[20] Events in the A-series approximate Sartre's existential temporality, the flowing sequence in which past and future are divided by a flowing present or now. The future blends into the past by means of the ever present now. But events can also be distinguished according to the relation of "earlier than" and "later than" (the B-series), and these events retain their relationship regardless of changes in the A-series. In other words, the fact that Caesar crossed the Rubicon prior to his assassination remains true whatever events may subsequently occur. We recognize something like Sartre's "in-itself of the for-others" in the events of the B-series. The hard facticality of the sequence of events must be incorporated by whatever consciousness might encounter it. The concept of simultaneity reflects this series of events.

Where Sartre's usage breaks with the concept of the B-series is in the notion of "presentness" that his ontology requires we retain from the A-series as McTaggert describes it. For the temporal ekstases are not merely psychological experiences, as McTaggert seems to believe, but are constitutive of the very being of human reality. This is the present life of the letter-writer, for example, whose consciousness strikes me as a dagger blow. It is past, no doubt, and ever will be (a member of the B-series), but it is capable of being experienced in its historical present. This is something McTaggert's B-series resists at the price of remaining a kind of sterile numerical sequence.

So when Sartre describes the "absolute" event, he is approximating McTaggert's B-series. When he speaks of dating that event and making it "of the world," he is closer to the A-series, though, again, he would deny that the events in this series are merely psychological or unreal. But when he refers to the dagger blow of simultaneity, he is moving beyond McTaggert's dichotomy, synthesizing features of each in our experience of the historical present.

In order to shed some light on this complex term, let us consider the three places where he discusses simultaneity in *Being and Nothingness*. Not surprisingly, all appear in the context of the interpersonal or being-for-others. The first occurs in Sartre's famous phenomenological description of the look (*le regard*) as rendering evident the existence of other consciousnesses. Recall Sartre's example of the voyeur who suddenly hears what he takes to be the footsteps of a third party (the Other) looking at him gazing on another. The Other's look is not only spatializing, he insists, it is also temporalizing: "The appearance of the Other's look is manifested for me through an *Erlebnis* [lived experience] which was on principle impossible for me to get in solitude—that of simultaneity" (*BN* 266–67).[21] Simultaneity is a function of being-for-others and, specifically, of "the temporal connection of two existents which are not bound by any other relation," else each would subsume the other in its world. The lived experience of simultaneity supposes "the copresence to the world of two presents [subjectivities] considered as presences-to." In an implicit appeal to the Bergsonian function of simultaneity (time and duration) as mediator of comparative temporalities, Sartre explains that each subjectivity refers the other to a "universal present" as to a "pure and free temporalization which I am not." Without having clarified the matter any further, he concludes with a metaphor: "what is outlined on the horizon of that simultaneity which I live is an absolute temporalization from which I am separated by a nothingness" (*BN* 267). That absolute temporalization "outlined" by the lived experience of simultaneity would seem to be the locus of the "absolute event" introduced in the *War Diaries* to combat Aron's historical relativism. Here too event and simultaneity are correlative.

Sartre returns to the matter of simultaneity for the second time as he concludes his discussion of the existence of others in *Being and Nothingness*. If he had employed "simultaneity" in the *War Diaries* to register the fact of the conversation's taking place, here he uses the term to denote the mutual negation of myself and other that both constitutes our respective being-for-others and makes any synthesis into a totality inconceivable. Sartre finds here "a kind of limit of the for-itself which stems from the for-itself but which qua limit is independent of the for-itself" (*BN* 300). He calls it "something like facticity." It rides on the back of the factical duality of these negations, "as the expression of this multiplicity . . . as a pure, irreducible contingency." In sum, "It is the fact that my denial that I am the Other is not sufficient to make the Other exist, but that the Other must *simultaneously* with my own negation deny that he is me." He concludes: "This is the facticity of being-for-others." Recall that in the *War Diaries* he had located the event in the special in-itself (facticity) of for-others. Here "simultaneity" unites as it separates consciousnesses among themselves. As with Bergson, it mediates a multiplicity without reducing it to homogeneity. Years later Sartre will attempt to achieve this delicate balance of sameness and otherness, of unity and difference, with his dialectical notion of totalization. But the problematic concept of simultaneity is being pressed into similar service in Sartre's predialectical thought.

He makes a final reference to "the fact of simultaneity" toward the end of the book when elaborating the social dimension of being-in-situation by appeal to "techniques for appropriating the world," most notably, language:

> Each man finds himself in the presence of *meanings* which do not come into the world through him. . . . In the very act by which he unfolds his time, he temporalizes himself in a world whose temporal meaning is already defined by other temporalizations: this is the fact of simultaneity. We are not dealing here with a limit of freedom; rather it is *in this world* that the for-itself must be free; that is, it must choose itself by taking into account these circumstances and not *ad libitum*. (*BN* 520; F 603)

Whence he concludes that "it is by choosing itself and by historializing itself [*s'historialisant*] in the world that the For-itself historializes [*historialise*] the world itself and causes it to be *dated* by its techniques" (*BN* 521; F 604). He will develop this concept of "historialization" in subsequent works, especially in the *Notebooks for an Ethics*. But the unifying role of "simultaneity" is gradually subsumed by other terms.

Though Sartre has not yet sorted out these distinctions, much less organized them into an ontology of temporality, it is already clear that the understanding of historical fact which grounds his realism presumes a concept of event and its correlate, simultaneity, that are more than the transitory nothingness of consciousness but less than the inert solidity of physical things. And his "existentialist" intuitions demand a unity that respects the plurality of consciousnesses in their respective individuality and presence. In an ontology that comprises only three categories of being, namely in-itself, for-itself, and for-others, the locus of events and hence of history remains problematic. At this early stage we find

Sartre stretching this threefold ontology to accommodate the historical event. In *Being and Nothingness* the ontological status of the event seems scarcely to have concerned him at all.[22]

Aron's Appeal to *Verstehen*

Aron discussed at length the major distinction drawn by German philosophers between explanation and understanding (*Verstehen*). Since Dilthey, the latter had been considered the proper method of the human sciences (*die Geisteswissenschaften*). Unlike the causal explanations of the natural sciences, the human sciences and especially history allow the possibility of an "inside" account, as it were, from the viewpoint of the intentions of the agents of sociohistorical change themselves. The challenge is to achieve this inner viewpoint, and that is where the method of comprehension or understanding enters. Is it the exercise of some esoteric faculty? Is it merely a refined form of analogical reasoning? Though Sartre adopts the method for the existentialist psychoanalysis he proposes in *Being and Nothingness,* he will not address this disputed issue at any length until *Search for a Method.*[23] But he is already disturbed by Aron's use of *Verstehen.*

Sartre agrees with Aron that, whether it be a question of explanation or of understanding, the same historical event can carry different layers of meaning (*signification*). The First World War, for example, can be judged in terms of Anglo-German colonial rivalry, Bismarck's Pan-Germanism, or the militarism of the Junker class (to limit oneself to Sartre's anti-German alternatives at the time). As a diplomatic historian, one can read the conflagration in light of Bismarck's alliances with Russia and Austria. Or one can discover the seeds of the conflict in the court and the person of the kaiser.[24] But Sartre questions the *irreducible parallelism* of these "systems of interpretation" that Aron accepts from Weber, namely, the belief that each account is true of the event under a different description. For, Sartre objects, these descriptions and explanations *never converge.* In fact, it is to his lack of a concept of simultaneity as just described that Sartre attributes Aron's "historical skepticism" (*WD* 296; F 359). Indeed, if one were to seek an early antecedent for Sartre's dialectical concept of totalization, it would lie in this suggestive but undeveloped, rather ambiguous and nondialectical notion of simultaneity.

UNITY OR TOTALITY?

Is the intelligibility of History fragmentary or total? Fragmentary, says Aron. Total, replies Sartre, and he cites his old school chum to refute him more precisely.

—Etienne Barilier, *Les Petits Camarades*

Sartre has always been a realist in epistemology and an individualist in metaphysics.[25] His response to Aron and Weber builds on this foundation by insisting that these different levels of signification are human and that their unity depends on that of the primitive project of human reality.[26] The rivalries in Europe on the eve of the Great War, for example, are human choices, not the expression of impersonal, larger-than-life forces. Sounding like a full-blown existentialist, Sartre explains that it is human agents who decide the meaning (*sens*) of any given situation and "man is a unitary totality" (*WD* 298).

But the First World War is what Durkheim calls a "social fact." How can even a plurality of individuals account for its unity, if such there be? At this juncture Sartre seeks social unity with a bow toward Heideggerian *Mitsein* (being-with), which he reads in a sense that will later cause him to deny its ontological primacy: "*Mit-sein* . . . means that each time one wishes to find in an individual the key to a social event, one is thrown back from him to other individuals" (*WD* 298). In effect, one is sent on a trip to infinity, Hegel's "bad" infinite that knows no synthesis. It is ironic that Sartre will labor under this same handicap in his philosophy of history until he develops an adequate social ontology in the *Critique* nearly twenty years later.[27] In the meantime, he has at his disposal only the ontological triad of being-in-itself, -for-itself, and -for-others. As he explains, every fact is a fact-for-others.

That Molière presented a particular play at the Hotel de Bourgogne on the sixth of May, 1680, though produced by the convergence of a plurality of consciousnesses (*Mitsein*), *as a fact* ("an undated lapse of time [*écoulement*]" confers a kind of synthetic unity on these consciousnesses "in the mode of in-itself." "And that unity," Sartre adds, "is opaque and inexhaustible; it is a veritable absolute. . . . Its content is entirely human, but the unity itself insofar as it is existence *in-itself* is radically nonhuman [*inhumain*] (*WD* 299; F 363). This is the facticity of the for-others discussed earlier and to which Sartre will return briefly in

Being and Nothingness. Sartre now identifies it as the event (*l'événement*) and draws his conclusion:

> Thus the *event* is ambiguous: nonhuman [*inhumain*], inasmuch as it clasps and surpasses all human reality, and inasmuch as the in-itself recaptures the for-itself which escapes it by nihilating itself; human, in that, as soon as it appears, it becomes "of the world" [*du monde*] for other human realities who make it "blossom" [*éclore à soi*]—who transcend it, and for whom it becomes a *situation.* (*WD* 300; F 364)

The ambiguity of the historical event will be a guiding theme of the *Notebooks for an Ethics* when he resumes his reflections on history after the war.

The major role of the event surfaces as he explains: "for it is this event in its absolute existence that the historian intends [*vise*]." This is the absolute reality Sartre believes will meet Aron's challenge and save him from the ravages of historical relativism. But it will not do so easily. As he admits, "the profound ambiguity of historical research lies in the need *to date* this absolute event, that is to say, to place it in human perspectives" (*WD* 299; F 363). So the possibility of multiple interpretations arises from the "for-others" character of the event, that is, from its availability to and assumption by consciousness. But its status, as in-itself and simultaneous, accounts for its factical condition.

The event joins that line of ambiguous phenomena and "metastable" conditions that populate Sartrean thought, symptomizing a basic tension in his own work and perhaps in the human condition as well. In the present case, because there is an event-in-itself (the "absolute event," as he calls it), one can distinguish the interpreted from its interpretation. In other words, one is not left with a Nietzschean infinity of interpretations of interpretations. So there are "absolutes" in Sartre's thought. One such is the historical event; another is individual choice. As we shall see, the two are not unrelated.[28]

Three Levels of Historical Analysis

Sartre's reflections on simultaneity and the event lead him to the most important methodological prescription of the *War Diaries,* namely, that the historian must move on *three planes:* "that of the for-itself, where he tries to show how the decision appears to itself in the historical individual; that of the in-itself, where this decision is an absolute fact, temporal but not dated; finally, that of the for-others, where the pure event is re-captured, dated and surpassed by other consciousnesses as being 'of the world'" (*WD* 300; F 364). By discounting the "absolute event" and simultaneity (with the totality of events at that point), Aron and Weber have had to accept the parallelism that, Sartre believes, leads to relativism. But as a result and more seriously, in Sartre's eyes, they have neglected the primary role of the individual agent in historical causality. Anticipating his criticism of structuralists a quarter century later, he objects that, by focusing on the situation acting on the man, such philosophers of history have left us with a disjunction of significant levels. Proposing the counterhypothesis, Sartre will consider "the man projecting himself [*se jetant*] through situations and living them in the unity of human reality" (*WD* 301; F 365). In other words, he is sketching the core of an "existentialist" theory of history. But his sought-after historical unity seems to be approaching the idealist's "totality"—what Dilthey called "the coherence of life" (*Die Zusammenhang des Lebens*). Indeed, in *Being and Nothingness,* he will make it "the principle of [existential] psychoanalysis . . . that man is a totality and not a collection" (*BN* 568). So in March of 1940 Sartre enunciates the strategy he will pursue for the next thirty years in his attempt to elucidate at one and the same time the epoch and the individual agent.[29]

THE KAISER'S WITHERED ARM

In short, this is an attempt to trace from the idiosyncrasies of a monarch the direct evolution of international political events—from his essential nature, the course of his country's destiny.
—Emil Ludwig, *Wilhelm Hohenzollern* (p. x)[30]

Having established provisionally three levels of historical investigation, Sartre turns to the one which will hold his lifelong interest, that of the individual project as historical cause. The actuality of the German threat directed him to its analogy with the First World War. In the intellectual framework we have just described, his reading of Emil Ludwig's biography of Wilhelm II suggests the first statement of a theme to be repeated with variations throughout his career: can we find an "internal relation of comprehension" (*WD* 301; F 365) between Germany's English policy and the kaiser's withered arm? Let us summarize Sartre's early thought on the meaning of history with a survey of his answer to this question, fully aware that he intends it as "an example of method and not . . . a factual historical truth." In other words, his creative response is a thought experiment, "a metaphysics of 'historiality' [*historialité*]" to show "how historical man freely 'historializes' himself [*s'historialise*] in the context of certain situations" (*WD* 301; F 366).[31]

Sartre begins his hypothetical analysis with a warning against a simple psychoanalytic answer which, by its implicit naturalism, is antihistorical. In words that reverse in advance a famous phrase of Foucault, he insists: "History can be understood only by *the recovery and assumption of monuments*" (*WD* 301); in other words, only by turning monuments into documents.[32] Without such assumption of the past, one may have causal sequence but not history properly speaking. So the challenge Sartre sets himself is "to draw a portrait of William II as human reality assuming and transcending situations—in order to see whether the different signifying layers (including the geographical and social layer) are not found unified within a single project, and in order to determine to what extent Wilhelm II is a *cause* of the '14 war" (*WD* 301). From what follows, it is clear that his principal concern is the kaiser, not the war.

So Sartre sets out on the first of his "existential psychoanalyses." As he will do with increasing thoroughness in the cases of Baudelaire, Tintoretto, Genet, himself, and especially Flaubert, Sartre marshals the facts to be interpreted: facts of empire, of inter- and intrafamilial relationships (Sartre has always been at his best in psychological descriptions), of the personnel serving the crown, of Bismarck's political legacy, of social, economic, and geographic circumstances, and, above all, of the fact of the emperor's congenitally disfigured left arm.[33] He makes much of the fact that Wilhelm as crown prince succeeded his grandfather, that a marked generation gap intervened between the ruling groups and that the young emperor, choosing to live his infirmity by demonstrations of autonomy from the liberalizing influence of his English mother, became the person he was, a "human totality," precisely in the way he appropriated the aforementioned facts. In other words, Aron's parallel levels of explanation-comprehension *converge* when we treat the historical personage in terms of the unity of his "historialization" (*WD* 318; F 386).

Sartre raises the obvious objection that he has turned a historical study into a biographical sketch (*une monographie*) which merely reveals the individual as artisan of his own destiny.[34] What of his influence on others? What of the historical agent? What of Wilhelm as *responsible* for World War I? Sartre is better at raising such difficulties at this stage than at answering them. But, clearly, these are the questions that matter to him.

The basic issue in the philosophy of history, as Aron sagely observes, is that of the relation between the individual and the social.[35] Sartre feels the press of this question as well, but his answer will remain unsatisfactory even to himself as his subsequent reflections in the *Critique* make clear. At this early stage, he offers three considerations in response.

First, while admitting the existence of historical "forces," whether religious, cultural, or economic, he presses the protoexistentialist thesis that "their resistance must be felt" (presumably by the individual in question) in order to be worthy of consideration. Against the Marxist view, for example, that myth is the effect of a state of affairs on consciousness, Sartre argues that very state of affairs is itself constituted by the project of a human reality for whom the choice of myth is one possibility. This is a view that he will defend, if later in somewhat chastened form, throughout his career.

But which human reality should we investigate? Historians typically speak of collectives, of the Prussian government's Pan-German policy, for example. Sartre seeks an answer in the concept of *situation*.[36] The situation and the individual are interrelated but, as he wryly warns, "that doesn't mean one can get the situation back into the individual by squeezing a bit" (*WD* 330). The relations of signification between ideas, movements, tendencies, and claims—in sum, the traditional métier of the historian—all are real but nonsubstantial in the ontological sense. Though they depend upon the agent's appropriation for their existence, they modify her situation as being-for-others. The *Mit-sein,* as Sartre calls it, requires that "one is oneself only by projecting oneself freely through the situations constituted by the Other's project" (*WD* 330). This is an idea he will expand in *Being and Nothingness* under the rubric of "techniques for appropriating the world." These techniques denote social realities such as signposts and natural languages that exist (in act) only as appropriated by us but whose meaning, as we saw, has been established by others. Sartre implicitly acknowledges Durkheim's "social facts" when he admits that the partition of Germany and Pan-Germanism, though meaningful only for individuals, by nature infinitely surpasses any sum of individuals but without thereby requiring appeal to any collective consciousness. In effect, these facts qualify each

German's situation after the First World War and each in turn, by his mode of appropriating this common phenomenon, enriches the situation *for-others* (see *WD* 330–31).

It is the ontological primacy of the individual agent, albeit modified by her historical situation, that warrants the third claim in Sartre's response, namely, that the description of the concrete development of an ideology in terms of political givens, for example, should be accompanied by a biographical study (*une monographie*) of one of the important personages of the time "in order to show the ideology as a lived situation, and one constituted as situation by a human project" (*WD* 331). Only by means of such a biography, Sartre seems to think, can the reader be delivered from remote abstractions such as the movement of imperialism and from the dull chronology of meaningless events to the lived reality where agents experience the risk of choice and the pinch of the real. Such a move would afford us the desired "synthesis of signification" from the most diverse layers of historical analysis. Otherwise, we are left at most with Aron's parallel levels of signification, which, in effect, are merely "abstract conditions of possibility for a concrete, human phenomenon" (*WD* 331).

So, at the same time that Sartre is fashioning the ideas that will gain him renown in *Being and Nothingness,* he is likewise reflecting on the philosophy of history. Alive to the core problem of such an enterprise, namely, the metaphysics of the collective-individual relation, he rejects both atomic individualist and "collectivist" solutions. But his concepts of being-for-others and situation as well as reference to the role of others in constituting historical facts and situations leave us little more than the hint of a resolution to the problem of relating the individual and the social. Yet of greatest importance at this early stage of his career, and a portent of his major achievement in the philosophy of history, is his insistence on the biography-history dyad for uncovering the lived reality of otherwise abstract and externally related significations. His underlying questions, "How do we understand a man in his totality?" and its converse, "How do we understand a totality in the man?" will remain the driving Sartrean queries for the rest of his career.[37]

Chapter Two

The Dawning of a Theory
of History

T hough Sartre's masterwork, *Being and Nothingness* (1943), contains valuable thoughts on temporality, facticity, and the human project, its looking/looked-at model for interpersonal relations leaves us at best with a philosophical anthropology but not a social philosophy properly speaking.[1] His phenomenological description of being gazed upon as I covertly view another (*le regard*) is both his experiential answer to the philosophical problem of "other minds" and the paradigm for interpersonal relations in his existentialist ontology. The interpersonal (being-for-another) in this classic text resembles a game of mutual stare-down. Indeed, the individualist spirit conveyed by that work left many in doubt that an existentialist philosophy of history was even possible.[2] In his subsequent *Notebooks for an Ethics* Sartre seems to sanction this view with a Nietzsche-like aphorism: "Existentialism against History through the affirmation of the irreducible individuality of the person" (*NE* 25). Yet these same *Notebooks* contain some of Sartre's most sustained reflections on the nature and scope of historical thought.

If the *War Diaries* are, among other things, an extended debate with Raymond

In History, too, existence precedes essence.

—Sartre, *Notebooks for an Ethics*

Aron about the meaning of History, the chief interlocutor in the *Note-books* appears to be Hegel as interpreted by the French Hegelians, Alexandre Kojève and Jean Hyppolite.[3] Though Sartre was not among that illustrious group, which included Jacques Lacan, Georges Bataille, and Maurice Merleau-Ponty, who attended Kojève's lectures on Hegel's *Phenomenology of Spirit* in the 1930s, he quotes liberally from their published version in his *Notebooks* and, to a large extent, adopts the Russian émigré's Marxian Heideggerian reading of the text, with its emphasis on the master-slave dialectic and the moving power of labor in the narrative.[4]

Jean Hyppolite's two-volume translation of Hegel's *Phenomenology* (1939–41) was followed by a two-volume commentary on the same, which appeared in 1946. The former is regularly employed and the latter is frequently cited, especially early in the *Notebooks,* sometimes to balance a Kojèvian reading.[5] In fact, Sartre had an explicit exchange with Hyppolite about phenomenological immediacy and the dialectic at the time he was composing these *Notebooks* (1947).[6] So when Sartre admits, "I knew of [Hegel] through seminars and lectures, but I didn't study him until . . . around 1945," we can assume it was with the aid of these commentators that his study progressed.[7]

Notebooks for an Ethics comprises the sketches and working notes for the moral philosophy that Sartre had promised at the conclusion of *Being and Nothingness* but never produced. Written in 1947 and 1948, they reflect the ethics of authenticity that characterize Sartrean existentialism at its apogee. These posthumously published notes reveal a more positive, optimistic thinker than the author of *Being and Nothingness* is popularly taken to have been.[8] Still, despite their number and extent, Sartre's thoughts on history in the *Notebooks* offer at best intimations of a theory of historical understanding. As they stand, they constitute a jumble of phenomenological "arguments," outlines, and aphorisms, waiting for the organization and review they never received. To assess their meaning and worth, I shall order his remarks under two cardinal headings in this chapter, namely, the historical event and the conditions of historical activity, reserving consideration of the dialectic of historical understanding and the nature of History itself for the next two chapters respectively. Since the event and the historical agent are commonly discounted by the New Historians in France, among whom Foucault is often listed, we must determine how Sartre understands and employs these concepts in his developing theory.

THE AMBIGUOUS HISTORICAL EVENT

At the conclusion of his survey of the New History in France, François Dosse observes that "any renascence of the historian's discourse demands the resurrection of what has been rejected ever since the beginning of the *Annales* school, i.e., events."[9] Though scarcely an *Annaliste,* Sartre was aware of the pivotal role of the historical event as well as its problematic nature. Early in the *Notebooks* he muses: "Perhaps History is an unsolvable problem but one that is posed in ever better ways" (*NE* 27). The chief source of this insolubility is the *ambiguity* of the historical event, which, as we have seen, had already disturbed Sartre in his *Diaries.* In a set of essays entitled "What Is Literature?" published the year the *Notebooks* were begun, Sartre sees as a major task for literature in his day to find "an orchestration of consciousness which will permit us to render the multi-dimensionality of the event."[10] This basic ambiguity stems from several interrelated considerations.

Human Reality. First of all, 'the historical event is a human, not a natural, phenomenon. But human reality, as we know from *Being and Nothingness,* is a "detotalized totality."[11] So too is the historical collectivity that incorporates it (see *NE* 20, 85, 122, 490) and ultimately for the same reason, that is, because of the "inner distance" proper to human consciousness, which Sartre terms "presence-to-self," and which constitutes the ontological ground of Sartrean freedom.[12] "Human reality," in Sartre's lapidary phrase, "is what it is not [its future, its possibilities] and is not what it is [its past, its facticity]" (*BN* 123). Whatever it is, it is in the manner of nonbeing it, that is, as its internal negation or "nihilation" (*BN* 34). Races, nations, classes, sexes as well as social predicates such as exigency, obligation, and duty (*CM* 269; *NE* 258)—all are permeated with that otherness, freedom, and lack of self-coincidence that characterize their component human realities. They will never be entirely what we say they are—another lesson from *Being and Nothingness.*

"In History, too, existence precedes essence [that is, representation]," he now writes. "*Separation* in History brings it about that it is never totally what one thinks it is" (*NE* 32; F 38). It follows, Sartre believes, that the resultant dualities of contingency-necessity and of part-whole will have to be suppressed in favor of one or the other of their terms by those who deny (Pascal) or apotheosize (Hegel) history respectively. Given these typically Sartrean dualities, the quest for unity in history, announced in the *War Diaries,* becomes acutely problematic. Here, as later in his existential biography of Jean Genet, *Saint Genet,* Sartre counsels us not to subordinate one side of the dichotomy to the other but to grasp both terms boldly "to describe and demonstrate their ambivalence" (*NE* 21). Given that Sartrean authenticity demands choosing to live our lack of self-coincidence with the anguish such lack of identity entails, we are, in effect, being invited to adopt an "authentic" posture toward History, though he does not use the word.[13] As consciousness (the for-itself) always surpasses the givens of its situation, so we are always "more" than our history. We are our history in the manner of not-being ("nihilating") it. This lack of full coincidence with our historical facticity is the ontological source of our freedom and our hope, both individually and as a collectivity.

Ontological Status. The second reason for the ambiguity of the historical event is its ontological position "intermediary between physical fact and free *Erlebnis*" (*NE* 36). As such, it exhibits features of both the causal (physical) and the noncausal (free) orders that Sartre adopts from Kant. As part of nature, the event is subject to the laws of the physical universe (for example, I can send a message via carrier pigeon) and to its hazards (the bird may be killed by a predator). Yet the event is the product of purposeful human action, limited by the detotalizing activity that is human freedom but allowing us to grasp the agent's intention. It is this ambiguity, Sartre holds, that enables the Marxists to appeal to causal, not dialectical, explanation when dealing with concrete phenomena, since "the dialectic, as stemming from Hegel, suppresses inertia and multiplicity" (*NE* 37). Revealing a sensitivity to the weakness in his own dialectic that both Aron and Claude Lévi-Strauss will later point out, Sartre adds: "A dialectic without unity is inconceivable. What is more, once represented (reflection), every dialectic acts through the representation of the dialectic, therefore nondialectically" (*NE* 37). This will emerge a decade later as the problem of discussing dialectical Reason in necessarily nondialectical language.

Contingency. From the ontological status of the event, that is, its bifocal nature, follows the further ambiguity of the necessity-contingency relationship. Thus a given undertaking can be said to have succeeded both because of human initiative in overcoming obstacles and because these obstacles were not greater. If my enemy had not had the sun in his eyes as I passed by, I should not have achieved my mission. Yet it is up to me to preclude foreseeable dangers. "Possibles," Sartre writes, "get realized *in terms of probability*. Freedom," he adds, "lives within the sphere of the probable, between total ignorance and certitude" (*NE* 335). He takes this ambiguity to be the warrant for statistical reasoning in the social sciences. But like the Marxist "causal" explanations, such reasoning succeeds only by focusing on one side of the ambiguity, in this case mathematical probabilities, and ignoring the other, namely, human purposiveness. It thereby manifests the "analytic" mind-set that Sartre is combatting.[14]

The historical event is thus subject both to the uncertainties of chance, which affect it as physical nature, and to the unforeseeabilities of human freedom. In this last regard Sartre mentions the historian Jean de Pierrefeu, whose quip he had cited in the *War Diaries* to the effect that if Wellington had been smart enough to realize he was beaten at a crucial point in the battle of Waterloo, he would have withdrawn and proved himself correct (see *WD* 298). And the ambiguity of the event is compounded by the *reversal* of this nature-freedom relation inasmuch as an agent "as thing" becomes predictable while historical "things," the consequences of a scientific discovery, for example, become unpredictable. The unpredictability of scientific discoveries has always constituted a difficulty for unreconstructed historical materialists. For Sartre, it simply underscores the ambiguity of the historical event.

Where the *War Diaries* spoke of the historical fact as being-for-others recaptured by being-in-itself, the *Notebooks* refer to "necessity within contingency but taken up again by contingency" (*NE* 60). The reversal is instructive. Earlier, Sartre was struck by the brute recalcitrance of the historical fact as having occurred, the event as "absolute." Now it is its lack of necessity that interests him. One suspects that moral considerations (appropriate in the context of the *Notebooks*) and their ontological foundation have overshadowed the epistemological problems of history in the *Diaries*. He discovers a "threefold historical contingency" in the historical event based on "the tool, the body and the other" (*NE* 53).

It is via the instrument, the tool, Sartre claims, following Heidegger, that "the whole world is inserted into History" (*NE* 73). Despite his misgivings about historical periodization, he admits, for example, that the appearance of the cannon marks the end of the Middle Ages. In fact, he chides the historical materialists for failing to recognize that, on their own principles, the explosion of the atomic bomb is more significant historically than the Russian revolution![15] But his point is that this "original contingency" could not have been predicted. Its appearance was as gratuitous as any human invention.[16]

The body contributes a specific dimension of contingency to the historical event. First, it is the original contingency of every consciousness, as *Being and Nothingness* affirms with striking imagery.[17] But of greater relevance to our topic is the fact that embodiedness implies that the event is a counterpart of human *work*. Sartre has not yet accepted the Marxist primacy of labor,[18] much less developed a praxis-centered philosophy. But he is aware of the inertia and passivity to which embodiedness exposes the historical agent: "If Cromwell had not had a gallstone . . . yes, but if one had only known how to cure him" (*NE* 53). Though the body generates contingency and hence ambiguity in Sartre's emerging theory, lack of a phenomenology of the body makes Heidegger's many references to historicity abstract in comparison with the reflections of Sartre and Foucault, where embodiedness predominates.

Ontologically constitutive of the historical event in its facticity as the in-itself of being-for-others, the Other accounts for the event's ambiguity, first because of its own contingency. Since *Being and Nothingness,* Sartre has argued that the existence of the Other is my original "fall," playing the role in historical contingency and unrepeatability that Pascal reserved for the biblical event ("man is a being to whom something has happened" [*NE* 58]). I cannot deduce the original existence of the Other, I can only encounter it. Moreover, there is no rule or limit to the number of people on the planet. The demographic factor is a major contingency affecting the nature of a historical event; for example, the defeat of the southern Swedes (Vikings) by their more numerous northern brothers.

As he grew older, Sartre seemed to become increasingly sensitive to the differences among the generations. It figures centrally, for example, in his account of the artistic options of the young Flaubert and his contemporaries, as we shall see. In view of the tendency of many critics to read Sartre's subsequent dispute with Foucault in terms of the conflict of generations, this is particularly ironic. In the *Notebooks* he observes: "The distinction between generations therefore, by its very nature, renders a historical phenomenon heterogeneous with itself. It provides this phenomenon with dimensions which in their concrete content, escape its witnesses as well as its actors, yet which haunt and influence their actions" (*NE* 136–37). The same event, the outbreak of the Great War, for example, will carry different meaning and significance for those who fought it and for those of Sartre's generation who were conscripts in the Second World War.

But it is chiefly by means of *interpretation* that the other consciousness contributes to the ambiguity of the historical event. The interpretation of its meaning is constitutive of the event since it is primarily via interpretation that the Other is related to the event. "The manner in which the event is lived," Sartre concedes, "is part of the event itself" (*NE* 35). These multiple interpretations, these ways of living the event, are distinct from and irreducible to one another—hence the plurality and "otherness" that invest each event with an ambiguity that turns it back on itself and moves it along. No doubt, this accounts in part for the perspectivism of Nietzsche and perhaps of Aron as well.

In this respect, Sartre refers to the ambiguous reading of one's neighbor's attitudes during the Dreyfus affair: "It is this relationship of outside and inside," he muses, "that makes the event escape each and every one of us. Its inertia, its weight, do not stem from some physical inertia, but from a perpetual regrasping" (*NE* 35). It is this "inertia" that statisticians try to capture.[19] But the sheer plurality of consciousnesses, Sartre implies, contributes an ineliminable element of chance to the historical event (see *NE* 31).[20]

To say that interpretation ("the manner of living the event") enters into the very constitution of the event ("is part of the event itself") sounds suspiciously like Aron's position in the *Introduction,* which Sartre had strenuously opposed. What it seems to yield is a plurality of lived events, each as "true" as the other, whose incorporation into a particular history is mainly a function of the historian's goals and interests. In the *War Diaries,* recall, Sartre had distinguished three levels at which historical inquiry occurred, namely, those that considered the event as in-itself, as for-itself, and as for-others. Does his subsequent incorporation of interpretation into the event itself ensnare him in the relativism that this distinction of levels was meant to avoid? The answer appears less clear now than it had been in the *Diaries.*

As an example of what he calls "the structure of otherness in the historical fact," Sartre cites the flight of gold out of France during the prime ministry of Leon Blum. From a welter of individual facts, each having its subjective signification (let us call it the fact/event as for-itself), one must discover an *objective* signification, first in the minds of the leaders of the Popular Front, who see in it the capitalists' distrust as Other (the fact as for-others). This interpretation is a subjectivity turned against and projected on the Other. It becomes what Sartre calls "subjectivity-object," or specifically, a "capitalist maneuver." On this reading there is no question of individual subjectivity, which is discounted as "just the soul of the fact." The capitalist bourgeoisie, on the other hand, lives this fact as *pure necessity;* the flight of capital is an unavoidable consequence of Blum's politics. Here the subjective element is totally suppressed, even as a factor mediating the flight and the politics. Finally, there is the popular interpretation, which, in Sartre's view, is "more animist (and in principle truer)," that seeks the *persons* behind this maneuver, the banks, for example, or the "two hundred families." Of course, this last interpretation, with its insistence on the individual, moral aspects of impersonal, collective responsibility, accords most with Sartre's overarching concern to connect History and morality.

Sartre concludes from this example that this historical fact is grasped in three different ways, ranging "from the purely economic consequence (a determinism of the type of the natural sciences) to a cynically deliberate ruse (Machiavellianism), passing by way of the maneuver of a class or a group whose subjective intention is not expressed in any particular subjectivity but is rather like a noumenal reality and the intelligible choice of such subjectivities." In conciliatory fashion, he grants that "naturally it is not a question of three errors but of three historical categories for apprehending a fact. This naturally leads to three modes of particular actions stemming from this fact" (*NE* 415).

This does not contradict Sartre's earlier claims in the *War Diaries* about the three levels of historical investigation, the in-itself, the for-itself, and the for-others. Without denying the level of the fact as in-itself, he is elaborating the other levels, especially the for-others, on which the fact/event receives its "pluridimensionality." So the fact (as in-itself) remains demonstrative, but what it demonstrates is a matter of interpretation.

The final source of contingency and so of ambiguity for the historical event that Sartre mentions is the historical *object* as distinct from the event. Consider the battle of Waterloo. One can see it as what Sartre terms a "material event," for example, cannon balls, loss of caloric energy, or death as a biological phenomenon. But the historian is concerned with what we have termed the "historical collectivity" such as the regiment. And that in turn requires, for example, that we consider its institutional form as something that antedates its members and that we respect the "subjective unity" of camaraderie and loyalty among its members, its esprit de corps, its leader and symbols and the like. And each of these in turn offers a multifaceted visage to the prospective inquirer. Sartre has come to recognize that history deals with social facts, but his best account of their ontological status does not move beyond the categories of *Being and Nothingness:* they are being-for-others. In sum, the historical object is "material, organic and spiritual at the same time" (*NE* 29).

So whether we view it from the perspective of the human reality that produces it, the ontological status it enjoys, or the threefold contingency that infects it, the historical event, as Sartre interprets it, is a thoroughly ambiguous phenomenon. Can the history fashioned from such events be any less so?

THE ABSOLUTE EVENT

This is not to say that Sartre has simply succumbed to historical perspectivism. The same rage for realism that drove him, at Aron's suggestion, to study Husserl in Berlin enlists Husserl against whatever hint of relativism the foregoing reflections might contain. He appeals implicitly to the Husserlian theory that a perceptual object must reveal itself in "profiles" (*Abschattungen*), each of which affords a valid, if limited, view of one and the same object. In effect, Husserl argues, one always perceives a certain aspect or "adumbration" of the same object. Sartre claims that the historical event is likewise "pluridimensional" but that each of the facets (*Abschattungen*) it displays to the investigator is the *entire* event under that aspect.[21]

He uncovers six "layers" of the historical event, ranging from the first layer "of original contingency" through layers of generality (e.g., general use of cannon), passivity, statistics, and tradition, to the sixth layer of invention, which he calls "freedom of the historical agent." After

which point he confesses: "In fact, these are not layers since the historical event is given as a whole across each one of them. Rather, [they are]
Abschattungen" (*NE* 73).[22]

This echoes the Husserlian defense he is making of the "absolute
event" at about the same time in *What Is Literature?*: "For *us* too [like the
idealists] the event appears only through subjectivities. But its transcendence comes from the fact that it exceeds them all because it extends
through them and reveals to each person a different aspect of itself and
of himself" (*WL* 158 n). Although Sartre does not develop this thesis of
the multiple profiles or facets of one and the same event, it clearly constitutes an attempt to accommodate the acknowledged ambiguity of the
historical event to his abiding sense of its absolute facticity.

Conditions of Historical Activity

No less problematic for the new historiography in France are the nature
and import of historical action. The much criticized narrativist paradigm
of historical understanding is linked as closely to the agent and to the
event for its unfolding. And, existentialism being the proverbial philosophy of individual choice and responsibility, an existentialist theory of
history must likewise respect the decisive role of the responsible agent
in historical narrative. But it is the conditions of *historical* action that concern us here. So under this rubric we can gather four general concepts
from the *Notebooks* essential to any philosophy of history that Sartre
might be in the process of formulating, namely, agent, Other, inertia or
matter, and temporality. If historical action is to occur in a Sartrean setting, all four factors must come into play.

The Agent

The eminent *Annaliste* historian Emmanuel Le Roy Ladurie entitled part
4 of his *Territory of the Historian* "History without People."[23] The expression articulates a major feature of recent French historiography: its ne-
glect of, if not outright disdain for, the concepts of agency, personal
responsibility, and teleology so central to traditional historiography. If
the New History is history without people, it is also history without he-
roes and villains. As another prominent French historian remarked, unlike the old history with its emphasis on narrating the drama of human
choice, the new history "focuses primarily on what underlies those
choices, on what determines them and makes them inevitable despite

the appearance of freedom. It prefers to analyze deeper trends rather than superficial changes, to study collective behavior rather than individual choices."[24]

In a clearly traditionalist sense, Sartre writes early in the *Notebooks:* "A philosophy of history . . . must first ask itself the question of the nature of *action*"(*NE* 50).[25] One finds the basic features of an existentialist philosophy of action discussed throughout *Being and Nothingness,* but especially in part 4, "Having, Doing and Being," where Sartre defends the superiority of the second of these "cardinal categories of human reality" (*BN* 431).[26] The for-itself is the being "which defines itself by *action*"(*BN* 431; F 507). This self-defining, indeed, self-creative, activity is conscious, purposive, situational, and free in the sense of transcending its facticity, that is, the "givens" of its situation. It is also eminently *biographical* rather than historical in nature, which constitutes its specific difficulty in the present context. For how are we to reconcile individual and social action, the biographical and the historical?

In his reflections on historical activity, Sartre employs several tactics to resolve this problem. First, he conceives of actions as "internalization of exteriority and externalization of interiority" (*NE* 51), a phrase that will figure often in his subsequent works.[27] Though the expression looks Hegelian and will eventually generate Sartre's own dialectic, he still warns against subsuming it into the classical dialectical triad, suggesting rather that we regard these movements as a "bringing together of two contraries" (*NE* 65).[28] As internalization, action is both an interpretation and an appropriation of the past as facticity; as externalization, it is the transcendence of this facticity and the casting of one's lot with the uncertainties and vulnerabilities of the world, with what we shall discuss shortly as the realm of "inertia." In no sense is action the overflow of an inner subjectivity. On the contrary, internalization/ externalization is a functional replacement for "subjectivity" in Sartrean discourse from now on.[29] In other words, Sartre is coming to see "action" as a dialectical appropriation of one's transformed material world—as what he will later call "praxis" and all that the term entails.[30]

On the one hand, this interiorization/exteriorization is a unifying activity, as is history itself. Out of a welter of possibilities, the agent fashions an actuality that, from the viewpoint of responsibility, is of his or her own choosing. Yet, on the other hand, no historical action is exclusively one's own. Exteriorization counters solipsism with an essentially public world, that of the in-itself and the for-others, subject to failure and to opposing interpretations as well as to a host of counterfinalities that he will elaborate in the *Critique*. The point of any action, Sartre notes, is "to realize quasi-syntheses within the context of inertia. To introduce unity into what is by definition multiplicity, synthesis into what is juxtaposed, but also at the same time to make these syntheses passive and to affect them with exteriority. To introduce the notion of the *fragile* into the world." The "fragile" which action introduces he describes as "that which rebels against synthesis, that which is bent by force to make up a whole and which perpetually tends to return to the multiplicity of juxtaposition" (*NE* 51). As the totalities of human reality are detotalized, so the syntheses of human action are "quasi" because in both instances the agent, who can never extract himself entirely from his actions, is a "being of distances."[31] These concepts of fragility and detotalized totality should be recalled whenever one is tempted to equate Sartrean historical totalization with totalitarianism, as Hannah Arendt, Karl Popper, Jean-François Lyotard, and Foucault are wont to do.[32]

It is worth noting at this juncture the link Sartre forges between historical action and a social ideal, especially in view of his entrance into mass politics at that time.[33] He sees an antinomy in the fact that "every historical action in its essence can only be finite . . . and yet it sets itself a goal at infinity." As a possible resolution, he suggests "finite action on finite objects (in the infrastructure) with an opening to the infinite." By this he means "to put forth one's action to others, as action/testimony, to accept being put *at risk* by others yet to come, as solicitation." But, he adds, "it is as a *maxim of action* that this claim on infinity has to inhabit action," and to do so as inspiration and practical ideal, not as a blueprint for some social engineer (*NE* 84). In fact, he considers the idea of socialism to be just such a "maxim directive of action" (*NE* 102). Presumably, one should commit oneself to action in the socioeconomic sphere (the infrastructure), guided by the *als ob* of socialist brother- and sisterhood, but without discouragement at its continual recession into the horizon. An index of the role of imagination in Sartre's philosophy, such regulative ideas will continue to figure in his view of society throughout his career.[34]

Sartre's theory of action broadens when he discusses the relation of agent to product (*oeuvre*) in the case of collective enterprises such as the legal code, the conquest of Algeria, or the triumph of a temperance league. Here the common effect (*l'oeuvre commune*) refers me back to "a concrete WE wherein my I gets fixed and gets lost" (*NE* 130). He has not yet resolved the issue of collective action as he will in his account of the group-in-fusion in the *Critique*. Failure to do so constitutes the chief obstacle to an adequate theory of history in the *Notebooks*. But he notes that "what is impossible at the level of the For-itself and the Project (the ontological organization of a We), becomes real on the anthropological level of some common work" (*NE* 130). Each and every member of the enterprise can take credit for the common work. But to the extent that he does so, he shares "an abstract I" with the rest. Recalling his existentialist theory of responsibility, Sartre adds: "The infinite thickness of this I, the contraction of a thousand concrete I's, has a reassuring solidity. At the same time, it also has a density of being that allows me to avoid the anxiety of being responsible for my I" (*NE* 130). This is the kind of collective responsibility criticized by Arendt and others who insist that if everyone is responsible, no one is responsible. It can easily slide into the anonymity of the "they" (*l'on*), precursor of the serial being of the *Critique*.

Action and Historical Intelligibility. The intelligibility of human action depends on the agent's intention since, as *Being and Nothingness* explains, the project is intentional. Yet as exteriorization, it requires a work (*l'oeuvre*), and it is this work that principally concerns the historian. He must judge not only its meaning (which, as we have seen, is ambiguous) but its historical significance, its success or failure, as well. But Sartre wonders how one can assess a historical work's success or failure accurately when "the end [*fin*] [of an action] is the entire world" in its concreteness (*NE* 436; *CM* 451). It is this holistic penchant, expressed in the *War Diaries* as "simultaneity," that distinguishes Sartre from Aron even as it underscores the failings of his own existentialist social ontology.

Sartre offers detailed reasons why the comparison between projected and realized end is impossible.[35] In sum, they stem from several roots: (1) the interconnectedness of historical events, that is, the "simultaneity" of the *War Diaries* and what earlier in the present work he called "the fibrous unity of the historical universe" (*NE* 35; F 41);[36] (2) the freedom and complexity of the human personality intending the end; (3) the constant mutability of what John Dewey called the end-in-view; (4) the impossibility of the achieved end's resembling the originally projected one in every respect; and (5) the ambiguity with which the plurality of consciousness (the *Mitsein*) invests the finished product. His conclusion is that it is a *free decision* of the agent whether a historical action is a success or a failure. He may decide it is a failure, given the ambiguities we have spoken of and especially given his "inner distance" from his own act. But here, as everywhere in Sartre's existentialist thought, the decision carries a *moral* weight, that is, it occurs in good or bad faith.[37]

Historical intelligibility is a dialectic of *contingency* and *necessity*.[38] The brute facticity of an agent's being is countered by the *absolute origin* of his fundamental "choice" or project. We know from *Being and Nothingness* that no motive or reason can "explain" such a project in the causal sense. Sartre recapitulates this view in the *Notebooks* when he writes:

> Every man as such is for himself and for others an ahistorical absolute within History. It is precisely because he is this absolute that he cannot be completely recuperated [*récupéré*].[39] To be recuperable he would have to become *relative* to the whole. It is because he is this absolute that History is not ideal but *tragic* and it does not suffice to comprehend it. But he is absolute insofar as he decides and acts, . . . insofar as he historializes himself [*s'historialise*] in History. . . . But in relation to others, who are equally free—above all, in relation to other generations that will arise when he is dead—this absolute is relative, precisely because they are themselves absolutes. . . . History appears to this absolute through the very fact that this absolute *happens,* as something that becomes relative. . . . History is a relativizing and perpetual upsurge of first beginnings. (*NE* 89–90; F 96–97)

Talk of "upsurges" and "first beginnings" is vintage existentialist Sartre. (Just how directly it contrasts with Foucault's relativism without absolutes will appear in volume 2 of this study.) Sartre continues these remarks by noting that "the denseness of History, its tragic quality and its reality, even its unpredictability imply that its very course must be absolute (otherwise everything falls into relations with nothing to support them)" (*NE* 90; F 97). Did we not have ample evidence of Sartre's antisubstantialist concept of consciousness, this last remark would seem inconsistent. In fact, it should be read more as supporting his metaphysical realism than as a plea for substance in any traditional sense. Whatever absolute figures in Sartre's theory, the absolute event, for example, will be a function of the in-itself; consciousness, though he considers it a "nonsubstantial absolute," as internal negation of the in-itself is inherently relative. But reference to the "absolute upsurge" of the for-itself accords well with his theory of the necessity and unjustifiability of the basic project, and again contrasts neatly with Foucault's structuralist claims regarding the derived status of the agent-self from prior relations.[40]

The Engineer and the Artist. Before concluding this discussion of human action as a basic dimension of Sartre's nascent theory of history, let us consider two models of human agency that he sets forth in the *Notebooks,* namely, the engineer and the artist.[41] These types lend a certain unity to Sartre's reflections on history by their implicit anthropologies. Their contrast will reverberate throughout his subsequent writings.

The world of the engineer originates in need, is itself reduced to pure instrumentality in meeting that need, and appeals to an underlying determinism in the process. We recognize in this portrait images of technological man sketched previously by Weber, Heidegger, and others as well as hints of Sartre's later depiction of "scarcity man" (*l'homme de rareté*) in the *Critique.* Sartre notes a kind of "magic materialism" at work in the engineer's world that in the final analysis is alienating.

Quite other is the model of the artist. Here we find that mixing of imagination, creativity, and freedom that has emerged as a fundamental Sartrean value since *The Psychology of Imagination* (1940). The artist's *oeuvre* is neither an instrument nor a thing in the technician's sense. It is what Sartre calls an "analogue"; its relation to the other's freedom is one of gift, invitation, or, at most, exigency—terms that will recur as we elaborate the aesthetic dimension of his theory.[42] In the next chapter we shall see that the interpretation of another's freedom in the optimal case is like active aesthetic contemplation. In the present context, it is worth noting that the corresponding optimum of activity is like artistic creativity. We shall have much more to say about this "type" of human action when we address Sartre's "poetics of history."[43] Most human actions, like the societies in which they unfold, are imperfect reflections of both of these images.[44]

The Other

Being-for-others is one of the basic categories in Sartre's ontology. So the "other" must figure in any analysis of the conditions for existentialist action. We have remarked that its "for-others" character qualifies an action as historical. If the historical event is the in-itself of the for-others, the action it records, insofar as it is historical, must likewise refer to others, at least implicitly.

If other consciousnesses invest the historical event with ambiguity, according to Sartre, they alienate it in the basic sense of "objectifying" it as well.[45] Indeed, Sartre believes at this point that "History will *always* be alienated" (*NE* 49). He explains, "History is the *Other*. . . . [It] is the history of men insofar as they are all for each one and each one for all *the others*." And he adds in criticism of Hegel and Marx that "History is *also* the history of Spirit perpetually seeking to escape otherness and never succeeding" (*NE* 46, 48). This escape from alterity will be a major theme of the *Critique*. But for the moment it suffices to note that Sartre's talk of "spirit" and in later works of "objective spirit" should not be taken as symptomatic of idealist tendencies (though his lifelong struggle with philosophical idealism has not left him unscathed). It merely evidences his special form of "materialism" that will allow for intentionality and permit the movement of a nonmechanical dialectic.[46]

Although Sartre's position on alienation is problematic, it will not do to say he equates alienation with otherness *simpliciter*.[47] He adds two cryptic notes in this regard: "The Other in History: women, the preceding or succeeding generation, the other nation, the other class" (*NE* 47) and "The Other, in history: the Orient (China, India, Japan)" (*NE* 60), observing that the Hegelian and Marxist dialectics treat only a portion of humanity. But however we finally sort out Sartre's position, it is clear that for him one cannot live history as we know it without becoming alienated. As he states the matter: "To act in History is to accept that this act will become *other* than what it was conceived to be. Here is the true synthesis of unity and duality: to regrasp the act *become other* and penetrate it again with subjectivity (the synthesis of the same and the other), to reappropriate it" (*NE* 47–48). One's very thoughts, the apparent core of subjectivity, once expressed assume a life and weight of their own (that "inertia" others confer on them) as the history of Christianity or of Marxism attests.

If that "otherness" which constitutes the historical event as historical (for-others) will never be overcome, Sartre leaves hope for escape from what, following Marx, he sometimes calls "prehistory" or "alienated" history, so termed because its "result always turns back into an object and because there is an unperceived historical evolution, or one that is denied by the agent of History." With this he contrasts "History [that] attempts to get hold of itself again," by which he means "action trying to become aware of its future objectivity, or, if you will, the agent trying to grasp the significance of his act" (*NE* 50). The latter resembles what Marx praised as "disalienated labor" or "man producing himself" rather than becoming "the product of his own product," except that Sartre at this stage seems less enthusiastic about the categories of economic determinism than he will later be. Genuine "History" in what is emerging as Sartre's valuative sense will require the overcoming or "reappropriation" of some forms of "otherness" while respecting other forms that stem from the sheer multiplicity of agents and intentions. But at this stage he still lacks a social ontology adequate to the task.

Inertia (Matter)

Sartre is fully aware that the possibility of and the threat to historical action lies in the realm of physical matter. His entire ontology throughout its evolution can be read as a dialectic of spontaneity and inertia, doubtless part of his Bergsonian heritage.[48] In the case of historical action this duality surfaces not only in the ambiguity of the fact, which we have just considered, but in the agent-inertia relationship as well. As Sartre avows: "We are therefore in the untenable situation that nothing comes *from the outside* to cut off our efforts so long as they are lived in freedom [his principle of historicity (*historicité*)][49] and yet these efforts have their destiny outside of themselves" (*NE* 82). To the extent that the action is the bearer of meanings ascribed to it by others, including subsequent generations, it lives a life quite independent of our original intent and purpose.

Being-in-itself, Sartre insists, is nondialectical (*NE* 64, 451). Doubtless, this is due to its "inert plenitude," its lack of negativity on which the dialectic turns. Whatever dialectical relationships enter the world do so through the mediation of consciousness or the for-itself, which is the locus of possibility, negativity, and lack.[50] This is his major difficulty with the communist doctrine of a dialectic of nature.[51] And yet he does allow that freedom and necessity reveal themselves Janus-like in the concept of *destiny*. And this clearly requires a dimension of the in-itself (see *NE* 94, 107).

In *The Psychology of Imagination,* Sartre had argued that "it is not determinism but fatalism which is the converse of freedom." Determinism belongs to natural processes but does not apply to consciousness.

Whereas determinism argues *a tergo,* from antecedent cause to consequent effect, fatalism, Sartre explains, being at home in the realm of consciousness, "posits that such an event should happen and that it is this
coming event that determines the series that is to lead up to it" (*PI* 61).
What Sartre calls the "chained consciousness" of someone in a dream is
the paradigm of fatalism. It is a world where the concept of the possible
has collapsed and yet consciousness continues to function. Though he
uses the terms "fate" and "destiny" interchangeably, the latter predominates as the role of inertia in society and history grows more pronounced. So in the *Critique* he will describe destiny as "an irresistible
movement [that] draws or impels the ensemble toward a prefigurative
future which realizes itself through it" (*CDR* 1:551). To the extent that
human action becomes what he calls "process" (alienated behavior),
"goals lose their teleological character. Without ceasing to be genuine
goals, they become destinies" (*CDR* 1:663). Such is the relationship of
the proletarian to the machine, for example.[52] Given this ever-present
inertial factor, Sartre concludes: "The social world is thus a perpetual
dialectic of three concepts: that of recognition of absolute freedom . . . ,
that of fatality or destiny . . . , and that of determinism" (*NE* 339; F 352).
If he were to criticize the New History at this point in his career, it would
be for neglecting the first concept in favor of the other two.

Speaking of the relation between individual intentions and general
interest in an action, Sartre distinguishes two levels that often overlap.
The first is the plane where the individual agent (subjectivity of the intention) discovers that he has become objectively a historical agent
(destiny). In this case the agent's consciousness is without connection
with the objective efficacy of the work. Sartre cites in this regard an example close to the plot of his play, *Dirty Hands:* I kill my wife's lover and
discover that I have deprived of its leader a party about to seize power.
In the second volume of the *Critique,* Sartre will analyze Stalin as such a
man of destiny in constructing "socialism in one country."[53]

The second level of analysis is that of subjectivity, where I cannot
will the singular without doing so in the context of more general, more
open social forms that surpass my present and my life. In this case, my
claim is "perfectly and authentically conscious." In explanation, Sartre
begins an argument echoing that of his famous, if unconvincing, lecture
on existentialism and humanism, delivered two years earlier.[54] In
choosing myself, he begins, I choose myself as communist, for example.

But in so doing, I choose the party as the "open future" for humanity and I choose to subordinate myself to the party and to its victory.[55] Yet, reciprocally, "in choosing the C.P., I choose a certain type of man and of ideal human relations (in a classless society) in terms of which I define myself: I insert myself into History, justify myself and give a meaning to my action." In words whose anti-Hegelian significance we shall assess in chapter 3, he summarizes: "I save myself through the infinite Future" (*NE* 420; F 436). Of these two levels on which an action can be analyzed, the second is the plane of existential freedom and responsibility; the first, that of inert determinations and natural necessities. Yet both are intrinsically related to the inertia of the physical or social world, whether via social causality or the circulation of meanings.

As historical "cause," as one of a sequence of events that account for untold and unforeseeable consequences, the action as exteriorization is invested by inertia with a force and a passivity (malleability) that escapes the control of the individual agent. This is the point of his appeal to destiny in his search for historical intelligibility. It is also the basis for the significant category of oeuvre that Sartre refers to frequently. We know another's specific freedom, as we shall see, by grasping his oeuvre. In words worthy of a structuralist, Sartre directs against defenders of a transcendental Ego or subjective idealism these two aphorisms: "The real *Me* [is] in the work [*l'oeuvre*]" and the Nietzsche-like "To live without an Ego" (*NE* 414). These remind us of the import Sartre accords the inert and the impersonal even in his "existentialist" period.

We have seen that it is the inertial aspect of the event that makes it liable to the chance happenings of the physical and the social world, and that, as "inert," action bears that "fragility" which we saw exteriorization bring into the world. The inertial aspect of action underscores my embodiedness as agent in that I must "make myself inert," for example, by pushing on buttons, moving a pen, or simply uttering a sound in order to work in the world. This is one of the more obvious senses in which action for Sartre is consciousness (the for-itself) as "internal [negative] relation of the in-itself with itself" (*NE* 52). As embodiedness, inertia figures in Sartre's historical "realism" as well: first through the Bachelardian concept of "coefficient of adversity" (the amount of resistance the in-itself offers our projects) employed in *Being and Nothingness* (see *BN* 324) and, second, in the account his master narrative gives us of oppression. "Oppression," he argues, "is not some ideal. It is always some direct or indirect action that acts on the *body;* it is a constraint by means of the body" (*NE* 328). Finally, as embodiedness, inertia translates my basic *contingency*. In the ontological order, it is my first facticity.

From the temporal point of view, which we shall address next, inertia marks the heaviness of the past, what Sartre calls "time-object," as a kind of in-itself. It absorbs my past (the past which, as facticity, I have "to have been") into the past in-itself of humanity which, in turn, shades into the limiting case of the physical time that we retroject on the world before the advent of man (see *NE* 90). Sartre's time-object resembles Heidegger's *Vergangenheit* or ontic past, a kind of tomb into which previous presents have fallen, as distinct from the "living past" (*die Gewesenheit*), the past we say is still with us.[56] Yet as past, Sartre would insist, both forms share a kind of inertia proper to the event, that is, to the in-itself of for-others.

Temporality

Being and Nothingness argues that human reality "temporalizes" itself and the world according to the threefold "ekstatic temporality" of facticity, existence, and presence-to, which Sartre adopts from Heidegger (see *BN* 107–29). Without this temporality and its concomitant ontological freedom, there might well be a sequence of natural occurrences but there would be no history. In the *Notebooks* Sartre distinguishes historical from merely biographical temporality described in *Being and Nothingness:* "Historical time is both thing and spirit (owing to its radical breaks), while the time of the individual is completely consciousness" (*NE* 108). By "thing" Sartre is referring to the in-itself of the for-others, which, as we saw, gives the historical event an "absolute" dimension that Sartre believed would save him from Aron's "relativism." By "spirit" he is alluding to his version of Hegel's "objective spirit" that we mentioned earlier and shall discuss at length in chapter 8.

Sartre elaborates this distinction between historical and biographical time in terms of what he calls the threefold dimension of historical time. First, there is the time that "temporalizes itself with each absolute For-itself," in effect, individual temporality as a necessary condition for historical time. Next there is "the time of intersubjectivities," namely, the temporal unity of the mutual looks (*regards*) that is both subject-time and object-time, since each consciousness in Sartre's existentialist ontology is both looking and looked-at. The "temporal unity" between subject- and object-time that this dimension denotes recalls one of the functions of "simultaneity" introduced in the *War Diaries*. Finally, we have what may simply be called "the Past," that melting of my subject-time into a prior series of object-times for both myself and others, and that series' dissolution into the past in-itself of all humanity and thence into prehistoric, physical time, "that we retrospectively project on the world before man" (*NE* 90). So it is not the case that an objective, natural time gets "personalized" through a human project. Rather, the reverse is true: concrete, lived time in its three "ekstases" shades off into the common past and further into universal time, from whence an objective, natural time is drawn.[57]

This last, complex description of the Past is meant to underline its nature as in-itself, as facticity and, above all, as a *one-way* relationship with the present and the future. As Sartre observes: "Hence my time is always dated in the past in terms of universal time, while the present and the future are unjustifiable and undated time, absolute time." In other words, the "absolute time" of my lived project is rendered both in-itself and relative to the Other's projects by slipping into the past. As he said in *Being and Nothingness,* the dead are prey to the living. And he concludes: "In historical time there is a double rending apart: that of the Other (which is reciprocal) and that of the Past (which is without reciprocity). In the past there is just one time, the historical time that unites the dead: they are all *in the same time.*" Taking issue with Heidegger as he had in *Being and Nothingness,* he continues, "The essential ec-stasis is the *past* (since past, present, and future are alike in that they all *pass*) and this equivalence allows the retrospective illusion of explanation," namely, of the present by the past (*NE* 90).

Sartre uses a historical example similar to the one employed in the *Diaries* to underscore the second function of "simultaneity," its serving as the locus for the "totality" of past events in their historical facticality or "transcendence." Consider the fact of Napoleon's eighteenth Brumaire coup d'état. Though each of its components is temporal, "it is true forever that Napoleon carried out a coup d'état on that day." But the recalcitrance of the fact leads Sartre to distinguish the level of existence from that of signification. From the latter viewpoint, the truth of the event "is something transcendent." Indeed, Sartre likens it to that of "2 + 2 = 4," which is also "a thing transcendent to consciousness."

Sartre's point is not to defend the dubious thesis that mathematical "truths" are matters of fact, but to illustrate the independence of the fact from the biography of the historian. Translated into the discourse of existentialism, "this means that the past as past is *being* that I have to be. Hence each past event is a being to be taken up by humanity as a whole. Hence it has an origin but not an end. Truths *appear* in History, but when they are there, they stay there forever" (*NE* 109).

So the Greek circle of time that Nietzsche tried to reintroduce breaks on the rocks of the Sartrean Other and the object-time of the Past. Scarcely transcending the categories of *Being and Nothingness,* Sartre has undertaken an account of historical time that distinguishes it both from physical chronology and from individual time, while defending its directionality and the recalcitrance of the past.[58] Though there is no longer mention of "simultaneity" in the *Notebooks,* Sartre continues to face the same problem of unifying and ordering a past which, in some sense, is discovered or "given."

Our initial tour of the *Notebooks* has revealed how the ambiguity of the historical event and the conditions of historical action—agent, Other, inertia, and temporality—are explicitly addressed throughout the work. If not thoroughly discussed, much less interrelated, Sartre's claims clearly evidence a developing scheme whose elements are being sketched in these drafts. We must await the *Critique* for their elaboration into a full-blown theory. Although his conversation with the New Historians and with Foucault has not yet begun, we can already see the direction it will take.

Chapter Three
Dialectic of Historical Understanding

B y the time he starts recording his reflections in his *Notebooks for an Ethics,*
Sartre has come to realize that "existential
ontology is itself historical . . . the appearance of the For-itself is properly speaking
the irruption of History in the world" (*NE* 6,
11). And yet the "history" it grounds is as
ambiguous as human reality itself, and for
the same reason: both rely upon the open-
ended nature of human transcendence (*dépassement*). The nonself-coincidence that introduces possibility and freedom into the
world makes an end-terminus of History an
impossibility, or what Sartre in *Being and
Nothingness* called an "unrealizable," like
death itself. There is no one "outside" of
History to summarize and take its measure.
In this, he agrees with Aron, as we saw. But
he concludes, not to the perspectivism he attributed to Aron, but to the "rediscovery of
the absolute at the heart of relativity itself"
(*WL* 148). Every one of us is for ourselves
and for others "an ahistorical absolute
within History" (*NE* 89). Consequently,
"the end of History is the end of humanity"
(*NE* 422).[1]

Still, Sartre remains fascinated by the dialectic. His study of Hegel, Marx, and Hegel's
French commentators after the war has re-

The fact is that the purely
imaginary and *praxis* are not
easily reconciled.
—Sartre, *What Is Literature?*

Our job is cut out for us. Insofar as literature is
negativity, it will challenge
the alienation of work; insofar as it is a creation and an
act of surpassing, it will present man as *creative action.* It
will go along with him in
his effort to pass beyond his
present alienation toward a
better situation.
—Sartre, *What Is Literature?*

vealed a dialectic that resonates with many of the seemingly Hegelian concepts of *Being and Nothingness.* Indeed, some have argued that Sartre was developing his own kind of dialectic all along.[2] In contrast to causal explanations of human behavior, only the dialectic seems capable of accounting for the freedom of human action. After lamenting the fact that by 1947 Marxist doctrine "has been degraded to a stupid determinism," Sartre assures us that "Marx, Lenin, and Engels said any number of times that explanation by causes had to yield to the dialectical process" (*WL* 181). The very vehemence of Sartre's objections to the dialectic of history in the *Notebooks* suggests the seriousness of its challenge to his earlier views. He repeats Kierkegaard's objection: "If History does not end, . . . the dialectic cannot confirm itself." But he adds a promising alternative: "Marxism puts man at the heart of the dialectic: the dialectic has no end. Therefore it is just the object of a hypothesis." This is basically the position he will adopt a decade later in the *Critique.* As evidence that not everything is dialectical, he cites "Scientific Nature" and "technology" that "introduce an antidialectical factor into the dialectic itself" (*NE* 450). What he is struggling to discover is a function that he will later call the "practico-inert."

But the line is drawn in the *Notebooks:* speaking of the relationship between myself and the Other, Sartre insists that there can be "an alignment of one of these modes of being, in its specificity, in terms of the other but not a *synthesis.* No more than one can synthesize height and depth in space." Still, he admits "there can be reciprocity of action or a succession of reciprocal actions, but nothing more." It is this "reciprocity of action (praxis)" that will break the logjam that we have seen forming in Sartre's existential ontology and open the space for a more adequate social theory. Setting the stage for the social ontology he will finally construct in the *Critique,* he explains: "There can be a dialectic here only if we could consider the absolute lived experience that is the Other and the lived experience that I am as incomplete truths that a larger truth might subsume. But as we see: (a) there is no third term or totalization of these two terms. (b) Each one is an unsurpassable absolute" (*NE* 452). Earlier in the *Notebooks,* Sartre had underscored the issue with perhaps unwitting irony as one of parts and wholes: "If there is no whole (pure sum) there is no dialectic. And if reality is a detotalized totality then there is a pseudo-dialectic or an aberrant one" (*NE* 62). For "the true motor principle of History, which is otherness, is broader than the dialectic and encompasses it. The dialectic is one *species* of other-ness" (*NE* 56). The very "othering" character of human consciousness, its alterity, he is implying, both makes dialectic possible and resists its totalizing power.[3]

The problem is being stated with increasing clarity and so, too, its answer: Develop a social ontology that respects individual alterity as an absolute, while fostering practical reciprocity through the media-tion of a third term. It must likewise account for the seemingly anti-dialectical character of technological culture and the natural world—no small order!

A DIALECTIC WITH HOLES IN IT: THE STRIKE

Before venturing further through the morass of Sartre's *Notebooks*, let us pause to consider his application of this incipient method to a specific historical problem: the understanding of a labor confrontation. It is sig-nificant that Sartre's principal examples of dialectical relationships are forms of *struggle*, where the twin but opposing concepts of fraternity and violence are at work.[4] This will be even more pronounced in his ex-tended analysis of the boxing match in volume 2 of the *Critique*. There he will link the intelligibility of History as we know it with the comprehen-sibility of conflict as such. (Foucault likewise counsels that we seek the intelligibility of history in struggle, not in linguistic meaning [*significa-tion*].)[5] In the *Notebooks*, the Hobbesian world of the looking/looked-at is still operative. The battle for dominance, refined in Hegelian fashion to include recognition in the realm of consciousness, is waged in the meta-phor of glances mirrored to infinity. Once praxis supplants conscious-ness in the *Critique* and after, glances turn to blows and the dialectic materializes. At this intermediate stage, however, Sartre seems more concerned with combatting Hegelian idealism than with social reform.

Any analysis of a labor strike simply in terms of class struggle, Sartre insists, overlooks a crucial element, the striking worker herself. (We have come to expect this focus on the "self-historializing" agent in any existentialist approach.) For it is the worker who makes the strike a *subjective-objective* phenomenon: subjective insofar as it is hers, objective by virtue of its being others' and viewed by others. Because the histori-cal agents are never identical with themselves at any stage in the process (Sartre's existentialist anthropology), in other words, because they can each assume a position with regard to their *representation* of the phenomenon, the strike is "a prismatic object," Sartre argues, neither dialectical nor antidialectical, but comprehensible as "a dialectic with holes in it [*une dialectique à trous*]" (*NE* 459).[6] The "holes" are those "unsalvageable" freedoms that are always "more than themselves," as Sartre is fond of saying. It is their "otherness" that exceeds the dialectic itself.

His point is that both individualist and collectivist approaches to the strike, say in terms of specific instigators and spontaneous developments respectively, fail to grasp it in its open-ended nature, its untotalizable totality. This is precisely what an "existentialist" approach must try to capture. In fact, "the representation of the strike is a factor in the strike [itself]." And when it emerges in the consciousnesses of those involved as "a totality that *encompasses them* (insofar as they are looked at by all the other strikers)," the strike itself becomes the object that they are acting upon. For example, the undertaking changes its nature when the worker ceases to view it as her affair and relegates it to the concern of union leaders. In other words, "the historical event presupposes something immediate that can be dialectical, and a partial reflection whereby it passes to the status of being an object. This means that History presupposes (in assuming the most favorable case) a double action: that of the organic and dialectical development of the process and that of the representation of this dialectical development. And since there is a plurality of consciousnesses, the representation of the dialectic is not itself dialectical" (*NE* 549). So he can restate his earlier claim that otherness, not "dialectic," is the concept with the greater logical extension: "History is <u>dialectical</u>, the surpassing of the dialectic, and the interference between the dialectic and its surpassing. Or if you prefer: the dialectic is plunged into History" (*NE* 459).

Given the open-ended, precarious nature of the dialectic of History, one must live the present moment in uncertainty. That, Sartre has been insisting since the *War Diaries,* is the true absolute, what we might call the "existential present" with its ineliminable dimension of unforeseeability and risk. One might be able to integrate this strike into the larger process of class struggle, as Marx (and Hegel) would claim, but not the decision to join it, made at the risk of one's livelihood and in the uncertainty of being right. If History is the study of the dead past under the "retrospective illusion" of causal necessity, "historialization" is the revival of these past moments as "lived absolutes," with their contingency, possibility, and risk (*NE* 467).

And this exposes another facet of the challenge of an existentialist philosophy of history. For it seems such moments of lived experience of the uncertainty of the future are not recuperable by any subsequent reflection, only their objects are.

> This incertitude gives our time span its reality. We can expect that things will fall apart. And this Expectation as conscious of itself is an absolute. No subsequent synthesis will make sense of it. They will take up the object of this expectation, not the expectation itself. This expectation, decisions made in uncertainty, weighing things, choices, which are the characteristics of the human condition, cannot be integrated into any synthesis because they are precisely what is eliminated from any synthesis. (*NE* 467)

To the ontological problematic sketched above must be added the specifically historical one of capturing, representing, reproducing, or otherwise "making sense" of the "lived absolute" of the historical agent. This will be the problem of existential "historialization" or, as he will later put it, of arriving at the "singular universal."[7] It is an invitation to introduce the lived contingency of biography into historiography.

ART AND THE OTHER: BEYOND THE LOOK

An existentialist philosophy of history by definition is going to be a philosophy of freedom. Human action, for Sartre, is ontologically free. To understand history "existentially," we must comprehend that action in its free exercise. Sartre now asks how we can grasp another's freedom. His response tells us much about his epistemology and, by implication, about the comprehension of History. He quickly turns to aesthetics for a model of such comprehension, suggesting that aesthetic considerations have never been very distant from his reflections on history.

He recommends two ways of "unveiling" the Other as freedom. The first is the famous experience of the look (*le regard*) illustrated graphically in *Being and Nothingness* and in his play, *No Exit*. The point of those phenomenological "arguments" is to warrant the certitude we have of the existence of other minds, which surpasses the probability that standard reasoning from analogy affords us. But Sartre now admits that this yields an undifferentiated intuition of the other freedom in general (*NE* 500). What individuates and concretizes a freedom-project is its goal (*le but*). So the problem of historical understanding for an existentialist entails gaining access to the other's intention, to what Dewey called the other's "end-in-view."

It is here that Sartre resumes the discussion of comprehension (*Verstehen*) that he had been pursuing since the appearance of Aron's first books on historical thought. He summarizes tersely the distinction between scientific explanation and humanistic comprehension: "To explain is to clarify by causes, to comprehend is to clarify by ends [*fins*]" (*NE* 276; F 287). Borrowing from the Heideggerian lexicon, he claims that "I have a preontological [that is, a pretheoretical] comprehension of the original structure of every end." In other words, I know what it is to direct an action toward a goal. That awareness is part of my way of being-in-the-world. It is also "an original structure of the perception of the Other": I perceive the deed in terms of its goal, not in a mechanistic manner, the way I foresee the trajectory of a falling object, but by a practical, "sympathetic" reading of my own experience of goal-pursuing into the phenomenon. When he raises the question once more, in *Search for a Method*, he will insist that there is nothing esoteric about this method. We use it every time we play tennis, watch a movie, or simply walk down a crowded street. Comprehension, the *Verstehen* of German social philosophers, will play a major role in his theory of history.

Lest we overlook the ethical context of these reflections in the *Notebooks*, consider Sartre's phenomenological description of the act of helping someone in trouble. He distinguishes three attitudes that I can adopt in face of the other's intent. Significantly, he assesses them in terms of authenticity. The first inauthentic mode consists of transcending the other's action-end complex as simply another fact in the world, devoid of deeper meanings or further possibilities. In effect, I have suppressed the other's freedom, with the values and purposes it brings to the world. I "fail to understand," for example, why the person rushing for the departing bus cannot wait for the next one.

Another inauthentic way of relating to the goal-directed activity of the other is to incorporate it as merely a means toward my own end, like the kibitzer looking over your shoulder in a card game. Obviously this is the vice of "using" others, which has been decried long before Kant made it the object of a categorical prohibition. The other then becomes purely instrumental in my eyes, what Sartre calls "an absurd and contingent thing." The contradiction here lies in my recognizing a freedom that I fail to respect; my use of a freedom against itself. This approxi-

mates the traps, ruses, and feints, the "counterfinality," that will populate Sartre's later works, except that by then he will be armed with a
concept of the practico-inert to link inauthenticity and the sorcery of
matter.[8]

The only authentic way of relating to another's purposive activity is
to assist in its realization by "modifying the situation so that the other
can do it" (*NE* 279). Elsewhere Sartre had insisted that, although we
cannot act directly on another freedom, by "changing their situations"
we can influence the actions of others.[9] He calls this "comprehension"
because it respects the other's values and ends without compromising
their autonomy. I *recognize* the other's freedom without transfixing it in
the look. This form of sympathy blossoms into acts of generosity and
the mutuality of authentic love as Sartre will sketch them in the *Notebooks*. What is noteworthy for our purposes is his view of comprehension as practical, not merely speculative, and as involving commitment.
As such, it will constitute a major ingredient in his theory of "committed" history.

He cites our appreciation of an artwork to exemplify the authentic
way of grasping another's goal: "The artwork presents itself to me as an
absolute end, a demand, an appeal. It addresses itself to my pure freedom and in this way reveals to me the pure freedom of the Other." Sartre extends this experience: "If therefore I grasp the other's work
[*l'oeuvre*] (it matters little that it be an artwork) as absolute demand requiring my approval and my concurrence, I grasp the man in the process
of making it as freedom [*de faire comme liberté*]" (*NE* 500; F 516). He allows that this is an optimal case and that there are other ways to grasp
the freedom of one who denies his freedom—the more common situation. In the present case, I grasp the other in terms of his future which
appears as an unconditioned end for my freedom.

Sartre has in mind the "comprehension" (*Verstehen*) of German social
philosophers, which we spoke of earlier and which will later play so important a role in his theory of history. Although at this point he is thinking chiefly in terms of the existentialist categories of freedom and
authenticity, he makes a notable move toward social consciousness and
collective identity when he speaks of the "comprehension" that accompanies my appeal (*la demande*) that another freedom recognize my own,
as bringing about "a certain kind of interpenetration of freedoms which
may indeed by the human realm [Sartre's version of Kant's kingdom of

ends subsumed into Marx's reign of freedom]" (*NE* 290).[10] Unlike the looking/looked-at model of *Being and Nothingness,* Sartre assures us that "this [mutual] recognition is not alienation" (*NE* 280). My comprehension of another's end is sympathetic, not intuitive. It is "an original structure of the perception of the Other" (*NE* 276). He explains that "it presupposes an active, original intention that is the basis of its revelation. The other's end can appear to me as an end only in and through the indication of my adopting that end" (*NE* 277). Comprehension is distinct from "the look" not only in its specificity (that is, it reveals the *sens-fin* of *this* action) but in its non-objectifying (non-alienating) character. It is to this last feature that Sartre will later appeal in discussing his socio-historical ideal. Although he mentions "comprehension" in the context of grasping another's freedom, its function in the *Notebooks,* unlike in the *Critique,* is more ethical than epistemic.[11]

THE DIALECTIC AND HISTORY

We suggested in the previous chapter that the reflections on history in the *Notebooks* can be read as a conversation with the French Hegelians, specifically, with Kojève and Hyppolite. Even if the term had never been used, what we have said thus far about the ambiguity of the historical event and especially about the inherent otherness of historical action would suggest that Sartre views history in a dialectical light. But, as we have already seen, his is a peculiarly existentialist dialectic: it generates otherness and resists syntheses.[12] Take the following historical example.

Sweden in the seventeenth century was in a dialectical situation. Sharp conflict existed between the nobility and the monarchy. The nobles appealed to the Protestant Queen Margaret of Denmark to lead them in a unified Nordic state. But, simultaneously, the rise of nationalism in each country and resultant competition with its neighbors favored strong national monarchies at the expense of the nobles and an international state. Further, the introduction of religious reform both liberated Sweden from the universal church and pushed it closer to German religious suzerainty. Everything seemed ready for a synthesis, that is, for a military fusion of all three states into a central one with general sentiments replacing nationalist ones, and Sweden seemed the state to effect this unity. But in his description of the situation, Sartre observes: "Yet just *here* the dialectic stops. No synthesis. Because History is not a closed system and because in being posed, the problem was enlarged" (*NE* 105). He then refers to numerous factors that militate against such a synthesis, chief among them being the fact that a United States of Europe presumes an industrial and a cultural development quite different from what in fact obtained in Europe at that time. He concludes: "This is how, in fact, History proceeds. Thesis and antithesis frequently appear in it because the relation between consciousnesses is one of struggle and opposition, but from this very fact—or from the fact that *during this time* the world gets completely turned around—the struggle loses its meaning [*sens*] and is integrated into a new universe that is the negation of the possible synthesis and the forgetting of the meaning [*sens*] of the struggle" (*NE* 106).

At this point, Sartre would agree with Aron that there is no single meaning [*sens*] to history; and yet historical events are related dialectically. What kind of historical dialectic not only relies on "otherness" (alterity as "the true moving principle of History") but is encompassed by that same alterity? The sheer multiplicity of interpreters, not to mention the ambiguity of the interpreted itself, leads Sartre to conclude: "It is precisely the denseness of the multiple faces of History that makes this quasi dialectic just *one* of the historical dynamisms. . . . Far from the dialectic explaining History, it is History that closes in on all dialectic and digests it" (*NE* 55–56). Then, too, there is the inevitable problem of expressing this dialectic linguistically (Hegel's history as *narratio*), perhaps the chief instance of alterity among so-called postmoderns.[13] We have already observed Sartre offering this as an example of the greater logical extension of "alterity." As soon as one attempts to conceive the dialectical relationship, to represent it mentally, one slips into non-dialectical otherness. Sartre is already painfully aware of this limitation, yet it constitutes a major criticism that Lévi-Strauss and Aron will level against the *Critique* over a decade later.[14] Again, if a dialectic of history is to succeed, it must be "understood" and expressed in a more fluid discourse than that of standard "analytic" thought. Another form of discourse and an alternative form of "rationality" seem called for.

Nature of the Historical Dialectic

By "dialectic" Sartre understands the "synthetic unity of a totality spread out over time" (*NE* 456). It is a part-whole relationship, where each part assumes its meaning in relation to the whole that it constitutes but which reciprocally constitutes it as a part. In other words, it is like the organic relationship to which Aristotle appealed when he pointed out that the human finger separated from the living body is no longer literally a human finger.[15] But dialectic for Sartre is a temporalized totality, meaning that the reciprocal significance of part and whole depends on what each was and/or will be (see *NE* 457). In fact, it is the future, the "will be," that counts most in Sartrean dialectic. Of course, the existentialist project is essentially forward-looking. But Sartre will subsequently refer to "a certain action of the future [on the present]" as the touchstone of any dialectic.[16] In what sense does this apply to history? Can we speak of a historical as distinct from a merely biographical dialectic? And how can the "future" be said to act upon the past? The "not yet" upon the "no longer"? For it is often argued that neither term in this relationship exists.

Sartre allows that "in certain regions of being certain temporal forms develop dialectically." But he quickly cautions that "this in no way implies the possibility of affirming that *everything* is dialectical." Indeed, he insists that "no matter of fact [*constatation de fait*] can prove that dialectic is a universal law." Still, he acknowledges "three aspects of human historialization by which a certain 'dialecticization' can be introduced into History," namely, the ambiguity of the for-itself that generates tension between contraries, the subjective process of comprehension as a transcending (*dépassement*) that involves negativity and creation, and the relation between the for-itselfs or the detotalized totality (*NE* 450–51; F 465–66). We have already considered these potentially dialectical features of human reality, its actions, and its relations. The critical issue seems to be what kind of "totalities," if any, we can ascribe to the plurality of consciousnesses that yields history as a category of being-for-others. This is a matter that will assume increasing importance in the *Critique* and *The Family Idiot*.

Sartre's attitude toward totalities at this point and with it his understanding of a dialectic in history can be summarized in two theses and a set of contrasts. First, there are totali*ties,* not a totality, in history. Since *Being and Nothingness,* he has insisted that any totality of which the for-itself is a part must always be a "detotalized" totality (see *BN* 181). A totality in history is the kind of unity that respects the singularity of the historical event. This distinguishes it from the universality of a law and hence from the domain of sociology. Sartre writes:

> If History has its *own consistency,* if by itself it refuses to evaporate into
> sociology, it is precisely because of its uniqueness. The first historical
> event is that *there be* a history [a story, *une historie*]. And if there is a
> history, it contains the universal in itself as one of its abstract struc-
> tures rather than being able to be universal. Pascal saw this clearly:
> the original fault that makes all universalization impossible. Free, a
> sinner, historical, man is a being to whom something has happened.
> (*NE* 58)

Sartre, still the realist, is struck by what others have called the singularity or nonrepeatability of the historical event. If this is to be rendered
intelligible, however, and not simply listed in a chronicle, it must be incorporated in a totality of some kind. One would expect the analyst of
the kaiser's withered arm to totalize these events in a biographical narrative. Instead, here and in the *Critique,* Sartre opts for the "concrete universal" understood here as "those men who find themselves in the same
historical situation" (*NE* 7). It is only with his massive Flaubert study
that the two approaches converge. Human reality is "in society" the
way Heidegger's *Dasein* is "in the world" (*NE* 112); the concrete situation is the social one (see *NE* 7).

   The building block of history is human reality which, because of its
facticity and its freedom, is both opaque to historical rationalism and
unsubsumable into organic social wholes. Each individual is doubtless a
totalizing, absolute subject. But for that very reason he is not totalizable
without remainder. Whatever social whole he belongs to, for example, a
party or socioeconomic class, will be a "quasi totality," enjoying a quasi
unity and exhibiting a "quasi dialectic" that is frustrated by the insuperable exteriority-otherness of the for-itself-for-others relationship (see
NE 57, 456). The deep reason, again, for the failure of historical synthesis consists in the fact that "the dimension of the For-itself and that of
the For-others . . . are existential categories and incommunicable dimensions" (*NE* 468).

   As there are totalities, second, so there are dialectics in history, each
related negatively to the others. These dialectics are coterminous with
existentialist projects understood as transcendings of situations, negations that conserve as they surpass (see *NE* 462). While there are no
epistemological "breaks" in Sartre's account similar to the Bachelardian
ones later employed by Foucault, insofar as the for-itself is a "spontaneous upsurge" and Sartrean fundamental choice an absolute begin-

ning, Sartre's ontological landscape is riddled with "holes" that suffer
no explanation by appeal to antecedent conditions. Where they differ
from Foucauldian "gaps" is in their explanatory power: consciousness
and "choice" are ultimate explanations in terms of freedom, a thesis that
Foucault categorically denies.

Finally, Sartre's "dialectic" differs from the classical, that is,
Hegelian, dialectic in the following respects: 1) In the contingency that
pervades it. This stems both from the "spontaneous upsurge" of consciousness and from the hazards of the in-itself to which, as we have
seen, all action is liable. 2) In the irreducible heterogeneity of its basic
components, notably the in-itself and the for-itself. This does not prevent classical dialectical relationships at another level, for example,
among situation, choice, and goal (*but*). But it does preclude any ultimate synthesis. 3) In the role of the imaginary, both in projecting a totalizing goal and in the creative moment that Sartre attributes to
fundamental choice. 4) In the specific Sartrean understanding of creative
freedom.[17] Sartre agrees that "the dialectic is until now the only method
available for making sense of freedom, for rendering it intelligible, and
for at the same time preserving its creative aspect" (*NE* 466). Still, he
distrusts the Marxist version as he then understands it: "The connection
among the structures of the historical fact are much *looser* than Marx
would have liked them to be. This is necessary because man is not the
reflection [of his circumstances] but transcendence and invention. . . .
Each of his works reflects and expresses [his] situation . . . *by surpassing
it*" (*NE* 74; F 80). Perhaps, above all, Sartre's dialectic differs from the
classical one by its insistence against Hegel that if History is not finished, the dialectic becomes a *hypothesis* and human existence an absolute
(see *NE* 466).

Despite these major differences, Sartre's dialectic resembles the classical variety in being a revolving relation of same and other. The "otherness" (alterity) that permeates History comes from several sources, as
we have seen, but primarily from the nature of the historical agent. Explaining that "History escapes itself" (an implicit reference to being-
for-others and to detotalized totalities), he adds: "To act in History is to
accept that this act will become *other* than what it was conceived to be.
Here is the true synthesis of unity and duality: to regrasp the act *become
other* and penetrate it again with subjectivity (the synthesis of the same
and the other), to reappropriate it" (*NE* 47–48). And to do so without

end till death transforms the entire person into alterity. Thus, he concludes, "History will *always* be alienated" (*NE* 49).

In a striking anticipation of his master dialectic of series-group-institution in the *Critique,* Sartre observes that "the true historical dialectic . . . [consists in] the given Alienation, Apocalypse and alienation of Apocalypse" (*NE* 414). He explains "apocalypse," a usage borrowed from André Malraux, as "the human moment, the ethical moment" that paradoxically is most often also "the moment of violence."[18] As if to prophesy the spirit of the student events of May, 1968, he writes twenty years before the fact: "Festival, apocalypse, permanent Revolution, generosity, creation—*the moment of man.*" Against which he counters: "The Everyday, Order, Repetition, Alienation—the moment of the Other than man." And he concludes: "Freedom can exist only in liberation. An *order* of freedoms is inconceivable because contradictory" (*NE* 414). These Zarathustrian aphorisms form an apt manifesto for an anarchist politics but seem to leave "History" in the *Notebooks* as either a chronicle of alienation or a calendar of feasts.[19]

SCOPE OF THE HISTORICAL DIALECTIC

So there are dialectics because there are totalities. But is there in any sense *a* totality and hence *a* dialectic of History? This is the final question of the first volume of the *Critique* as well. At this stage of his reflection, Sartre warns against attributing the unintended results of our actions to the "cunning of Reason." For "to do this would require that there is *one* Reason, that is, a principle of unity situated behind individual consciousnesses and particular collectivities . . . or simply a real presence of the whole yet to come in the parts" (*NE* 106–7). In place of such Reason, he suggests that our actions are alienated and their meanings stolen by an "anonymity with a thousand heads" (*NE* 107; F 114). Still, these and other misgivings about *one* totality and *one* dialectic of History do not dissuade Sartre in the *Notebooks* from offering a tentative, positive answer:

> If we assume that a man can conceive the whole (the final state of humanity), we must also assume that this whole is now and always given. This is what I believe. It is always given as the whole of freedom (freedom as comprehension of the human condition and as implying the freedom of everyone). Except there is no longer a dialectic. To put it another way: either History is finite or we can grasp its dia-

lectic only partially, in the past and by extending it (a bit) through
extrapolation. (*NE* 467)

Reference to "the whole of freedom" is the point at which "History"
crosses over into moral philosophy and the dialectic assumes a valuative
stance. Here the style of life Sartre terms "authentic" enters his theory
of historical dialectic.

Though we shall pursue this ethical dimension in the next chapter,
let us note Sartre's picture of "the human condition" as it emerges
from this dialectical vision of the end-goal of History: "If the dialectic is
not a closed system, then we have to live with the incertitude of the
present moment. And this life of incertitude becomes an absolute. But it
is no longer the Hegelian absolute, it is the absolute of the lived [*le
vécu*]. . . . Expectation, decision made in uncertainty, oscillation,
choice—precisely the features of the human condition—these cannot
be integrated in any synthesis because they are exactly what are eliminated from a synthesis." From this he draws the conclusion and the
moral, "if each human being is a risk, humanity as a whole is a risk" (*NE*
467; F 483). His philosophy never lost this sense of risk or of hope as the
response. There is no guarantee that History will finally issue in lasting
freedom, harmony, and peace. The "absolute" consciousness may
choose unfreedom, discord, and violence instead. So *a* dialectic of History
as a given in the nature of things is ruled out of court, as we have seen. Still,
the possibility, the image, the *ideal* that can retrospectively turn histories
into History is beginning to take shape on Sartre's horizon.

LIMIT OF THE HISTORICAL DIALECTIC

But what of Sartre's "reign of freedom" and "city of ends" discussed
earlier? If it becomes an end-terminus, History is finished and so too is
humanity. We revive alienation in a closed society à la Bergson. But if
the end-goal is "*what we shall do* when these conditions are realized,"
then humanity realizes itself in a project of *transcendence*. As Sartre explains, "this is why every historical system that *stops* the development of
humanity at the phase of the self recuperating the self becomes a form of
authoritarianism. This, properly speaking, is the *totalitarian idea*" (*NE*
169). This would be the social equivalent of existential "bad faith" as the
attempted collapse of transcendence into facticity (otherness into identity). In the *Critique,* this authoritarian move will characterize the leader
and followers of the institution. On the other hand, it is this collective

project of transcendence as a practical *ideal* that constitutes the "action of the future on the past" which Sartre's existential dialectic demands.

The glimmer of hope that breaks forth from Sartre's theory at this stage springs chiefly from his existentialist thesis that meaning (*sens*) is created, not discovered. Whatever meaning in the sense of "synthesis" or "unity-totality" History bears will result either from our attitudes or our *oeuvres,* the subjective and objective views respectively. We have discussed the role of the "work" in revealing the project of another's freedom. Sartre has addressed this issue amply in his writings on aesthetics.[20] Here he repeats a claim made elsewhere that the aesthetic *oeuvre* is an act of generosity by the artist and an invitation to the spectator. Art, as we have seen, is Sartre's ideal form of communication among freedoms (where the looking/looked-at relationship of *Being and Nothingness* seems suspended or overcome). But he adds in the *Notebooks* that the nonaesthetic work can likewise suppress contradiction between self and Other, that it can unify "on the plane of the real, made object," that is, in the real as distinct from the imaginary world. Yet he speaks of "suppression," not "synthesis"; he insists that "this contradiction still remains within it" (*NE* 468).

What Sartre suggests in these notebooks is "a lived through solution, that is, [one that takes place] on the plane of actual experience, of consciousness." He is recommending what elsewhere he calls a "moral conversion," namely, a change in "existential attitude."[21] This entails "undertaking one's project *while taking into account* the double contradiction [between for-itself and for-others] or, if you will, extending a bridge between them, realizing through a perpetual tension, an attitude that takes account of both terms" (*NE* 468; F 484). For example, the constant attempt to be for-others what I am for myself (and the converse) requires that I live this contradictory status either by opting for one of the terms (inauthenticity) or by sustaining the perpetual tension (authenticity). The sustained tension that perpetuates without resolving the "dialectic" of my personal project becomes the recommended form of interpersonal relations as well as the (ideal) end-goal of History. This is what Sartre calls "the whole of freedom" (*NE* 467) and its foretaste, as later in the *Critique,* is the all-for-one-and-one-for-all of the combat group.

He extends this "authentic" mode of acting to one's historical existence earlier in the *Notebooks* when he writes, "The virtue of the historical agent is generosity. But here true friendship intervenes: the friend, the one for whom the other is the same. Combatants who together create a setting of intersubjectivity in their own way. In this instance, rather than the same being in the other, the other is in the same. Nuance of quasi objectivity in this common subjectivity" (*NE* 48). This extension of an existentialist "virtue" to the social realm prepares us for the positive values of mutuality and "free alterity" among group members set forth in the *Critique*. In fact, it is the concept of "free" alterity that resolves one of the problems of historical dialectic that we noted above, specifically, that of achieving a nonalienating otherness.

Sartre later repeats the move when characterizing the "conversion" of the authentic person as achieving a new relation of "accord with self," yielding a "unity of existence" instead of an [inauthentic] "unity of being." He sees this as a kind of solidarity (not solidity) of the person with himself that can later be modified into "solidarity with others," a special type of existence that excludes "possession" of self or others and which Sartre terms "ethical unity" (*NE* 479). In the second volume, we shall question whether Foucault's "aesthetics of existence" and "constitution of the moral self" formulated toward the end of his life make possible an analogous social solidarity.

The foregoing could be termed a "practical" synthesis of otherwise heterogeneous elements. Sartre will elaborate but not deny such a resolution of his basic antitheses later in his career. It accords with the *moral* dimension of his theory of History, which we shall examine in the next chapter.

COLLECTIVE REALITIES: THE SUBJECT OF HISTORY

Elsewhere I have charted the evolution of Sartre's social ontology from *Being and Nothingness* to the *Critique of Dialectical Reason*.[22] Such an ontology is integral to any complete philosophy of history since it addresses the issue of the ontological status of those entities such as armies, prime ministers, and socioeconomic classes of which historians speak.

Briefly, *Being and Nothingness* adopts what I have been calling the "looking/looked-at" model of social relations grounded on Sartre's well-known description of the "look" (*le regard*). The upshot of this approach is that social relations are viewed as intrinsically objectifying-alienating and the social subject, the "we" of collective identity, as a purely psychological phenomenon. This has been a view favored by so-called methodological individualists in the social sciences.[23]

The *Critique,* on the other hand, introduces what I have called the more versatile "praxis" model of social ontology, which we shall discuss later. What the *Notebooks* employ is a more supple theory than *Being and Nothingness* but one still in thrall to the existentialist model of the social. It is a transitional position that highlights its own inadequacies.

To begin with, Sartre allows that the individual intends objects that largely surpass his historic personality. We have noted this kind of historic causality earlier, ascribing it to the Other and to inertia as components of historic action.

Second, he admits that a "collective unity" is never abstract: "It is the unity of the *doings* [*faire*] of Others" (*NE* 110; F 117). Such, for example, is the postal service, which is united for me by its common function, its end, and its rules. Significantly, Sartre speaks of a whole set of "relations among individuals" that constitute this "collectivity." He lists six, without any claim for completeness: a form of work, a condition of life, interests, a hierarchy, rituals, and frequently a myth. But as evidence of his abiding existentialist ontology, he cautions, "society exists when I am conscious of it," and adds, "I first become conscious of it *in the gaze of the other*" (*NE* 111).

Thus far, Sartre has merely elaborated his remarks on the "Us" and the "We" in *Being and Nothingness,* passages he later judged as "particularly bad."[24] He distinguishes an "internal objectivity"—the "look" of another member of the collectivity—from the "external objectivity" of the nonmember's gaze. The former, since it is *qua* member that the other is looking at me, Sartre characterizes as "recognition of the totality by itself" (*NE* 112). At best, what the collective unit consists in is a revolving series of objectifying (and hence alienating) looks—what he will criticize as "serial" relationships in the *Critique.* Suggesting his analysis in this later work, he notes that I am both *within* and *without* this totality, since I can take perspective on it and appropriate my own membership as I wish. As we have come to expect, "the historical collectivity is a detotalized totality" (*NE* 20).

But the advance over his earlier thought appears when Sartre concludes, "Hence, Society is a real, noematic being,[25] but one that is neither the sum of individuals nor their synthesis. It is always the synthetic totality of persons insofar as this totality is brought about by *others*. Hence it is always and everywhere present without *ever being*" (*NE* 113). Sartre grants society the ontological status of the "objects as meant" (*noemata*) in Husserlian phenomenology. These are knowable, efficacious, and "real" in the sense that they are not simply imaginative figments. Yet if social phenomena are noematic, not all noemata are social. This led Husserl, when discussing social groups, to speak of "personalities of a higher order."[26] Sartre will not pursue the problem of the specificity of the social or develop a social ontology until the *Critique*. But the infection of social wholes with otherness, their inevitably objectifying character, is another reason why History in the *Notebooks* is judged alienating. If Sartre is to give a plausible account of History as disalienated, he must defend its ontological possibility with an alternative theory of collective reality.

True to his individualistic proclivities, he adds that society is torn in three segments that cannot be conjoined: exterior and interior objectivity as well as "the intimacy of alienation" (that characterizes me as being both inside and outside). But society is *real*, he insists, because whichever of these segments I choose to deny, the others force themselves upon me. Finally, as another sign of the existence of Society, he appeals to its (collective) representations (again, Durkheim's term for an essential constituent of social life), and what we would today call "social facts" (another Durkheimian term) such as the banking system, an ideology, or the network of diplomatic relations between states. They cannot be ascribed to an individual nor produced by one (*NE* 112–13).

This marks a notable advance beyond the "purely psychological *Erlebnis*" to which Sartre had consigned the "We" in *Being and Nothingness,* especially when these remarks are conjoined with others about "interpenetration" of freedoms, a concrete "We," and "the common *oeuvre*" (*NE* 130; F 138). But throughout the *Notebooks,* this theory remains hobbled by its ocular model.

The Marxist *Sens* of History

We know that there was an evolution in Sartre's attitude toward historical materialism (which, following the Soviet custom, he usually distinguishes from dialectical materialism [DIAMAT] or the materialist metaphysics that includes a dialectic of nature). His opposition to dialectical materialism is voiced unequivocally in "Materialism and Revolution," published in 1946. The *Notebooks* addresses historical materialism, the Marxist theory of history and society. There Sartre both expands and softens this opposition in significant ways. This is best observed in his response to three major theses of historical materialism: the explanatory ultimacy of economic considerations (so-called economic determinism "in the last instance"), the crucial role of class struggle in historical progress in the West, and the possibility of and hope for the advent of a classless society at the end of "prehistory."

In remarks scattered throughout the *Notebooks*, Sartre indicates that, while respecting the importance of economic conditions in the directing of history, equal value must be accorded technological considerations and primacy reserved for individual choice and hence moral responsibility in determining the course of history. Locating economic considerations in the realm of facticity, he argues that "a man is always beyond the economic, which, moreover, he conserves as a surpassed foundation" (*NE* 76; F 82). It is easy to attack a crude understanding of the ideological superstructure merely "reflecting" an economic social base. Sartre sometimes aims at such simple targets. But when economic determinism is read as technological determinism, as it is by some current authors,[27] the matter becomes more complex. As we noted earlier, Sartre acknowledges this interpretation when he writes: "Even in the name of Marxism, the most important event in the last fifty years is not the Russian Revolution, but the atomic bomb." But he turns the argument against historical materialism as he understands it when he continues: "Marxism is true only if we assume that industrial discoveries are secondary and occur *in the same direction* as preceding ones. A discovery as important as the steam engine suppresses the very conditions in which Marxism had a chance of being true. It suppresses its own future and replaces it by a *true* future" (*NE* 81). Although the validity of this objection will be denied by many, my point in citing it is to indicate Sartre's assessment of historical materialism at this stage of his career.

But it is his lengthy reflections on the Engels-Dühring controversy over the relative importance of political and economic considerations in historical explanation (see *NE* 340–48) that best reveal his studied opinion at this stage. Despite the idealist motivation for Dühring's support of the political, Sartre preferred it for respecting moral categories, for example, the "just and unjust," grounded in human choice. These are the same reasons why Sartre would later favor "les Maos" over the French Communist Party.[28] According to Sartre's Dühring, "in every given material situation, the decision for association or oppression must be possible" (*NE* 341). This resembles Sartre's own remarks about consciousness-freedom. But the matter is complicated when Sartre agrees with Engels that Dühring's "freedom" is abstract and ahistorical. Sartre's Engels goes on to claim that "the dialectic of economic forces suffices to place men in a situation of oppressor and oppressed" (*NE* 341). In fact, he finds Engels's position ambiguous in that it allows a degree of personal freedom-responsibility in *The Origin of the Family* that it denies in *Anti-Dühring,* works written within a few years of each other. Sartre's conclusion suggests the program he will follow in the *Critique:*

> Therefore we arrive at the necessity of attempting a synthesis of Düh-ring and Engels. Oppression is not a gratuitous decision, however it is a human fact. It appears in a favorable economic situation, but this situation by itself is not sufficient to give birth to oppression without at the same time dehumanizing it and making it lose its meaning. The original communitarian society may or may not decide to have slavery and if it does so, this is not just an economic fact. The addition of some size of labor force to that of the tribe is a decision that implies an affir-mation affecting the existence and value of man and is possible only on the basis of some prior relationship of man to man. (*NE* 348)

This effort to concretize and "humanize" the most abstract phenom-ena by linking "fact" to "decision" continues to be the mark of an exis-tentialist approach to history. What Sartre regards as a union of Engels and Dühring, Aron will later criticize as Sartre's impossible synthesis of Kierkegaard and Marx.[29]

As for the second Marxist thesis, Sartre argues that "the class 'struggle' determines none of the important phenomena in ancient his-tory: neither the struggle for the Mediterranean, nor the constitution of Empires. Nor the appearance of Christianity" (*NE* 453). Though far from denying the fact of conflict among socioeconomic classes, Sartre is opposed to the quasi-automatic interpretation he believes Engels gives it in *Anti-Dühring.* "What happens," he asks, "to the class *struggle?* . . . A principle of economic disequilibrium cannot be likened to a struggle. In fact, there is a universally accepted system, but one that contains within itself the seeds of its destruction. There is no opposition between men.

Here man is an epiphenomenon" (*NE* 345; F 359). This will continue to be an existentialist criticism of all historical determinisms. We can already sense the stirring of Sartre's self-proclaimed mission ten years later "to reconquer man within Marxism" (*SM* 83).

Finally, despite the functional similarity and common Hegelian inspiration of the Marxist and the emerging Sartrean ideas of the "end of prehistory" as a unifying historical concept, Sartre's is a socioethical ideal that does not deny the individual transcendence (*dépassement*) synonymous with human freedom nor the element of chance involved in the "conversion" of an entire generation. In contrast, for Sartre, the Marxist ideal casts a retroactive necessity over the movement of prehistory that fails to respect the contingency of the ideal, much less the loose historical connections leading up to it.[30]

In sum, the Sartre of the *Notebooks* remains a critic of historical materialism in its attempt to discover *the* philosophy of history based on "objective" historical necessities, whether strictly economic or technological. And yet he is more sensitive to the economic factors conditioning the historical situations than the popular reading of *Being and Nothingness* would have led us to expect. Although scarcely presenting a systematic theory of history, the remarks gathered in these notebooks represent Sartre's most serious and sustained, if still hypothetical, reflections on the topic thus far in his career. They presume the anthropology of *Being and Nothingness* but evidence a greater respect for historical, especially economic and technological, conditioning than his earlier work allowed. In particular, they attest Sartre's growing awareness of his task as a committed philosopher of history to somehow synthesize individual freedom and socioeconomic necessity—Dühring and Engels. Yet the word "synthesize" is scarcely appropriate. The Sartrean "dialectic" as continued from *Being and Nothingness* remains truncated, resembling rather the Kierkegaardian in its move to push each antithesis to its extreme.

The *Notebooks,* itself an ambiguous work due to its posthumous publication and aphoristic style, carries as its chief message for a philosophy of history the multifaceted *ambiguity* of the historical fact. This derives primarily from the inherent otherness of the fact as historical (a gloss on Sartre's remark in *Being and Nothingness* that the dead are prey to the living [*BN* 543]), from the hazards of being-in-itself, and from the nonself-coincidence that grounds individual freedom.

Sartre respects the need to base a philosophy of history on an ontology of action by addressing the questions of the individual and the social subject, the Other, temporality, and inertia—all essential to historical agency. But the ambiguity of the historical fact coupled with the "inner distance" of the human agent leads him to essay a properly (that is, quasi-Hegelian) *dialectical* approach to meaning in history, one that appeals to otherness or negativity, to the intrinsic temporality of the phenomena in question, and to the telic unity of a (detotalized) totality conveyed by the practical ideal of the reign of freedom. On the other hand, this ideal articulates the characteristically Sartrean marriage of the moral and the historical (means-end; violence-fraternity); on the other, it differs from its Marxist equivalent, the classless society, by its status as practical, moral ideal. It is to the Sartrean concept of History as ethical ideal that we now turn.

Chapter Four

History as Fact and as Value

There is little doubt that the later Sartre, author of the "Marxist" *Critique of Dialectical Reason,* subscribed to a theory of history in the grand style of his nineteenth-century predecessors, though he did it as he did everything else, in his own way. But it is often assumed that his "discovery" of History coincided with his "discovery" of society during the German occupation of France in the Second World War. Indeed, Sartre implied as much.[1] In this chapter, I shall expand my initial claim that the "pre-Marxist" Sartre had a lively interest in the philosophy of history by continuing to analyze how that theory developed along characteristically "existentialist" lines. I shall appeal chiefly to the same posthumously published evidence to exhibit Sartre's concept of the historical process evolving from a descriptive, through an interpretive, to a valuative view. These texts reveal, in effect, that soon after the war, without discounting the concept of historical fact so central to his early reflections, Sartre adopted a concept of "History" as value to be fostered in our social life. An appreciation of this valuative dimension of his thought, confirmed by his contemporaneous theory of "committed" literature, softens considerably the scandal of his final

> The absolute is not God's point of view on History, it is the way in which each man and each concrete collectivity *lives* its history.
> —Sartre, *Notebooks for an Ethics*

> But what makes our position original, I believe, is that the war and the occupation, by precipitating us into a world in a state of fusion, perforce made us rediscover the absolute at the heart of relativity itself.
> —Sartre, *What Is Literature?*

interviews with Benny Lévy, so criticized by Simone de Beauvoir and others.[2] More importantly, it should serve to temper an excessively Marxist reading of his subsequent work in theory of history.[3]

Concomitant with this valuative concept of History is Sartre's unique attempt to conjoin historical "objectivity" with existential authenticity—values that are commonly taken to be mutually exclusive. What he calls "historialization [*historialisation*]," a defining feature of what I am calling an "existentialist" theory of history, is both the vehicle for achieving "authentic" history and the key to understanding a historical period in its lived contingency, not as a museum piece.

AGAINST RELATIVISM: THE ABSOLUTE FACT

We have observed two absolutes stabilizing Sartre's notoriously Heraclitian philosophy. One is consciousness-freedom, which, as a "spontaneous upsurge," simply appears, without cause or ground. This may seem to afford an odd kind of stability, if one forgets that Sartre's philosophy is primarily moral and that the "buck" of moral responsibility stops with individual consciousness-freedom. Talk of grounds or causes, Sartre believes, would simply pass the buck elsewhere and ultimately to natural processes. Consciousness thickens into the "lived absolute" (*le vécu*) in the *Notebooks,* where its historical, as distinct from ontological, relevance is more easily appreciated.

Sartre's other anchor is the in-itself in its various functions. In the theory of history it serves as the basis of the recalcitrance of the historical event or fact. The status of the historical fact as the in-itself of for-others conveys hard facticity to the human condition and as we have seen, gives history its *unidirectional* character: Pascal's "something happened to man." Henceforth, every attempt to dissolve history in a liquor of interpretations of interpretations must stop at the insoluble facts: the grain of sand in Cromwell's gallbladder, the failure of Grouchy to arrive on time. It is in this recalcitrance that the historical "realist" Sartre has sought refuge from the ravages of relativism since his initial conversation with Aron in the *War Diaries.*[4]

And yet from the start he has been keenly aware of the plurality of interpretations to which a fact or event is liable. We have seen him insist on the perspectival nature of our grasp of a historical epoch, the "pluridimensionality" of the event (*NE* 35). How shall we reconcile this perspectivism with existential facticity in history? What kind of historical "realism" is possible for an existentialist?

HISTORICAL REALISM AND THE THREE LEVELS

To begin to answer these questions, we must return to the three levels on which Sartre claims the historian labors, namely, those of the for-itself, the in-itself, and the for-others, corresponding to the basic dimensions of his ontology. At this point, we shall focus on each level in terms of historical realism and the absolute fact, reviewing these same levels from the perspective of "History" as a valuative concept later in the chapter.

Recall that in the *War Diaries* Sartre had appealed to the plane of the in-itself and the event "in its absolute existence" as "what the historian intends." What makes this claim interesting but problematic is his insistence that the absolute event is "temporal but not dated" (*WD* 300; F 364). Recall, too, that Sartre attributed Aron's "relativism" to lack of the concepts of "absolute event" and "simultaneity." In chapter 2 we saw how these concepts were related, although the functions of "simultaneity" were subsequently absorbed by "facticity" and "totality." We listed temporality as one of the conditions for historical activity and noted Sartre's distinction between historical and biographical time as well as the unidirectionality of the former and the "absolute" status of the latter. Let us now pursue this last topic as the key to his historical "realism."[5]

Sartre seems to think that the second plane, that of the "absolute event," belongs to the chronicler or the potential chronicler. Presumably, the absolute event has an "objective" status, available for discovery and interpretation. One would think that the event or fact, as temporal though not "dated," stands in sequential relation to its predecessors and successors, however one might choose to interpret that relationship, very much like the events in McTaggart's B-series mentioned in chapter 1. That Brutus stabbed Caesar, for example, is a fact, but not the reverse. So too is its sequential relation to the battle of Actium.

One could object that, in the ontology of *Being and Nothingness* which is anticipated in the *Diaries,* being-in-itself has no relations; relations are introduced by the for-itself or consciousness (see *BN* 184). Still, relationality seems predicable of the event, particularly insofar as it is temporal. Moreover, Sartre does refer to "that original temporality of being-in-itself" (*BN* 124). Clearly this is relevant to the historical fact inasmuch as the fact is being-in-itself of for-others. What, then, is one to make of the "undated" temporality of the "absolute" event?

The solution Sartre offers in *Being and Nothingness* appeals to his concept of "universal time," the objective time dated by chroniclers and measured by clocks. It is here that he locates the temporality of the in-itself. He admits that the in-itself, being essentially self-identical, "is not adapted to temporality precisely because [temporality] is a being which is perpetually at a distance from itself and for itself" (*BN* 204). Universal time, though it arises with consciousness, nonetheless is discovered "*on being* [-in-itself] [*sur* l'être]"; that is, it reveals itself as "objective," as "already there." He explains: "It is not true therefore that the non-temporality of being [-in-itself] escapes us; on the contrary, it is *given in time,* it provides the foundation for the mode of being of universal time" (*BN* 205).

But this mode of being is primarily the past: "Thus there is only one Past, which is the past of being or the *objective* past *in* which I was. . . . It is through the past that I belong to universal temporality" (*BN* 208). We must admit, however, that Sartre never pursues further the meaning of the undated temporality of the historical event, other than to locate it in the horizon of universal time, a dimension prepared by his earlier concept of "simultaneity," even though the issue arises by implication in *Being and Nothingness.* We can presume that it includes the "datability" of which analytic philosophers would later speak, but fixed, however problematically, in the inert facticity of the in-itself.[6]

Sartre both confirms the ontology of undated temporality in *Being and Nothingness* and opens a path for understanding the two other planes in the context of his historical "realism" when he writes:

> We shall see later that we continually preserve the possibility of changing the *meaning* of the past in so far as this is an ex-present *which has had a future.* But from the content of the past as such I can remove nothing, and I can add nothing to it. In other words the past which *I was* is what it is; it is an in-itself like the things in the world. The relation of being which I have to sustain with the past is a relation of the type of the in-itself—that is, an identification with itself. (*BN* 116)

Note his distinction between content and *sens* (meaning/direction). It is crucial to our thesis in the next two chapters that, for Sartre, the meaning/direction of history is decided, not discovered. No doubt one discovers the raw material for history (its "content") from the facts and events of the past, including the "coefficient of adversity" exerted by

these facts as we try to marshal them in one direction rather than another. But these mute monuments must be rendered vocal not only by
the questions we address to them but by the chain of relationships into
which we introduce them, including our present freedom and possibility. Further, the "dead" past of inert facts and events can be vivified
only by incorporating the choice of the present and the risk of the future,
that is by "situating" them in the existentialist sense of uncovering the
tension between facticity and transcendence that they conceal. This is
the task of "historialization," which we discuss below.

The first plane of historical research that Sartre delineates, that of
"the man projecting himself [*se jetant*] through situations and living
them in the unity of human reality" (*WD* 301; F 365), need not detain us
here. It entails its own kind of "absolute," what he calls "historialization." We shall discuss this level and the term that distinguishes it when
we consider the valuative dimension of Sartrean History later in the
chapter.

DIFFICULTIES WITH THE THIRD LEVEL

But problems arise when we move to Sartre's third plane of historical
investigation, what might be called the "historical" properly speaking.
This is the field of the for-others, the social realm, and it takes note of the
event's being "dated" and becoming "of the world." Several difficulties
surface at this level. Let us consider four.

First, there is the question of the "world" in which the event becomes
ingredient. From the Husserlian perspective that Sartre presumably is
adopting with this term, there is only "one" world. On the other hand,
Sartre from the outset has denied any transcendental ego—the Husserlian vehicle of world singularity. Given the relation between consciousness and world in *Being and Nothingness* ("Without the world there
is no selfness, no person; without selfness, without the person, there is
no world" [*BN* 104]), "world" assumes a valuative cast, correlative to
the project which constitutes my self. By becoming "of the world" at
this third level of investigation, the event enters a circle of relations
formed by the projects that subsume it. Absent a transcendental ego,
"objectivity" in a realist sense seems difficult, if not impossible, to attain. Again, we encounter the fundamental ambiguity of the "given"
and the "taken" in Sartre's thought, a difficulty that haunts his entire
corpus.

The next problem is ontological. What is the status of these "others" who "surpass" the event in constituting their "world"? If the event is by definition a form of being-for-others, then the concept of a "private" event would seem contradictory. Of course, one could respond that the "other" in question is purely conceptual, a feature of the "embodied-ness" of the event, like the wind rustling the bush in Sartre's famous example of "being-looked-at" (see *BN* 276). But if there is indeed a being-in-itself of being-for-others, and if this is the locus of the histori-cal event, then any adequate theory of history will have to examine that peculiar ontological state, its "publicness."

Thirdly, what does it mean to "date" an event? Is this equivalent to incorporating it into a narrative? Sartre would have no trouble with this account, as long as it did not reduce the ontological to the discursive, being to the language of being.[7] After all, he agrees with Aron and Paul Veyne that the historian's craft produces *un roman vrai* (a novel that is true).[8] But he would resist what Fredric Jameson calls "the fashionable conclusion that because history is a text, the 'referent' does not exist."[9] Sartre's point in insisting on the second plane of historical investigation is to underscore a referent that is real, not imagined. If Sartre nods to-ward linguistics (as he will do in *Search for a Method,* for example), it is in order to underscore the primacy of lived experience. As Denis Hollier encapsulates it: "I myself am the signifier (*Le signifiant, c'est moi*), says Sartre in all simplicity."[10]

Nonetheless, as narrative (*un roman*), the historians' history is a form of "doing" and is subject to the moral categories of good and bad faith. Insofar as history can be "committed," in the sense to be described shortly, Sartre can be presumed to consider "detached" narrative a form of bad faith, that is, an unacknowledged acquiescence in the economic and political status quo (see *WL* 201). Since "to be dead is to be a prey for the living" (*BN* 543), we are free-responsible to read the past as we choose. But the "text" through which we read (realism) is an instrument of our own creation (constructivism). We shall discuss this claim in chapter 6.

Finally, what is the relation between these three "planes"? In particu-lar, how should we connect the first and the third, biography with his-tory in the strict sense? In many ways, the remainder of our volume is the answer to this last question.

We have already situated the first difficulty in the larger context of the ambiguity of the given/taken disjunction in Sartre's thought overall. Let us examine each of the remaining problems in order. The question of ontological status is resolved indirectly after *Being and Nothingness,* when Sartre exchanges his looking/looked-at concept for the praxis model of social relations. It then becomes possible to account for group action in a way that enriches individual projects without dissolving them in some organic whole. Whereas a plural "look" is impossible except in a purely psychological sense, group "praxis" is a quite common, ontological phenomenon. And the increased "power" of group membership enhances historical causality considerably.[11]

Similarly, the matter of "dating" the event emerges as the problem of "totalizing" the fact(s) in an ongoing project. Whoever reads or tells a story is engaging in a "totalizing" act. The individual agent's way of "subsuming" historical events into a life project—which is his or her "story," no doubt, but presumes a "choice" of goal and action in-the-world, in addition to an "account" of where one is heading (*sens*)—this carries a moral value that transcends the "story" and is presumed by it. The very use of narrative presumes a moral to the tale. As Hayden White observes, "where, in any account of reality, narrativity is present, we can be sure that morality or a moralizing impulse is present too."[12]

This third-level question helps focus the existentialist view of historical understanding as it moves from *Being and Nothingness* into the dialectical relations of the *Critique.* For it reminds us never to overlook the primacy of individual praxis, to which responsibility can be ascribed in a moral sense. So if "to make the event 'of the world'" means "to incorporate it into a narrative," as we said, Sartre would insist that the narrative be *performative,* not merely descriptive. When the rioting Parisian shouts "we are a hundred strong," he is not only incorporating his project into the collective narrative known as the French Revolution, he is *effecting* a qualitative enrichment of his individual undertaking: "interiorizing" multiplicity, as Sartre will later put it, and creating History, not merely being drawn in its wake as some isolated flotsam.

As for relating biography and history, the individual and the social, though this is faced in the *Notebooks,* it is not resolved until *The Family Idiot,* his monumental study of Flaubert's life and times. But by then the matter of historical fact (and of facticity in general) has been incorporated into the issue of "History" as practical ideal, to which we now turn.

History as Value: Fraternity and Violence

If the terminus a quo of Sartre's theory of history is a somewhat naive understanding of historical facts or events as seeming to await our selection like fruit for the picking, its terminus ad quem is a rather subtle defense of "History" as the ideal achievement of our common strivings. This image surfaced in the interviews Sartre gave Benny Lévy toward the end of his life. There he spoke of "fraternity" and a morality of the group in terms that shocked those who had grown used to the rugged existential "individualist," leading some to speak of senility (in Sartre) and/or betrayal (in Lévy). By focusing on several passages from the *Notebooks,* I hope to show that these ideals were not so novel, that Sartre had nurtured a quasi-communitarian concept of History as value even from his vintage existentialist days.

Among the issues of relevance to the philosophy of history discussed in the *Notebooks,* one emerges as a leitmotiv that will henceforth sound throughout Sartre's work, namely, the recurring antithesis of fraternity-violence. This value/disvalue duality employs a parody of the social contract to introduce the historical efficacy of the pledged group in the *Critique.* That each member swears loyalty to all the others, each being considered "the same" as every other (fraternity), and does so under pain of death (terror), is a well-known feature of the later Sartre's social thought. But his mature position on violence is already enunciated in a work contemporary with the *Notebooks,* where he writes: "I recognize that violence under whatever form it may manifest itself, is a setback. But it is an inevitable setback because we are in a universe of violence; and if it is true that recourse to violence against violence risks perpetuating it, it is also true that it is the only means of bringing an end to it" (*WL* 200). Moreover, the voluntarism of Sartre's philosophy generally and the appeal to direct action and counterviolence in his polemical writings in particular are aspects of his thought in the sixties and seventies that linked him with the ultra Left and "les Maos."[13] Toward the end of his life he avowed: "But in all truth, I still don't see clearly the real relationship between violence and fraternity" ("LW" 415).

A number of passages from the *Notebooks* strikingly reveal the valuative nature of "History" as Sartre is coming to use the term. In one, he redescribes his standard duality, totalization-detotalization, in terms of fraternity and violence respectively:

The more the historical agent chooses violence, lies, and Machiavellianism as his means, the more efficacious he is. But the more he contributes to division, the more he puts the accent on detotalization; the more he is himself an object in History and the more he defeats History (whose ideal existence would be in terms of totalization). The true historical agent is less efficacious; but by treating human beings as himself, he tries to make the Spirit exist as a unity, therefore [as] History. It is through him that a History is possible (through the writer, the philosopher, the saint, the prophet, the scholar). (*NE* 21–22; F 27–28)

In view of his subsequent *plaidoyer* for counterviolence, one is tempted to quote Sartre from another context against himself in this one: "When I read this, I said to myself: it's incredible, I actually believed that!" (*BEM* 34). But given his view of violence as a necessary evil and of our current "prehistory" as the locus where ethics is both necessary and impossible—a thesis he later articulates in *Saint Genet* but which he is already implicitly defending in *What Is Literature?* and the *Notebooks*—this text is compatible with his later work and certainly corresponds to the position expressed in his final interviews.

Read in light of Sartre's social ontology of series and groups developed in the *Critique* ten years later, these remarks indicate that "History" denotes both an objective process (totalizing unity) and an ideal term (that set of positively reciprocal relations among freedoms that here he terms "spirit," but which he often calls the "reign of freedom" or the "city of ends"). In a way reminiscent of Hegel and Marx, he warns that one can be the "object" of this totalizing process, whereas, presumably, it is better to be its "subject." One cannot fail to note here the disvalue of detotalization as that which divides and separates, much as the practico-inert in the *Critique* will falsely "unify" in serial impotence those alienated individuals whom mass society produces and sustains.

This is the first example of Sartre's conception of "History" as value to be fostered. It is a clear synthesis of "fraternity" or the rule to "treat others as one does oneself" and those social functions and roles that are nonexploitative by nature. Sartre has not yet incorporated the concepts of seriality and praxis fully into his vocabulary, much less has he adopted the historical materialist discourse of "forces and relations of production."[14] But he is already in possession of a concept of history that includes a normative ideal by which to assess the disvalues of violence, division, and alienation. His imminent "conversion" to Marxism is thus not the *volte-face* it is commonly taken to be.

Nowhere else in these notebooks does Sartre better describe that amalgam of moral vision (fraternity) and sensitivity to the contrary forces of the times (violence) with an antistatism that we may call "political existentialism"[15] than in the following paragraph, which bears quoting at length:

> History will *always* be alienated. There may be happy periods, but though the opposition of interests is not so strong, otherness remains. Our actions are stolen from us just the same. If however we imagine a utopia where each treats the other as an end—that is, takes the other person's undertaking as an end—we can imagine a History in which otherness is recuperated by unity, even though, ontically, otherness always remains. But no *State* as mediator between individuals can realize this situation since the State cannot deal with individuals as free. It takes an ethical determination of the person to treat other persons as ends. So the passage from pseudo-History to true History is subjected to this ahistorical determination by everyone to realize what is ethical. The historical revolution depends on moral conversion. What makes this utopian is the fact that the conversion of all at the same time, though always possible, is the least probable combination (because of the diversity of situations). One must therefore seek to equalize these situations to make this combination less improbable and to give History a chance of getting beyond pseudo-History. At present, we are historical agents within pseudo-History, because we act on these situations in the hope of preparing a moral conversion. That is why it is absurd to declare that people nowadays are too evil for anyone to devote himself to them. For, in fact, one devotes oneself to what they might be, how they might be better if the situation were changed. (*NE* 49; F 54–55)

In his *Anti-Semite and Jew,* written shortly before the *Notebooks,* Sartre had argued: "Since [the anti-Semite], like all men, exists as a free agent within a situation, it is his situation that must be modified from top to bottom. In short, if we can change the perspective of choice, then the choice itself will change" (*AJ* 148). Now he encourages us to work for greater equality among situations (only in his openly Marxist works will he emphasize socioeconomic equality) in order to facilitate a *conversion* from individualistic egoism to generous cooperation among freedoms respecting one another. For Sartre as for Marx, the passage from pseudo to true History requires an end to the state (though at this point Sartre does not elaborate that claim) and bears a kind of moral significance. Admittedly, the significance of "morality" is ambiguous for both thinkers; but in either case the change from false to true History is *disalienating*.

That Sartre places such stock in moral conversion (and in its objective conditions) to overcome selfish individualism and, in an as yet vague way, in friendship and community building as well, presages his later stance on morality and fraternity.[16] In other words, it is beginning to appear that the "problem of History" for Sartre is primarily moral rather than ontological or epistemological. For the committed thinker, it is a humanistic concern. This reflects his belief that "man is *also* a value and that the questions he raises are always moral" (*WL* 203).

Addressing the insurmountable inequality between totality and singularity, Sartre again raises the issue of morality, this time in the context of the ideal end of History:

> The end [*fin*] of History is supposed to be the advent of Ethics [*la Morale*]. But this advent cannot be provoked from within History. It is a chance combination since it requires that *everyone* be moral at the same time, which presupposes an infinite chance relative to each individual consciousness. Moreover, morality is not the fusion of consciousnesses into a single subject, but the acceptance of the detotalized Totality and the decision from within this acknowledged inequality to take each consciousness in its concrete singularity as a concrete end (and not in its Kantian universality). *NE* 88–89; F 95)

Sartre's ideal, again, is a city of ends where each freedom respects the others' freedoms in their singularity and multiplicity. There is no talk yet of praxis or even of common projects. But Kantian formalism is under attack as the paradigm of a morality that stands in direct opposition to lived historical realities. That is why he can speak of looking "beyond the antinomy of morality and History" (*NE* 104). The morality he is criticizing is abstract and universalist, and the History he envisions, concrete and totalizing. Yet, repeating an argument used in "Existentialism Is a Humanism" he believes that every historical agent proposes for himself a goal that "presumes a certain conception of man and of values; it is impossible to be a pure agent of History without an ideal goal [*but*]."

Whence he concludes that beyond this antinomy of morality and History one glimpses "a concrete ethics that is like *the logic of effective action*" (*NE* 104).

This contrast between pseudo and true History restates the view of History as value which we have been proposing. The ideal of "a History in which otherness is recuperated by unity, though ontically it still perdures," presupposes a "moral conversion" from individualistic formalism to "a concrete ethics." In another interview toward the end of his life, Sartre describes his collaborative effort with Benny Lévy (being composed on tape because of Sartre's blindness) as formulating an "ethics of the We [*une morale du* NOUS]"[17] Though the ontological foundation for such an ethic is laid in the *Critique,* especially in those sections that describe the "resurrection of freedom" in the apocalyptic emergence of the group from serial impotence, such texts as the present one reveal that the search for an end (*but*) to history as a normative quest is not just a feature of his later, neo-Marxist thought.

Toward the end of the second notebook, Sartre finally sketches his projected existentialist ethics in a numbered series of topics. All of the entries in his proposed second section deal explicitly with history. In what are cryptic notes to himself as he plans this investigation, he claims that alienation "gives the meaning [*sens*] of history: alienation—negation of alienation—new Alienation" and that "the suppression of alienation must be universal [because of] the impossibility of being ethical alone."[18] He continues: "Whence the problem: History ↔ ethics [*morale*]. History implies ethics (without universal conversion, there is no meaning [*sens*] to evolution or to revolutions). Ethics implies History (no morality is possible without systematic action on some situation)." And he notes under "Man's role in History": "The *true* (concrete) ethics: to prepare the realm of ends by a revolutionary politics that is finite and creative" (*NE* 471; F 487).

Translated into the language of Sartre's subsequent works, this means that the *historical* (chiefly socioeconomic) *conditions* for mutual recognition among freedoms and for concrete moral ties of generous cooperation, that is, the conditions for true *fraternity,* must be realized before we can expect this otherwise merely utopian end to prehistory to come about. The question of a meaning-direction (*sens*) to History becomes a function of the *moral* imperative to liberate all humankind from its historical bond of alienation. Sartre's project of *giving* a meaning to

History, however, remains programmatic in the *Notebooks* and without a social ontology to sustain that union of personal conversion and socio-economic revolution which it clearly prescribes. Moreover, the historical source of disvalue (of exploitation, oppression, and violence in general), which he will subsequently discover in the "fact" of scarcity, will make its appearance only with the *Critique*. But, by then, its defeat, or even its diminishment, seems to require some kind of technological victory issuing in a "socialism of abundance" (*FI* 5:171).

THE THREE PLANES REVISITED

We noted that in his *War Diaries* Sartre distinguished three levels at which historical scholarship might be carried out, what we might designate the factical, the autobiographical, and the historical properly speaking. We raised but did not address the question of how the last two, history and (auto)biography, were interrelated. Although the topic is so complex and important in Sartrean thought that I shall devote chapters 8 and 9 to its explicit discussion, what we have just said about history as fact and as value may serve to broach the topic and begin to illuminate the biography-history question. In the following section, under the rubric "History and Historialization," we shall examine this question from another perspective, this time reflecting on the matter of auto-biography. In chapter 3 we treated the epistemological issue of how our understanding (*compréhension, Verstehen*) of an agent's life project contributes to our grasp of the meaning-direction (*sens*) of a large historical phenomenon such as the First World War and vice versa. Let us now concentrate on the valuative aspect of the existential project and histori-cal unity, turning to the problem of how the project and the historical enterprise are interrelated. The concept of "conversion" will serve as a helpful bridge from the *Notebooks,* connecting biography with History as value.[19]

In a frequently cited footnote to *Being and Nothingness,* Sartre speaks of "the possibility of an ethics of deliverance and salvation," but warns that "this can be achieved only after a radical conversion which we can not discuss here" (*BN* 412 n). Given the individualistic context of that work, "deliverance" from the reefs of sadism and masochism on which desire founders seems to require a radical change in fundamental pro-ject. Specifically, it seems to call for the willingness to live in creative tension the impossible desire to coincide consciously with oneself—

that playful state of "chosen" contingency and unjustifiability that Sartre terms "authenticity." But, of course, at the time of that footnote this condition was notoriously asocial.

Yet the texts cited from the *Notebooks* indicate that "moral conversion" entails both the rejection of alienation and a positive respect for the other's freedom that adds an interpersonal dimension to "authenticity." Although he qualifies this prospect as a "rubric" and an "ideal direction," Sartre claims that "we can conceive an absolute conversion to intersubjectivity. This conversion is *ethical.* It presupposes a political and social conjuncture (suppression of classes and of the State) as its necessary condition, but [he warns] this suppression is not sufficient by itself" (*NE* 407).

The insufficiency of such "situational" determinants as political and social conditioning leads us to the "lived absolute" of individual freedom-responsibility and Sartrean biography. The biographical plane of historical research enables us to determine the contingency of this individual's living his situation in the totalizing process that constitutes his project. How, for example, did Flaubert "live" the debacle of Sedan or the entire Second Empire? A major thesis of *The Family Idiot* is that the novelist, living in a society of massive bad faith, "totalized" his age as a "demoralizer," whose "choice" of the imaginary (the literary as "unreal") resonated with the self-deception of his Second Empire reading public. In other words, this was "art as subversion" of bourgeois values, not in favor of "fraternity" and History, but for its own nihilistic sake. Not all art is salvific nor every conversion "moral."

Thus "existential psychoanalysis" illuminates the singular way a historical event or period is assumed by an agent even as it contributes to a moral assessment of that agent and his age. Without this personal aspect, talk of "morality," much less of "moral conversion," in Sartrean terms is useless. This yields the concrete ethic (*morale*) that Sartre characterized in the *Notebooks* as alone compatible with History in its valuative sense. In other words, the moral ideal of History as the "reign of freedom" or the "city of ends" is unthinkable without the "conversion" of individual projects from negative to positive reciprocity, from conflict to mutual respect. Whether this will happen is a matter of fact to be established empirically. But its general occurrence is a sufficient condition for the advent of History, and anyone who would work for its realization must be guided by "fraternal" aspirations here and now. Such is the "true historical agent" described earlier.

So the nineteenth-century socialist ideals of fraternity and solidarity are revived in Sartre's view of History, duly modified to require more than just a change in the material conditions of life. This convergence of the social and the ethical, of History and biography, which emerges from the notebooks for his "existentialist" ethics, forms the focal point of Sartrean *hope*. It shines brightly even near the end of his life when he reflects to Benny Lévy: "The world seems ugly, evil and without hope. Such is the tranquil despair of an old man, who will die in that despair. However, I resist, and I shall, I know, die in hope. But this hope must be well grounded." Setting the task for the ethical study he and Lévy are engaged in, he continues: "We must try to explain why the world of today, which is horrible, is only one moment in a long historical development, that hope has always been one of the dominant forces of revolutions and insurrections, and how I still feel that hope is my conception of the future" ("LW" 422).

HISTORY VERSUS HISTORIALIZATION

"We make one kind of history and *another one is written.*"
—Sartre, *Truth and Existence*

"Hegel's philosophy," Sartre observes, "is a History in the sense that History is a discipline turned toward the past. Not a *historialization* [*historialisation*] in the sense that it really unveils the future dimension. For the future dimension is ignorance, risk, uncertainty, a wager. If each human being is a risk, humanity as a whole is a risk" (*NE* 467; F 483).[20] Recall from the *War Diaries* Sartre's concern to describe the way a concrete individual "historializes" himself, that is, how he distills abstract conditions and atomic facts into a situation (facticity and transcendence) unified by his individuating project:

> William is nothing but the way in which he *historializes himself* [*s'histo-rialise*]. And one can see that, in the unity of that historialization, the most disparate layers of signification are linked: the reign reveals the disability, which in its turn exposes the family, England, the anti-liberalism and the Prussian militarism. It's not a question of one single thing, but of situations that are hierarchized and subordinated according to the unity of a single original project. (*WD* 318; F 386)

The principle of existential psychoanalysis introduced in *Being and Nothingness* is "that man is a totality and not a collection." Its goal is "to *decipher* the empirical behavior patterns of man" in order, by an appropriate hermeneutic, to lay bare the fundamental choice that gives meaning and direction to these patterns (*BN* 568–69). In Cartesian fashion, Sartre announces its criterion of success as "the number of facts which its hypothesis permits it to explain and to unify as well as the self-evident intuition of the irreducibility of the end attained" (*BN* 574). This evidential grasp of the individual's existential decision is confirmed, Sartre suggests, by the testimony of the person in question when such is available. But, of course, Sartre would be the first to admit that the subject could misread himself and mislead us.[21]

As if to gloss his remarks about William in the *Diaries,* Sartre explains in *Being and Nothingness:*

> If we admit that the person is a totality, we can not hope to reconstruct him by an addition or by an organization of the diverse tendencies which we have empirically discovered in him. On the contrary, in each tendency the person expresses himself completely, although from a different angle. . . . But if this is so, we should discover in each tendency, in each attitude of the subject, a meaning which transcends it. A jealousy of a particular date in which a subject historializes himself [*s'historialise*] in relation to a certain woman, signifies for the one who knows how to interpret it, the total relation to the world by which the subject constitutes himself as a self. (*BN* 563; F 650)

At this stage, Sartre is still less interested in history than in biography. But reference to "totality" and "total relation to the world" suggests that the concrete individual is not the atomic agent but the historical individual—a thesis defended in the *Notebooks.*[22] The agent enters history by his or her project. History enters the agent via the existential situation.

If the project transforms circumstances into "situation," situation colors the original project. "Situation and project are inseparable, each is abstract without the other and it is the totality, project and situation, that defines the person" (*NE* 463). Moreover, this totality is dialectical in nature; its goal guides and unifies the process, but has no existence except as sustained by the ongoing choice of the project. Because of the creative nature of existential choice as well as the "not yet" character of the goal, dialectic is essentially tied to the *imaginary* (see *NE* 464). Given the pivotal role of the imaginary in Sartre's philosophy in general, it is not surprising that it figures centrally in dialectical relations as well.[23]

Sartre uses *s'historialiser* quite often in his reflections on history in the mid to late 1940s. It occurs in "Materialism and Revolution" ("MR" 227; *S* 3:181) and frequently in *What Is Literature?* (*WL* 80, 147, 148, 175, 190). He continues to employ *historialisation* in *The Family Idiot* (for example, *FI* 5:397; F 3:429). But only in *Truth and Existence* (1948) does he discuss the distinction at any length:

> I distinguish historiality [*historialité*] from historization [*historisation*]. To me historiality is the project that the For-itself makes of itself in History: by deciding to undertake the coup d'état of the 18th Brumaire, Bonaparte historializes himself. And I call historization the passing of historialization to the objective. It results in historicity, or belonging objectively to an age. It is evident that historialization is the objective transcendence of the age and that, on the other hand, historicity is pure expression of the age. Historization is the outcome of transcendence from the point of view of a subsequent age, or the passage from historialization to historicity.

From which he draws the inevitable moral:

> Thus there is perpetual mystification. And for a transcendent and *noncommitted* [emphasis mine] consciousness, completed history would be the historicity of all mankind, that is, the free historialization of men turned into congealed Destiny. We make one kind of history and *another one is written*. Kaiser Wilhelm II decides to struggle against British imperialism and this historialization falls back into historicity: through Wilhelm II a civil war began on a world scale opposing the proletariat to the propertied classes. But what must be understood is that it is in historialization that the concrete absolute, and the unveiling of truth to the absolute-subject, reside. The mistake is in seeing an epiphenomenon of historicity there, instead of seeing historicity as the meaning conferred on my project insofar as it is no longer lived or concrete, but pure abstract in-itself. (*T* 79–80)

In what is a virtual repetition of a passage quoted earlier from the *Notebooks* (*NE* 490), he concludes:

> Therefore we must make ourselves historical against a mystifying history, that is, historialize ourselves against historicity. This can be done only by clinging to the finitude of the lived experience as interioriza-

tion. It is not by attempting to transcend our age towards the eternal or towards a future of which we have no grasp that we will escape from historicity; on the contrary, it is by accepting to transcend ourselves only in and through this age, and by seeking in the age itself the concrete ends that we intend to propose to ourselves. . . . I most certainly do not escape from historization, but it is a *minimal* historization: only of my age. (*T* 80)

For Sartre, history (on the third level of the historians) is now a matter not only of how we "date and make 'of the world'" the actions of previous generations but of how future generations see us. It is a question of how the living prey upon the dead. Inauthenticity and flight from historialization merge in the futile act of self-justification by which, for example, Franz, the guilt-ridden suicide of *The Condemned of Altona,* makes a tape recording of his "defense" to be played to the denizens of another century. Sartre warns: "By not pretending to be living with my grandchildren, I keep them from judging me by their standards. By giving them my act as a *proposition,* in order that they may do with it what they want, I escape the risk that they do with it something other than I wanted" (*T* 80). He twice remarks: "A long time ago we got rid of our grandfathers' ghosts. We should now get rid of our great-grandchildren's ghosts" (*T* 8 n).

To the extent, then, that *historicité* is related to *historialisation* as history to biography, this distinction forms a subplot running through our entire study. Thus, the existential historian, *committed* to the value of individual and collective freedom, must focus on such phenomena as the kaiser's *historialisation,* if he or she will give us concrete history and not the "Destiny" of impersonal "laws" and historical "necessities."[24]

HISTORIALIZATION AND HISTORICAL AUTHENTICITY

The concept of historialization presumes that action is "revealing/unifying" and that it reveals Being "from *my* point of view" (*NE* 486). Far from being a disadvantage, Sartre sees this as providing our access to the concrete. One must resist the illusion of universality, that is, the claim to grasp reality without a point of view. That would be a matter of contemplation, not action, and would yield only abstractions. Rather, he urges, "uncovering the *concrete* is done by claiming myself as *this* point of view." Using an expression that de Beauvoir had employed in her *Ethics of Ambiguity* and which he will repeat in his manuscript,

Truth and Existence,[25] Sartre insists that the sole aim of such an action must be "unveiling the *maximum of being* by being oneself to the utmost (not as Me but in terms of ipseity)." The allusion to de Beauvoir is not unimportant; it reminds us of the valuative dimension to Sartre's theory, which we have been pursuing in this chapter. But of greater relevance to the matter at hand is his claim that by intensifying my authenticity, the circle of selfness by which I both constitute the world as *mine* and transcend it toward an ideal, I reveal "the *totality of being*," albeit from my perspective (*NE* 487).[26]

Recall the ambiguity that infected the absolute event in the *War Diaries* as soon as one attempted to date it and concretize it in-the-world. Sartre now extends the revelatory assumption of contingency to the very date at which one finds oneself in history: Whatever I do, in effect, my historical presence calls into question the "course of the world," and a refusal to call it into question is still a calling into question and an invented answer. My concrete situation is defined as a particular point of view on my historical situation. "I-am-in" History and every one of my acts will provoke a modification of the course of the world or, on the contrary, will express this course (*NE* 489).

Hegel resolved this problem of perspectival truth by placing himself at the end of History where "the Truth is the Whole." But since History is not finished, Sartre concludes:

> I can assume my contingency and make it the absolute that I defined above only by assuming it within History. And that is precisely what is called historializing oneself [*s'historialiser*].
>
> So I historialize myself in laying claim to myself as the free consciousness of an epoch in a situation within that epoch, having its future in the future of this epoch, and being able to manifest *just* this epoch, not being able to surpass it except by assuming it, and knowing that even this surpassing of my epoch belongs to this epoch and contributes to its taking place. Hence my epoch is mine. . . . I am nothing other than its pure mediation. Except this mediation, being consciousness (of) self and assuming itself, saves the epoch and makes it pass over to the absolute. (*NE* 490–91)[27]

Consider the famous example from *Being and Nothingness* of the thesis that, for Sartre and his contemporaries, the Second World War is "my war" and that "it is in my image and I deserve it" (*BN* 554). There the point is to elucidate the meaning of "being-in-situation" and the bad faith entailed in trying to deny that fact. Elsewhere, he says that "in choosing myself, I choose all men" (*EH* 291). These claims converge in the concept of historialization: "To will myself is to will *my* epoch" (*NE* 490). As he explains, I cannot wish to abolish war in general. We lack the means at hand to do so and, besides, the next generation could use their freedom to reinstitute it. But I can wish to do away with *this present war,* and to do so by appealing to the same principles used by pacifists to suppress war in general. In other words, "I can want *my time* to be one where a certain imminent war was avoided" (*NE* 490).

It is not simply that I am thinking and acting concretely, with full awareness of the tension between my facticity and my freedom (as "authenticity" demands). It is that my incorporation of the moral principles of my age into my project, as in the present example, vivifies an otherwise abstract and lifeless phenomenon with my absolute freedom. And so it is for all my contemporaries as well.[28] "For an epoch *is nothing if no one thinks about it,* it is at the heart of every thought that it attains itself. So it has a thousand absolute facets but is never the *unity* (detotalized totality) of these facets, even though in each of them it is unified." Once again, Sartrean anthropology of nonself-coincidence, of the inside/outside relation between individuals and the whole, generates what we might call "historical authenticity":

> Each of them, as thinking and changing this epoch, remains *outside of it* as what upholds it within the absolute—and when thought and unified as one epoch by another they are *within it.*
>
> Each facet, therefore, will attain absolute authenticity if it realizes the tension of thinking its epoch as the absolute that attains itself can think it and itself think itself (the passage to the objective) in that epoch as the others think it. (*NE* 491)

Within the limits of a looking/looked-at model, this "authentic" relationship to one's era is the most Sartre has to offer.

Yet a real glimmer of hope, albeit one incompatible with the ocular model, dawns in the *Notebooks* when Sartre links historialization with the dialectic as he does in the following:

> In fact there are three aspects of human historialization through which a certain *dialecticalization* of History may be introduced: 1st, the ambiguity of the For-itself, the tension between contraries; 2nd, the subjective process (grasped in the *cogito*) of comprehension as surpassing

(therefore as negativity—creation); 3rd, the relations among For-itselves or detotalized totality. (*NE* 451; emphasis mine)

Although he hastens to add that these aspects also show us the limits of the dialectic, I shall argue that his whole-hearted adoption of the praxis model (internalization of the external and externalization of the internal) as it has already begun to insinuate itself will allow the "dialecticalization of History" to flower.

Still, the problem of understanding a historical object, the First World War, for example, by grasping how someone historializes himself, continues to press Sartre. What he now calls an "antinomy"—that great figures both express their epoch and transcend it—is more intensified than resolved by his existential dialectic:

> So before manifesting my epoch to itself, before changing it into itself and for itself, I am nothing other than its pure mediation. Except this mediation being consciousness (of) self and assuming itself saves the epoch and makes it pass over to the absolute. This is what allows us to resolve the following antinomy: it is said that great men express their epoch and that they surpass it. The truth is: I can *express* my epoch only in surpassing it (to express in a surpassing the given—and furthermore expression is marginal. One expresses in a surpassing meant to change) but this surpassing is itself part of this epoch—through me my epoch surpasses itself and contains its own surpassing. For my epoch, being a detotalized totality of transcendences, is itself a transcendence. (*NE* 490)

Only in his extended study of Flaubert's life and times twenty-five years later will Sartre arrive at his mature solution to this problem when he states as a heuristic principle: "A man—whoever he is—totalizes his era to the precise extent that he is totalized by it" (*FL* 5:394).[29]

MORALITY AND HISTORY: THE SECOND ETHICS

In the manuscript room of the Bibliothèque Nationale in Paris, alongside copies of rare medieval codices and diaries of seventeenth-century explorers, one can consult the quadrated papers on which Sartre penned his "second" thoughts on substantive ethics. Along with two other manuscripts conserved elsewhere, these pages constitute what Sartre called indifferently his "dialectical" ethics, his "realist" ethics, or simply his "second" ethics.[30] Although access to this material remains limited and I have not seen the second manuscript, my reading of the other two confirms their pursuit of the close relation between history and ethics sketched in the *Notebooks,* even if Sartre's position by now has shifted to a new and "realist" phase.[31]

It is this first manuscript, known as the *Rome Lecture Notes* because it consists of material for a talk given at the Gramsci Institute in that city on 23 May 1964, that de Beauvoir described as "the culmination" of Sartre's ethics.[32] In it, Sartre develops his remarks from the *Notebooks,* now couched in language from the *Critique.* He writes, for example,

> It is nonetheless the case that history and ethics are mixed together [*se confondent*] in the sense that history affirms its unity against historical pluralism only by revealing itself *in struggle* as what is continually lost in the system and as what is always regained by its unconditioned possibility for destroying *from within* the system that imprisons it. True ethics founds and dissolves alienated moralities in that it is the meaning [*sens*] of history; that is to say, *the rejection of all repetition* in the name of the unconditioned possibility of *making man* [*faire l'homme*]. (*RLN* 47)

He is explicit about the normative character of history: "But we do not share the idealism of 1848, because we think that history as *norm,* that is to say, as *pure future,* is always concealed [*voilée*], even for the exploited and the oppressed, by the institutional ensemble and by the alienated moralities maintained by the dominant classes, which are inculcated into the disadvantaged classes from their childhood" (*RLN* 46).[33]

In a way that leaves his Marxist orthodoxy in question, Sartre charts the relation between morality and history by affirming that "history is the rigorous combat between the practico-inert and praxis," not between socioeconomic classes (*RLN* 45).[34] In other words, from the normative perspective, it is the praxis/practico-inert distinction that counts, though historically the moral agonistic reveals itself in class struggle.

He fleshes out the ethics which is the *sens* of history with the humanist claim that the ongoing realization of integral humanity "is what gives history its human meaning/direction [*sens*]" (*RLN* 50). "Integral humanity" (*l'homme intégral*) is the value concept that dominates these manuscripts. It denotes associated organic individuals in positive reciprocity, free from the alienating force of material scarcity, as I shall show in my discussion of the *Critique* in chapter 6. Its counterconcept is "subhumanity," which denotes our present alienated condition, mired in a static morality ("repetition" as a form of the practico-inert) and subject to the violence of material scarcity. Still, it would be naive to read this as a simple humanism *sans phrase*. For the nature of the ethical radicalism in the Cornell manuscript and the indications from the second manuscript warn us against subscribing to some easy reconciliation of fact and value, some final synthesis of praxis and the practico-inert as the realization of the ethical and the end of History.[35]

From the other direction, *need* ("felt exigence") is the moving principle of these manuscripts that gives the second ethics its quasi-naturalist character. Consider, for instance, the following: "The root of morality is *in need,* that is to say in the animality of man. It is need which poses man as his own end, and praxis as domination of the universe *to be effected through work.*"[36] I say "quasi-naturalist" because the unresolved ambiguity of the "given" and the "taken" (in this case, fact and value) in Sartre's ontology returns to haunt his dialectical ethics as well.[37]

In sum, History stands to "prehistory" as "integral humanity" stands to "subhumanity"—and they coalesce in a common ideal, or value and disvalue. Humanity, as Sartre explains, "is the end [*fin*]—*unknowable,* but graspable as *orientation*—for a being that defines itself *by praxis,* that is, for the incomplete and alienated men that we are."[38]

The third, Cornell manuscript bears a title that could have been the subtitle for the *Notebooks,* "Morality and History."[39] These are the unpublished notes for the Messenger Lectures that Sartre was to deliver at Cornell University in 1965. They too incorporate the vocabulary of the *Critique of Dialectical Reason,* in the same way that the *Notebooks* employed that of *Being and Nothingness.* They take a major step toward constructing that "concrete ethic" he spoke of earlier, what we shall soon be calling "committed history." Such an ethic must be one of situations, and these situations, after the *Notebooks,* are seen to be historical.

By an examination of several cases, Sartre lays bare what he calls "the paradox of ethics," namely, that the ethical moment, which he terms the moment of "unconditional possibility" or "invention," is a dimension of historical *praxis.* As such, it is subject to the inertia and ambiguity of historical institutions and events, including what Weber would label the "routinization" of creative moral choices. Coming after the *Critique,* with its analysis of the only history we know as a tale of conflict and violence due to the pervasiveness of material scarcity, the paradox of ethics recalls Sartre's thesis in *Saint Genet* that ethics in our day is both inevitable and impossible (*SG* 186 n.). Every action as unconditional contains an "ethical moment," namely, the surpassing of its conditions toward an end (nonbeing, the correlate of creative imagination), which is human autonomy. But in that very surpassing it reveals its historical conditioning and practico-inert destiny. This dimension of unconditionality, Sartre writes, "if it could fully bloom [*s'épanouir*], would make historical action and ethical action homogeneous."[40] But for that to occur, the alienating effects of the practico-inert would have to be nullified. And this seems impossible short of that "socialism of abundance" he will speak of in *The Family Idiot* (5:171). To put it another way, this paradox seems to be the ethical elaboration of the maxim of Sartrean humanism that "you can always make something out of what you have been made into" (*BEM* 35; *S* 9:101). Ethical action ("authentic morality") in an alienated world is this project of living the unconditional despite one's historical link with the practico-inert (institutions, imperatives, rules, values, and the like) and because of it.

A decade earlier, in *What Is Literature?*, Sartre had spoken of the "paradox of ethics" in simpler terms as the need in a society such as ours to "take advantage of oppression in order to do good" (*WL* 190). Here, he insists that "the moral requirement [*demande*], whatever its conditions, remains inert. Consequently, the undertaking in interiority [*l'entreprise en intériorité*] becomes unconditional because it can act on the conditions rather than on the norm." But this means that "the unconditional obtains when the pure future is subjected to an inert and repetitive past," a formula that Sartre admits has "something absurd and indefensible about it." But in Juliette Simont's judgment, this constitutes "the point of no-return for Sartre's reflections on the ethical, and the reason why he always abandoned these reflections rather than ever completing them." But, as she is quick to add, this does not keep one from assuming the ethical as a paradox and living it from within as "*effectively absolute.*"[41] It looks as if Sartre's second, "realist" ethics in a society of "subhumans" is necessarily an ethics of "dirty hands."[42]

We have noted throughout Sartre's work a fundamental ambiguity between the "given" and the "taken" in every being-in-situation. This ambiguity finds its fullest expression, appropriately, in this "paradox of ethics." The autonomy of consciousness, its "absolute" character, entails its being value-constituting or "inventive," as he sometimes says. The paradox arises from the internal relation that obtains between consciousness and the *content* of moral judgments, in other words, between moral invention and what one invents as well as the resultant example and ideal image that accompany this creative act. It is often overlooked that the argument of Sartre's problematic "Existentialism Is a Humanism" lecture turns on the "image" of what humans ought to be that is implicit in every moral choice.[43] This value-image is a form of the impossible ideal of conscious self-coincidence (being in-itself-for-itself) that we recognize from *Being and Nothingness*. It recurs in the Cornell lectures as what Simont calls "an imaged coincidence [*une coincidence phantasmée*]" of the self and its moral character.[44] It is a question of the historicity of the ends chosen and the inert permanence of the action taken, on the one hand, and the unconditioned, "pure" future of the ethical choice involved, on the other. The conflict between ethics and History arises precisely from the tendency of the ethical ideal to crystallize into inert rules and maxims—that is, into the same inauthentic, repetitive mode that (in the *Critique*) characterizes "serial" existence in general. One would die for the honor of one's family, for example, in some societies and in some periods but not in others. Simont points out the tension that obtains between Kantian formalism and Marxist naturalism in Sartre's argument here and, we might add, henceforth.

The *Rome Lecture Notes* conclude with the recommendation that we create an "ethics of history," that is, "the identification of history with the dramatic development of morality" (*RLN* 162). In his own vocabulary, this constitutes an appeal for a committed history.

History and Commitment

Over several issues of his newly founded journal, *Les Temps modernes,* Sartre published a series of essays that later appeared as the book *What Is Literature?* There he elaborated his theory of committed literature enunciated in the inaugural issue. I do not intend to rehearse the rather well-known concepts developed in that remarkable opus—its distinction, for example, between poetry, which could not be committed, and prose, which could be, or its trenchant critique of surrealism. But since history is already emerging in Sartre's mind as a form of literature, we shall gain insight into his existentialist understanding of history by briefly considering his remarks on committed literature in that seminal text, published the year the *Notebooks* began. To begin with, the following observations are a virtual gloss on what we have said about History as value:

> The prose-writer is a man who has chosen a certain method of secondary action which we may call action by disclosure. It is therefore permissible to ask him this second question: "What aspect of the world do you want to disclose? What change do you want to bring into the world by this dis-

But if perception itself is action, if, for us, to show the world is to disclose it in the perspectives of a possible change, then, in this age of fatalism, we must reveal to the reader his powers, in each concrete case, of doing and undoing, in short of acting.
—Sartre, *What Is Literature?*

closure?" The "engaged" writer knows that words are action. He knows that to reveal is to change and that one can reveal only by planning to change. He has given up the impossible dream of giving an impartial picture of Society and the human condition. (*WL* 14)

Sartre is raising the question of the social responsibility of the writer and, by implication, of the historian as well. We are responsible for the aspects of the world we choose to unveil.

It is clear that Sartre as a "committed" historian has also sacrificed the impossible dream of an impartial picture for the (possible?) one of a disalienated society, that is, of History in the valuative sense. He cannot simply follow Engels's "choice" of one History through a dialectic which appeals to "the viewpoint of totality—classless society," because Engels thereby "transforms a hypothetical determinism into an apodictic necessity" (*NE* 347). In Sartre's eyes, this removes the essentially moral core of history, a criticism he will level against Marxist economism in *Search for a Method*. Rather, the sole "authentic" choice of a meaning-unity-totality for History is the moral one of the career of freedom-fraternity, which thereby furthers the advent of that value which directs the original choice.[1]

Of immediate relevance to our present topic are three theses ingredient in this committed literature that apply equally to written history as we have been discussing it. First, Sartre claims that freedom, of which literature is an expression, is both negative and constructive in its critique of unfreedom or alienation. He writes:

> Our job is cut out for us. Insofar as literature is negativity, it will challenge the alienation of work; insofar as it is a creation and an act of surpassing, it will present man as *creative action*. It will go along with him in his effort to pass beyond his present alienation toward a better situation. If it is true that to have, to make, and to be are the prime categories of human reality, it might be said that the literature of consumption has limited itself to the study of the relations which unite *being* and *having*. . . . We, on the contrary, have been led by circumstances to bring to light the relationship between *being* and *doing* in the perspective of our historical situation. . . . What are the relationships between ends and means in a society based on violence? The works deriving from such preoccupations . . . will present a world not "to see" but "to change." (*WL* 163–64; *S* 2:262–63)

So committed literature performs the practical, "moral" function of bringing our alienated condition to critical awareness, while proposing the possibility of change. (In this respect it performs a task Foucault would later assign to his archaeology: revealing the contingency and possibility that underlie the supposed "necessities" of our practical and theoretical lives.)

Secondly, committed literature is one of *praxis* as distinct from a literature of *hexis* (habit): "*Praxis* as action in history and on history; that is, as a synthesis of historical relativity and moral and metaphysical absolute, with this hostile and friendly, terrible and derisive world which it reveals to us. There is our subject. . . . It is not a matter of choosing one's age but of choosing oneself within it" (*WL* 165–66). We recognize here the call to "historialization" as "historical authenticity," though neither term appears in the text. Nor are we astonished to hear Sartre speak of a moral and metaphysical "absolute." If there is any absolute "value" in his thought, it is certainly "freedom," a term that is growing in extension as Sartre's social sense develops. This concrete, historical freedom is realized in the "socialist collectivity," his Kantian "city of ends," for he insists, "Only in a socialist collectivity would literature, having finally understood its essence and having made the synthesis of *praxis* and *exis*, of negativity and construction, of doing, having, and being, deserve the name of *total literature*" (*WL* 166). But it is precisely in these terms that he has described the end of "prehistory" or "alienated history" in the *Notebooks*. It is perhaps no coincidence that the concept of "total history" was being propounded by certain *Annales* historians at that time.[2]

The third thesis concerns the very content of committed literature. It is moral in nature and focuses on our experience of the impossibility of living a moral life in an immoral society.

> It is up to us to convert the city of ends into a concrete and open society—and this by the very content of our works. If the city of ends remains a feeble abstraction, it is because it is not realizable without an objective modification of the historical situation. . . . But if we start with the moral exigence which the aesthetic feeling envelops without meaning to do so, we are starting on the right foot. We must *historialize* [*historialiser*] the reader's good will, that is, . . . provoke his intention of treating men, in every case, as an absolute end and . . . direct his attention upon his neighbors, that is, upon the oppressed of the world. But

we shall have accomplished nothing if, in addition, we do not show him . . . that it is impossible to treat concrete men as ends in contemporary society. (*WL* 190; *S* 2:297)

This is the ideal that will unify and direct Sartre's writings from then on: "The freedom of the person *and* the socialist revolution" (*WL* 190; *S* 2:297).

Sartre continued to wield his pen as a sword on behalf of the exploited and the oppressed of society. His existentialist emphasis on the primacy of individual praxis, which we shall study in the *Critique*, requires that he emphasize oppressive praxis over institutional exploitation. But his works of imaginative literature, including his existential psychoanalyses of Baudelaire, Genet, and Flaubert, must be read as forms of the literary commitment proclaimed in *What Is Literature?* Each in its own way intends to "historialize" our good will, luring us into thoughts, as he once said, "traitorous to our class."

This same existential primacy of praxis leads Sartre to write history in such a manner that individual biography becomes integral to its unfolding. This is not simply because, as he proclaims at the outset of his multivolume study of Flaubert, he is keen on learning "what we can know about a man nowadays." His overall aim is to comprehend our common project in order to "objectively modify" our historical situation so as to liberate us from exploitative social relations. The panoply of technical terms that we shall see him introducing in the *Critique*—praxis, practico-inert, process, passive activity, and the like—is marshaled to construct a social ontology that leaves space for moral responsibility while respecting the specificity and efficacy of social wholes. This is what I am calling "committed history" at its inception. We shall review its progress in chapter 6.

This study opened with the question of whether Sartre, feeling the sting of current history, would allow for *a* meaning to it *all*. His answer to this question completes the foregoing guide to the elements of an existential philosophy of history. It can be summarized by a brief reconstruction from previously discussed material.

Given the multiplicity of consciousnesses, the ambiguity of historical facts, and the noematic status of social wholes, whatever meaning (*sens*) history has will be a product of creative *decision*, not discovery. The Marxist concept of one History as a scientific law or cultural fact, for example, can be dismissed as an expression of "social and metaphysical prejudices" (*NE* 80). We have seen that, for Sartre, in history as in individual life, "existence precedes essence" (*NE* 32); in other words, meaning in both cases is chosen, with all the risk and anguish attendant upon such commitments. And in both cases Sartre "chooses" authentic unity-totality on *moral* grounds, that is, in pursuit of the socioethical ideal of mutual recognition of freedoms (fraternity), the city of ends.[3]

Sartre does not defend these maxims in the *Notebooks,* but he does acknowledge the need for totality (not yet realized but as to-be-realized, that is, as an ideal [maxim]) to confer unity—that is, meaning—on History. In other words, his concept of a "science" of history is that of a committed thinker whose reading-interpretation of the ambiguities of history will occur from the valuative perspective of maximizing the conditions of freedom for all. In effect, this means extending to the historian the concept of "committed literature" that Sartre was making famous at about the same time.

Hayden White has warned: "Take the vision out of Marxism, and what remains is a timid historicism of the kind favored by liberals and the kind of accommodationist politics that utilitarians identify as the essence of politics itself" (*C* 143). Sartre's existentialist approach to history, even in this first phase, clearly issues from a philosophy of vision. That he is a philosopher of the imagination is as much in evidence here as in his aesthetic writings. His early adoption of imaging consciousness as the paradigm of consciousness *tout court* has continued to touch every facet of his work. If Etienne Barilier could confront Sartre and Aron on their respective conceptions of the relation between thought and reality, between the imaginary and the real,[4] it is because the decisive role of imaginative vision gave Sartre's entire philosophy an aesthetic flavor which the sober Aron never managed to produce. Whether "committed history" is a cover for ideology or whether it honestly voices the social responsibility of the historian cannot be decided fairly until we have the full dossier at hand. But in this initial stage of our inquiry and of his formulation, it is evident not only that Sartre writes with a certain set of values and disvalues in view, but that the conjunction of the historical and the moral permeates his thought and seeks resolution in a writing that effects what it portrays. Such is the message of this existentialist philosophy of history in its first phase.

PART TWO

It is often overlooked that the conviction that one
can make sense of history stands on the same level
of epistemic plausibility as the conviction that it
makes no sense whatsoever. My point is that the
kind of politics that one can justify by an appeal to
history will differ according to whether one proceeds on the basis of the former or the latter
conviction. I am inclined to think that a visionary
politics can proceed only on the latter conviction.
　　　　—Hayden White, *The Content of the Form*

Chapter Five
History Has Its Reasons

It is worthwhile recalling at this juncture that we are addressing the general issue of reason in history. Sartre is not a rationalist, not even like Hegel and perhaps Marx, a dialectical rationalist. One feature that marks his theory as existentialist is its insistence that we have a choice in the reason we employ. Not that there is a menu of rationalities from which we can select to suit our needs or whims. His point is that our life-directing project includes the valuing or the disvaluing of the rational as we understand it. And if there are kinds of rationality, our manner of being rational is part of our self-definition. So we cannot avoid responsibility even for being rational.

Reasoning has a human air. And it is not merely the objective presentation of arguments (as in a philosophy class): it is also struggle and tactics. There is a will in that voice which wants to find me wrong.
—Sartre, *Notebooks for an Ethics*

A CONFLICT OF RATIONALITIES

Sartre seems to believe that historical "reason," or sense-making, at least in the West and in our day, is of just two kinds, the analytic and the dialectical, and that each fosters a corresponding set of values. In fact, he argues that "at a certain level of abstraction, class conflict expresses itself as a conflict of rationalities" (*CDR* 1:802).

Put somewhat crudely, the analytic sums but does not totalize; it is blind to social wholes and, hence, to class conflict. It is atomistic and determinist, atemporal and formal (structural). In the face of historical events, the most analytic reason can offer is statistical generalizations and abstract causal laws. It is the rationality proper to the engineer in the *Notebooks*. Sartre sometimes calls it "bourgeois" reason since, in its passion for the "objective" as the value-free, it roundly endorses the status quo: "One makes oneself bourgeois by once and for all choosing a certain analytic vision of the world which one tries to impose on all people and which excludes the perception of collective realities" (*S* 2:19). Dialectical reason, on the other hand, is totalizing and temporalizing. It is not deterministic, though the kind of (positive) freedom it advocates is much disputed. And it is developmental; its "truth," as we have seen, is a "becoming" truth in a sense redolent of pragmatism.

With "dialectical Reason," we have reached the core of Sartre's theory of reason in history. He encapsulates that view when he writes in *Search for a Method:* "Without these principles [of his progressive-regressive method], there is no historical rationality. But without living men, there is no history" (*SM* 133). The rationality he refers to is dialectical. Its proper field comprises those ambiguous facts, conflicting interpretations, objective contradictions, and time-bound realities that make up history in the concrete. Since his mature theory of history turns on his notion of dialectical reason, we must scrutinize that term in its many aspects. In addition to the concepts of comprehension, totalization, and progressive-regressive method to be discussed in this chapter, "dialectical reason" entails two basic forms of mediation by means of which the abstract individual enters concrete history, namely, the practico-inert and praxis. For clarity of exposition, we shall defer consideration of these until chapter 6.

Sartre's first systematic treatment of the issue of historical understanding is *Search for a Method*. In the nine years that separate it from the *Notebooks*, he has followed his own advice regarding the committed historian and has entered the political arena via a series of essays, interviews, and politically oriented plays, not to mention his participation in protest movements of various sorts.[1] Yet his belief in the mission of the political Left to further the conditions for realizing the "city of ends" does not blind him to the theoretical difficulties such a project entails. "Do we have today the means to constitute a structural, historical anthropology?" he asks at the outset. And he answers with the conditional, "if such a thing as a Truth can exist in anthropology, it must be a truth that has *become,* and it must make itself a *totalization.*" Showing the fruit of his long conversation with Hegel and the French Hegelians in the *Notebooks,* he adds that such a becoming, a totalizing truth which refers both to being and to knowing is what Hegel meant by "dialectic." He takes it as a basic postulate of the book that "such a totalization is perpetually in process as History and as philosophical Truth" (*SM* xxxiv). With the help of this postulate, his task is to offer provisional solutions for the internal conflicts of philosophical anthropology.

Sartre seems to have laid aside the perplexities about History/ histories that bothered him in the *Notebooks.* He now allows that his postulate is incompatible with the "positivists'" (and his own former) claims that "there are *several* Histories and several Truths." Yet acknowledging that his "postulate" must in some sense be defended, he describes his task in *Search for a Method* as answering the question "whether there is any such thing as a Truth for humanity."[2] This translates into the challenge to show a relation (*rapport*) between historical totalization and *totalizing Truth,* his code word for historical materialism. That relation he calls "dialectical Reason," and he devotes the formidable *Critique of Dialectical Reason* published three years later to its defense.

Unlike Kant's *Critique of Pure Reason,* Sartre's *Critique* must answer not only the *quaestio juris* (How does one warrant the claims of dialectical Reason?) but also the *quaestio facti* (Is there such a thing as dialectical Reason at all?). In this he joins the post-Kantian philosophers of history such as Dilthey, Heinrich Rickert, Georg Simmel, and Weber, who seek to establish the *quid facti* as well.[3] Yet it is not a matter of "discovering" a dialectic the way one discovers a planet or even a mathematical proof, for dialectical reason by definition encompasses the inquirer along with the stated object of inquiry.[4] Rather, the dialectic must emerge, must come to consciousness in such revelatory moments as the experiences of negation, necessity, counterfinality, and *dépassement* (translated as "transcending" or "overcoming"). But these moments, like the dialectic of which they form a part, demand the counterposition which Sartre calls "positivist, analytical Reason" (*CDR* 1:823). The negative side of Sartre's justification of the dialectic is his argument that analytic Reason fails to render human reality comprehensible.

In his introduction to the *Critique,* Sartre warns that volume 1 will comprise a theory of practical ensembles "as moments of totalization," whereas volume 2, the notes for which were published posthumously in

1985, will consider "the problem of totalization itself; that is to say, of History in its development and of Truth in its becoming" (*CDR* 1:824).

Making Sense of History: *Search for a Method*

Turning to a more detailed examination of the first of these works, we find Sartre's theory of history hinged on three cardinal concepts: comprehension, totalization, and the progressive-regressive method. As the previous quotations indicate, these are to be understood dialectically, that is, with a certain spiraling reciprocity, though the dialectic as such will be reviewed with the *Critique*.

Comprehension of Oneself

Recent philosophical literature is replete with articles and books assessing the difference between understanding and explanation as well as the specificity of the former to the human sciences.[5] Indeed, Raymond Aron has remarked that "understanding [*la compréhension*] is fundamentally the decisive problem, one could almost say the sole [*unique*] problem, of the logic of history."[6] Since the *War Diaries,* we have seen that Sartre has accepted the concept of comprehension (*Verstehen*), if not uncritically. But only in *Search for a Method* does he examine it closely. There and in the *Critique,* he sees it as the nonreflective awareness of praxis, heir to the "self-translucency" of the for-itself in *Being and Nothingness*. In other words, Sartre differs from classical *Verstehen* theorists by insisting that one begins by understanding the field of one's own practical concerns, one's "circuit of selfness."

The same lingering Cartesian ideal of unqualified self-awareness from *Being and Nothingness* permeates *Search* and the *Critique*. In Sartre's case, however, that clarity is not theoretical but practical and is vulnerable to a very un-Cartesian mystification.[7] Because the historical agent understands what he is about, Sartre is arguing, we have the possibility of comprehending him as well. But what we comprehend ideally is his *own* comprehension of his project, the "inside" of the action, if you will, the first of the three "planes," according to the *Diaries,* on which the historian moves (see *WD* 300). Since this self-comprehension is prereflective (and in many ways a functional equivalent of Freud's unconscious), it is conceivable that we can (reflectively) know an agent better then he (reflectively) knows himself, the ideal of historical hermeneutics since Dilthey.[8]

In an important passage in *The Family Idiot,* Sartre explains a distinction he has used virtually without comment since *The Psychology of Imagination,* that between the prereflexive and the unreflected:

> [Comprehension] is itself lived experience [*vécu*], and I shall call it *prereflexive* [*préréflexive*] (and not unreflected [*irréfléchie*]) because it appears as an undistanced redoubling of internalization. Intermediary between nonthetic consciousness and reflexive thematization, it is the dawning of a reflection, but when it surges up with its verbal tools, it frequently falsifies what is "understood": other forces come into play . . ., which will divert it or compel it to replace meaning [*sens*] with a network of significations, depths glimpsed through verbal and superficial generalities. (*FI* 3:429; F 2:1544)

Close to what G. E. M. Anscombe calls "non-observational knowledge,"[9] and closer still to what Dilthey terms "reflective experience," comprehension is an intensification of our immediate awareness that is neither objectifying, as is reflective knowledge, nor simply immersed, the way nonthematic (nonthetic) being-in-the-world appears to be. As an "undistanced redoubling of internalization," comprehension might appear to be more on the "subjectivizing" than on the "objectivizing" side of the dialectic of internalization-externalization. But Sartre's use emphasizes its telic, externalizing character as well. In sum, comprehension is our lived, fallible awareness of what we are about.[10]

Comprehension of the Other

The way is open for such a hermeneutic of another's action because, as Sartre puts it, "man is for himself and for others a *signifying* being . . . a creator of *signs*" (*SM* 152). It is this grounding of semiotics in the signifying power of human praxis that maintains its "existentialist" character: "*Le signifiant, c'est moi,*" in Denis Hollier's summation of Sartre's view.[11] As examples of such interpretation, Sartre cites the participants in a boxing match (a case that will figure centrally in *Critique 2*) and the people in a stuffy room who observe someone walking toward the closed window (see *SM* 157, 153 respectively). We understand the other's project in a practical way. Neither a special faculty nor an arcane talent, "comprehension" is described by Sartre as "the dialectical movement that explains the act by its terminal signification in terms of its starting conditions" (*SM* 153). We must note this reference to the end and the initial conditions because comprehension, though originally progressive, may be entirely regressive or both at once. In fact, what he will call the "progressive-regressive method" aims at just such "comprehension" of a concrete historical action.

In the *Critique*, he explains: "Whenever a praxis can be traced to the intention of a practical organism *or a group*, even if this intention is implicit or obscure to the agent himself, there is comprehension" (*CDR* 1:76, emphasis mine). The reason is that consciousness is intentional, and "praxis" in Sartre's later works has subsumed the "directionality" of the for-itself in his earlier writings. But of special note for the philosophy of history is Sartre's claim that there may be a group intention and that this can be discovered. We shall not pursue this matter until we have discussed the origin and nature of the group. But it is already clear that Sartre wishes to carry into historical understanding that comprehension he ascribes to individual awareness. A kind of social hermeneutic is entering the list of Sartre's methodological tools. Although he employed an individual hermeneutic in the existential psychoanalysis of *Being and Nothingness* (see *BN* 569), he was in no position to extend this to the collective. But until he does so, his comprehension of history remains seriously impaired. Still, the application of "comprehension" to groups requires a change in Sartre's social ontology. If the individual is absolute, what kind of purposiveness can one ascribe to collectives? Though he steadfastly rejects Durkheim's "collective consciousness," Sartre in the *Critique* will occasionally speak of "collective representations" and refer to the constraint we feel from phenomena like public opinion—evidence of collective consciousness for Durkheim. In other words, the matter of collective intention is as much ontological as epistemological, as we shall see.

Sens and *Signification*

It is in the context of comprehension that we must distinguish *sens* from *signification* in Sartre's theory. Though both words can be translated as "meaning," *signification* refers to a static, conceptual meaning whereas *sens* denotes the ongoing unity of a lived process, what he sometimes calls a "presence." As such, the terms seem consonant with analytic and dialectical reason respectively. Significantly, Sartre first employed the distinction in aesthetics where he differentiated between images, which "presentify" *sens,* and signs, which communicate *signification.* As he insists, "I shall say that an [aesthetic] object has *sens* when it is the incarnation of a reality that surpasses it but which cannot be grasped aside from it and whose infinity does not allow adequate expression in any system of signs; it is always a case of totality: totality of a person, a milieu, an epoch or the human condition."[12] Thus the paintings of Paul Rebeyrolle, for example, are said to present the *sens* of the Cold War.[13] The terminological bridge to Sartre's later dialectic of history consists in the equivalence he sees between *sens* and what he calls the "singular universal."[14] The latter term, of Hegelian inspiration, appears more frequently in the later Sartre. Just as life is in every part of the body but is identical with none, and just as the soul, in medieval parlance, "is where it acts," so Sartre argues, is the entire Renaissance present in Michelangelo's *David* or in the Mona Lisa's smile.[15] This equivalence of *sens* and singular universal will lend a key to understanding the crucial, related terms "totalization" and "incarnation" to be considered next. Sartre recapitulates the relation between "comprehension" and *sens* when he later describes "comprehension, a silent adjunct to lived experience [*le vécu*]," as "an obscure grasp of the *sens* of a process beyond its significations."[16]

In the introduction, I referred to Sartre's "poetics" of history. I have already noted one aspect of this in his likening comprehension of another's free action to that of a work of art. In "Existentialism Is a Humanism," he even repeats the Nietzschean maxim, echoed by Foucault, that we make of our lives a work of art. But the similarity between history and art in Sartre's view grows closer still in the above passage where the aesthetic object is described as capable of *incarnating* an infinite reality which is nonetheless a totality, such as a milieu or an epoch.[17] What makes the "incarnation" aesthetic, we can presume, is, among other things, its occurring through an image and not a "system of signs." Now this reference to the *sens* of an epoch such as the Renaissance suggests that "History," not as an analytic system of signs to be summarized in a conjunction of objects or attributes but as a dialectical totalization, might "incarnate" the "spirit" of a person, a people, or an age. This would presume a "poetic" use of the language of history that Sartre has not yet acknowledged, but which Jules Michelet, for example, championed in French historiography.[18] And Sartre's aesthetic theory is ready to accommodate the *sens-totalization* relationship that he now discerns in the historical realm.[19]

It is one of the assumptions of Sartre's theory of history that collective as well as individual lives have a *sens* that is comprehended by their agents and, given the proper hermeneutic, is available to others as well. The only evidence he offers for this momentous presupposition, as we have seen, is the understanding it confers on the otherwise disparate events under consideration. The method for unlocking this *sens* is both progressive and regressive.

Another major assumption of Sartre's method is that "common action and individual praxis exhibit a real homogeneity." This is necessary lest the agent not understand the action of his own group. But it has the added advantage of leaving historical action in principle open to the outsider as well. This is not to deny the specificity of social facts. Sartre allows that "group status is indeed a metamorphosis of the individual." But he continues, "the formal structure of the objective and of the operations is still typically individual" because, as we shall see in detail shortly, only individual praxis is constitut*ing;* group praxis is entirely constitut*ed* by its individual members.[20] As Sartre points out: "If the objective of the group is by definition incapable of being *realized* by an isolated individual, then it can [at least] be *posited* by such an individual (on the basis of need, danger or more complex forms)" (*CDR* 1:510). In other words, "the dialectical rationality of common praxis does not transcend the rationality of individual praxis" (*CDR* 1:538). What remains for Sartre to account for, lest his postulate be dismissed as mere question begging, is the cognitive homogeneity that obtains in the midst of an ontological heterogeneity between the individual and the social. He will attempt this in the *Critique* by distinguishing constituting (individual) from constituted (group) praxis.

Totalization

From the introduction to *Search for a Method* through the final pages of the *Critique 2,* the term "totalization" dominates Sartre's theory of history. Mikel Dufrenne called it the key term to unlocking the *Critique.* He also acknowledged that its meaning was difficult to delineate.[21] Georg Lukács is credited with introducing the term into Marxist literature. Sartre was familiar with the latter's *History and Class Consciousness* and the Marxist humanism it propounded.[22] Whatever his conceptual borrowing from the Lukács volume, it will suffice here to grasp the term's function within the emerging Sartrean system.

"Totalization" denotes the unifying function of "praxis" once this has replaced "consciousness-project" in the Sartrean vocabulary. "Praxis" signifies roughly "purposive human activity in its material-social environment."[23] We noted Sartre's early criticism of Aron's failure to correlate or unify the plurality of significations to which the action or event was subject. Twenty years later he continues to warn that "we lose sight of human reality if we do not consider [these] significations as synthetic, multidimensional, indissoluble objects, which hold individual places in a spacetime with multiple dimensions." As he explains, "the mistake here is to reduce the lived signification to the simple linear statement which language gives it" (*SM* 108–9). In other words, one must adopt a dialectical discourse in order to respect human reality and its lived meaning (which, were he observing his own distinction at this point, he should call *sens*). Totalization "as a movement of History and as a theoretical and practical attempt to 'situate' an event, a group or a man" seeks to capture this unity: "what totalization must discover is the multidimensional *unity* of the act" (*SM* 111; emphasis mine).

One of the major differences between Sartre and Foucault, as we shall see, is their respective assessments of this "multidimensionality" of the act (event). Where Sartre strives to gather these dimensions into the unity of a praxis-project, Foucault will insist on their irreducible multiplicity.[24] As befits a poststructuralist, he is opposed to totalizing acts of any kind.

So praxis is totalizing. But it is likewise dialectical. Its practical totalization is no mere "summing up." Nor is its unity that of the abstract universal concept or term such as Aristotle advocated. Indeed, it was his preference for such universals that led Aristotle to deny any "science of the singular." No doubt Aristotle too favored the knowledge of "the many through one." But the one he championed was abstract and eternal, not concrete and historical. Sartre joins Hegel, the German Aristotle, and dialectical thinkers thereafter in trying to respect the unique character of the individual while appreciating the greater degree of understanding conferred by relating individuals among themselves and to the whole. Individual organic praxis does not suppress its components but constitutes them as parts in a dynamic, ongoing whole. Organic praxis alone is "constituting" of such wholes; what Sartre terms the "group" is constituted by such organic praxes. Although "synthetically enriched" in group praxis, the individual retains ontological primacy. Where there is praxis there is dialectic. This ontological primacy of organic praxis renders Sartre's dialectic "nominalistic," as we shall see. Constituting dialectic characterizes the individual; constituted dialectic, the group.

Later, in *The Family Idiot,* Sartre will distinguish "the simple *Aufhebung* of a given from the totalizing return that we effect upon it at one and the same time to integrate it in the organic unity that we are trying to be and to prevent it from undermining the same." For, he explains, "in human reality . . . the multiple is always haunted by a dream or a memory of synthetic unity; so it is detotalization itself that demands to be retotalized and the totalization is not a simple inventory followed by a totalitarian constant, but an intentional, oriented enterprise of re-unification" (*FI* 2:3; F 1:653). Sartre seems to see totalization as both an ontological and a psychological necessity, analogous to the "futile desire to be God" in *Being and Nothingness.* He now focuses on our totalizing drive toward the impossible goal of full integration into the social unit conceived as an organic whole.

Totalization is a practical act (as is comprehension) that effects this interrelation and focus of acts and environment. Like Husserlian consciousness, it is meaning-giving (*Sinngebende*), but this meaning-direction (*sens*) is primarily telic and practical. For example, Sartre observes in the *Critique* that the single group in process of formation is, from the methodological viewpoint, "the most simple form of totalization" (*CDR* 1:407).

But totalization is a *valuative* act as well, though Sartre seldom speaks in such terms. It assesses what is and what is not relevant to an end-in-view. And, more important, it establishes that end itself, as in classical Sartrean existential choice and in the sense of committed history discussed in chapter 4. This is the point of his remarks on the Kronstadt uprising during the Bolshevik revolution:

> The condemnation of the insurgents at Kronstadt was perhaps inevitable; it was perhaps the judgment of history on this tragic attempt. But . . . this practical judgment (the only real one) will remain that of an enslaved history so long as it does not include the free interpretation of the revolt *in terms of the insurgents themselves* and of the contradictions of the moment. . . . The historian, by consenting to study facts at all levels of reality, liberates future history. This liberation can come about as a visible and efficacious action only within the compass of the general movement of *democratization,* but conversely, it cannot fail to accelerate this movement. (*SM* 99 n; emphasis mine)

A good example of "committed history," Sartre's advice is likewise an expression of the Marxist "unity of theory and practice" which his existentialism has always maintained. In the present case, it indicates that the *goal* of historical description should be the liberation of the oppressed. By paying attention to the level of choice-freedom-responsibility ("historialization," in his earlier discourse), in other words, by respecting the "praxis" dimension of historical events, the historian saves human reality from submersion in antecedent "necessities" and impersonal accounts. She makes the reader feel the pinch of the real, the contradictions of the situation. She likewise contributes to the advent of the reign of freedom by raising the social consciousness of historians and others who read her work.

Finally, totalization is ongoing. It is correlative both to praxis and to the fact that human reality and the social wholes human reality constitutes are at best "detotalized totalities" (see *BN* 165 and *CDR* 1:407). Sartre gives the reason why individual and social wholes will always be unfinished and ambiguous when he notes: "A totalizing praxis cannot totalize itself as a totalized element" (*CDR* 1:373).

One consequence of this open-ended character of social wholes is that the outsider who would "comprehend" a group praxis stands in the same condition as one who would join the group; total integration as if into some organic whole is impossible in either case, and for the same reason: the "inner distance" of the individual agent-consciousness. No doubt, a certain interpenetration of interests-ends is possible, not unlike the "fusion of horizons" (*Horizontverschmelzung*) of Gadamer's hermeneutic.[25] As the group members can subordinate their personal interests to "ours," so the historian can practice a kind of ascesis, what Sartre calls a "practical negation of the negation which defines his life," in order to comprehend the process, not "wie es eigentlich gewesen ist," but as the participants understood it themselves.[26] Hence the importance of the project, both individual and group, in understanding the *sens* of a historical event. To the extent that events have a meaning-*sens,* they are the effects, countereffects, or intersection of human projects. This is the *principle of the primacy of praxis* that guides Sartre's theorizing on society and history for the remainder of his career.[27]

Sartre formulates what we may call the *principle of totalization* in his philosophy of history when he claims that "a man—whoever he is—totalizes his epoch to the precise degree that he is totalized by it" (*FI* 5:394; F 3:426). He was groping for such a principle as early as the *War*

Diaries when he spoke of the kaiser's withered arm and again, in the *Notebooks,* with his discussion of surpassing and expressing one's epoch through historialization. He approached significantly closer when he related Michelangelo's *David* to the *sens* of the Renaissance. But despite the distinction between *sens* and signification, one could dismiss these totalizations as merely symbolic.[28] More difficult to dismiss (or to account for adequately otherwise) is the totalizing reciprocity that directs Sartre's massive study of Flaubert, *The Family Idiot.*

He gives some indication of this reciprocity when in *Search* he recommends that the progressive-regressive method be fortified by "cross-references between the *object* [*Madame Bovary,* for example] (which contains the whole period as hierarchized significations) and the *period* (which contains the object in its totalization)" (*SM* 148). Thus, Leconte de Lisle, as both signifier and signified (*signifiant-signifié*), "signifies . . . the unspoken and lived *sens* of the epoch by his singular appropriation of the sign," for example, by wearing a monocle (*FI* 5:399–400; F 3:432). In the case of Flaubert, Sartre explains, "the man and his time will be integrated into the dialectical totalization when we have shown how History surpasses this contradiction" between how Flaubert was and how his age took him to be (*SM* 150). The point is not simply to note these facts, nor merely to connect them chronologically, causally, or even narratively. Totalization requires that we grasp the dialectical necessity of the contradiction, for example, between these two views of Flaubert, in terms of the praxis of the agent and the inertia and contrary praxes of his society. In other words, the historian's task is to bring to light the "synthetic bonds of History," its bonds of "interiority," as he had said in the *War Diaries.* Sartre's dialectical investigation aims to determine what, in the process of human history, "is the respective role of relations of interiority and exteriority" (*CDR* 1:56–57).

Reflecting on culture as a "temporalizing totalization" in the *Critique,* Sartre points out that each of us *qua* cultured, totalizes himself by "disappearing as a cultivated individual and emerging as the synthetic bond between everyone and what might be called the *cultural field*" (*CDR* 1:54). What he means is that we are dialectically conditioned by the totalized past and totalizing future of the process of human development. A cultural object, as it were, wears its history, and we are internally related to the field of cultural objects in which we act.[29] Sartre admits that talk of an individual is merely a methodological point of departure, that one's short life soon becomes diluted in the "pluridimensional human ensemble which temporalizes its totalization and totalizes its temporality." Anticipating the theory behind his Flaubert study, he adds:

> To the extent that its individual universals are perpetually aroused, in my immediate as well as my reflective life, and, from the depth of the past in which they were born, provide the keys and the rules of my actions, we must be able, in our regressive investigation, to make use of *the whole of contemporary knowledge* (at least in principle) to elucidate a given undertaking or social ensemble, a particular avatar of praxis. (*CDR* 1:55)

Totalization can be either synchronic (structural) or diachronic (historical). The former is the terminus of a regressive argument in Sartre's vaguely Kantian sense of reasoning from the fact to the formal conditions of its possibility. Thus the first volume of the *Critique* employs a mainly regressive method to arrive at "the elementary formal structures" of sociohistorical development, namely, the series, the group, the institution, and their dialectical interrelation (*CDR* 1:818).

Diachronic totalization, also called "temporalization," is an essential feature of individual praxis. And since only organic praxis is constitutive of social wholes, its diachronic totalizations constitute History. Indeed, Sartre claims that "History is a totalization that temporalizes itself" (*CDR* 1:54). In other words, history is to be grasped by a "progressive" movement, one that comprehends its "end" and its means. In that respect, history is more about the future than the past, though as history it will be the future *perfect.* The second volume of the *Critique* was to pursue this movement. Sartre's Flaubert study, in many ways the culmination of his theoretical work, employs both synchronic and diachronic totalizations.

Finally, and in a way that invites our analysis of the Flaubert case in chapter 8, Sartre distinguishes *micro-* and *macro*totalization. A rich, if extended, instance is the following:

> So in each totalization in progress, one must always envisage in their dialectical relations the direct connection between the general totalization and the singular totalization (a totalization of the singular by the concrete generality), that is, of the whole to the part. And one must keep in mind the same dialectical relationship of the macrocosmic totalization to the microcosmic totalization *through the mediation* of the historical moment [*la conjuncture*]—of the *concrete universal* produced by it, retotalized by every part, and determining individual singularity at once by the historical event (the totalized *incarnation* of the totaliza-

tion) and by the general face of the world (i.e., by the real relation among all the parts, not insofar as they directly express the whole but as they are distinguished from it by their movement to retotalize it— in order to reexternalize it as it was internalized by them). (*FI* 5:399 n; F 3:432 n; third emphasis mine)

The difference between the micro and the macro seems to be one not only of scope but of quality and even of kind. This is an elucidation of the principle of totalization mentioned above. It both guides and warrants Sartre's Flaubert study. In explaining the principle, as always, we must begin with the praxis of the organic individual. The individual is a signified-signifier. Sartre has long accepted the Husserlian notion of consciousness as meaning-giving. He now conjoins this with the semiotic concept of man as sign-giving, in a sense, the social side of the Husserlian position. The individual finds himself in the midst of a network of signs that designate him as a class member, a professional, and the like, but also as a man of his times (or a misfit). These are *macro*totalizations; they occupy the space between organic individual praxis and physical nature, in other words, the cultural, historical world.[30] Those like Hollier and Jean-Marie Benoist, who see Sartre as insensitive to the specificity and relative autonomy of linguistic meaning, seem to discount his claim that the individual is *signifié* as well as *signifiant*.[31] This will come to the fore in our discussion of the practico-inert in chapter 6.

Yet, unlike the structuralists, Sartre sees this signifying network both as itself historical (the "sedimentation," in Husserl's term, of prior totalizations) and as *dialectically* related to the totalizing praxes of organic individuals, that is, to micrototalizations. What counts in this respect, Sartre writes, is the "action of the *future* as such" (*SM* 94). We must consider society as penetrating each action-motivation from the "perspective of the future" (*SM* 96). In fact, micrototalization emerges as the proper way to "appropriate" historical meaning as called for by the *Diaries* and the *Notebooks*. In pursuing his own end, the agent "interiorizes" his social world, using it as an instrument in his totalizing project. But he thereby concretizes that same world, moves it forward in time and changes it the way a colonialist, for example, brings his culture to another people while distancing himself in several senses from that very culture, to which he can never fully return.

The relation between micro- and macrototalization is dialectical, and the dialectic is mediated by what Sartre calls the "singular" or "concrete universal" (*FI* 5:399 n.)—for example, the monocle *as* worn by Leconte de Lisle, which, as we saw, signified "the unspoken and lived *sens* of his epoch," or the practice of bourgeois "respectability" *as* maintained in late nineteenth-century France (*CDR* 1:774). The paradigm, of course, is *Madame Bovary*, which is not a type but a singular universal (*FI* 2:390). But again, it is the novel *as* written by Gustave Flaubert. The concrete universal "incarnates," in Sartre's term, the objective spirit of an age, but it does so as more than a symbolic form.[32] It mediates praxis enabling the generation of *sens* (meaning/direction) out of the interrelation of individuals with each other and with their cultural environment. In this sense the Victorian practice of respectability both signified and effected a certain oppressive relation between the bourgeoisie and the working class. The pivotal role of "incarnation" in Sartre's theory of history comes to the fore in his study of Stalin and Soviet society in volume 2 of the *Critique.*

Before moving to our last conceptual element of a philosophy of history from *Search for a Method,* we should distinguish "totalization" from the "invisible hand" of the utilitarians and the "cunning of Reason" of the Hegelians. Despite a superficial resemblance—all three theories of history view the individual as bearer of a message she may not be able to translate herself—Sartre's differs from the others significantly. He conceives the relationship between individual intention and common result dialectically, unlike the utilitarians, who understand it in merely cumulative terms or after Newton's model of the parallelogram of forces. But what distinguishes him from Hegel and the orthodox Marxists in this regard is his emphasis on the constitutive role of individual totalizing praxis. Throughout *Search* Sartre's recurrent criticism of Marxism is that it "lack[s] any hierarchy of mediations" (*SM* 56). We recognize a form of his initial critique of Aron. Indeed, this respect for individual praxis sustains the specifically existentialist tilt of his theory of history.

THE PROGRESSIVE-REGRESSIVE METHOD

"I have a passion for understanding men" writes Sartre in the course of his extended introduction to Jean Genet's collected works (*SG* 137). His three-volume study of Flaubert confirms that claim. Sartre's interest in history flows from that passion as well. He approaches history via the singularity of an individual existence (the principle of totalization) in order to clarify the one by illuminating the other. This bifocal method, so appropriate to an existentialist theory, lends greater precision to what has motivated his approach to historiography from the start, namely, the desire to attain that mutual comprehension of the kaiser and the war. Brought to reflective awareness in *Search,* this procedure is christened the progressive-regressive method. It consists of three stages.[33]

Sartre recommends we begin with a rigorous phenomenological description of the object of our inquiry at the general level of its *eidos* or intelligible contour. This resembles the method employed in *Being and Nothingness* to reveal the essential structure of "human reality." We have recorded those structures as being-in-itself, -for-itself, and -for-others. But if the point of Sartrean existentialism is to ferret out the unique, the concrete individual from the faceless human mass, the descriptive analyses of *Being and Nothingness* are but the end of the beginning. They uncover the basic elements of the human condition and, above all, reveal that human reality, the existentialist everyman, is not a self but a presence-to-self, this being the ontological root of its freedom. Moreover, these phenomenological descriptions show that our fundamental project, not space-time or matter, is what individuates each of us.

But such descriptions do not capture that project and hence our individuality in its uniqueness—nor could they. Of their nature, phenomenological descriptions are static or timeless. Their fruit is the *Wesensschau* or immediate grasp of the essence (*eidos*) of the object in question. Phenomenology continues to yield "concepts," not "notions" in Sartre's technical sense of those terms. Though he continues to employ arresting descriptions of paradigmatic cases in his later works, he no longer calls his method "phenomenological."[34] It is becoming clear to Sartre, even in *Being and Nothingness,* that another, supplementary method is required in his search for the concrete, one that "reads" *this* agent's actions as expressions of a unique life project or what we have been calling the agent's "historialization." Such is the hermeneutic of existentialist psychoanalysis, introduced in that same text.

The second, regressive stage of Sartre's method, like its Kantian counterpart, moves from facts to the conditions of their possibility. Sartre sometimes calls these conditions "formal" (see, for example, *CDR* 1:671). The mediating factors in Sartre's social ontology that we shall discuss in the following chapter—praxis, practico-inert, mediating third, and praxis-process—are examples of such "formal" conditions of social possibility. So too are the concepts of class identity, economic base, and ideological superstructure so dear to historical materialists. In fact, Sartre believes that Marxist economism is the result of concentrating on this regressive method to the exclusion of its "progressive" complement. "Marxism as a method," he argues, "gives us 'general particularities,' i.e., abstract, universal relations masking as particular, historical realities" (*SM* 24). But not all of the structures or conditions that regressive analysis yields are formal. Some are clearly material or existential, for example, the details of Flaubert's early childhood milieu. The latter make intelligible those factors, especially intrafamilial relationships, that mediate more abstract forms and structures. In a remark that alludes to his existential psychoanalysis of Jean Genet and foretells his massive study of Flaubert, Sartre insists that we achieve the required link between socioeconomic constraint and personal project "if we understand that everything took place in childhood" (*SM* 60). For he has come to believe that "the particular family [serves] as mediation between the universal class and the individual" (*SM* 62). So existential psychoanalysis—the hermeneutic of the signs of an individual's self-defining life project—is "concerned above all with establishing the way in which the child lives his family relations inside a given society" (*SM* 61). The regressive analysis must be completed by a progressive grasp of the individual's "personalization" or what in our historical context he calls "historialization."

The agent's progressive advance through a dialectical spiral of totalization and retotalization, Sartre believes, will account for what he calls the "inner necessity" of the historical phenomenon. A more complete comprehension of the agent-event is achieved when it is linked with the macrototalization of social ensembles. He studies Flaubert in the context of the rise of the modern novel as a bourgeois art form and the social and political ambiguities of the Second Empire. Similarly, his sketch of a study of Stalin is framed in the dialectic of the dictator's personal choices and the objective possibilities in the 1930s for building "socialism in one country." This greater specification yields more concreteness in the quasi-Hegelian sense that Sartre has come to adopt.[35] Our historical investigation will have succeeded when we have comprehended their respective comprehensions of their epochs—their unique manners of "historializing" their times.

The last two movements in the method constitute a kind of synthesis of existential psychoanalysis and historical materialism. Without an existentialist hermeneutic of the signs of an original choice (the progressive movement), we would have to be satisfied with such "general

particularities" as "the Soviet bureaucracy" or "the petite bourgeoisie"—terms Sartre associates with Marxist economism. Biography
would be dissolved in impersonal history. But without the dialectical
interplay of micro- and macrototalization (the regressive movement),
history would shrivel into biography.

As we conclude our discussion of the key concepts of Sartre's philosophy of history introduced in *Search for a Method*, we should reflect on the
relation of this work to the *Critique*, for it is a curious one. One of Sartre's
most astute commentators, Klaus Hartmann, argues that the former has
little to do with the latter, that their respective methods are quite independent of one another.[36] Indeed, Sartre himself seems rather unclear
on the matter. In his preface to the edition that contains them both, he
notes: "Logically, the second [the *Critique*] should have come before the
first, since it is intended to supply its critical foundations. But I was
afraid that this mountain of notes might seem to have brought forth a
mouse" (*CDR* 1:821). So he retained the chronological order in which
they appeared.

By his own admission, *Search* takes for granted what the *Critique* aims
to establish: "whether there is such a thing as a Truth of humanity."
Recall that this was the issue in the *Notebooks* on which the reality of a
dialectic of History hung (see *NE* 460). Sartre now assumes that this
truth is totalizing, that a dialectical movement characterizes both being
and knowledge. As we said at the outset, the *Critique* must establish both
the existence and the warrant of dialectical reason. And yet Sartre admits
that the method of the *Critique* "must also be dialectical" (*CDR* 823). So
we should not be surprised to find him shifting from regressive to progressive movements in the course of his argument in the *Critique*, even
though the general direction of the two volumes is supposed to be regressive and progressive respectively. Such circularity in methodological questions in inevitable; as dialectical, it is by definition not vicious.

We live in a polyvalent world, Sartre argues, with a plurality of
meanings. "Our historical task . . . is to bring closer the moment when
History will have *only one meaning*, when it will tend to be dissolved in
the concrete men who will make it in common." He repeats a claim we
saw him make in the *Notebooks*, namely, that these plural meanings can
be dissolved "only on the ground of a future totalization" (*SM* 90). In
the next chapter I shall argue that this task is more a matter of *decision*

than of discovery and that it is hence intertwined with ideal vision and moral responsibility as befits a properly "existentialist" theory.

Totalization thus assumes both a moral and an epistemic task in *Search* that links it with the earlier works and with the *Critique*. It is the leading instrument of the committed historian. "The real problem of History," as Sartre surveys it at the close of the *Critique* volume 1, is whether we can *totalize* the vast plurality of totalizations with their partly erased, partly transformed meanings "by an intelligible totalization from which there is no appeal."[37] This, in effect, is the problem of "totalization without a totalizer." He challenges himself and us to seek "its motive forces and non-circular direction" (*CDR* 1:817)."

Chapter Six

The *Sens* of History:
Discovery and Decision

I f the "objectivity" of analytic Reason masks a certain commitment to the status quo by disregarding its vain effort to be a viewpoint without a point of view, dialectical Reason avows its involvement in the contextual and valuative nature of comprehension. Sartre joins a line of distinguished thinkers who have attempted a critical justification, a "critique," of historical Reason to complement Kant's famous critiques of theoretical, practical, and aesthetic Reason. But his method, though vaguely Kantian in its regressive-progressive movements, is not transcendental.[1] Sartre has never relented in his opposition to a transcendental Ego, which he rejected in one of his first philosophical publications.[2] Rather, he undertakes a dialectical investigation (*l'expérience*) of dialectical experience (*l'expérience*) in order to reveal the formal conditions of the "dialectical necessity" that we encounter in our dealings with one another and with our history.

The ambiguity of the word *l'expérience* is crucial. It attests to Sartre's abiding phenomenological conviction that we must witness the overlap, though not the identity, of the logical and the ontological, of the "rational" and the "actual," as Hegel would say,

Some day I am going to describe that strange reality, History, which is neither objective nor ever quite subjective, in which the dialectic is contested, penetrated, and corroded by a kind of antidialectic, but which is still a dialectic.
—Sartre, *What Is Literature?*

in order to bring our investigation to an end. If this is epistemological foundationalism, it is of a very attenuated sort. It labors in the mode of a hypothesis: "*If* something like socioeconomic classes exist . . ." Sartre cautions. Despite frequent lapses into the language of apodicticity, the two volumes of the *Critique* remain hypothetical. Their plausibility stems from the explanatory force of their master concepts—totalizing praxis, practico-inert, and mediating third—and what I shall term the "moral" force of their larger picture, their invitation to make sense of history by fashioning it into a narrative of oppression and liberation.[3] This ethicopoietic dimension of Sartre's project, to which I alluded in chapter 5, will become increasingly important throughout the remainder of our study. But the "making evident" of dialectical Reason as the "logic" of history will be a function of its ability to account for the "dialectical necessity" that we experience in our lives.

BASIC FORMS OF MEDIATION

Foucault's former professor, Louis Althusser, once described Sartre as "the philosopher of mediations par excellence."[4] It is the absence of mediating concepts (or their reduction to functions of the objectifying "gaze") in *Being and Nothingness* that accounts for its basic poverty as a social ontology. But it also helps explain the remarkable absence of a theory of history operative in that masterwork composed at a time when, as we have seen, Aron had awakened Sartre to the philosophy of history. If Sartre is to formulate a theoretical approach to history, he must move beyond his looking/looked-at model of interpersonal relations. Something must mediate the harsh objectification of the alienating gaze.

Dialectical Reason is a logic of mediations. The key to Sartre's theory of history is the nature and scope of the forms of mediation that he introduces to account for our "dialectical experience" (*l'expérience*). Marx captured this phenomenon when he distinguished between an "alienated" society in which people are "the products of their products" and a properly human one in which workers "produce" themselves via their labor. For Sartre, this instantiates the dialectical principle that "man is mediated by things to the extent that things are mediated by men." This reciprocity must not be lost sight of. He considers it to be "the crucial discovery of dialectical investigation [*expérience*]" (*CDR* 1:88). "In a sense," he insists, "man submits to the dialectic as to an enemy power;

in another sense he *creates it;* and if dialectical Reason is the Reason of History, this contradiction must itself be lived dialectically, which means that man must be controlled by the dialectic insofar as he *creates* it, and *create* it insofar as he is controlled by it" (*CDR* 1:35–36). So the meaning/direction (*sens*) of history is a dialectical interplay of mediations that both thwart and foster historical agency.

The Practico-inert

Recall that a theory of the historical agent is central to Sartre's enterprise. Absent such an emphasis on agency, history loses the moral dimension that we saw is essential to his existentialist approach. But this leads to criticism such as this from F. R. Ankersmit: "Philosophy of action can never speak the language of the unintended consequences of human action. As a philosophy of history, philosophy of action is only suited to prehistorist historiography. Being unable to transcend the limitations of methodological individualism, it is historiographically naive" (*HT* 35). Aron, arguing from Sartre's ontology, draws a similar conclusion, namely, that "the *Critique* tends towards the following objective: *to establish ontologically the foundations of methodological individualism.*"[5] In fact, both critics miss the point of Sartrean mediation. The mediating factors that I shall now examine, especially what I call the "mediating third," serve to keep Sartre from the extremes of both individualism and holism in the social sciences. This nuance of Sartre's "dialectical nominalism" seems to have eluded his critics. And the practico-inert as the vehicle of counterfinality accounts for those unintended consequences that provide the evidence which dialectical Reason demands.

Functional heir to "being-in-itself" of the earlier Sartre, the concept of the practico-inert is antidialectical in the sense that it negates the constituting dialectics, "not by destruction or dissolution, but by deviation and inversion" (*CDR* 1:340). Sartre's now classic examples are Chinese deforestation and Spanish hoarding of New World gold (see *CDR* 1:161 ff.). In both cases the achievement of certain intended consequences entailed unintended results that undermined the original end in view. The Chinese peasants lost land to flooding and the Spanish lost the buying power of their gold to inflation. Thus Sartre points out that "within praxis . . . there is a dialectical movement and a dialectical relation between action as the negation of matter . . . , and matter . . . as the negation of action" (*CDR* 1:159).

"Practico-inert" denotes that realm of worked matter, sedimented praxis, passivity, and counterfinality—matter as the negation of action. It extends and refines the notions of "otherness" and recalcitrance that Sartre, since the *War Diaries,* has attributed to the historical event as in-itself. It applies these notions to the social field of collective objects like the newspaper or the Gothic cathedral, to ideas and systems like racism and colonialism, and to institutions like the army or the state bureaucracy.[6]

But he refines these earlier uses of the in-itself, and so of the historical event, when he describes the practico-inert as "simply the activity of others insofar as it is sustained and diverted by inorganic inertia" (*CDR* 1:556). The sustaining function of the practico-inert accounts for what philosophers of history have called the "trace,"[7] which for Sartre is simply the "worked matter" that mediates our social and historical relations even as it preserves the sediment of past praxes. It is this "dialectical," that is, mediating, role that distinguishes the practico-inert from other, analytical uses of the term. Unlike the analytical "trace," the practico-inert is intrinsically subject-referring; it functions *as* practico-inert only while interiorized-totalized in our activities.

Moreover, despite its antidialectical character (Sartre limits his dialectic to the interpersonal realm, joining revisionist Marxists in questioning a dialectic of nature), the practico-inert does exert a kind of negative, deforming influence on individual and collective projects. Sometimes Sartre refers to this as a "*force* of inertia" (*CDR* 1:278). It appears, for example, in the "objective, negative exigencies" (*CDR* 1:159) made by the colonialist or the capitalist systems on their practitioners,[8] in the logic of a series of human decisions that entails unintended, contrary consequences such as the inflation and concomitant devaluation that followed upon Spanish gold policy under Philip II (see *CDR* 1:165 ff.), or in the "serial rationality" of the Great Fear of 1789 (see *CDR* 1:295). In effect, the practico-inert serves to connect a class of automatic and impersonal processes with underlying praxes, while retaining a certain rationality of its own: "there is a *rationality* of the theoretical and practical behavior of an agent as a member of a series [a social whole mediated by the practico-inert]," Sartre insists (*CDR* 1:266). It is the logic of otherness, of exteriority, of passivity, of alienation, of social impotence and "flight." Indeed, Sartre refers to such "serial Reason" as "a special case of dialectical Reason" (*CDR* 1:642). It is in our experience of these counterfinalities that Sartre locates the "dialectical necessity" that we said is so critical for justifying historical Reason.

"Social objects," that is, what since Durkheim has constituted the subject matter of sociology, Sartre observes, "are at least in their basic structure, beings of the practico-inert field" (*CDR* 1:253). Those objects, divided into "collectives" (series and institutions) and "groups" are the concern of the historian as well, first because, in Marxist terms, they constitute the object and the subject of History respectively (see *CDR* 1:255), and, second, because as *practico*-inert they transmit sedimented past praxis into the present field of action. No doubt, these are ideal types since concrete reality is an admixture of both in various degrees. Still, Sartre admits, "we can identify, at the extremes, groups in which passivity tends to disappear entirely . . . , and collectives that have almost entirely reabsorbed their group" (*CDR* 1:254).

A social object of major importance for Sartre's theory of history is the socioeconomic class. He claims that "on the ontological plane . . . class-being is practico-inert" (*CDR* 1:686). As long as society remains divided into classes, he is claiming, the practico-inert will "mediate" social relations. In the language of the Other and the Same that he employs throughout the *Critique,* class relations link individuals *as* Other, that is in exteriority; they are alienated and alienating.

The practico-inert mediates at the level of meaning as well. Recall that the human is a signified-signifier. Regarding the practico-inert, Sartre notes that each agent's actions are situated "within a framework of exigencies that cannot be transcended; they simply realize everyone's class being. Everyone makes himself signify by interiorizing, by a free choice, the signification with which material exigencies have produced him as a *signified being.* Class-being, as practico-inert being mediated by passive syntheses of worked matter, comes to men through men" (*CDR* 1:238). In fact, he defines "objective class spirit" as "milieu for the circulation of significations" (*CDR* 1:776). As the young man in the *Diaries* inherited a facticity that included the Great War, so the working-class youth of the *Critique* discovers himself "signified" by his class status, and his possibilities limited by this same class being. The vehicle for such signification and objective conditioning is the practico-inert.

This provides the second major instance of practico-inert mediation in Sartre's theory of history, his concept of "objective spirit" or "culture as practico-inert" (*FI* 5:35). Objective spirit combines the semiotic and the historical. Sartre introduces it in the *Critique* mainly to account for that "medium for the circulation of meanings" which enables the members of a class to interpret the meaning of a particular event, practice, or institution in light of the class struggle. In that context, he calls it "objective class spirit." So the Parisian Commune of 1871, the bourgeois practice of respectability (exchanging calling cards, social and economic Malthusianism, personal abstemiousness and the like), the great governmental bureaucracy as well as the aesthetic and religious norms of an epoch are all aspects of objective spirit. In the context of material scarcity, that is, in Western history with is haves and have-nots, these forms of practico-inert mediation constitute a kind of violence, what Sartre calls "the judgment of things on persons" (*FI* 5:589).[9]

It is practico-inert mediation, therefore, that supplies the "materiality" requisite for the artifact, the trace, the historical residue as well as that numerical multiplicity which figured so prominently in the reflections of the *Notebooks*. In so doing, it separates as it unites (what Sartre calls "serial" unity or "unity in exteriority"). This unity-in-otherness effected by practico-inert mediation is exemplified in the "passive activity" of "serialized" agents like the television-viewing public or the lynch mob. Sartre sees ideology likewise as a "practico-inert determination" (*FI* 5:193 n). It, too, bears the marks of serial "otherness" such as passive activity and unity in exteriority that he associates with practico-inert mediation. In fact, he promises to show in volume 2 of the *Critique* that "exteriority [that is, quantity, Nature, the practico-inert] is the inert motive force of History in that it is the only possible support for the *novelty* that places its seal on [exteriority] and which exteriority in turn preserves both as an irreducible moment and as a *memory of Humanity*" (*CDR* 1:72; last emphasis mine). This role of the practico-inert in the novelty-memory relationship yields a past that is both nonrepeatable and cumulative; in other words, a past that is historical.

We have pointed out the analytic and structural reason that finds its basis in the practico-inert field. But the practico-inert also grounds a kind of rationality (serial rationality) proper to human activity (what Sartre sometimes calls "serial praxis") in a space otherwise consigned to brute facticity.[10] This cannot simply be reduced to generically "analytic" reason, because, as praxis, it is inherently dialectical, even if that dialectic has been countermanded and rendered socially impotent by practico-inert mediation. The ontological source of Sartre's historical optimism, of his utopian hope for an end to prehistory, if you will, is this dormant seed of organic praxis in the humus of seriality.

Finally, and perhaps most important, as modified by the brute fact of material scarcity (*la rareté*), the practico-inert marks human history as a continuous violent interchange. Assessing the human enterprise thus far, Sartre concludes: "Man lives in a universe where the future is a thing, where the idea is an object and where the violence of matter is the 'midwife of History'" (*CDR* 1:181). One can scarcely exaggerate the role of violence, which Sartre describes as "interiorized scarcity," in his social theory and his philosophy of history in particular. Given our pursuit of the role of reason in history, it is important to note that for Sartre "human violence is meaningful." Not only does it render intelligible the tragic course of class conflict in the Western world, including conflict within what were then socialist states, but it emerges as itself something more than "the contingent ferocity of man," namely, "everyone's intelligible reinteriorization of the contingent fact of scarcity" (*CDR* 1:815). It is for this reason that he devotes so much space in volume 2 of the *Critique* to a phenomenology of the boxing match as the intelligible incarnation of struggle in general and of class conflict in particular.

If the fact of scarcity's rendering practico-inert mediation violent gives a tragic tone to the voice of history, the contingency of scarcity, its superability, offers hope that Sartre's reign of freedom might be realized in a true "socialism of abundance" (*FI* 5:171). This is the factical dimension of his historical ideal.[11]

Structure, not Structuralism

In his drive for dialectical intelligibility, Sartre has not claimed complete historical rationality. First among the limits to such intelligibility is the surd of material scarcity itself. There is a sense in which even this can be subsumed in a society of abundance that technology may usher in. But, of course, the ontological scarcities of time and space remain, not to mention that ultimate facticity which hovers over Sartre's existentialist universe. So the dream of complete historical transparency remains just that.

A limiting form of facticity that directly implies temporality is what Sartre calls "the depth of the world" (*CDR* 1:541). By this he means those serialities of the society out of which the group is engendered along with the "memory of humanity" mentioned above. Just as the for-itself relies on the in-itself of which it is the internal negation, so the group carries with it those practico-inert serialities that it is continuously overcoming. They cloud its intelligibility even as they condition its being.

Besides the limits established by facticity in general and scarcity in particular, complete historical (dialectical) intelligibility comes to grief on three additional obstacles. First, the antidialectic of practico-inert *process,* such as the capitalist or colonialist systems mentioned earlier, in its very serial rationality masks the irreducibility of individual praxes deformed by practico-inert mediation. Agency in these contexts is limited to passive activity like the impotent actions of the public before the mass media or the "impossibility" of the factory owner's meeting the labor union's demands.

An additional limit stems from the fact that totalization, as we have seen, cannot include the totalizer himself. This generates the traditional problem of perspectivism or what Sartre calls "situated knowledge." Despite the homogeneity of individual and group praxis, and not withstanding the power of comprehension, the anthropologist or historian cannot entirely escape her own situation. This renders especially acute the problem of "totalization without a totalizer," the overarching issue of the *Critique.*

The final obstacle to full dialectical intelligibility in history arises from the impossibility of free organic praxis being completely integrated into the group. The social dialectic of the group (the "constituted dialectic") is a totalization by its members, not a totality; full organic unity is at most a Kantian ideal (see *CDR* 1:708).

Praxis and the Mediating Third

The two most significant conceptual innovations in the *Critique* are the practico-inert and the mediating third. The former accounts for the otherness and, modified by scarcity, the violence that colors human history as we know it. The latter carries the intelligibility of organic praxis to the interiority of the group. According to Sartre, each organic individual *is* a third, but this feature is submerged in serial dispersion. "Nevertheless," he insists, "it *does* exist in each of us as alienated freedom" (*CDR* 1:366). Disalienated freedom, then, is the actualization of our status as mediating thirds: we are free, so it seems, only in the practical group.

Because the third is a function of praxis, let us first consider that fundamental term.

"Praxis" is purposive human activity in its material, social, and historical context.[12] Sartre will often identify it with "labor" in the Marxist sense that includes mental as well as physical work (see *CDR* 1:90, 124). In fact, he claims that "the essential discovery of Marxism is that labor . . . is the real foundation of the organization of social relations" and adds that "this discovery *can no longer* be questioned" (*CDR* 152 n). In his commentary on *Critique 1,* Joseph Catalano distinguishes praxis from action, describing "action" as "praxis stripped of its historical relations and limited to a very local context," which underscores the totalizing and social nature of praxis as such.[13]

Sartre develops what I call "the principle of the primacy of praxis" in the *Critique* when he writes that "praxis alone . . . is, *in its dialectical freedom,* the real and permanent foundation (in human history up to the present) of all the inhuman sentences which men have passed on men through worked matter" (*CDR* 1:332). Elsewhere, I have elaborated this principle by discussing the threefold primacy of praxis—ontological, epistemological, and moral—in Sartre's social ontology.[14] I shall not repeat that argument here, except to note that what I have said about comprehension as the self-awareness of praxis and about the moral ascriptions for collective effects to individual moral agents indicates how the epistemic and ethical primacy are linked to the ontological primacy that we are exhibiting at present. This threefold primacy comes into full view with the concept of the mediating third.

The true "subject" of history is the closely knit group, in the sense that only in the group does one overcome the passiveness and exteriority of the practico-inert and achieve a degree of mutual recognition among freedoms that Sartre visualizes as the "reign of man." He has in mind those combat groups he experienced, if only vicariously, during the Resistance as well as those spontaneously formed bands of revolutionaries that sprang up during the French Revolution. "Our History is intelligible to us," he writes, "because it is dialectical, and it is dialectical because the class struggle produces us as transcending the inertia of the collective towards dialectical combat-groups" (*CDR* 1:805). Notwithstanding his abiding interest in biography and his commitment to the ontological primacy of individual organic praxis, Sartre has admitted that historically the solitary individual is impotent.[15]

We need not pursue that revolving set of practical relations that constitutes the inner life of the group. The "mediating third" is a functional concept denoting the praxis of the organic individual *as* group member, that is, as communicating identity of interest and purpose (each member is "the same" for the others in that regard and each action occurs "here" in terms of common concern), without claiming an impossible unity within some superorganism. This example of what Sartre calls "dialectical nominalism" allows for a true "synthetic enrichment" of individual praxis, justifying such social predicates as "power," "function," "right/ duty," and "fraternity-terror," while ostensibly avoiding the collective consciousness of Durkheim or the organic theories of idealist social philosophers generally.

Above all, the function of the mediating third is to foster the fullest possible mutual comprehension among the members of the group. This is the Sartrean ideal of positive reciprocity which forms the countervalue to alienation in his writings after *Being and Nothingness.* Indeed, his discussions of "the gift" and "authentic love" in the *Notebooks* reveal him as prizing positive reciprocity already in his vintage existentialist days (see *NE* 370, 508). In the *Critique* he explains: "In reciprocity, my partner's praxis is, as it were, at root *my praxis,* which has broken in two by accident and whose pieces, each of which is a complete praxis on its own, both retain from their original unity a profound affinity and an immediate understanding" (*CDR* 1:131). Again, the affinity is valuative and the understanding practical. The partners have cast their lots together.

By calling the group's life and action "constituted dialectic" and that of the organic individual "constitutive," Sartre again underscores the principle of the primacy of individual praxis. He sees the impossibility for a union of individuals to transcend organic action as a strictly individual model to be *the basic condition of historical rationality;* in other words, "constituted dialectical Reason (as the living intelligibility of all common praxis) must always be related to its ever present but always veiled foundation, constituent rationality" (*CDR* 1:678). In fact, early in the *Critique* he redescribes his project: "When our whole investigation is complete, we shall see that individual praxis . . . is at the same time constituting Reason itself, operating within History seen as constituted Reason" (*CDR* 1:96).

The master key to the logic of History, therefore, is that sequence of mediations that enable organic praxis to effect group activities or that deviate and maintain praxes in serial impotence as passive, manipulated "objects" of history. Generically, Sartre's synchronic analysis has yielded praxis, the third, and the practico-inert as those crucial mediating factors. Sartre further specifies praxis and the practico-inert (the third is a specification of praxis), but he leaves us to establish empirically how they operate in historical fact. That is why he claims to deliver in the first volume of the *Critique* "not the real concrete, which can only be historical, but the set of formal contexts, curves, structures and conditionings that constitute *the formal milieu* in which the historical concrete must necessarily occur" (*CDR* 1:671; emphasis mine). It is the double circularity of the constituted dialectic, namely, static (horizontal and vertical) and dynamic (perpetual movement that sooner or later degrades groups into collectives), "that constitutes the final moment of the dialectical investigation and, therefore, the concrete reality of sociality" (*CDR* 1:671). More specifically, his intent is to demonstrate that "*if* classes do exist," then one is forced to choose either to grasp them by static, analytic reason that allows them "no more unity than the compact inertia revealed by geological sections" or to understand that "their moving, changing, fleeting, ungraspable yet *real* unity" comes to them from a "practical reciprocity of either a positive [cooperative] or a negative [violent] kind" (*CDR* 1:794). (This not-so-veiled critique of structuralism also asserts the link between historical intelligibility and unity that he has been seeking since his initial debate with Aron.) Comprehension will terminate in discovering "a real project of violence [or counterviolence]" between members of opposing classes (*CDR* 1:794). For a society such as ours, divided along class lines, this is the understanding that dialectical Reason accords to History as we know it. Its emblem will be the boxing match.

Praxis-Process

Sartre distinguishes three "modalities of human action": individual praxis, common, constituted praxis, and praxis-process. They are, he insists, "in themselves distinct from the practico-inert process and are its foundation" (*CDR* 1:789). By itself, the term "process" denotes that impersonal sequence of events proper to the practico-inert field. "The social field," Sartre writes, "is full of acts with no author" (*SM* 163–64). What he calls the "systems" of colonialism and capitalism, for example, are processes. "In this [practico-inert] field," he explains, "everyone's action disappears, and is replaced by monstrous forces which, in the inertia of the organic and of exteriority, retain some power of action and unification combined with a false interiority" (*CDR* 1:319). *Praxis*-process reminds us that the "monstrous forces" whose effects we witness and whose exigencies we feel are deviations and mutations of a praxis that simultaneously sustains and is sustained by the necessities of the process. His crucial example of the boxing match in *Critique 2* will appeal to the unity and intelligibility "of a very particular praxis-process, since the process is defined here as the deterioration of one praxis by the other" (*CDR* 2:11). Again, he points out "the human features of praxis, as a lived aspect of praxis-process and as the motor of the process itself" (*CDR* 2:182). This fruitful, hybrid concept figures in Sartre's historical accounts of systems, institutions, and historical customs and practices.

TEMPORALIZATION

Praxis is not only totalizing, it is also temporalizing. Like Sartrean "consciousness," which it supplants in the later works, praxis brings into play a specifically human time, the "ekstatic" temporality of facticity, presence-to, and *Existenz* or transcendence. But the omnipresence of praxis in Sartre's social theory temporalizes not only the constituted dialectic of the group but the antidialectic of the practico-inert as well. It is, after all, *practico*-inert. So let us examine each dimension of temporalization as it affects Sartre's philosophy of history.

The Future

Sartre argues that "dialectic as a movement of reality collapses if time is not dialectic; that is, if we refuse to recognize a certain action of the future as such" (*SM* 92 n). This "action" of the future is, first of all, that yet-to-be-achieved totality toward which praxis transcends (*dépasse*) the present. It unifies and directs present praxis through the spirals of dialectical advance. This is the classic existentialist concept of the future as possibility. But it has undergone a modification reflecting Sartre's praxis philosophy and his discovery of Marx. Besides being the "lack" which illumines present reality, the possible serves as a limit in that it counterpoises the *im*possible. Thus, Sartre speaks of "the real and permanent future which the collectivity forever maintains and transforms," for example, the need for more doctors that industrialized society creates (*SM* 94). He continues, "the most individual possible is only the internalization and enrichment of a social possible" (*SM* 95). This is the future as objective possibility. This new understanding of the future signals a major shift in Sartre's concept of freedom (toward so-called positive freedom) and constitutes a prime factor in his tilt toward a Marxist theory of history.

But not only does the "future" unify and direct present praxis, it also reveals "scarcity" and its correlate "need" for what they are. Recall that material scarcity, in Sartre's eyes, accounts for the violence that mars human history as we have experienced it. Dialectically, he characterizes scarcity as negation and need as "negation of negation."[16] Totalizing praxis creates both the lack *and* the need by virtue of its intrinsic reference to the future as the whole. So Sartre can summarize the "dialectical experience [*l'expérience*]" at the start of the *Critique* as follows: "It is the existence of this nothingness, which is both active (totalization positing its moments) and passive (*the whole as the presence of the future*), that constitutes the first intelligible dialectical negation" (*CDR* 1:86). It is within this totalization that negation of negation becomes affirmation (the violent fulfillment of need, for example, becomes counterviolence). Thus the historian, if she will comprehend the historical event, must grasp this "action" of the future as well.

The Present

The Sartrean "present" is elusive precisely because of its dialectical nature. As presence-to-self, the Sartrean subject is nonself-identical and hence ontologically free. We saw this ontological freedom translate spatially into an "inner distance" and temporally into the "is-been" (*est-été*) that marks the agent as free of causal determinacy properly speaking. Sartre's discussion of "human reality" anticipates the postmodern rejection of a logic of identity by Gilles Deleuze and others. The famous Sartrean "choice" continues to operate within a praxis context, not only as creative of meaning/direction ("recuperation" in the *Notebooks*, "appropriation" and "internalization" in the *Critique*), but now as translator of possibility into facticity for which responsibility is incurred in characteristically existentialist fashion.

The Past

It is here that Sartre's concept of the practico-inert joins his earlier reflections on the in-itself of the for-others to yield a distinctive theory of the historical event and especially of the subsequent agent as "man of the event" (*l'homme événement*). An occurrence becomes part of History by its happening for-others. It is "registered" in the practico-inert like "an inert universal memory" (*CDR* 1:122), thereafter to modify the situations of those who interiorize it in their own projects. This influence takes the form of "exigency," deforming consequences, counter-finalities, and all the other types of "inertial force" we have attributed to the practico-inert. Unfortunately, Sartre never hierarchizes these practico-inert antecedents (as his early concept of simultaneity might have suggested he do). Thus he misses an important chance to refine his theory of practico-inert mediation, for example, by determining "degrees" of exigency and the like. So the past exists not only in memory or even in the traces of monuments and documents. For Sartre, it is operative in the practico-inert mediation of the colonialist system, for example, and of Malthusian practices by third-generation French industrialists as well as in the "necessary" choice of neurotic art that faced young would-be writers under the July Monarchy. Whereas existentialism affirms the "specificity of the historical *event*," the Marxists, Sartre believes, tend to reduce it to a pure symbol (*SM* 124) or relegate it to chance and the nonsignifying (*SM* 126). The challenge to an existentialist theory is "to discover a supple, patient dialectic which espouses movements as they really are and which refuses to consider a priori that all lived conflicts pose contradictions or even contraries" (*SM* 126).

Let us consider a favorite Sartrean example of a historical event that changed the relations between succeeding generations, the massacre of unemployed Parisian workers by the *Garde Mobile* during the uprising of June 1848. His thesis is that before that confrontation the French bourgeoisie and proletariat could have maintained the illusion of a common interest in the industrialization of the country, but that after the massacre this was objectively impossible. The event had raised consciousness, but it had also changed the very identity of the respective sides. From that moment on each would face the other as massacrer and massacred respectively: not just psychologically or because of family ties with those directly involved in the event, but because the respective "class-being" (the practico-inert bond that unites/separates each collective) is partially determined in relation to that affair. As *l'homme événement*, each bears the mark of that historical catastrophe. That is why the French bourgeoisie differs from its British counterpart: it is the practico-inert heir to another history—a point Sartre thinks eludes Marxist "econo-mists."[17]

The Search for a "Supple, Patient Dialectic": The Theory Established

History is not chronology, the mere concatenation of facts along a tem-poral trajectory—what critics and skeptics dismiss as "one damn thing after another." Historical facts, if they are to make any sense, must en-joy a relationship closer than mere temporal sequence. And yet that linkage cannot be so tight as to squeeze out every last drop of freedom (understood in the general sense of "could have done otherwise") or history is transformed into something else—something akin to "natural history." Sartre is convinced that what he calls "analytic Reason" (for example, the binary functions of modern logic or the Aristotelian princi-ples of noncontradiction and excluded middle) cannot escape this dilemma—but neither can a Marxist economism that models history on a natural science. Sartre insists that his concepts of practico-inert, medi-ating third, and totalization belong to a dialectical Reason that renders history intelligible while enhancing, not compromising, the character of human freedom.

In *Being and Nothingness* he had criticized Heidegger's concept of *Mit-sein* (being-with) as originative, saying that unless one starts with the individual, one will never arrive at him (see *BN* 244 ff.). So too in histor-ical understanding. If the goal is intelligibility not only of a social fact such as the battle of Waterloo but also of the adventures of the historical agent, Napoleon or Wellington, for example, a method must be found to respect the *specificity* of each. For Sartre, this means that one begins with the individual and moves toward his or her "constitution" of social prac-tice, whereas the structuralist typically will begin with the social prac-tice and reserve a functional placeholder for the individual.[18]

But if history is to be *one* and yet remain history, it must be a totaliza-tion or a detotalized totality, not a simple totality—which it could be only for a subject outside of history (a hypothesis Sartre has rejected since the *War Diaries*). Its unity must come from "within," not from "without" as in some preestablished plan. So Sartre begins with the question, "Is there a sector of being in which totalization is the very form of existence?" The answer, of course, is the field of free organic praxis.

The Historical Agent (Again)

Sartre's point of departure in seeking historical intelligibility is "the immediate, simple lived praxis" (*CDR* 1:56) which we now know is dialectical and temporalizing as well as totalizing. But if praxis is conceived as purposeful human activity in its material environment, we have watched Sartre join Marx in taking this constitutive activity primarily as *work*. What his analysis of scarcity adds to the Marxian thesis (and he admits that the idea of scarcity [*la rareté*] is not a Marxist notion)[19] is the concept of an inert material "negation" of praxis, interiorized by the agent as violence. One might call this "structural violence" in order to underscore its objective, conditioning function in *all* human relations where material scarcity reigns, not just in relations of production. Given the fact of scarcity, violence permeates human history. But Sartrean violence is always a relation between free, organic praxes mediated by "worked matter."

The chief epistemological reason for beginning with "simple lived praxis" is what Sartre considers the "total, translucid dialectic of individual praxis" (*CDR* 1:318). This is what I have termed "the epistemological primacy of praxis." We have already noted that this Cartesian legacy from the for-itself of *Being and Nothingness* is liable to mystification. Sartre nonetheless seems convinced that we can be and usually are sufficiently aware of what we are doing that we understand one another and incur responsibility for our actions (the moral primacy of praxis).

The agent is aware of the resistance of the physical world to his praxis; he relies on that resistance as he carves out a world of worked matter. He is moved, directed, and limited by the need that his basic totalizing project generates as it reveals to him here and now the scarcity of the world's goods. But his awareness attains a potentially higher stage when it encounters the counterfinality of this worked matter itself. Again, a good example is the way deforestation by Chinese peasants actually diminished their arable land. As Sartre explains, "insofar as, having achieved our goal, we understand that we have actually done *something else* and why our actions have been altered outside us, we get our first dialectical experience of necessity" (*CDR* 1:222). This initial experience of necessity occurs "when we are robbed of our action by worked matter, *not* insofar as it is pure materiality but insofar as it is materialized praxis" (*CDR* 1:224).

It is not surprising that, as Sartre pursues his regressive and progressive study of historical action, he will appeal to the model of the ambush and especially of the boxing match. As we said, a major portion of his notes for volume 2 of the *Critique* is devoted to an analysis of the praxis-process of boxing. Sartre seems especially interested in the unintended consequences of human actions—a topic which has engrossed philosophers of history from the start. But in his case, the focus of concern is the counterfinalities with which the practico-inert affects free praxes. His panoply of concepts from social ontology—praxis, the practico-inert, and the mediating third—is intended to render intelligible not the fact but the possibility of *un*intended historical consequences, especially insofar as these are contrary to our desires and violent in nature. A large part of history, he implies, can be included in this domain and its "dialectical necessity" grasped by our personal experience of the same.

Ever the phenomenologist though always in his own way, Sartre places great stock in the experience of dialectical necessity in our quotidian lives. Transgressing his initial caution that the argument of the *Critique* is hypothetical, he claims this experience of dialectical necessity is apodictic, that is, its evidence is necessary, "universal," absolutely certain and indubitable. It satisfies our intellectual curiosity and puts an end to our inquiry in this regard.

But his is a historical, dialectical phenomenology. To support this claim he sometimes refers to the principles, laws, and terms of dialectical reason such as "reciprocity" as *individualized universals.* His point is that dialectical necessity can be the "reflexive" experience of anybody. But he respects the totalizing nature of his own theory as well as the situated condition of the historian by adding that this "anybody" refers to anyone at *our* stage of historical development. Anticipating what in *The Family Idiot* we shall call his "principle of totalization," he explains that "if the historical totalization is to be able to exist, then any human life is the direct and indirect expression of the whole (the totalizing movement) and of all lives to precisely the extent that it is opposed to everything and to everyone" (*CDR* 1:49–50).[20]

This experience of dialectical necessity is ongoing and *retrospective,* that is, it confers a new meaning on the action underway by referring to the results, especially those counter to the agent's intention but which the agent helped bring about by doing what he intended. As Sartre describes it, "the basic experience of necessity is that of a retroactive

power eroding my freedom, from the final objectivity to the original decision, but nevertheless emerging from it. . . . It is the historical experience of matter as praxis without an author, or of praxis as the signifying
inertia that signifies me" (*CDR* 1:226). Elaborating on what he had written in *Notebooks* about the oeuvre-trace as illuminative of the *sens* of a
praxis, he adds: "The agent's real aim and . . . the agent himself can only
be assumed in the light of the result. It is Madame Bovary who illuminates Flaubert, not the reverse" (*CDR* 1:226). By parity of reasoning, it
is Waterloo that illuminates Napoleon and the gulag, Stalin. History
like biography must be read backwards.

The dialectical experience of practico-inert necessity ushers in a new
level of awareness, that of seriality mediated by the practico-inert. Sartre refers to the practico-inert as "fundamental sociality" (*CDR* 1:318).
Both logically and temporally, the initial social ensembles are serial.
Whatever groups appear originate in opposition to serial otherness, dispersion, impotence. In a famous phrase, Sartre refers to the practico-
inert ensemble as "both the matrix of groups and their grave" (*CDR*
1:635). It is at this level of fundamental sociality, we have seen, that he
locates class being. In fact, it is in the dialectical context of the general
conditions for the *inversion* of relations between men and matter that the
more specific issue of the conditions for the rise of capitalism (as studied
by Marx), for example, should be located (see *CDR* 1:152). Sartre intends to show "how classes are possible" and so how our history is intelligible by his notions of practico-inert mediation, seriality, and
scarcity, culminating dialectically in the lived experience of dialectical
necessity.

If we understand individual praxis as (abstract) freedom in the classic
Sartrean sense, then the historical dialectic can be understood in terms
of freedom and necessity. The phase of serial otherness through
practico-inert mediation in a context of material scarcity is the alienation
of freedom in necessity. This is how Sartre seeks to understand the historical dialectic of interest and destiny that characterizes relations between industrial capitalists and the proletariat in the nineteenth century.
But a new phase of historical intelligibility, namely, the constituted dialectic, opens with the advent of the group understood as "freedom as
necessity," in other words, as "necessity freely accepted" in the pledge
(*CDR* 1:671). So Sartre allows that "there are *two* quite distinct dialectics
at work here: that of individual praxis and that of the group as praxis"

(*CDR* 1:319). If the group affords the individual the power to act historically, the pledge gives the group the permanence to do so through a
diversity of members and in a variety of circumstances.

The spontaneous group, which Sartre characterizes as "the sudden
resurrection of freedom" (*CDR* 1:401), once the external threat that led
to its being formed subsides, preserves itself by a kind of oath of mutual
loyalty under pain of death. The resultant "fraternity-terror" fashions
the context in which group membership perdures. Sartre describes the
pledge as self-imposed inertia (see *CDR* 1:419). The artificial (*factice*)
inertia of the pledge forms the apex of his social dialectic in terms of
freedom-necessity and yields the "common individual" (group member
as such) as the effective positive agent of history. Because of its efficacity and its relative permanence, he refers to the pledged group as "the
origin of humanity" (*CDR* 1:436). He further describes the group as
"the free milieu of free human relations" and concludes: "Thus the
group is both the most effective *means* of controlling the surrounding
materiality in the context of scarcity and *the absolute end* as pure freedom
liberating men from alterity" (*CDR* 1:673).

If the experience of dialectical necessity brings to our consciousness
the counterfinalities of the practico-inert, another experience, that of the
interiorization of multiplicity, makes us aware of our potential historical
efficacity. This is the practical awareness of each group member's being
"the same" and of everyone's praxis occurring "here" as opposed to the
"other" and "elsewhere" of serial dispersion. By the experience that
"we are a force to be reckoned with," the agent achieves the practical
unity of the common individual ("we") as comprehended in the exercise
of historical efficacity (". . . are a force"). This new experience becomes
reflective as fraternity-terror is ushered in with the pledge. It thereby
advances to the experience of "freedom as necessity," that is, as self-
imposed inertia. If the individual harnesses her spontaneity to some extent, she thereby gains the efficacity and permanence required of a historical agent.

As the "grave" of the group, the practico-inert reintroduces serial
otherness through the institution, whose paradigms are the army and
the state. The logic of this move is once more that of deviated intentions
and alienated consequences by means of worked matter, particularly the
bureaucracy. We need not pursue the details of Sartre's position here
except to recall that both the constituted dialectic of group praxis and the

antidialectic of the collective and the institution have their own rationalities, which are sustained by the "constitutive dialectic" of free organic praxis.[21] This lived dialectic gives access to the "interiority" of the
resultant social ensembles, even to that of the partially "exterior" relations of the collective and the institution, which are, after all, *practico-
inert*. It is the original experience of dialectical necessity that reveals the
practico-inert.

Dialectical Circularity

Recall that a basic hypothesis of Sartre's critical investigation is "the ontological identity and methodological reciprocity" between "an individual life and human history" (*CDR* 1:70). The methodological
reciprocity expresses itself in the principle of totalization that we discussed earlier. The ontological "identity" would seem to refer to the primacy of individual praxis; that is, to the fact that group praxis, though it
is a synthetic enrichment of individual praxis, is nonetheless constitut*ed*
by individual praxes, which alone are constitut*ing*.

A certain dialectical circularity seems inevitable here, as we noted
earlier. Sartre is fully aware of the challenge of this position: "In reality," he allows, "the hypothesis which makes the critical investigation
feasible is precisely the one which the investigation aims to prove"
(*CDR* 1:70). As a hypothesis, it requires "proof"; as a hypothesis of dialectical Reason, this proof must emerge as the experience of dialectical
necessity and common *freedom* during the practical task of progressive
and regressive argument. The investigation is successful, he believes, if
it reveals "the rocky sub-soil of necessity beneath the translucidity of
free individual praxis" (*CDR* 1:70–71). It is an effect my experience of
dialectical necessity, which Sartre terms the temporal development of a
"practical intuition" (*CDR* 1:94), that confirms this identity/reciprocity
of individual life and history. He claims to prove "that *necessity,* as the
apodictic structure of dialectical investigation, resides neither in the free
development of interiority [which he later rejects as Hegelian idealism]
nor in the inert dispersal of exteriority [historical positivism or Marxist
economism]; it asserts itself as an inevitable and irreducible moment in
the interiorization of the exterior and in the exteriorization of the interior" (*CDR* 1:71). But such internalization/externalization has been the
mark of dialectical praxis since the *Notebooks*. He describes this experience graphically as finding oneself "carrying out the sentence which a

'developing' society has pronounced upon us and which defines us a priori in our being" (*CDR* 1:71).[22] Its most significant instance for historical intelligibility lies in class conflict read as just such a dialectical necessity. In this case, the circularity arises from the fact that one requires dialectical Reason to recognize the very socioeconomic classes whose conflict yields that authenticating experience of dialectical necessity.

But the circularity extends to historical comprehension as well; not only to the comprehension of another agent's comprehension but to our situated understanding of any historical praxis-process. Of course, given the epistemological primacy of praxis, our understanding of the latter is related to our comprehension of the former. Sartre discusses these aspects of circularity in volume 2 of the *Critique*.

Praxis-process, which he seems to equate with "enveloping totalization" in *Critique 2,* operates according to a feedback relationship: "its consequences react upon its principles and its outcomes upon the forces that have produced them." But, in our present society, with its class division and material scarcity, the feedback is negative, "since its effect is to warp praxis rather than to correct it" (*CDR* 2:283). He allows the possibility that "in a society in which science and technology were more advanced" a system of compensating devices might "automatically correct the deviation by its effects." But, reaffirming the primacy of praxis, he insists this would happen "through the labor of men" and that in any case the suppression of primary deviation "would engender a reflexive circularity with second-level deviations" (*CDR* 2:283–84).

Given this feedback phenomenon, he must now ask:

> From the viewpoint of historical knowledge, does circularity allow a total comprehension of praxis-process? For we know that the comprehension of constituted actions [pledged and organized group praxis], although itself different from constituent comprehension, is nevertheless possible—and wholly appropriate—so long as an organized action is involved. For comprehension is *praxis* itself, nothing else. As constituted comprehension of a common praxis, it emanates simply from the historian, inasmuch as he can make himself into a common individual by virtue of a pledge. But the enveloping totalization comprises a turning back of the inert upon the agent, to recondition him. Is it the task of comprehension to grasp this process of involution? We

must frankly reply: yes. For such reconditioning at all events eludes positive Reason. (*CDR* 2:284; translation emended)

The Stalinist bureaucracy, a prime example of praxis-process, is dialectically intelligible because the practico-inert "was refracted through the dialectical medium of totalization" (*CDR* 2:284–85). What distinguishes its intelligibility from that of nondictatorial societies is that the closed society seeks to "integrate the field of the anti-dialectic into the totalization as a constituted dialectic." This occurs via the totalizing praxis of the dictator as unique sovereign. Showing little sympathy for this historical phenomenon, Sartre explains that "praxis (as a constituted dialectic) [is, in this case] poisoned from within by the antidialectic." But from the epistemological viewpoint, "those various transformations [whereby the antidialectic reconditioned the dialectic] did not transcend the limits of constituted comprehension" (*CDR* 2:285).

What he has called the progressive-regressive method in the example of Stalin's bureaucracy would move down from the dictator's sovereign praxis to the masses and the new modifications of the practico-inert, and then up through new abstract statistical determinations (such as the one analytic sociological reason can supply us) to the sovereign once again, but now as reconditioned by the new results of this method. Sartre concludes, "So circular intelligibility is always comprehensible, since the historian never has to deal with anything but praxis and discovers the inert like a residue at the bottom of the crucible of action. So the movement of his comprehension is regressive, then progressive; for he will discover the inert by the deviation, and interpret the other by the former" (*CDR* 2:287).

The Historian's Task: Reconstituting Praxis

In his approach to aesthetics, John Dewey distinguishes the studio from the gallery view of an artwork. Thus far we have been considering the "studio" view of history, the viewpoint of the historical agent. The corresponding "gallery" view pertains to the historian, who would make sense of others' historical activity. Sartre calls this operation "reconstituting praxis." He undertakes it in his "biographies."[23]

The point of departure for reconstituting praxis is the self-awareness that the historian shares with any historical agent. This includes a practical comprehension of his life project, of the group praxes he shares with other members, and of the serial impotence and practico-inert counterfinalities that plague his private and public existence. If the investigator is to be totalized by history, Sartre warns, "he should re-live his membership of human ensembles with different structures and determine the reality of these ensembles through the bonds that constitute them and the practices that define them" (*CDR* 1:52). Sartre's first recommendation is that the historian not rest content with a superficial positivism of facts and dates. The reality to be dealt with is practical and totalizing. So too must be the method of the historian who would grasp it.

We have noted Sartre's principle of the ontological and epistemological primacy of individual praxis. He reaffirms this epistemic primacy as he summarizes his study of constituted Reason, the rationality of the social whole: "Thus constituted Reason derives its very intelligibility—as the structural logic of common action—from constituent Reason: and if our critical investigation enables us to grasp the formal genesis of the second dialectic, in its double character as praxis and process, with its scope and its limits in terms of the practico-inert and of dissolutions of seriality, this is enough" (*CDR* 1:663). The first volume of the *Critique* is a social ontology of collective action as well as an explanatory scheme of historical movement in general.

Aron had pointed out the historian's perspectivism. Sartre, as we saw in our discussion of "historialization," has by and large come to agree. But he urges that "the first necessity for the situated investigator (assuming that he has the necessary information and that he is approaching his facts within a period whose main features are already known), is to *comprehend the comprehension* of the regulatory third party" (*CDR* 1:696; emphasis mine). As individual praxis reveals itself by its goal or project, common praxis is manifest by its objective. But the latter must be interpreted by the Third. "It is the tension of this future in the practical present," Sartre notes, "and the progressive and regressive decoding of this fundamental relation, that furnish the first elements of intelligibility [of a group praxis]" (*CDR* 1:387).

The historian must grasp the third party's comprehension as "free group praxis," that is, "as transcendence which preserves the conditions it transcends." A structuralist like Levi-Strauss, Sartre objects, would rest content with such formal relations to account for phenomena like matrimonial practices in primitive societies. But Sartre considers such explanations merely way stations on the road to full, dialectical intelligibility. A dialectical account of cross-cousin marriages, for example, would refer to the purpose which directs the agents following these rules, their way of interiorizing scarcity of women—again, the kaiser's withered arm.[24] The dialectical historian is like Clifford Geertz's interpretive anthropologist, who wants "to grasp the natives' point of view" in order "to figure out what the devil they think they are up to."[25] Regressive analysis reveals the formal structure of the group, its pledge, for example, as self-imposed inertia. The historian must temporalize this structure by grasping how the common individual totalizes that particular situation. This understanding of the common individual is available to the historian, Sartre urges, because he is a group member and hence a common individual himself, and "a common individual [is] capable of understanding *any* common praxis" (*CDR* 1:508; emphasis mine).

But Sartre expects a similar comprehension of the serialized individuals. Thus, the dialectical historian, he claims, "must comprehend the project of the Other (of the institution) in its real unity (within the institutional group) and on this basis he must be able to grasp the *transcended conditions.*" Sartre concludes optimistically, "the *sole* limitation on the power of comprehension here is not due to the complexity of the object, but to the *position of the observer*" (*CDR* 1:696). The class-being of the investigator, for example, can function "as a *limit* to his practical comprehension" (*CDR* 1:509). In addition to exemplifying the valuational dimension of historical knowledge, this advice constitutes a major concession in view of Sartre's earlier Cartesian insistence on the translucidity of praxis. It anticipates and in a sense expands what we have seen will be his subsequent admission that mystification can cloud even the self-comprehension of individual praxis.[26]

The praxis of the professional historian as a member of an organized group is modified in terms of "function, power and ability." This "membership," Sartre points out, is exercised by "a synthetic, individual decoding of the practical field . . . [which] in this case, is constituted by certain documents and monuments through which a *common* signification must be rediscovered." This means that his "professional" act of reconstructing the past brings with it a "double comprehension: that of the common function of the scholar and that of the common *praxis* of the past group" (*CDR* 1:508–9). The values and norms of the historical profession are interiorized by the member in his very act of exercising his métier. Sartre's distinction of dialectical from analytic Reason is a way of pointing out the inevitable value component in the practice of a profession, even one whose goal is historical truth. If Sartre's challenge to the dialectical historian is to determine "in the process of human history, what is the respective role of relations of interiority and exteriority" (*CDR* 1:57), like a good psychoanalyst, the historian must focus this determination originally on himself.

So it is the historian's task to reconstitute the relevant totalizing praxes with their experience of dialectical necessity and necessary freedom in order to bring to critical, reflective awareness these practical intentionalities and mediating factors in their continued functioning as the "depth of the world" in which we are presently struggling. *Reconstituting praxis,* the historian's proper craft, Sartre observes, "constructs past, that is to say, transcended, reality by rediscovering it in the present transcendence which preserved it; and it is itself constructed by this resuscitated past which transforms it insofar as it restores it. Furthermore, as a transcended past, the reconstituted praxis necessarily forms part of our present praxis as its diachronic depth" (*CDR* 1:56). The historian must perform a hermeneutic of the signs of the individual and group projects which constitute History as the field of freedom. But he must likewise uncover "the world of humanized materialities and materialized institutions" that prescribe a "general future" to every agent (*CDR* 169). It is becoming clear that existentialist history is as much about the future as it is about the past!

It is in this sense that Sartre understands Fernand Braudel's characterization of the Mediterranean as "a unit, with its creative space, the amazing freedom of its sea-routes . . . , with its many regions, so different yet so alike, its cities born of movement."[27] "This is not a metaphor," Sartre explains. Just as a house to be a dwelling must be inhabited, and as the reconstituting praxis mediates between the exterior and the interior, so "one can speak of 'the Mediterranean' as a real symbiosis of men and things and as tending to petrify man in order to animate matter" (*CDR* 1:169). Like all praxis, reconstituting praxis mediates the "exterior" and the "interior." But in the case of the historian's praxis, this mediating activity entails comprehending the historical agent's comprehended past in light of that same agent's projected future. But such reconstitution is not speculative and detached; it becomes part of the "diachronic depth" of the historian's own world, subject to the kind of sense-making that her own project confers on its situation. Commitment is unavoidable for any form of praxis.

If dialectical history is totalizing praxis, it is something one does with and to the practico-inert and other praxes. Just as the serialized individual's practical coming to consciousness of his numerical force in the performative, "We are a hundred strong!" totalizes the events imaginatively antecedent by interiorizing his multiplicity, so the historian "sees" the *sens* of History as a struggle between haves and have-nots in a field of scarcity. Something like Wittgenstein's "dawning of an aspect" takes place. But the scarcity is real; so too are the group relations that constitute the social bond. In other words, Sartre is arguing that the historian will not comprehend History unless she interiorizes the class struggle, that is, unless she is committed.

History and Commitment

We would misconstrue the *Critique* and Sartre's philosophy of history if we regarded this collection of concepts and principles as serving a primarily speculative end. The historian's praxis, like everyone's, is totalizing in virtue of a certain end-goal. If she would comprehend a particular historical action, she must not only grasp the agent's understanding of what he was about as well as how others read the meaning of the action, but she must relate those understandings to the movement of History as a whole, of which she, the historian, is a part. Where analytic, positivist Reason rests content with causal sequences punctuated by "chance events," Sartre urges that the historian do "as dialectical rationality requires [and assume] that there is a larger totalization," for example, by locating an individual strike within the history of the trade-union movement in a particular country (*CDR* 711). But we have seen that history, for Sartre, can be a whole only if it is a totalization of totalizations, that is, only if it interrelates these comprehensions to a comprehended goal. Hence we are faced again with the global question of whether History is going anywhere, whether it has a goal.

What Sartre's concepts render intelligible is the possibility of class struggle and the retrospective necessity that the status quo would not be what it is if the past had been other than it was. This possibility is a function of the practico-inert in a field of material scarcity; the retro-spective necessity follows from "the synthetic bonds of History" (*CDR* 1:56), specifically, from the fact that transcendence (*dépassement*) defines itself in relation to that which it transcends and that dialectical negation is also a conservation that constitutes what Sartre calls the "diachronic depth" of our praxis. If existence precedes essence, essence stalks existence in History as in life.

But transcendence is always toward something, and dialectic, as we have seen, presupposes a certain "action of the future as such." What is this telos that can retrospectively unite, direct, and give meaning (*sens*) to the whole of History? It cannot be an existing state of affairs or History would be finished. But neither can it be the natural consequence of mechanical or even organic forces, like the stops on a tramline or the flower in the bud, lest history cease to exist. Rather, as the *Notebooks* lead us to expect, Sartre sees this goal of History as a moral value and a social choice. He recommends that the historian "totalize" the human enter-prise as a search for relations of full reciprocity among freedoms, that is, for "fraternity" or what he calls the "reign of freedom." The class struggle and all the more concrete forms of historical mediation can then be "seen as" stages in this ongoing adventure. The events of modern history can be read in light of this value and, of course, the interpretation may contribute to its realization.

Like the committed literature whose praises Sartre sang in the late 1940s, "committed history" presumes a choice by the historian of the meaning-value which will guide her interpretation of admittedly ambig-uous historical facts. The historian's "reading," praxis that it is, is also a totalizing choice, in this case, of the exploited and oppressed whose cause her action serves. This is a far cry from Leopold von Ranke's history "wie es eigentlich gewesen ist" or from Weber's *Wertfrei* social science. But neither does it succumb to Nietzsche's skeptical "inter-pretation of interpretations." There is a basic historical agent, the or-ganic individual whose praxis has been diverted in the series or enriched in the group. By focusing on the alienation, exploitation, and oppres-sion of this agent, the historian is furthering the advent of the classless society. (Recall Sartre's remarks about class conflict at a certain level of abstraction being one of rationalities.) The historian's very choice of subject matter as well as of the categories of dialectical intelligibility constitutes this totalizing commitment. If Sartre agrees with the opponents of value-free social science, he also subscribes to the thesis that freedom is the foundation of all values and that no one can be free concretely until all are free.[28]

But if historical events and situations sustain such an interpretation, do they demand it? Thus, obviously alluding to the Russian revolution, Sartre insists that the first moment in constructing a socialist society could only be "the indissoluble aggregation of bureaucracy, of Terror and of the cult of personality" (*CDR* 1:662).[29] The upshot of the critical investigation, he notes, is the practical, ongoing insight that *if* classes exist, these dialectical relations *must* obtain (see *CDR* 1:794). He has consistently claimed that analytic (causal or functional) reasoning is blind to class identity and struggle, that the latter requires a telic and developmental method foreign to nondialectical thought.[30] The necessity conferred on historical events and situations accordingly is telic and retrospective: the apodictic experiences to which Sartre appeals throughout the *Critique* are seen as necessary in relation to the end just achieved and to the moral goal to be realized, namely, a disalienated society. We could say that Sartre's "reading" of History takes the form of the challenge: either work for an end to alienation for all humankind, in which case History will be justifiably seen as a series of events leading to the "reign of freedom," or persist in exclusively analytic Reasoning with its attendant resignation to inevitable strife-alienation and to the ultimate meaninglessness of History.

Despite the fact that Sartre uses the language of Kantianism, for example, in his regressive method generally and, specifically, by its application in volume 1 of the *Critique* ("*if* classes exist"), the necessity to which he appeals, let me repeat, is not transcendental but ongoing and dialectical. It emerges with the corresponding totalizing insight which links the elements-become-parts into a meaningful whole.

One might object at this juncture that this resembles more the "likely story" of analytical philosophers of history than the "cunning of Reason" of either Hegel or Marx.[31] Of course, Sartre believes his dialectical nominalism, that is, his antiorganicism, distances him from Hegel. But he claims a necessity for historical relations that surpasses the merely "likely." Calling it "dialectical" removes it from the context of determinism, but it does not illumine the meaning of the term. Sartre insists that the *experience* of dialectical necessity is self-justifying. Since he is referring to an alternative form of reason, we have little choice but to follow along the path of critical investigation and test those experiences ourselves.

But, more seriously, could one not simply revive the objection leveled against Sartrean commitment in the heyday of existential authenticity, namely, that Sartre gives us more a style than a content, and that existential authenticity is compatible with the most morally reprehensible behavior? The possibility of an "authentic" anti-Semite was suggested as a counterexample at the time. Could one not cite the committed fascist or Stalinist historian to undermine Sartrean optimism regarding committed history?

In both cases, Sartre would respond that one cannot consistently commit oneself to unfreedom and that such "historians" are *eo ipso* propounding not History but the continuance of prehistory as alienation and oppression. While this is not the place to assess his defense of freedom as value, it should suffice to show that Sartre does not hold all commitments to be of a kind or all "histories" to be authentic.

A basic but seldom articulated premise of Sartre's philosophy of history is that, on the "history" side of the dichotomy history/nature, only praxis is explicative of praxis. And yet the break between history and nature is not neat; human reality is not pure praxis in the *Critique* any more than it is pure consciousness in *Being and Nothingness*. The "organic individual" must "make himself material" to fashion "worked matter," and the group likewise must materialize in "power" to realize its objective. Hence we must appeal to the "inertial force" of the practico-inert to account for that sequence of "actions without an agent" that characterizes what Sartre terms practico-inert "processes," such as the necessities entailed by colonialism or economic Malthusianism as a policy. But even here, as we have seen, it is the *practico*-inert to which appeal is made. So history, like the human reality whose adventure it records and expands, must instantiate just this basic dialectical "structure." As Sartre explains apropos of class struggle, the test case for his theory of history,

> If it is a practico-inert structure (a passive contradictory reciprocity of conditioning) or if it is *hexis*, [then] the human order is strictly comparable to the molecular order, and the only historical Reason is positivist Reason, which posits the unintelligibility of History as a definite

fact. But, on the other hand, if [class struggle] is praxis through and
through, the entire human universe vanishes into a Hegelian idealism.
(*CDR* 1:734)

Sartre's middle way depends on a totalization of totalities, but *without* a
totalizer (see *CDR* 817).

I am suggesting here that this is possible according to his own principles only if the aimed-for totality remains ever an ideal, a form of that
nonbeing which Sartre terms "value" in *Being and Nothingness* and which
in his social theory emerges (negatively) as the end to alienation and
(positively) as fraternity. This suggests as well that Sartre's "theory" of
history is shot through with implicit reference to the imaginary. In our
penultimate chapter we shall complete our account by examining that
realm.

The Given and the Taken

The ambiguity of the given and the taken, of facticity and transcendence, of the event and its interpretation, of signification found and
meaning (*sens*) constructed, has recurred like a leitmotiv throughout
Sartre's theory. Whether his appeal to a "supple, patient dialectic" resolves these ambiguities or merely serves to intensify them in a
Kierkegaardian manner is decisive for his project of historical intelligibility. Dialectical circularity suggests that we live with the ambiguity. So too does the resistance of consciousness and later of praxis to
the logic of identity. As early as *Being and Nothingness* Sartre had insisted
that "situation" was an inherently "ambiguous phenomenon in which it
is impossible for the for-itself to distinguish the contribution of freedom
from that of the brute existent" (*BN* 448). His later reference to dialectical necessity and to evidence "beyond appeal," on the one hand, while
insisting on the contextual and perspectival nature of historical knowledge ("the experimenter is part of the experimental system" [*SM* 32n]),
on the other, reveals his own ambivalence on this basic matter.

If this ambiguity is endemic to the human condition (if not to a "human nature" that Sartre would reject), perhaps the solution is to be
found *ambulando,* in the very praxis of historiography as openly committed to a social ideal. It appears that only a shift to the imaginative
mode and the practical commitment to a socioethical ideal will help us

face these ambiguities. While leaving them theoretically unresolved, such a move would enable us to live with them, perhaps even to foster them as the situation requires.

But if this is to be something more than wishful thinking, the shift must be consonant with the facts or events that constitute one term of the dialectic. Sartre's realism seems to demand such fidelity to the facts. Like the person who connects the dots in a puzzle, the existentialist historian must imaginatively link the actions, events, facts, and states of affairs so as to yield the desired form of intelligibility. And here is where discovery gives way to decision. If the facts do not connect themselves (the dot matrix approach to historical intelligibility) and if a variety of intelligible forms can be sustained by the multiplicity of "dots," then the meaning which emerges will depend on the historian's commitment to Truth and the resultant choice of methods. This is Sartre's lesson to analytic rationalists. If a dialectical method fosters "living history" and "integral humanity," then a decision in its favor is a step toward realizing these values. At times Sartre writes as if there were only one way to achieve this goal: "one Truth of History." Yet at other times he is more hypothetical. But, always, he is proposing that History is both a fact and a value and that, both as written and as lived, it is the creation of human praxis for which moral responsibility must be assumed. One's choice of rationalities carries a clear ethical price.

Chapter Seven

History and Biography:
Critique 2

The year after Sartre published the *Critique 1* (1958), the American sociologist C. Wright Mills wrote that "social science deals with problems of biography, of history, and of their intersections within social structures. These three—biography, history, society—are the co-ordinate points of the proper study of man."[1] Though not an admitted existentialist and without mentioning Sartre, Mills echoes what we have seen is the ideal of Sartre's approach and anticipates his subsequent characterization of his massive "biography" of Flaubert: "*The Family Idiot* is the sequel to *Search for a Method.* Its subject: what, at this point in time, can we know about a man?" (*FI* 1:ix). Perhaps their common inspiration is German *verstehende Soziologie,* especially Dilthey and Weber. The presence of these authors in Sartre's approach to historical comprehension is becoming increasingly evident.

Throughout this study I have been arguing that a properly existentialist theory of history must respect the role of biographical factors in any adequate historical account. To the extent that history is "alive," that is, insofar as it yields the living and not the dead past, *le passé présent,* not *le présent passé,*[2] it must capture or, better, reproduce those

The men History makes are never entirely those needed to make History.
—Sartre, *Critique of Dialectical Reason 2*

In short, the subject (and its substitutes) must be stripped of its creative role and analyzed as a complex and variable function of discourse.
—Foucault, "What Is an Author?"

experiential dimensions of choice, risk, and responsibility that mark the event as properly human. Sartre reaffirms this point, while appealing to the primacy of praxis, when he speaks of recovering "the *hazardous* aspect that characterizes every human undertaking: it is necessary to take risks and to invent. . . . We thus discover the human features of praxis, as a lived aspect of praxis-process and as the motor of the process itself. . . . For the situated historian, [this ignorance of the future] is thus not an *obscurity* (as for the agent) but a translucid intelligibility" (*CDR* 2:182). Otherwise we are left with a sequence of occurrences and their prior conditions that resembles astronomy more than history. The existentialist historian's task of reconstituting praxis, which we delineated in the previous chapter, is intended to reintroduce the human into historical narrative. If this resembles the construction of a historical novel (and the similarity has emerged early in our inquiry), it must at least be a "novel which is true," as Sartre described his study of Flaubert. We shall address this objection in our concluding chapter.

The editor's subtitle for the unfinished second volume of Sartre's *Critique of Dialectical Reason* is "The Intelligibility of History." It purports to constitute the "progressive" movement that complements the more formal, "regressive" arguments of the first volume. But like most of Sartre's major works, it remains a torso. Only Russian society after the revolution, what Sartre calls a "directorial" (i.e., dictatorial) society, is treated at length, and even these pages remain chiefly regressive in character. His consideration of bourgeois democracies ("nondirectorial" or "disunited" societies) is brief and introduced mainly by way of contrast. The content of the remainder of the work, though barely sketched, leaves the impression that he intended to undertake the herculean task of applying his principles and method to Asian societies and to world history in general. This was doubtless a major reason for abandoning the project at his advanced age.

The Intelligibility of Struggle: The Boxing Match

We have seen that the only history we know is a tale of conflict and violence due to the scarcity of material goods. In fact, Sartre describes violence as "interiorized scarcity" (*CDR* 1:815). If we are to make sense of this series of events, we must understand the meaning of struggle. Conversely, if struggle is simply an intellectual surd, a brute fact, or even an essential characteristic of human nature, then history remains either unintelligible as a whole or comprehensible only in its hopelessness. Neither option is acceptable to Sartre. So he seeks ways other than appeal to a Hobbesian human nature to render intelligible this most fundamental historical relationship: the use of freedom against itself by another freedom. His paradigm is the boxing match.

Sartre, who was himself an amateur pugilist, has used the example of the boxer's feints and jabs on other occasions to illustrate both our comprehension of another's praxis and the counterfinality of someone's being frustrated in their long-range projects by the success of their immediate actions.[3] His point was to reveal the role of the practico-inert in the deflection and deviation of praxis and to underscore the fact that "the only conceivable violence is that of freedom against freedom through the mediation of inorganic matter" (*CDR* 1:736). Now he wishes to make comprehensible the expanding spiral of mediating factors that are "enveloped" by the practice of prize-fighting and "incarnated" by a particular match. Let us observe his use of these terms in his discussion of a boxing match as the prelude to analyzing their technical meaning in detail. We can then observe their historical application in Sartre's dialectical account of Stalinist Russian in the 1930s.

Describing a specific contest between two professional boxers, Sartre moves beyond a mere detailing of their comparative records, their distinctive physical features, or even their respective styles of fighting. Such statistics, even if augmented by "human interest" considerations about the personal lives of each contestant, yield at best an analytic account that misses the specific unity of the event. The latter is available only to a dialectical reason that understands the totalizing praxis that sustains this event as well as the practico-inert mediation which such praxis subsumes. The potentially infinite amount of information that one might amass as the social and historical context of the match widens is "compressed" into the activity of these fighters in this ring on this evening. Not that they are thinking of it at the moment. Each has been trained to keep his guard up, to "read" his opponent's body as he "thinks" with his own. In this respect, each bears in his own person the history of his training, the sedimentation of years of upbringing and practice. It is for the dialectical historian to interpret this message in the action of the evening.

Inasmuch as every praxis is dialectical, each forms a distinctive locus of intelligibility. As praxis, each is a totalizing temporalization of the givens of a situation, including the ignorance and attendant risk essential to such a contest. But insofar as it is a dialectic of internalization/externalization, praxis responds to "external" exigencies and actualizes objective possibilities even as it entails unintended consequences in a process of which it may be only dimly aware. Sartre asks the question that, mutatis mutandis, forms the theme of the entire volume and the key to historical intelligibility: "How could there be *one* dialectical intelligibility of the ongoing process?" (*CDR* 2:5).

The answer will lie with Sartre's expanded notion of "situation," which in the *Critique* includes the agent's biography and socioeconomic condition as well as with the dialectical nature of praxis as internalization/externalization. For the boxers are not atomic entities. Though an analytic approach might grasp each of two contrasting viewpoints in the ring, at best it would dissolve the social fact of the contest itself in a calculus of probabilities. But as professionals, these fighters are social agents. Not only is x fighting y and y, x; they are together fighting one another.[4] Both men are united in an antagonistic reciprocity that realizes its historical and social conditions (interiorization) even as it modifies those conditions by its absolute particularity (this match will never recur; any rematch would be merely similar, not the same). In other words, each fighter is mediated by the match in his practical relation to the other. It is the mediating and totalizing functions of rationality that analytic Reason by definition misses.

Chief among the "conditions and grounds" of the conflict, which their praxis interiorizes, is the fundamental scarcity of the "material conditions of their existence" (*CDR* 2:9). Sartre sees this as the "deepest source" of their violent combat. Whether it be in the blood oath that founds and sustains the group or in the implicit appeal to the life-and-death struggle which scarcity of goods imposes on us, Sartre reads society and history in terms of this ultimate dichotomy. In a most telling remark, he observes:

> The absolute is *above all* the difference separating life from death—in my own case and, for me, in every other case. It is the gap between existence and Nothingness. It is neither *life* that is an absolute for a start, nor death: but death, inasmuch as it comes to threaten fundamentally what lives; or life, in so far as it is stripped from the real by the death that threatens it, and in so far as it can hurl itself of its own

accord to shatter intentionally upon the reef of death. . . . Every violence-event is produced, lived, refused, accepted as *the absolute.* (*CDR* 2:31)

In the case at hand, it is the knockout, "always risked, always awaited by the crowd—[which] is a public realization of death."

Later, Sartre will note that "human praxis has a non-transcendable aim: to preserve life" (*CDR* 2:385). He will speak of life as "the unitary process grounding the dialectic" (*CDR* 2:341) and will characterize violent death as "at least one case where we experience absolute exteriority within interiority," that is, the "inassimilable and non-recuperable reality" of praxis-process (*CDR* 2:310, 309). Once again, Sartre is resisting both idealism and relativism in his search for historical intelligibility, this time by appealing to the absolutes of life and death.

Anyone reading the Sartrean corpus carefully cannot help but be struck by the pervasiveness of the life/death dichotomy in his reflections. From the "one can always choose suicide" of his vintage existentialist options to the "fraternity-terror" relationship that sustains society with the fear of death, Sartre joins Marx and others in valorizing the Hegelian master-slave dichotomy between victor and vanquished in terms not only of recognition but of physical survival.[5] Yet if the possibility of violent or unexpected death shows that rationalist History is "riddled with holes" (*CDR* 2:313), the actual threat of such an ending, which scarcity constitutes, is what gives the unity he seeks to an otherwise haphazard concatenation of actions and events. Far from being merely a psychological phenomenon, this threat of violent death is as real as scarcity itself.[6]

In attempting to understand natural phenomena, Aristotle appealed to three principles that came to dominate what was called "physics" for over a millennium. These were the famous pair "matter" and "form" as well as the enigmatic "privation."[7] Without their concomitant influence, motion and nature (mobile being) remained unintelligible, caught between Parmenidean inertia and Heraclitean flux.

My point in recalling this bit of natural philosophy is to underscore both the explanatory role of "negativity" as Hegel, the German Aristotle, came to understand it and the importance of "death" as privation in Sartre's theory of history. For Sartre claims that history has two principles: human activity and inert matter (see *CDR* 2:135–36). But the foregoing suggests that he could have added violent or unexpected death, thereby reviving the ancient trio. And just as Aristotle distinguished between mere absence or negation (a stone is without sight) and privation (only animals can be blind), so "my death," for Sartre, is essentially life-referring and is nothing in itself but a surd, what he calls in *Being and Nothingness* an "unrealizable" (*BN* 547). Not only does this understanding of death as what we might call "finite life" distinguish Sartre's approach to history from that of the early Heidegger, whose ultimate horizon was "finite being" or "mortal temporality," it frees him from many, though not all, utopian theories.[8] Moreover, it challenges him to incorporate the absurdity of unexpected death into a comprehensive theory of historical totalization. We shall see him meeting this challenge in the case of the aging Stalin.

But the praxis of these boxers as Historical (in the case at hand) must be shown to be a de facto collaboration in a common task, a "new and living *process,* which is born of man yet escapes him" (*CDR* 2:13). This is the theoretical role of praxis-*process* in a dialectic of interiorization and exteriorization. It accounts both for the dimension of material scarcity that infects human history and for the objective possibilities, exigencies, hierarchies, sedimented praxes, and counterfinalities that supply its depth.[9]

Consider what Sartre calls the "contractual moment" of the praxis-process of boxing. Here one party sells his violence as a commodity in order to escape his class limitations while the other purchases the same in order to realize profits, the way one buys the labor-power of a worker in Marxist theory. Sartre sees this as "the decisive instant of incarnation" (*CDR* 2:37), both of the boxing world and of the larger, bourgeois society that envelops it. The class struggle comes into high relief in this exchange of violences. For this moment and the series of conflicts to which it explicitly commits the boxer constitute as many incarnations of all oppressive and exploitative systems, namely, "alienation of the violence of the oppressed" (*CDR* 2:45).

If the hierarchy of mediations by which these events are linked to increasingly more general conditions and significations, mounting from the technical training that produces "the boxer," through class conflict, to the "original struggle" or "fundamental violence" of life-and-death, which is the historical legacy of material scarcity—if this nest of concentric circles *envelops* its lesser members, the lesser, in turn, *incarnate* their more "abstract" components (*CDR* 2:23, 25). These circles are an ensemble of possible meanings and practices: one cannot perform a "hat trick" in boxing, for example, or be the champion unless recognized by the commission. As "enveloping totalizations," they reveal themselves in the limits they impose as well as by the "incarnations" (objects and events) they render possible or exclude. But it would be a category mistake to believe that boxing existed anywhere except in the act of boxing as praxis-process. Sartre's nominalism will allow for the "in-itself" of externalization only in the real threat of death, which is carried into the arena with every punch. All lesser forms of envelopment are themselves enveloped.[10] Correspondingly, "every boxing match incarnates the whole of boxing as an incarnation of all fundamental violence" (*CDR* 2:27). Not that violence fails to exist elsewhere—in the mugging, for example, that is taking place simultaneously in the dark alley behind the arena or in the honking horns of angry motorists delayed by traffic coming to the match. But it is a thesis of dialectical rationality that "an act of violence is always all of violence, because it is a reexteriorization of interiorized scarcity" (*CDR* 2:28).[11]

This overview of Sartre's application of the technical terms "enveloping totalization" and "incarnation" to an avowedly conflictive relationship introduces us to the specific problem of his theory of history: how to discover a unity amid the dispersive antagonisms of historical relations. It is on this unity that the intelligibility of History turns. As we prepare to study a concrete historical example, let us first examine these expressions themselves, for they are proper to the dimension of his theory of history elaborated in *Critique 2*.

HEGEL RECUMBENT: TWO DIALECTICAL NOTIONS

"An absolute mind without *development* (intuition) could not *comprehend* History. It has to be historical itself" (*CDR* 2:453). In other words, the positivist historian's ideal of abstract and timeless objectivity is not only futile, it is distorting. Sartre was developing this view as early as 1947, when he addressed the French Philosophical Society on the need to synthesize contemplation and transcendence, Husserl and Heidegger:

> I believe we have need of both: a becoming truth and, nevertheless, a certitude such that one can judge. And I believe that if one reintegrates temporality into the categories, that is, if one notices that the grasp of consciousness by reflection is not the grasp of consciousness of a

snapshot, but of a reality which has a past and a future, then a temporal truth is possible, often probable, but it sometimes carries an apodicticity which does not depend on the totality of history or the sciences.[12]

This early version of the structure-history controversy reminds us of the epistemological role of dialectical necessity, which we observed in volume 1 of the *Critique*. One can understand history without either rendering it static or waiting for its termination. It also challenges the dialectical historian to "comprehend" the "temporal truth" of a fluid reality. The vehicle for expressing these temporalized categories is the "notion."

Already in 1946 Sartre had distinguished the static "concept" of analytic Reason from the dynamic "notion" (Hegel's *Begriff*) of dialectical rationality.[13] Later he made tactical appeal to the distinction to combat the perceived antihistorical tendencies of structuralism. As he explained: "In order to oppose Althusser, I was forced to reconsider the idea of 'notion' and to draw a series of consequences from it" (*S* 8:286). Elsewhere he defines "notion" in Hegelian fashion as "a synthetic effort to produce an idea which develops by contradictions and successive overcomings and which is thus homogeneous with the development of things."[14] He elaborates the contrast in a way that, by implication, brings the *situated historian* into the picture: "A concept is a definition in exteriority which is likewise atemporal; a notion, to my mind, is a definition in interiority and includes in itself not only the time supposed by the object whose notion it is but also its own time as [an act of] knowledge. In other words, [notion] is a thought which introduces time along with it" (*S* 10:95). The matter of the notion's "own time" as praxis, which is what is at issue, has yet to be addressed. It figures throughout Sartre's theory as the problem of the "situated historian." We shall turn to it shortly. But first we must consider the two principal notions of *Critique 2,* "enveloping totalization" and "incarnation."

Enveloping Totalization[15]

Sartre portrays "enveloping totalization" metaphorically as "*the act overflowing the man* that is totalized" (*CDR* 2:238). In more technical terms, he describes it as "a turning back of the inert upon the agent to recondition him" (*CDR* 2:284). Enveloping totalization is "material" in the sense of being human and practical. In the categories of *Critique 1,* it is a temporalization of praxis-process and, as such, both draws its unity from its transcendence toward a goal (praxis) and forges passive syntheses and multiplicities (process). As the editor of *Critique 2* notes, Sartre sometimes calls enveloping totalization a "system" (*CDR* 2:183n), a term that evokes the "systems" of capitalism and colonialism whose exigencies, necessities, and "destinies" he scrutinized in polemical essays over the years.[16]

The expression "enveloping totalization" is unique to *Critique 2*. What it adds to "totalization" *tout court* from volume 1 is a greater intensity and a broader scope. It is more comprehensive than isolated organic praxis in both senses of the term: it is more inclusive of the mediating relationships that render abstract organic praxis concrete and, correspondingly, it yields greater understanding of the praxis in question. Sartre writes that "every singular totalization is *enveloping* as a totalization as well as *enveloped* as a singularity" (*CDR* 2:49, emphasis mine). It is a unifying notion (historicizing praxis-process), not an atemporal concept, that subsumes our praxes as parts of a dynamic whole. In fact, Sartre is quite explicit that the boxing match, for example, as a dialectical reality cannot be conceptualized, though it can be understood (see *CDR* 2:45–50).

The singularity of the totalization comes from its unique locus as the nodal point and matrix of an indefinite multiplicity of relationships. Its enveloping character arises from the linkage it constitutes (both in knowledge and in being) to the entirety of these relations.

Sartre calls this aspect of envelopment the "law of immanence," namely, that "every man is linked to every man, even if they are unknown to one another, by a reciprocal bond of immanence" (*CDR* 2:282, 247). Such immanence obtains within the practical field unified by a sovereign individual like Stalin, as we shall see. But it seems to hold also for nondictatorial societies, as the boxing example suggests. In fact, Sartre has this immanence in mind when he refers to the "synthetic interiority of the historical field" (*CDR* 2:384). He describes this immanence, presumably in its most integrated state, as "the living unity of the common activity" (*CDR* 2:231). It appears to be a feature of every practical field as such.

Sartre's enveloping totalization resembles a Leibnizian monad in its "mirroring" of the universe. And not unlike the "compossibility" of Leibnizian monads in our actual world, it "supports, by itself and in itself, the hierarchy of signifying structures and the inert movement of the process." In practice, this means that "through this highly structured system, [enveloping totalization] marks the place of every possible incarnation, and the ensemble of correspondences that makes of each—in its place and within its perspective—the incarnation of all" (*CDR* 2:231).

But Sartre's singular totalization differs from the monad first of all in being as radically contingent as is the "theodicy" he builds upon it.[17] In addition, it is dialectical, not analytic; in other words, the singular totalization is a synthesis of these relationships and their relata, not their mere summation or "reflection," as Leibniz would have it. Moreover, these relata include the chance events and unintended results of the process sustained by a totalizing praxis. In this respect, the enveloping totalization forges a "dialectical link between the intended result (with its foreseen consequences) and the unforeseeable consequences of that result, inasmuch as its incarnation in the totalization of the practical field has to condition from afar all the elements of that field, including the agents themselves" (*CDR* 2:242). Furthermore, as dialectical, this totalization is temporalizing: it is date-progressive. And as we have come to expect, enveloping totalization is never complete; it is a temporalizing totali*zation,* not a totality—or History would have come to an end. Every totalization presumes a detotalization of which it is the ongoing negation or retotalization (see *CDR* 2:448).

True to his dialectical nominalism, Sartre gives "enveloping totalization" a somewhat different meaning as its referent shifts.[18] So the enveloping totalization of an organized group is "the integration of all concrete individuals by praxis" (*CDR* 2:86), whereas that of the directorial society is "*autonomous* praxis asserting itself as such, *inasmuch* as it produces, undergoes, harbors and conceals its own heteronomy as the passive and reactualized unity of its own by-products" (*CDR* 2:242). We shall find a directorial society such as Russia under the Bolsheviks, totalized by the autonomy of the party of which Stalin was the incarnation in the 1930s: "society turne[d] itself into an individual in the person of the dictator," thus rendering his practical role historically decisive (*CDR* 2:219). And the famous "cult of personality" will emerge as more a symptom than a source of Stalinist envelopment. The virtual identification of dictator and disciplined society is not merely psychological. It is ontological and epistemic. But in its own way, this applies to such enveloping totalizations as the boxing world in a bourgeois society as well. To understand Russian society or the boxing profession in the 1930s, aside from the analytical grasp afforded by statistical generalizations or sociological "laws," we must comprehend the dialectical internalization/externalization (praxis) of their respective milieus by Stalin or by specific boxers. The ontological basis of this claim is the "law of immanence," namely, that if Stalin and the pugilists were "made" by their respective societies, they each returned the favor.[19]

In its most comprehensive form, enveloping totalization may be seen as a version of that "totalization without a totalizer" on the possibility of which Sartre hangs the meaning of History in volume 1. Retaining the hypothetical mode of these volumes, he writes early in *Critique 2:* "We do not even know yet if the enveloping totalization can exist. We shall see further on that it is the foundation of any intelligibility of History" (*CDR* 2:33 n).

Its function resembles that of Hegel's famous "cunning of Reason" in that it enables us to set the "necessary margin of indetermination in which chance . . . may operate" and entails a higher order unity of which its agents may be unaware. But as we have come to expect, praxis remains the engine of historical totalization: "However surprising the outcome may appear to contemporaries, chance—as an intervention of the practico-inert at the heart of the dialectic—merely executes the verdict delivered by praxis itself" (*CDR* 2:92, 93). The problem, of course, is to establish the details of that "verdict." Just how limiting and how "determining" are those "sentences" handed down by prior praxes through the practico-inert? Inevitably we encounter the ambiguity of the given and the taken in Sartre's basic ontology.

Sartre even notes the conceivability of an enveloping totalization being produced "*in itself* and *for itself.*" This ideal, if not limit, concept would require "a technology and economy entirely conscious of themselves," he concedes, as well as "the application of a transformed and developed cybernetics to the internal organization of an enterprise-society." He seems at least to be toying with, if not subscribing to, a technological version of historical materialism, especially when he lists as an additional condition for this in-itself-for-itself of the enveloping totalization "a more advanced form of withering away of the State" (*CDR* 2:283). The amphibious notion of history as fact and as value continues to be operative.

Sartre distinguishes two possible dialectical procedures in analyzing one and the same social reality in terms of enveloping totalization: "decompressive expansion" or "detotalization," and "totalizing compression." The former is popular with Marxist analysts, who situate the reality in the larger ensemble of mediations as "non-singularized concrete totalities." Recall that this yields the heavy-handed Marxist "economism" which Sartre criticized in *Search* with the remark that, although Valéry was a petit bourgeois, not every petit bourgeois was a Valéry (*SM* 56). Analysis of historical change in terms of class struggle, for example, though a necessary condition for intelligibility, is insufficient for comprehending the lived reality of historical agents.

It is totalizing compression, Sartre insists, "which alone is capable of grasping the dialectical intelligibility of an event." This procedure grasps "the centripetal movement of all the significations attracted and condensed in the event or in the object" (*CDR* 2:49). In fact, in this compressive movement, enveloping totalization is equivalent to "incarnation."[20] It forms what we have called the "intensive" dimension which distinguishes enveloping totalization from Sartre's earlier totalization *sans phrase.* In a manner resembling Hegel's "determination" of the concrete universal via the mediation of its multifarious relationships, Sartre's compressive procedure is a recognition of the ways in which the abstract violence of our society is realized (not merely exemplified) in this evening's boxing card or in Stalin's decision to liquidate the Kulaks. But what makes the dialectic peculiarly "existentialist" is its continued emphasis on the primacy of organic praxis: "It is actually *through the project* which condenses them that the mediating fields receive a new status of efficacy" (*CDR* 2:49). Indeed, sensing the vulnerability of his own jargon, Sartre assures us: "It would be quite impossible to escape idealism, if you forgot that everything—be it a battle or an execution—is always *human labor*" (*CDR* 2:272).

Incarnation

Earlier we pointed out Sartre's use of the term "incarnation" in an aesthetic context: Michelangelo's *David* incarnates the Renaissance and Rebeyrolle's paintings, the Cold War. From an aesthetic viewpoint it was a question of "presence" rather than of intelligibility or truth.[21] Sartre repeats this usage in *Critique 2* when he speaks of the baroque age being "presentified" in the performance of a Bach fugue.[22] But in *Critique 2,* "incarnation" is introduced as a correlative to "enveloping totaliza-tion."[23] It is an "internal and local temporalization," a "moment," to speak like Hegel, of the ongoing totalization (*CDR* 2:77). One is re-minded of Plato's famous and equally difficult concept "participation," except that, unlike those of Plato, Sartre's "universals" are dynamic wholes, concretized or temporalized by the praxis or praxis-process at issue. Every move of the boxers in the ring "incarnates" the fundamen-tal violence that permeates the historical process in a field of scarcity. It appears that, because of its overt appeal to physical force, its direct link to conflict in our lives, the match serves better than a Renaissance statue or even the depicted violence in Rebeyrolle's paintings to "incarnate" human history as marked by scarcity. And its indirect connection is formed by the social, economic, and historical factors that mediate our social existence and, as our facticity, constitute the "profundity of the world" (*FI* 5:297). The upshot of this quasi-Hegelian stance is that "*box-ing in its entirety* is present at every instant of the fight as a sport and as a technique, with all the human qualities and all the material conditioning (training, physical condition, etc.) that it demands" (*CDR* 2:20).[24] Speaking of a dictatorial society, but without limiting himself to that context, Sartre insists that "in one way or another every event—however 'private' it may be—must be considered as an incarnation. And each event, as an enveloped totalization, incarnates all the others via the mediation of the enveloping totalization" (*CDR* 2:237).

Like its correlate, "enveloping totalization," the term "incarnation" is rather fluid in denotation. In fact, Sartre speaks of a "hierarchy of in-carnations" (*CDR* 2:188). There are the "incarnation of the summit," the sovereign of a directorial society, for example, and "subordinate incarnations" (*CDR* 2:255, 231). The latter denote "the retotalization of the enveloping totalization by every event, every praxis and every par-ticular *hexis*" (*CDR* 2:265). If the term covers a family of interrelated uses, the prime analogue, the "head" of this family, once again, seems to be the totalizing praxis of the organic individual in its practical relation-ships.

Incarnation is "the concrete universal constantly producing itself as the animation and temporalization of individual contingency." In the case of the boxing match, this means that "*one* punch, like *one* dance, is indissolubly singular and universal" (*CDR* 2:40). If, as we suggested, incarnation is the "compressive" pole of the enveloping totalization, as a dialectical notion, it necessarily points toward the other, "decompressive" pole. Again, this is a consequence of praxis being a dialectic of internalization/externalization. Internalization—which does not mean "incorporating into one's 'inner' life," a notion from which Sartre's use of "intentionality" presumed to have freed us once and for all—entails dialectical temporalization (*CDR* 2:231).[25] In words that echo his earlier remarks about enveloping totalization, Sartre points out, "Every incarnation is tied in two ways to the historical ensemble: on the one hand, in fact, it realizes in itself the latter's condensation; on the other hand, it refers back in a decompressive blossoming to the ensemble of practical significations which determine it in its belonging to the social and historical field" (*CDR* 2:188). This particular boxing match might take place in a climate of historical tension, the day of the Anschluss of Austria by Nazi Germany, for example, which would be incarnated here by the small size of the crowd.

Let us clarify Sartre's understanding of "incarnation" by distinguishing it from the exemplification of a concept, on the one hand, and from the conceptualization of an experience, on the other. In light of his earlier, aesthetic use of the term, we should contrast it with the symbolization of a person or period as well. What distinguishes it from the purely conceptual is its practical and temporal character. Incarnation is never contemplative. It is praxis or praxis-process. And its intelligibility comes from the dialectical comprehensibility of praxis itself, not from an abstract concept which it instantiates or from an equally "abstract" (in the Hegelian sense) isolated example.[26] Hence, neither is it a purely semiotic phenomenon.

Still, we know that human reality, for Sartre, remains a "signified signifier" (*significant-signifié*) and that praxis accordingly is signifying as well as significant.[27] The practice of incarnating accordingly will refer to "structures and significations," at least as a "bond of exteriorized interiority" that tends toward the disintegration of the group as well as to a "background of immanence" which is the "*living* unity of the common activity" (*CDR* 2:230–31). In other words, as process and as exteriorized praxis, incarnation requires *signification* and "concepts." But as interiorizing praxis, incarnation yields *sens* articulated in "notions." So the hybrid praxis-process, which we saw was a dimension of incarnation, if not its mirror image, is not fully conceptualizable. Although incarnation as signifying does involve symbols, Sartre insists that "an incarnation is not a symbol" (*CDR* 2:226).

In a way that deepens his remarks about meaning (*sens*) and signification in an aesthetic context, Sartre notes that meaning is "what is lived in interiority," that is, it is what we could say is "incarnated" in the temporalizing praxis at hand. He completes the circle by linking meaning with original violence, as we saw earlier, when he adds that there is a "primary meaning (*sens*)" which is grounded in biological need and material scarcity (*CDR* 2:402).

Sartre's raising of the semiotic issue may seem to involve him in inconsistencies. But in fact it directs our attention toward the two constellations of terms revolving around analytic and dialectical Reason respectively. Whatever ambiguity may surround his occasional semiotic references stems from the problematic interrelation of these forms of rationality and, in the final analysis, from the indeterminability of the "given" and the "taken" in his epistemology and ontology—a weakness we have watched plague him from his earliest works.

Unfortunately, Sartre does not scrupulously respect his own distinctions between meaning (*sens*) and signification and between their respective articulations in notions and concepts.[28] But when he is speaking strictly, he will link signification with the exterior and conceptual and *sens* with the interior and notional. For example, in an extended description of a working-class woman who innocently buys and wears clothing commonly preferred by prostitutes, he pauses to explain that his aim is to offer us "the *sens* of the person rather than the signification of her behavior" (*CDR* 2:293). It is clear that he expects the same of the dialectical as opposed to the positivist historian, for it is in "historical reconstruction," he insists, that "praxis-process is disclosed as a temporalization that has taken the form of *realization of a meaning* [*sens*]" (*CDR* 2:294). And while implying that enveloping totalization is not conceptual, he claims that "the same reality will be *enveloping totalization*, inasmuch as it is produced by the temporalization of the historical agents, and a *meaning* [*sens*], inasmuch as it is reactualized by the labor of the situated historian" (*CDR* 2:297). For it is the historian who "transforms the past event into its meaning [*sens*]" (*CDR* 2:299). But, ever the historical realist, Sartre cautions: "It should not be concluded that this *meaning* [*sens*] is relative to the knowledge the historian gains of it. It must first be noted that it exists implicitly in and through every particular action—and in the very interiority of praxis—inasmuch as every enveloped totalization incarnates also the relation of the latter to the future, as a product and as a destiny" (*CDR* 2:287).

It may look as if Sartre is getting caught in what Roland Barthes calls "the great mythic opposition of the *true-to-life* (the lifelike) and the *intelligible*,"[29] for we have watched him contrast concept to notion as intellection to comprehension and as signification to lived reality (*le vécu*). But that is precisely the point. The intelligibility Sartre seeks in historical "reality" is *dialectical*. Without denying the function and import of structural considerations—they are, after all, the terminus of regressive analysis and the starting point for progressive totalization—he seeks to situate them in the ongoing project that is our historical adventure. To paraphrase Foucault, Sartre would read Barthes's simple equation of intelligibility to analytic rationality as an instance of the "blackmail of the Enlightenment."

Sartre's reference to a primary *sens* that is grounded in biological need and scarcity reminds us not to ignore the materialist connotation of the term "incarnation." "The concrete reality," he repeats, "is *a-man-shaping-matter-by-his-labor*" (*CDR* 2:228). Like the for-itself of *Being and Nothingness,* praxis-process is a reality "that is not the condition of its own possibility." In fact, its triumph over things in the world presupposes that it is "*tolerated* by the Universe" (*CDR* 2:308). Sartre means to stress the practical efficacy of a network of relationships in the singular reality of a historical action or an event as well as the essential "coefficient of adversity" of the material reality being worked. Aside from their embodiment in this individual, which they simultaneously make possible and limit in its singularity, these relationships remain abstract and distant. But so too does the "raw material" with which it works. One can speak of the world of boxing and point to its instruments and symbols such as the professional organization, the contracts, and the physical arena, but these objects, though significant, are without meaning (*sens*) until the praxis of agents brings them into play. Like medieval angels, these relationships "are where they act." In nominalist fashion, Sartre assigns their reality to their concrete efficacy.

Not that this means that, when it comes to historical intelligibility, "anything goes," as in some kind of anarchist epistemology. Incarnation is also a totalization and, as such, conserves what it surpasses—

whether this be a sequence of diminishing contracts for an ex-champion or the gum under the seats in the arena. Facticity or what Sartre calls the "trampoline of transcendence" modifies whatever praxis would transcend it, a lesson we have learned from *Being and Nothingness* but whose dialectical import emerges only in the *Critique*. The sense-making dimension of incarnation entails reference to the future with its risks and responsibilities as well as to the retotalized past. It is in this sense that Sartre can claim that "every history . . . is the incarnation of History" (*CDR* 2:453). By incarnating the past in present praxis, the historical agent renders it liable to the vagaries of fortune and to the reinterpretation that it inevitably undergoes. The championship match, for example, may reveal improprieties which in turn discredit the profession in the eyes of the public and lead to the demise of the sport as a business. The very meaning of the Bolshevik revolution was changed by the Gorbachev era.

I noted at the outset that Sartre's approach to the meaning of History could be read as the search for unity among historical agents and events. Recall that lack of such unity formed his chief criticism of Aron's theory of history. He devotes almost twenty pages in *Critique 2* to the category of unity and its status as the product of synthesizing praxis.[30] But given the adversarial mark which material scarcity has stamped on historical relations, this search must focus on the possible unity to be discerned in antagonistic relations among praxes. In other words, the answer to the question of the meaning of History turns on a positive response to the question, "Is struggle unifying?"

In brief, Sartre intends to show that conflict is intelligible only because it involves praxes, for praxis is dialectically intelligible (see *CDR* 2:91, 332). Of course, one could approach the matter via the quantitative, atomistic methods of analytical reason. But such forms of "exteriority" are blind to the totalizing, integrating character of praxis. They must read conflict as disunifying and seek an external unity elsewhere, for example, in appeal to the parallelogram of forces, in a calculus of probabilities or in the use of statistical generalizations.

Finally, "incarnation" is an especially apt notion for integrating idiosyncrasies and biographical considerations into the historical account, as befits an existentialist theory. This follows from praxis as a dialectic of necessity and contingency: the necessity of our contingency (the facticity that shapes and colors every attempt to overcome it) and the contingency of our necessity (the "freedom-transcendence" to which we were "condemned" in vintage existentialism) (see *CDR* 2:77).

Without subscribing to some kind of perfect fit between individual and historical task (à la Plekhanov [*CDR* 2:218]), Sartre emphasizes the personal contingencies that the agent incorporates in the collective contingencies of historical action. He cites a case where "the ignorance and blindness intrinsic to every undertaking that casts itself towards an insufficiently determined future are identified with the ignorance, the blindness, the intellectual limits and the obstinacies of *one* particular individual" (*CDR* 2:205). Again, this affords the historian an intelligibility which the agent by definition is lacking.

Were we writing the history of angels, we could ignore such "imperfections." But our is a history of human agents, with their excesses and inadequacies, their errors of judgment and their unreasonable demands. As Sartre remarks, "those jolts, those accelerations, those brakings, those hairpin bends, those acts of violence which characterized Stalinism—they were not all required by the objectives and exigencies of socialization. *Yet they were inevitable,* inasmuch as that socialization demanded, in its first phase, to be directed by an individual" (*CDR* 2:209). Let us now consider this object lesson of the incarnation of an enveloping totalization in a dictatorial society, namely, the person of Joseph Stalin and the construction of Soviet socialism immediately after Lenin's death.

Stalinism as a Venture

"The men History makes are never entirely those needed to make History" (*CDR* 2:221)—this capsulizes Sartre's existentialist theory. On the one hand, it acknowledges an order of objective possibilities and historical exigencies that charts the limits of historical action in any given situation. It thereby adds the dimension of objective possibility to Sartre's early concept of existential situation, opening "situation" to social and historical considerations seemingly absent from his vintage existentialist discussions. But, on the other hand, it reveals a crucial gap (*décalage,* one of Sartre's favorite terms)[31] between situation and situated agent. It is in that space that biographical factors become relevant to the historical scheme and that existential freedom and responsibility are preserved. Dialectical reason enters via the transformations and deviations of agent and situation that ensue.

The Circularity of Incarnation

As he begins this portion of his dialectical investigation, Sartre warns us that "the psychoanalytic interpretation of Stalin as an incarnation of Stalinism remains inopportune" (*CDR* 2:223). It is not false, however, as the thesis from *Search for a Method* concerning the child realizing the singularization of generalities through his family situation makes clear (see *SM* 57 ff.). In other words, we would not be mistaken to see in Stalin's harshness and inflexibility both the totalization of the life experience of a former Georgian seminarian and the incarnation of the Soviet regime. But it is inappropriate at this stage of an inquiry that is interested not in biography as such (the "singularization of the social") but in history as the subsumption of chance events and personal idiosyncracies (the "socialization of the singular") (*CDR* 2:216). So if inflexibility, for example, is called for by this historical situation, it need not be the kind issuing from a provincial seminary. In a thesis pivotal to his theory, Sartre claims that this generic quality becomes specific in a dialectic by which Stalin makes himself (and is made) the man of the hour: a transformation of the individual and a deviation of the social function (see *CDR* 2:219). It is this reciprocal modification, this transformation and deviation, which Sartre calls the "circularity of incarnation" (*CDR* 2:194), that determinists like Plekhanov overlook.

Still, despite his emphasis on practical necessities and objective exigencies (the work of praxis-process and the practico-inert), Sartre maintains that "the importance of the sovereign-individual . . . manifests itself *in the differential:* i.e., in the gap separating the objective exigencies from the realization. And in the world of scarcity [of goods and men]," he continues, "this gap ultimately means only *the deviation of praxis by its incarnation*" (*CDR* 2:225). Contingency and chance enter the historical scene through the deviation of praxis that facticity (the practico-inert) and other freedoms guarantee.

The Plan

Consider Sartre's analysis of the decision to collectivize land and force industrialization on the Soviet Union in the summer of 1928 as an example of the circularity of incarnation. The event was historical and singular at the same time. Given the resistance of the peasant class to socialism, the threat of famine, and the external menace to a still feeble socialism that summer, the historical situation demanded an immediate and radical response. The speedy decision to adopt Trotsky's plan seemed to be the only possible reaction. "And this praxis," Sartre points out, "was to begin the grandiose, terrible, and irreversible temporalization that in History was to take the name of *Stalinism*" (*CDR* 2:195).

But Sartre intends to present us with "Stalinism-as-a-venture, containing within it its own temporalization, and not Stalinism-as-a-prototype" (*CDR* 2:296). A prototype loses its temporal determinations and is universalized as a *signification* to be applied like a concept to similar situations in other historical periods. But what that leaves us, Sartre claims, is sociology, not History in his understanding of that term, for "meaning [*sens*] has disappeared with History" (*CDR* 2:295).[32] As he explains, in the present case, "what we shall call meaning [*sens*] is the indissoluble unity of Stalinism with the *unique* and *peerless* temporalization that constitutes it." Articulating the relation between dialectical method and *sens*, Sartre describes the latter as:

> the perfect reversibility—at the heart of that unity [of Stalinism and temporalization]—of two movements: one regressive . . . [toward historical events and conditions]; the other progressive, which in the circular comprehension of a unique adventure sees the gradual production . . . of deviations, always practical, always individual, always *invented as much as suffered,* whose ensemble will become *Stalinism* as a system when they are already part of the transcended past. (*CDR* 2:295–96)[33]

The decision to collectivize and industrialize forcefully occurred at a conjuncture of events that left the Rightists in impotent opposition and Trotsky under house arrest. So the decision to coopt Trotsky's solution, Sartre argues, realized "the total victory of Stalin the *individual* over all his adversaries" (*CDR* 2:195). It was not a case of Stalin's being the instrument of the situation, as Marxist determinists often claimed, nor simply of Stalin's "opportunism," as Western theorists have argued, but of Stalin "[making] himself the man of the situation by the reply he gave to the exigencies of the moment" (*CDR* 2:196). Again, the crux is to capture "historialization"—the kaiser's withered arm. The day when the first Plan was decided constituted both a dialectical transformation of the agent and a deviation of the praxis: collective leadership was replaced by the sovereignty of a single individual.

Personal Power

Sartre has analyzed in volume 1 how the sovereign individual exercises power by exploiting the serial impotence of the subgroups and their members. He elaborates that point in the present context when he insists that "as soon as Stalin had taken power, he was incarnated in the pyramid of ruling bodies and that pyramid was incarnated in him." In other words, "this common individual, as a sovereign, was *in addition* a collective individual," as institutional. But, as with every incarnation, "Stalin was *more* and *something other than* that sovereign as common-collective . . . just described. . . . [In] his concrete existence he was the *facticity* of that sovereign praxis and that pyramid." And this is what interests us here: Sartre's account of the "historical reality of Stalin, a militant formed on the basis of his milieu and his childhood by the circumstances of this past struggle" (*CDR* 2:199).

Stalin's case is peculiar in that he succeeded in exercising his authority as personal power, not simply as an institutional function the way a dauphin might assume the throne on his father's death. This brought a multiplicity of human and personal factors to bear on the first phase of the revolution. For example, the mortality of the leader affected the aging of the regime and, with his death, introduced a rupture in the movement whose consequences were unforeseeable. But it also entailed a series of conditions that arose from Stalin's facticity, from the "necessity of his contingency" (*CDR* 2:204). Stalin's being less cultured than Trotsky, for example, would reproduce these shortcomings in his regime. The same could be said of his provincialism, his dogmatism, and his paranoia. Sartre concludes: "In so far as the exigency of those purges and the 'Moscow Trials' was not contained in the totalizing objectivity of industrial growth in an underdeveloped country, the origin of the slippage *must* be imputed to Stalin, for the simple reason that he was at once the sovereign totalization and the singularity of an individual" (*CDR* 2:206).

This last conclusion suggests a revival of analytical reasoning, namely, the positing of two independent lines of causation, the personal and the social, with their intersection as a matter of irrational *chance.* Sartre recognizes this possibility but questions the alleged independence of the causal chains, especially in the case of a dictatorial society. By now we are in a position to see that the dialectic of internalization and externalization does not allow for totally independent lines of causality except in the abstract. The production of ten million tons of pig iron via bloody coercion (executions, concentration camps, and the like), for example, is not comparable to a similar quantity produced without coercive measures. There is a deviation of the praxis-process at work here. And in a society where the organs of sovereignty are shaped by and for the sovereign individual, that individual's facticity marks the ensuing praxis with its idiosyncrasies. "The personal factor *cannot* be eliminated," Sartre insists, "if the sovereign is *one* person" (*CDR* 2:208).

Historical Intelligibility

The foregoing examples of the boxing match and of historical Stalinism, coupled with our analysis of the basic "notions" of enveloping totalization and incarnation, lead us to the conclusion that if history is not rigorous in the sense of conforming to a universal schematism such as Marx, Oswald Spengler, or even Arnold Toynbee have proposed, neither is it a plurality of random events and their causes (the positivists' "one damn thing after another"). The individual and chance character of praxis, the fact that praxis "overflows" into process or that the contingencies of individual facticity are ingredient in social action—this in no way implies that history occurs haphazardly. "Contingency appears only through strict exigencies. Through all its deviations and all its sidetracks," Sartre assures us, "we shall see later on that the *historical process* continues on its path. Only this path is not defined a priori by the transcendental dialectic" (*CDR* 2:226). As we have come to expect, it is determined by praxis and the practico-inert.

HISTORY AND CHANCE

In his inaugural lecture at the Collège de France, Foucault announced his project of restoring "chance as a category in the production of events" (*AK* 231). Sartre was fond of citing Pascal's appeal to the unrepeatable event ("something happened to man") as the limit to any rationalizing of history.[34] Both authors are combatting a certain Hegelian and Marxian fetishization of history. But whereas Foucault seeks to leave us with a plurality of discursive formations and axes of intelligibility,[35] Sartre is firmly committed to a unifying praxis on which to ground historical reason, socioeconomic freedom, and moral responsibility. Indeed, with his refusal to place himself "under the sign of a unique necessity," Foucault, the self-styled "happy positivist," seems intent on avowing just those methods and objects that would dissolve Sartrean "history" into "sociology"![36] Though the matter is far more complex than that, as my study of Foucault will reveal, the contrast in this respect is not unfounded.

The transformations and deviations entailed by incarnating such abstractions as the Russian Revolution (and, a fortiori, the proletarian revolution) into the person and praxis of Stalin, far from submitting History to contingency, Sartre insists, reveal "how History *integrated* chance occurrences and contingency as the manifest signs and necessary consequences of its own facticity" (*CDR* 2:227; F 2:238). In other words, we are once more referred to the Sartrean "situation" with its twin dimensions of transcendence and facticity, now ontologized respectively as praxis and the practico-inert. So, discussing Stalin's death as a chance event whose significance was being fashioned by the internal contradictions at work in an "already de-Stalinized" Soviet society, Sartre points out: "However surprising the outcome may appear to contemporaries, chance—as an intervention of the practico-inert at the heart of the dialectic—merely executes the verdict delivered by praxis itself" (*CDR* 2:93). Even chance is subject to the primacy of praxis in historical intelligibility.

The factical dimension of human reality, its inevitable contingency and irreversibility (*CDR* 2:277)—the fact of someone's being born Jewish, for example, or Genet's having been caught in the act of stealing— makes us singular and thus nonconceptual (Pascal's point). But these chance events as assumed in a project become ingredient in biography-history and thereby achieve comprehensibility. "Chance · is nonconceptual," Sartre insists, "and it makes man non-conceptual; conversely, however, man making himself discloses chance in its dialectical intelligibility." He continues, "the same will be the case in all events: there is always (even [for an event] wholly suffered—apart from death) an *appropriation*" (*CDR* 2:451).

Paul Veyne, quoting Jacques Maritain, once referred to the "sane philosophy of man" that historians acquire in the course of their reflections on the past.[37] As if to anticipate an objection from Foucault and other poststructuralists against the existentialist self, while relating his philosophy of man to his theory of history, Sartre remarks:

> History is essential to man in so far as it makes him into the non-essential intelligible. Man is never essential (other than in the past [Hegel's "das Wesen ist was gewesen ist"]). He is, in himself, a *being-other* (because he makes himself an interiorization of the world); but that *being-other* does not presuppose that there is a *being-yourself* blocked from underneath. Being-yourself is precisely the recuperation of being-other. It is the dialectical movement of comprehension. (*CDR* 2:451)

In *The Archaeology of Knowledge,* on the other hand, Foucault exults that his "diagnostic" method "establishes that we are difference, that our reason is the difference of discourses, our history the difference of times, our selves the difference of masks. That difference, far from being the forgotten and recovered origin, is this dispersion that we are and make" (*AK* 131). One could epitomize the similarity and the contrast between their respective approaches to historical intelligibility by comparing Sartrean *being-other* with Foucauldian *being-difference.* I shall begin such a summary comparison in chapter 10.

THE SITUATED HISTORIAN

From his first encounter with Aron's theory of history, Sartre has been concerned to avoid historical relativism (which seems to entail moral impotence or at least acquiescence in the status quo) without subscribing to a transcendent view of reality. I have addressed this issue in terms of committed history and the discovery/decision dichotomy in chapter 6. Reflection on the facticity both of history and of the historian suggests considering this matter once more.

Early in *Critique 1,* Sartre observes that a critique of dialectical Reason "could not appear *before* historical totalization had produced that individualized universal which we call the dialectic. . . . Nor could it occur *before* the *abuses* which have obscured the very notion of dialectical rationality and produced a new divorce between *praxis* and the knowledge which elucidates it." In other words, dialectical investigation "could not occur *in our history,* before Stalinist idealism had sclerosed both epistemological methods and practices" (*CDR* 1:50). Sartre's point is that the nature of critique as "corrective" and "warrant" required as its historical condition both the errors of Stalinism and the distance afforded by the post-Stalinist period. The "comprehension" which the progressive-regressive method both employs and produces "takes the form of individual attempts to grasp the moment of historical totalization through one's own life, conceived as an expression of the whole. In its most immediate and most superficial character," Sartre concludes, "the critical investigation of totalization is the very life of the investigator in so far as it reflexively criticizes itself. In abstract terms, this means that only a man who lives within a region of totalization can apprehend the bonds of interiority which unite him to the totalizing movement" (*CDR* 1:51). In other words, he must be situated.[38]

Sartre's advice is that the situated investigator exploit his very situatedness. He should "re-live his membership in human ensembles with different structures" by a regressive move that enables him to grasp through his own living mediation the formal structures of various practical multiplicities. "He must be able to leap from his individual life to History simply by the practical negation of the negation which defines his life" (*CDR* 1:52). Lest we think he is doing "traditional" history, Sartre warns: "We are not trying to reconstruct the real history of the human race; we are trying to establish the *Truth of History*" (*CDR* 1:52). And that "truth," as we have come to see, is as much valuative as descriptive.

Sartre reminds us of the personal sovereignty, that is, the totalizing praxis, of the historian himself, who "realizes the retemporalization of the entire praxis-process, when he temporalizes himself in the present by operating as a historian." By examining the sources in terms of an expanding circle of practical unities such as the paragraph, the book, the profession, the national ensemble, and the like, the situated historian's explanation of the meaning (*sens*) of the individual reality will be a dialectical re-production of certain enveloped totalities. No doubt the historian deals with the objectification of praxis in a *past*. And he does so from the social and practical ensemble to which he belongs. And we have seen that the historian transforms the past event into its meaning (*sens*). But Sartre insists that the resultant meaning (*sens*), though limited by the historian's situated status, is not relativized thereby (*CDR* 2:298). This is so even though the historian is further situated in relation to other scholars and finds himself totalized in turn by "Universal History" that prescribes an infinite task to future generations of historians. Sartre revives his early phenomenological convictions to underscore the fact that it is resultant knowledge, not the "known" that is relative: "What is in fact revealed through the [historian's] situated reconstruc-

tion is that part of Being which the chosen perspective allows to be discovered. And this part of Being is totally and fully real. All that is relative is *the limit* which separates within it the known from the unknown,
and reflects other limits: those of present-day historians" (*CDR* 2:299;
emphasis mine).[39]

The historian as such, Sartre insists, "contributes to the praxis-
process, is temporalized in the enveloping temporalization and towards
its short-term and long-term aims, and—in himself and through all his
activities—makes himself an enveloped totality. For through *History in
progress,* the meaning (*sens*) of completed History is transformed" (*CDR*
2:299). It is in this transformation and completion of History that the
valuative dimension of Sartre's theory of history again comes to the
fore.

CONVERGENCE: THE "ONE WORLD"

Recall Sartre's criticism of Aron's plurality of historical accounts of the
same phenomenon: they fail to converge.[40] He returns to this objection
in *Critique 2* when he asks:

> Is History not perhaps, at the level of large ensembles, an ambiguous
> interpenetration of unity and plurality, dialectic and anti-dialectic,
> meaning and meaninglessness? Are there not, according to the cir-
> cumstances and ensembles in question, *several* totalizations—with no
> relation between them other than coexistence or some other relation-
> ship of exteriority? Is it not up to the historian alone, in his historical
> investigation, to determine the directions in which a single praxis-
> process sees itself resumed and retotalized at different levels, and to
> demarcate the signifying constellations to which a single event gives
> rise in the most disparate milieux? (*CDR* 2:120)

Such an approach, that admits dialectical sequences into a history that
remains pluralistic and analytical, remains "positivist."

What analytical Reason misses, Sartre reminds us, is that "men make
History in so far as it makes them." Specifically, it ignores the scarcity-
need relationship and its resultant "impossibility of living" that confers
on human praxis and its practico-inert counterfinalities a certain necessity and ultimacy beyond which there is no appeal. He explains: "In the
present instance [that of class struggle], this means that the practico-
inert is engendered by the counterfinalities of praxis precisely in so far as
serialities of impotence, by producing the impossibility of living, give

rise to the totalizing unity that transcends them." In a capsulation of the argument of *Critique 1,* he concludes that the "movement of historializa-tion" has three phases:

> In a first phase, a common praxis transforms society by a totalizing action whose counterfinalities transform the results obtained into practico-inert ones. In a second phase, the antisocial forces of the practico-inert impose a negative unity of self-destruction upon soci-ety, by usurping the unifying power of the praxis that has produced them. In a third phase, the detotalized unity is retotalized in the com-mon effort to rediscover the goal by stripping it of counterfinalities. (*CDR* 2:120–21)

The challenge that faces Sartre (and humankind) is to develop a system of self-monitoring that controls the counterfinalities of worked matter. This requires both holistic thinking and dialectical comprehension, that is, "a certain [unifying] action of the future as such" (*SM* 92 n).

Sartre seems to be basing the superiority of unity over plurality, of dialectic over antidialectic, and of meaning over meaninglessness, not on professional interest or personal whim, but on the practical "apodic-ticity" of the life-and-death struggle itself. Given the primacy of praxis and the "immanence" of the practical field, the "choice" of life is the choice of history and conversely.

Without leaving the descriptive mode, he now distinguishes between the pluralism of past history based on the lack of communication and mutuality that persisted among different sectors of the world's peoples into the nineteenth century, and the "One World" (significantly, he uses the English term) of the 1950s. The latter has resulted from a multi-plicity of causes, including colonialism, the industrial revolution, impe-rialism, and technological advances that conferred on humanity a "unity of mutual conditioning" (*CDR* 2:299).[41] He insists that "these separate ensembles are *constituted as convergent* by their future unity." This future appears as their "Destiny."

In an almost Whiggish manner, Sartre speaks of contemporary histo-rians' "reclassification" of prior history in ways that attempt to account for our current unity, which emerges as "the truth of History":

> One changes the *meaning* [*sens*] of a past totalization (*indirectly*) by act-ing upon the present situation (and, through repercussion, upon the *past-being* in its meaning), but not by reverting *to that meaning* in order

to know it. It is not *the historian* who imposes the convergence of their practices upon the former ensembles. He *discloses* it, on the abstract terrain of rigorous reconstruction of the past, because he *constitutes* it through a temporalization that envelops him and totalizes his partial action with those of all the others. This influence of the future on the past, far from idealizing the *meaning* . . . , confirms the reality of its *being*. (*CDR* 2:300; F 2:311)

And yet, like Moses at the Jordan, Sartre's theory stops short of the promised land of diachronic totalization and the "historical density" (*CDR* 2:107) that it would confer on what has been chiefly a "formal," synchronic analysis. The Stalin-Trotsky conflict and Stalin's anti-Semitism, for example, have yet to be located in their larger historical contexts, which would entail reference to xenophobia and racism in czarist Russia, details about the respective upbringing of each of the protagonists, and the like. Clearly, such "total" dialectical history must be a collaborative effort, one that Sartre never undertook.[42]

Nor did he apply even his synchronic analyses to nondirectorial society at any length. Indeed, he voices a certain hesitation about the attainability of enveloping totalization in bourgeois society: perhaps its multiplicity of significations, he muses, will "vanish into seriality or into the void" of positivist chance or exteriority (*CDR* 2:189).

TOTALIZATION WITHOUT A TOTALIZER

Sartre concludes the first volume of the *Critique* on a quasi-Hegelian note:

> History is intelligible if the different practices which can be found and located at a given moment of historical temporalization finally appear as partially totalizing and as connected and merged in their very oppositions and diversities by *an intelligible totalization from which there is no appeal.* It is by seeking the conditions for the intelligibility of historical vestiges and results that we shall, for the first time, reach *the problem of totalization without a totalizer* and of the very foundations of this totalization, that is to say, of its motive-forces and of its non-circular direction. (*CDR* 1:817)

This avowal has perplexed readers of this text from the very first. For it seems patently incompatible with Sartre's "realism," his "nominalism," and what we have seen to be the ontological and epistemic "primacy" of individual praxis in his social thought.[43] Totalization without a totalizer would resemble dialectic without an individual dialectical agent—something like the "cunning of Reason" or the "collective consciousness" that Sartre has always resisted.

And yet, he is clearly attracted by the idea from early in the *Critique* to this concluding promise to pursue the matter beyond the limits of its first published volume. Is there any way to make sense of the expression, using ideas that Sartre defends in either portion of the *Critique?* I think there is, and that, as he claims, such an "objective" totalization must be possible on his own terms lest the question of the "intelligibility of History" remain unanswerable and his project of a Critique of Dialectical Reason, futile. The resolution turns on his use of "totalization" and "totalizer" in this context.

Recalling his distinction between synchronic and diachronic totalization, he continues the extended quotation just given with the remark that "the regressive movement [of volume 1] has ended with a question: that is to say, it has to be completed by a synthetic progression whose aim will be to rise up to *the double synchronic and diachronic movement by which History constantly totalized itself*" (*CDR* 1:818; emphasis mine). What is this question with which the regressive movement of the first volume concludes? Precisely that of the possibility of "totalization without a totalizer." And how will the progressive spirals of the projected second volume furnish the answer? By establishing "enveloping totalization" as the *sens* of the concrete historical event which is its dialectical "incarnation." That "event" is the historialization of the epoch by the agent who, in turn, is totalized by it. The life of Stalin or, as we shall see in greater detail, of Flaubert is a totalizing project (the primacy of praxis); but it is also the incarnation of a set of real relations, both synchronic and diachronic, that Sartre calls their "epoch," and each is "totalized" by it to the extent that he "totalizes" it (the principle of totalization). Thus "totalization without a totalizer" does not refer to some "hyperorganism" or some transcendent reality, which Sartre would reject on principle. Rather, it denotes that set of objective relations or possibilities that are put in motion and sustained, even in their deviating and counterproductive functions, by individual and group or collective activity. This does allow for a "metanarrative" pace Jean-François Lyotard, and thus for a meaning-direction (*sens*) to History. But the plot is not scripted in advance.[44]

The link between the question of totalization without a totalizer and the unity of "History" as well as its "one Truth" is confirmed by the final sentence of the text: "If the truth is *one* in its increasing internal diversification, then, by answering the last question posed by the regressive investigation, we shall discover the basic signification of History and of dialectical rationality" (*CDR* 1:818). In other words, the unity of History and its single Truth are a function of the dialectical movement by which "History totalizes itself." This is the "totalization without a totalizer," the possibility of which Sartre is trying to investigate by a critique of dialectical Reason.[45]

More succinctly, dialectical Reason simply *is* that elusive "totalization without a totalizer" on which the intelligibility of History depends. The "totalization from which there is no appeal" is exhibited in the "experience" of dialectical necessity to which we have found Sartre appealing throughout *Critique 1*.[46] Early in that text, after pointing out that "the dialectic as the living logic of action is invisible to a contemplative reason: it appears in the course of *praxis* as a necessary moment of it," he adds that the individual thereby becomes acquainted both with his autonomy in the transcendence of his needs and "with the *law* which others impose on him in transcending their own." From which he draws the relevant conclusion: "Through the very reciprocity of coercions and autonomies, the *law* ends up escaping everyone, and in the revolving movement of totalization it appears as dialectical Reason, that is to say, external to all because internal to each; and a developing *totalization, though without a totalizer,* of all the totalized totalizations and of all the detotalized totalities" (*CDR* 1:38–39; emphasis mine). It is this "law" in its dialectical necessity that Sartre seeks to uncover in the *Critique*.[47] It is the key to historical intelligibility.

Chapter Eight
Biography and History:
The Family Idiot

Sartre already grasped the kernel of an existentialist theory of history in his early disagreement with Aron when he challenged theorists to reveal "an inner relation of comprehension" between, for example, Germany's policy toward England and the kaiser's withered arm (*WD* 301; F 366). At that stage of his writings this seemed little more than a hyperbolic remark, akin to suggesting we seek the start of the Trojan War in the intrafamilial squabbles of the gods. But we have watched Sartre raise the theoretical framework and forge the instruments to pursue this project at length. Existential psychoanalysis reveals a person's basic manner of "surpassing the givens" of his or her situation in good or bad faith. Sartre's shift from a philosophy of consciousness to one of praxis, understood as internalization of the external and externalization of the internal, places a "materialist" dialectic at his disposal and with it the various forms of social mediation introduced in *Search for a Method* and the *Critique*. The dialectical progressive-regressive method, without which Sartre's powerful phenomenological descriptions would be so many frames in an insightful slide show, enables him to comprehend historical praxis as lived

I would reproach psychoanalytic theory with being a syncretic and not a dialectical thought. . . . Psychoanalytic theory is thus a "soft" thought. It has no dialectical logic to it. Psychoanalysts will tell me that this is because there is no such logic in reality. But this is precisely what I am not so sure of: I am convinced that complexes exist, but I am not so certain that they are not structured.
—Sartre, *Between Existentialism and Marxism*

My aim is to try to demonstrate the encounter between the development of the person, as psychoanalysis has shown it to us, and the development of history. For at a certain moment, an individual in his very deepest and most intimate conditioning, by the family, can fulfill a historical role.
—Sartre, *Between Existentialism and Marxism*

(*le vécu*). It is in capturing historical agency *sur le vif* that the existentialist theory reaches its goal.

Gustave Flaubert was a lifelong interest, if not a passion, of Sartre's.[1] So it is fitting that a massive study of Flaubert's "life and times" should form the culmination of Sartre's work, conjoining his love of philosophy and literature with a rage to "understand a man" to the extent that the formidable tools now at his disposal allowed. Placed in the context of Sartre's abiding concern to unmask individual and collective bad faith, the three volumes of *The Family Idiot* constitute the paradigm of an existentialist approach to history, one that undertakes to comprehend an agent's comprehension of his historical praxis. As if to complete the circle of his philosophy of history, Sartre virtually repeats in his last work the original challenge from his *War Diaries* when he refers to "the organic bond of interiority" that is essential for claiming that a writer "expresses his times" (*FI* 5:391). A close examination of this connection will yield a deep comprehension of Flaubert the artist and of nineteenth-century French society. It may likewise be taken as an object lesson in an existentialist theory of history.

THE DECISIVE MEDIATION OF THE FAMILY

> I want to show the signifying relationship [of his disability] with William's English policy. It's necessary, first, to pass via the *family*.
> —Sartre, *War Diaries*

Freud has his family romance (*Familienroman*) and Sartre his dialectic of personalization. The latter refers to the spiral movement by which the infant or child appropriates the values and expectations placed on it by the agents in its milieu. In a reciprocal manner, it both assumes and transcends this network of relationships that are likewise sustained and surpassed by others. The ontological space in which the Sartrean agent operates is one of givens, sustainings, and surpassings. This is the classical existentialist "situation" of facticity-transcendence, but with two crucial modifications. The first is an increasing sensitivity to the individual's psychosocial development, especially to the role of familial relationships during early childhood. The second is the major emphasis now placed on "objective spirit" as constituting the sociohistorical dimension of facticity. The former qualification brings Sartre into dialogue with Freud and psychoanalysis; the latter with Hegel, Marx, and the French sociological tradition.

Sartre's relation to Freud and depth psychology is complex and nu-anced.[2] On the one hand, he denies its pivotal thesis of an uncon-scious, insisting that the famous Freudian "censor" is in bad faith, since presumably it both knows and does not know what is admissible to con-sciousness.[3] The point of this criticism, of course, is to defend his claim that human reality is "without excuse" in its choices and actions. Yet Sartre argues for a "prereflective consciousness" and a "preontological comprehension" that extend far beyond our (reflective) knowledge.[4] This enables him to exercise a hermeneutic on the intentions and mean-ing (*sens*) of agents and their praxes of which the agents themselves may be (reflectively) unaware. For example, it warrants his account of why Flaubert belittled the Legion of Honor during the July Monarchy, wore its rosette with pride during the Second Empire, and refused to show it after the debacle at Sedan.[5] Sartre is informing both us and the agent of what the latter may not know but doubtless comprehends. In fact, pre-reflective consciousness functions in the Sartrean scheme remarkably like the Freudian unconscious, except that appeal to the prereflective does not diminish our responsibility. To underscore this hidden-from-knowledge dimension of consciousness, he introduces in his Flaubert study the term "lived experience" (*le vécu*) as "the equivalent of consciousness-unconscious."[6]

So one need not be amazed to find Sartre distinguishing throughout *The Family Idiot* between Flaubert's (prereflectively) intentional choices and his (reflective) decisions or judgments. Apropos the murder of an older brother by his envious sibling in one of Flaubert's early stories, Sartre acknowledges: "It may be, for example—for all I know—that Gustave was never in on the secret of his [own] fratricidal intentions" (*FI* 2:292). Sartre exploits the prereflective in each of his "biographies," but never so much as in this work. In fact, Flaubert's way of living his epoch is mediated by his way of appropriating his relationship with his family, especially with his physician father.[7] This fundamental thesis al-lows Sartre to engage in an extensive hermeneutic of Flaubert's writings and to account for the nature and sequence of his literary production.

In *Search for a Method* Sartre already sets the agenda:

> It is, then, inside the particularity of a history, through the peculiar
> contradictions of *this* family, that Gustave Flaubert unwittingly served
> his class apprenticeship. Chance does not exist or, at least, not in the

way that is generally believed. The child becomes this or that because he lived the universal as particular. . . . The explosive mixture of naive scientism and religion without God which constituted Flaubert, and which he tried to overcome by his love of formal art, can be explained if we understand that everything took place *in childhood;* that is, in a condition radically distinct from the adult condition. (*SM* 58–60)

Strange words for the philosopher of freedom as conceived by café existentialists since the mid-1940s, but they state the guiding theme of *The Family Idiot.* Sartre finds the key to Flaubert's life in the "passive constitution" imposed on him by his mother: "He is deprived, *from the start,* of the cardinal categories of praxis" (*FI* 1:136). Since truth and knowledge are two such categories, Sartre's Flaubert remains strangely alienated from himself and his language. His ego is an "alter ego," the creation of others, his epistemic contact with the world, one of authority and belief ("the other in us"), rather than evidence and knowledge, and his action, what Sartre in the *Critique* calls "passive activity," the behavior of someone who reflects the praxes of others but avoids initiating his own.[8] It would seem that Flaubert's "choice" of the imaginary is predestined from infancy, at least to the extent that it is for him what William James would call a "live" option (unlike the choice of the active life of a revolutionary, for example, or an entrepreneur, which are excluded as options a priori).

But Gustave's passive "constitution" taken by itself is an abstract conditioning.[9] "No one can be alive without creating himself," Sartre insists in true existentialist fashion, "that is, without going beyond what others have made of him in the direction of the concrete" (*FI* 1:627). This is the role of *personalization.* Following Sartre's progressive method, it moves "toward the concrete," which is the agent totalizing and temporalizing his or her situation by a datable praxis.[10] It requires that we trace the curve of this choice through the phases of actor, poet, and finally writer (*écrivain,* not novelist)[11] as Flaubert settles accounts with his family throughout the crises of his life.

Because of its centrality to Sartre's argument, let us pursue the matter of Flaubert's passivity. Gustave was the fourth child born to Dr. Flaubert and his wife, Caroline. Of seven births, only three children survived—Achille, the firstborn, who bore his father's name and inherited his position, "the most distinguished medical appointment in Normandy"; Gustave; and his younger sister, named after her mother. Sartre makes much of the competition for their father's favor that consumed Gustave's relation with Achille, nine years his elder. But the older brother seems not to have felt the pressure nor suspected Gustave's rage, even when it became "somatized" in the "seizure" that felled the younger man and literally threw him at his brother's feet on a winter's evening in 1844. Sartre reads this crisis as the fundamental break in Flaubert's life, as the (necessarily passive) "choice" of the life of an invalid, free from the vocational demands of his bourgeois family to pursue the life of a literary artist. In other words, Flaubert's "neurosis" is not so much a problem as the solution to the problem of avoiding his father's expectation that he earn a degree in law while obtaining the leisure for his art, without resorting to disobedience or outright rebellion, precluded by his "passive constitution." In Sartre's view, Flaubert's attacks were psychosomatic and intentional; they were strategic moves.[12]

In a predictably Sartrean reversal, Gustave "becomes what others made him," the family idiot, incapable of pursuing a "liberal profession," destined to the life of a provincial *rentier* who busies himself with literature.[13] But unlike Jean Genet, who actively made such a sentence his own and turned it against the class that imposed it, Flaubert slid into a situation that, though intentional, was fatalistic in its conception and manipulative in its execution. He became an artist, *l'homme imaginaire*, who derealized himself in order to lure the bourgeoisie into the imaginary, the better to infect it with the pessimism and negativity that devoured him. On Sartre's reading, the Flaubertian oeuvre is a work of Nietzschean *ressentiment*.

What makes Flaubert's "choice" of the imaginary inauthentic, in contrast with that of Genet, the paradigm of Sartrean authenticity, is its passivity, its demoralizing aim, and, of course, its bad faith. Flaubert's practical attitude toward his world is one of "gliding"; he assumes a "spectator consciousness" (*conscience de survol*) that evades commitment. "But this passivity, we know, is active in the sense that it cannot even exist without becoming a surpassing of the given. Which must be understood in two ways at once: passivity has its own method—gliding—for achieving its objectives, but it is also haunted by the phantom of praxis, which is perceived at each surpassing as the thing of which it is a priori incapable" (*FI* 2:205). We should recall this remark when we note Sartre drawing a similar contrast between the make-believe world of Napoleonic posturing during the Second Empire and the harsh reality of the Prussian war machine; this will constitute an instance of his sought-after relationship between the individual and the historical collective.

Flaubert was a practical joker. But his humor was not simply for the fun of it. Sartre defines "demoralization" in a way that captures the genius of Flaubert's choice of the imaginary:

> To demoralize is . . . to ruin an existence by manipulating it through phantasms, to produce collapses, irrecoverable losses, shatterings, a deficit in reality through the representation of the unreal. But for the operation to be perfect, it is not enough to produce deceptions and fakeries: it is indispensable that the victim become conscious of their nonbeing—if not at the beginning of the process at least as quickly as possible—for it is at this moment of sudden consciousness that he will discover the being of nonbeing [appearances] and the nonbeing of being [finitude], each by means of the other, and that he will perceive in a stupor that all this was *nothing* and that this nothing has inexplicably corroded his life. (*FI* 3:201; F 2:1309)

The usual upshot of such a realization is laughter, an attempt to restore one's link with reality, momentarily broken by the joke. But the nihilistic intent of Flaubert's practical jokes, caricatures, and stories is to foster nonbeing for its own sake. This, in Sartre's view, is the true meaning of *l'art pour l'art* in his aesthetic. The laugh is Nietzschean, the gift poisoned.[14]

Yet Flaubert's game is in bad faith. He longs for the public acceptability he so roundly mocks: "*Renown* is what counts, this alone will satisfy his pride and his resentment" (*FI* 2:232).

The point of this excursion into Flaubert's inauthenticity is to underscore the subjective pole of a dialectic of internalization/externalization that "demands" or "necessitates" such behavior. The ultimate objective pole is French bourgeois society of the period, which renders authenticity improbable, if not impossible, as we shall see. Whether describing neocolonialism in Algeria, anti-Semitism in France, or the "system" of capitalism in general, the later Sartre pursues with a vengeance the traditional thesis that our social environment conditions our choices. If this appears to compromise his vintage existentialism, it contributes positively to the intelligibility of history ("chance does not exist").

What the family mediates in the child's personalization is not only its own particularities but the distinctive features of its society. It is initially and primarily via the family that the objective spirit is concretized in the life and person of the child. This, too, is programmed in *Search for a Method:*

> Existentialism . . . believes that it can integrate the psychoanalytic method which discovers the point of insertion for man and his class— that is, the particular family—as a mediation between the universal class and the individual. The family in fact is constituted by and in the general movement of history but is experienced, on the other hand, as an absolute in the depth and opaqueness of childhood. (*SM* 62)

A forceful example of this social mediation in practice is the lived "contradiction" that pervades the Flaubert family by the presence of two competing ideologies that divided French society in the first half of the nineteenth century.

Two Ideologies

Like the young Sartre of *The Words,* Flaubert grew up in a household torn between two conflicting worldviews, the religious, espoused by the mother, and the skeptical, freethinking, upheld by the patriarch.[15] In both cases the masculine predominated and tended to undermine religious belief to which it nonetheless proffered a calculated external respect. In the Flaubert family during the Restoration (1814–30) and the July Monarchy (1830–48), this tension pitted bourgeois faith in science and technological progress against a sense of hierarachy and tradition. Morally, this translated into a pragmatic utilitarianism versus an ethic of duty.

"To understand Flaubert," Sartre insists, "it must never be forgotten that he was forged by the fundamental contradictions of the period, but at a certain social level—the family—in which they are masked in the form of ambivalences and ironic twists" (*FI* 1:488). Typically, Gustave will work these out not in the real world but in the imaginary. One has only to consider the freethinking pharmacist and the village priest at Emma Bovary's wake to sense Flaubert's rehearsing this conflict from his own life *en famille.*[16] In fact, Sartre believes that "every time Gustave writes in the first person he is insincere" and that his most forthright statements about himself and his family are to be gleaned from his stories: "Gustave reveals himself the moment he invents" (*FI* 1:174).[17] Although Sartre's work is copiously documented with references to Flaubert's correspondence and that of his friends, *The Family Idiot* is in large measure a hermeneutic of and a commentary on Gustave's creative writings. Sartre regards Gustave's fiction as the equivalent of Freudian dreamwork. In other words, he is undertaking an imaginative reading of the imaginary man in order to gain access to the latter's reality.

Sartre concludes that "Gustave was forced to oscillate endlessly between two contradictory ideologies, each of which contained in itself the key to all problems, the answer to all questions" (*FI* 1:477). The contradiction is originally not in Flaubert but in "the family structures." In fact, family anguish and stress merely translate "the objective conflicts of the period" (*FI* 1:487). The Jacobin bourgeoisie had been dechristianized, but the Restoration revitalized organized religion and required that liberal anticlericals like Dr. Flaubert subscribe in public to an ideology they condemned in spirit. This awkward relationship continued through compromises between church and liberal bourgeoisie under the Citizen King. Young Gustave, like the generation he represents, feels the need for belief but is forever deprived of its object by the father's skeptical scientism.

OBJECTIVE SPIRIT

As we remarked above, Sartre's theory of history and society builds on a modification of classical existentialist "situation." In addition to the major role of familial mediation in the spirals of personalization, heir to the existential "transcendence" of facticity, Sartre has socialized the situation by appeal to objective spirit, a qualitative enrichment of existential "facticity." This opens his account to the world of collective consciousness and social facts and rules that the French sociological tradition has bequeathed us.[18] Sartre explicitly rejected a "collective consciousness" and insisted that "objective Spirit" (whose Teutonic capitalization significantly he usually retained) be shorn of any idealist connotation. Still, he occasionally employed the former term. More importantly, he often used Durkheim's example of the experience of collective consciousness, the "pressure" or "necessity" we feel as serialized individuals to conform to opinions, standards, or norms, when he discussed the practico-inert mediation of collectives.

But the context for Sartre's methodological holism is ultimately dialectical, that is, Marxist and Hegelian.[19] It is totalizing and materialist. This translates into a keen sense of the inertia of language (for example, Flaubert's saying that "words are stones") and a far greater respect for what Merleau-Ponty and the sociologists call "institutions" in analyzing social phenomena.[20] Yet it is a dialectical nominalism, as we pointed out earlier, that frees him from the extremes of organic social models, with their totalitarian proclivities. The principle of the primacy of praxis sustains synthetic enrichment that underpins relatively autonomous social structures. But it likewise combats tendencies to dissolve the organic individual in a holistic solvent.

Though the term is missing in *Being and Nothingness,* Sartre introduces "objective spirit" in his *Notebooks for an Ethics.* As we have come to expect from that text, the ideas are social and dialectical, but they are expressed in the consciousness language of his earlier work. Significantly, he employs the term to account for specifically "social" possibilities and constraints, but he does so in a manner that respects what we have been calling the "primacy of praxis":

> Hegel overlooks the image of intentionality and of transcendence. It is true that the objective Spirit is the work of individuals, it is also true that it surpasses them. . . . Precisely because it is their work, it is an *object.* Objective-spirit means object-spirit. Not just an object of knowledge but also an object within which one moves (as in space, as in the air one breathes). But precisely because it is these *surroundings,* it cannot *enter into* Consciousness any more than a tree can, and Consciousness can neither emanate from it nor get away from it. Consciousness is in the Spirit as Heideggerian *Dasein* is-in-the-world. As a consciousness engaged in multiple relationships with other consciousnesses, it is in-the-Spirit. That is, it surpasses the Spirit toward its own ends. Instead of the Hegelian image—it uproots itself from itself in order to return to itself—we have to assume the image of transcendence: consciousness perpetually surpasses the Spirit toward its own ends. . . . Spirit is the always transcendent and noematic unity of the multiplicity of For-itselves. However, it lacks their ontological irreducibility. (*NE* 92–93)

Still, the perennial problem of the individual and the social continues to plague Sartre. It surfaces in a tension between the two descriptions he gives of "objective spirit." On the one hand he describes it as the "me-

dium for the circulation of significations" (*CDR* 1:776). He subsequently complements this semantic description with an ontological one
when he characterizes objective spirit as "culture as practico-inert" (*FI*
3:44).[21] Both aspects of the term are ingredient in Sartre's theory of history as his account moves dialectically from the organic individual
through familial mediation of social relations and back again to the social individual as "concrete" or "singular" universal. Let us examine
both the semantic and the ontological uses of the term with reference to
French society during Flaubert's formative years and youth, the Restoration (1814–30) and so-called July Monarchy of Louise-Philippe
(1830–48).

Taken as the horizon within which meanings are communicated in a
society, "objective spirit" denotes the language actually employed by
the members of a society as well as the nondiscursive practices current
at the time—what Foucault would term the "archive" of a period.[22]
Consider the practices involved with the concept of "distinction" in
bourgeois society in Flaubert's day. Sartre interprets such practices as
the exchange of calling cards, the giving of dinner parties for friends and
business associates, the wearing of physically constraining clothing
(corsets for the women, starched collars for the men), as signaling to the
working class that they are "other": uncultured, unrefined, and self-
indulgent. These practices both constitute and convey a bourgeois humanism that establishes what it is to be properly human and excludes
those who do not qualify. On three occasions Sartre has developed this
thesis apropos three generations of nineteenth-century French bourgeoisie.[23] It is the first, accumulative generation that interests him now.
But in each case, the epistemic (intentional) dimension of objective
spirit—parades and processions, ideologies and institutions, bon mots
and *idées reçues*—serves to infect the members of the collective with responsibility. They understand what they are about even if reflectively
they do not know it. The stage is set for collective bad faith as an objective possibility.[24] Part of the popularity of Flaubert's work in the Second
Empire, Sartre argues, stems from its resonating with the pessimism,
guilt, and self-deception that characterized the ruling class at the time.
The imaginary is addressing the imaginary. "Objective spirit" taken in
this semantic sense is the vehicle for this implicit communication.

The implicit knowledge (*savoir*) that accompanies even the most elementary praxis, if left nonverbal, dies with that praxis. But, in remarks

that combine the semantic and the ontological uses of the expression, Sartre insists:

> Verbalized value systems and ideologies remain in the mind, or at the very least in the memory, because language is matter and because their elaboration has given them material inertia. Written words are stones. Learning them, internalizing their combinations, we introduce into ourselves a mineralized thought that will subsist in us by virtue of its very minerality, until such time as some kind of material labor, acting on it from outside, might come to relieve us from it. I call these irreducible passivities *as a whole* the Objective Spirit. (*FI* 5:38)

He is quick to add that "this definition has no negative intent." In a "society of exploitation" these structured wholes would become harmful. "But taken in themselves they simply manifest this necessity: matter is the mediating element between men to the same degree that through their praxis they become mediators between different states of matter" (*FI* 5:38).

When he defines objective spirit in terms of the practico-inert, Sartre adds that this applies to all its aspects: to the mode of production defined by the instrument as a form of worked matter as well as to "relations between men" insofar as they are established in *institutions* and are lived institutionally. In other words, his understanding of objective spirit is broader and more materialist than that of Karl Popper's "objective knowledge."[25]

It has become increasingly clear that the concept of the practico-inert is a major Sartrean contribution to social ontology. Its mediation serializes social relations and, when modified by scarcity, the practico-inert leaves a path of violence in its wake. It accounts for the continued effect of past praxes as well as the unpredictable consequences of present actions. In each case a praxis or a passive activity puts into motion a series of events that leads to conclusions unintended by or contrary to the intentions of the original agent. Indeed, the concept of original agency in a practico-inert context is seriously attenuated, though not renounced— as the case of Flaubert's passive "constitution" makes clear. This is the locus of such social phenomena as Marx's "fetishization of commodities" and Weber's "objective possibility." Above all, as we have seen, it is the vehicle for incorporating structuralist concepts into Sartre's social theory. But it does so in a characteristically Sartrean fashion, insisting on the "primacy of praxis" at work in the most impersonal imperatives and necessities of these social structures. We must never lose sight of the fact that we are dealing with the *practico*-inert. Sartre writes: "*Objective Spirit,* while *never* on the side of pure lived experience [*du pur vécu*] and free thought, exists *in act* only through the activity of men and, more precisely, through the activity of *individuals*" (*FI* 5:41; F 3:50).

Neurotic Art

> The third volume [of *The Family Idiot*] will show in what way Flaubert's neurosis is a neurosis *required* by what I call the objective spirit. . . . I think that the idea of art for art's sake does depend on neurosis.
> —Sartre, *Life/ Situations*

Sartre's project of melding biography and history in *The Family Idiot* comes to fruition in his extended analysis of "neurotic art" (*L'Art névrose*) during the reign of Louis-Philippe, when Flaubert and his friends were maturing in their vocations, and under Louis Napoleon, when their works came into their own. This is a study of one form of objective spirit—the literary—in a particular society within a specific time frame.[26] As such, it serves as an example and a model for the existentialist approach to historical understanding. Sartre observed on more than one occasion that a similar analysis could have been done of a political figure, Robespierre, for example, if one had at hand the wealth of material that Flaubert left us.[27] But the fact is that Sartre limits himself to "biographies" of artists and their epochs, no doubt because in these cases the "choice" of the imaginary is so patently at issue.

He states the guiding question clearly:

> And since [Flaubert] always remained faithful to his values, that is, to the transposition of his neurotic phantasms into canons of art and style, how could the work that was the issue of this fidelity become integrated into the Objective Spirit? In other words, how could one man's madness become a collective madness and even the *aesthetic reason* of his epoch? (*FI* 5:25; F 3:32)

Sartre devotes the better part of volume 5 of *The Family Idiot* to its response.

Simply put, his thesis is that an "objective neurosis" afflicted the artistic world of Louis-Philippard society according to which any would-be artist was obliged to break with psychological normalcy, or at least to seem to do so, in order to produce important art. Unlike the two previous centuries, when the writer was expected simply to be normal or even upstanding, *"un honnête homme,"* nineteenth-century French culture made new demands on its potential artists. This "imperative of *la littérature-à-faire,"* though unstated, was fully comprehended by the post-Romantic generation of artists. Its point of departure was the literary tradition (*la littérature-faite*), but viewed from the presumed aspect of a future public. "The literary form and content of an epoch," Sartre notes, "are inseparable from the real situation of the writer in society and consequently from the function this society actually assigns to literature" (*FI* 5:55). By placing impossible demands on the potential artist, the objective spirit (here, the example of the older siblings and the legacy of the previous generation as well as the expectations of the reading public) left him or her no choice but to reject the artist's life or to satisfy these imperatives by neurotic behavior: in short, it was necessary "to unrealize oneself in order to write" (*FI* 5:55). This structural disfunction in the society itself constrained the potential artists, not their art. It was the creators who were required to seem neurotic, not their creations.

Sartre proceeds to discuss in detail the contradictory demands of art and reality that French society imposed on its future artists in the post-Romantic age. In imitation of Gaston Bachelard, Sartre had psychoanalyzed a physical quality like the "sticky" in *Being and Nothingness.* He now undertakes the psychoanalysis of an entire society through his examination of neurotic art in the 1830s. Acknowledging that "neurosis always implies a certain refusal, a break with the real" (*FI* 5:20), Sartre sees in the demands of "the bourgeois century," with its commitment to analytic Reason, its scientism, utilitarianism, and boundless confidence in human progress, the challenge to its artists to produce either bourgeois art or nothing. By choosing the unreal, and for its own sake, these aspiring artists made the latter a genuine option. "This is called *the aesthetic attitude,* the rigorous requirement of a literature that claims its full autonomy just when the bourgeoisie wants a class literature. With this attitude the artist unrealizes himself and at the same time derealizes the world" (*FI* 5:128).

Here lies the root of that inversion of dominant values, the "vampirizing" of being (especially language), and "demoralization" that Sartre has associated with the other subjects of his biographies, Baudelaire, Mallarmé, and Genet. Each is reacting against bourgeois humanism and the self-deceptive optimism it fosters. Alluding to his generic distinction between analytic and dialectical Reason, Sartre observes: "In a way these new literary men have remained at the stage of pure negation for lack of another kind of reason, another tool" (*FI* 5:134). We are in the midst of a conflict of rationalities, which, as Sartre observed in the *Critique,* is one form of the class struggle. He traces the contradiction of ideologies and expectations to the ground level of class conflict: "The story of these men and their destiny can be understood only through the evolution of the middle class. This will allow us in our final volume to broach a difficult problem that has never been dealt with: what is the *class being* of a writer born into the professional class who produces *Madame Bovary?*" (*FI* 5:135). In other words, the fundamental contradiction is socioeconomic. This portion of Sartre's theory of historical movement is Marxist.

Elsewhere I have argued that Sartre's Marxism is adjectival to his existentialism.[28] But it cannot be denied that appeal to class conflict—the "motor of history" (*CDR* 1:789)—is integral to his philosophy of history and that it is decisive for his analysis of the objective neurosis that hobbles Flaubert's generation of artists. Though Sartre sees "the truth of the epoch" in these works of neurotic literature produced during the Second Empire, he insists that their truth remains incomplete, a phenomenon of the superstructure until it has been "engendered by the mode and the relations of production" (*FI* 5:297). The genesis of this neurosis in class conflict entails a story Sartre has recounted at length in the *Critique* and elsewhere. It involves the transformation of accumulative into expansionist capitalism at midcentury, accompanied by a rising class consciousness on the part of the workers and the anarcho-syndicalist dream of overturning bourgeois society by the general strike. These changes are structural and occur almost automatically—by economic necessity. As practico-inert phenomena, of course, they are subject to the primacy of praxis like everything else in Sartre's theory. But the possibility exists for denying personal responsibility in the face of enormous social movements. Nonetheless, to the extent that these conflicts are *practico*-inert, their (passively active) participants understand what is happening: *their moves are tactical.* Just as for Freud there are no "accidents," for Sartre, the link between objective spirit and economic change is not fortuitous. And, for that reason, the intelligibility of social phenomena does not end with brute facticity ("That's just the way it is") or shade off into innumerable microphenomena. The primacy of praxis and the related principle of totalization connect the personal with the social in a reciprocal bond.

What are the features of this neurotic art that arises in response to the objective exigencies of the social situation we have just described? Sartre sees Baudelaire, Flaubert, and Leconte de Lisle[29] exhibiting six characteristics: a disengaged attitude toward the world (*conscience de survol*), the view of art as noncommunication, a quest for personal solitude, the derealization of self and of the world, failure (*l'échec*), and nihilism (see *FI* 5:333 ff., 379–82, 389). The artist must assume an ironic distance on his world ("The viewpoint of Death"), pursue his art for its own sake, breaking the web of bourgeois instrumentalities and human ends, and eschew the company of men (Flaubert, the "Hermit of Croisset"). In valuing nonbeing over being and choosing the unreal, he must "derealize" himself (*l'homme imaginaire*), adopting the aesthetic attitude toward the world in general, which entails a life of failure, since the task, though imperative, is impossible ("You must therefore you cannot").[30] The result is an aspect of the nihilism that Nietzsche saw gathering like a storm cloud over Europe in the nineteenth century.[31]

THE IRRUPTION OF HISTORY: *L'homme événement*

At any given moment the historical agent resembles Pascalian man, in that he can *never* be the object of a concept. For Pascal, *human nature* as a pure essence existed when Adam left the hands of God; after the Fall it continued to exist but in perverted form, bumped off track by what may well be called the absolute event. . . . The consequence, for Pascal, is that man must be accounted for at once by conceptual universality and by the opaque irreversibility of a singular temporalization. . . . Pascal concluded that man is not *thinkable;* he envisaged him only as the object of an impossible intellection. It is characteristic of dialectical reason, by contrast, to understand this man-event (*l'homme événement*) as someone who endures history and at the same time makes it.

—Sartre, *The Family Idiot*

Thus far we have been working chiefly at the sociological, synchronic level, the regressive phase of Sartre's progressive-regressive method. We have focused on the structural conditions for Gustave's development, especially intrafamilial relationships and his passive constitution. The spirals of "personalization" are, of course, diachronic and progressive; our charting of their initial turns has implicitly referred to a back-and-forth movement between progressive and regressive phases

throughout Sartre's study. Still, the context for the progressive analysis
thus far has been primarily the family, not the larger social whole. We
could say that Sartre's account has accordingly been biographical and
interpersonal but not yet "historical" properly speaking. This is due to
the limited breadth of its reference, but also especially to the fact that it
has not yet sounded the diachronic depth of the unrepeatable event.[32]
Regarding social breadth, Flaubert might have passed his life in relative
if not total obscurity, and entered history merely as a statistic in the log
of some *Annaliste,* had he not figured significantly in the larger social
world.

But we know that history, for Sartre, deals with the harsh facticity of
being-for-others, the historical event: Pascal's "something happened to
man."[33] Respect for this phenomenon turns us toward the diachronic.
The inertia of the practico-inert retains sedimented past occurrences as
factical ingredients in current situations. When these events carry a socioeconomic significance, they are subsumed in what Sartre calls the
"collective memory" (*CDR* 1:358). The historical event, thus subsumed,
colors social relations thereafter.

Such were the "events of 1848" involving the February revolution—
the closing of the National Workshops, the resultant rioting and massacre of the striking workers by the National Guard in June, and the coup
of 2 December. Henceforth, relations between labor and ownership
were filled with mistrust, hatred, and guilt. In Sartre's view, this translated during the Second Empire into the demand for a class literature,
one in service to Napoleon III's religious politics and in homage to an
idealized beauty that the most splendid artworks had never achieved
(see *FI* 5:273). Above all, historical class literature had to be consonant
with a bourgeois public that had been unmasked by the massacres of
'48.[34] Class antagonism could no longer be smoothed over by imperial
ceremony. "These are the readers who will ensure [the future writers']
success, changing their neurosis into an objective expression of society"
(*FI* 5:273). Under the July Monarchy, developing artists chose art as the
refusal of their bourgeois identities, that is, as the antithesis of scientism,
utilitarianism, and the "real." But by the time their works began to appear (in the 1850s) the class conflict had prepared a reading public for a
literature of hatred.[35] The artist's mistake, Sartre concludes, savoring
the irony, "is to reject the human condition in order to escape the bourgeois condition, without realizing that the essence of the bourgeoisie, at

this time, is to establish the hierarchy on the rejection of the human condition" (*FI* 5:284). Artist and public are entering the same room from different doors.

So Sartre's account of the rise and function of neurotic literature as a key to the *sens* of Second Empire France entails a "structuralist" component in terms of both the formal conditions revealed by regressive analysis and the use of the Marxist base/superstructure dyad—this in addition to a "historical" dimension. But until the historical "profundity of the world" (*FI* 5:297) has been plumbed, the totalization is defective. The "oeuvre of hatred" and its model, the "man of hatred," are not simply the effluence of class warfare in general or the expression of some abstract *homo homini lupus.* As heirs to the massacres of 1848, society under the Empire "seems to be a circuit of hatred. This is a matter of *national* and historical fact." The events of '48 have given class struggle in France the character of "a permanent 'civil war'" (*FI* 5:296).[36]

Comprehension of the historical event that irrevocably qualifies subsequent social relations demands an appropriate dialectic. Implicit in the foregoing is a concept of dialectical Reason that Sartre had already enunciated in the early 1950s:

> A concrete fact is the singular expression of universal relations; but it can be explained in its singularity only by *singular reasons:* to try to deduce it from an absolute but empty knowledge or from a formal principle of development is a waste of time and trouble. In truth, there are dialectics and they reside in facts; it is for us to *discover* them there, not put them there." (*CP* 134–35; emphasis mine)

Like the post-Romantic writers Sartre is discussing, Pascal had courted the irrational because his only alternative was what Sartre calls "analytic reason."

FLAUBERT'S PROPHETIC FALL

Asked whether he considered *The Family Idiot* to be a scientific work, Sartre replied with a distinction that we have come to recognize as integral to his theory of history:

> No. And it is for that reason that I had the book published in the Philosophical Library series. "Scientific" would imply rigorous *concepts.* As a philosopher I try to be rigorous with *notions.* The way I differentiate between concepts and notions is this: A concept is a way of defining

things from the outside, and it is atemporal. A notion, as I see it, is a way of defining things from the inside, and it includes not only the time of the object about which we have a notion, but also its own time of knowledge. In other words, it is a thought that caries time within itself. Therefore, when you study a man and his life, you can only proceed through notions. . . . The distinction I make between concept and notion is similar to the distinction I make between knowledge and understanding. The attitude necessary for understanding a man is empathy. (*L/S* 113)

As a work of (psychoanalytic) hermeneutics, *The Family Idiot* entails guided imagination and empathy, carried out at the level of lived experience (*le vécu*). Sartre's goal is to understand the artist and his times, but not merely in juxtaposition or even in a relationship of reciprocal mirroring. From the outset, his methodological presupposition has been dialectical: notions, not only concepts, totalizing praxis, surpassings that deny, conserve, and raise to higher viewpoints.[37] We have been searching for an "organic bond of interiority," in Sartre's lapidary phrase, between Flaubert's neurosis and the career of *Madame Bovary*.

Whatever one may think of the evidence adduced, Sartre believes he has confirmed the hypothesis that the success of *Bovary* and the literature it emblemized was a mediated result of organic praxis (interiorization/exteriorization), practico-inert structure, and historical conjuncture. He ordered these factors according to the progressive-regressive method throughout the published volumes of *The Family Idiot*. The case he has built is enlightening, even plausible. Certainly, Flaubert scholarship must henceforth take it into account.[38] But the sign, if we needed one, that we have been dealing with something more than linear historical causality or simple historical narrative appears when Sartre inverts historical perspective. Foucault has argued that history deals with the present, not the past, and Sartre would seem to agree.[39] But now he attempts to find in Flaubert's crisis of 1844 a prophetic anticipation of the events of 1848; like the great speculative historians of our century, he is suggesting a history of the *future*, even if it is of the future perfect.[40]

We have seen Sartre insist that dialectical thinking entailed "a certain action of the future as such" (*SM* 92 n). At first blush, this is as unexceptionable as the traditional maxim, "First in the order of intention, last in the order of execution." But Sartrean dialectic, as we now know, is not limited to explicit intentions. Recall his example of the woman "carrying out the sentence" imposed on her by the praxis-processes of economic "necessity" when she procures an abortion. "In so far as praxis is process," Sartre explains, "goals lose their teleological character. Without ceasing to be genuine goals, they become destinies" (*CDR* 1:663). It is precisely this system of "nontelic goals" that Sartre denotes with the terms "praxis-process" and, in *Critique 2* "enveloping totalization." Remember that a major function of the practico-inert is to account for *counter*finality. What Sartre calls "destiny" is precisely a future inscribed in the practico-inert. He describes it as "an irresistible movement [that] draws or impels the ensemble toward a prefigured future which realizes itself through it" (*CDR* 1:551). The meaning-direction of history in our exploitative society is a function of such "destinies."

But there is another, related teleology operative in Sartre's theory of history. Thus far we have focused on the structural possibilities and limits of our historical society. In this context we have remarked Sartre's plausible extrapolation from present communication technology to the creation of "One World" and the sociopolitical ideal of the "city of ends" that it makes possible but in no way guarantees. But Sartre pursues his thesis still further with the claim that at least some biographical actions carry a historically "prophetic" meaning.

The test case for this new aspect of Sartre's theory is doubtless the anticipation of the moral "fall" of the bourgeoisie in the events of 1848 (the February revolution, the July massacres, and the December coup d'état) by Flaubert's physical crisis on a January evening four years earlier. Sartre is raising the age-old question of history's predictive value—except that here it is a case not simply of history repeating itself, but of relating a private episode to a future public occurrence. So it is appropriate to call this action "prophetic," for it resembles the behavior of biblical prophets who sometimes taught a moral lesson or foretold a future event by means of symbolic gestures. Of course, the bridge between the two events, in the Sartre-Flaubert case, will not be divine. Whatever necessity obtains between them will be retroactive, what nineteenth-century skeptics called "prediction after the fact" (*vaticinatio post eventum*). If we are to make sense of this biographical dimension of Sartre's theory, we must discover and analyze the link between private episode and future, public event.

The facts are that on an evening in January 1844, while driving a cabriolet with his brother on a dark, country road near Pont-l'Evêque,

Flaubert was startled by the sudden appearance of a wagon passing them on the right. He suffered a seizure, falling unconscious at Achille's feet, and had to be taken by his brother to a nearby farm for immediate treatment.

Sartre interprets this as the decisive event in Flaubert's life, matched only by the humiliating collapse of the Second Empire at Sedan. The one opens his artistic career and the other brings it to a close: "At Pont-l'Evêque a cycle was initiated; at Sedan, it was completed" (*FI* 5:559; F 600).[41] The immediate symbolism of the action—for it is a passive activity, intentional and tactical—is apparent from Sartre's account of Flaubert's constitution and personalization. With his physical collapse, Gustave is abdicating in the brother's favor any claim to their father's mantle or to the world of praxis. But this death to the real, to the arena of history, is also a resurrection to the life of an artist, *l'homme imaginaire,* neurotic but freed from the hated study of law to pursue his art at leisure. Given the nature of Sartrean comprehension and the shadowy awareness of *le vécu,* this is a plausible reading of the event. In view of what Sartre elsewhere calls the "pluridimensionality" of the act, other readings may also be plausible. But whence its prophetic link to the events of 1848, so that Flaubert need not bother about the revolution since

> the crisis of Pont-l'Evêque and its aftermath until the death of Achille-Cléophas [his father] would be *Gustave's* February and June days, *his* coup of 2 December, and *his* plebiscite; he would have lived, not symbolically but in earnest and in advance, the defeat and cowardly alleviation of a class which, in order to complete its destiny and realize its secret primacy, agrees to renounce its visible praxis (political action) and go into apparent hibernation to retrieve its "cover," its irresponsibility as an eternal minor? (*FI* 5:398)

In other words, how can one claim that he "had already constituted himself a subject of the Second Empire in 1844 [at Pont-l'Evêque]" (*FI* 5:621)? Again, what is the objective connection between these two phenomena? Dialectically speaking, what mediates their difference?

First of all, the "text" that Sartre interprets is not the historical accident itself but Flaubert's imaginary anticipation of the same in his juvenilia, especially in an early autobiographical novel.[42] It is the misanthropy of that work that he sees as mediating Flaubert's "fall" and that

of the participants in the events of '48. The story will capture the *sens* of
the February revolution and the December coup better, he argues, if its
author is someone "who did not experience them [firsthand] but whose
misanthropy has its motivations in his own protohistory"; in other
words, someone whose distrust of human nature is profound and long-
standing, not superficial and accidental. But the crucial point is that "the
deep and distant causes of this misanthropy must *also* be considered the
causes of the February movement" (*FI* 5:316). Otherwise, the connection between the theme of the story and the historically rooted distrust
will be purely fortuitous.

Sartre introduces Gustave's contemporary, Leconte de Lisle, to serve
as a control case. His misanthropy followed the failure of the February
revolution, his writings were generally ignored by the imperial public,
and he came into his own professionally during the subsequent bourgeois republic after Sedan—exactly the contrary of Flaubert. The former's misanthropy will be of merely anecdotal significance, whereas the
latter's will hit the reading public with "the abundance and obscurity of
a myth," and this because both his personal situation and the subsequent civil war, on Sartre's hypothesis, are "conditioned by the same
factors" (*FI* 5:317).

The simplest answer to the question of linkage would be to see both
individual and collective events as well as the published story simply as
incarnations of objective spirit in Sartre's sense of that expression. This
accords with his claim that Leconte de Lisle's interiorization of objective
spirit is explicitly not an incarnation of neurotic art because it occurs
after the events of '48 and, in Sartre's view, is opportunistic in motivation (see *FI* 5:381). And it has the advantage of employing a major term
from his established theory. Understood in this dialectical fashion,
Flaubert's seizure would be more than the symptom of a historical neurosis destined to break out collectively in four years, but less than an
instance of some abstract historical law to be repeated on the streets of
the capital later in the decade. The former is insufficient as an account of
the root of the disfunction; the latter, redolent of speculative historians
like Spengler and Toynbee, is too deterministic for Sartre. Aesthetically
re-presented in the work of art, Gustave's "fall" imaginatively totalizes
the internal contradiction that rends French society and its individual
citizens in the 1840s. Sartre's reading of the message in both events is

the same: "man is impossible" (*FI* 5:386). In other words, the task of revolutionary freedom, the "city of ends" that implicitly motivates every liberating struggle, is destined to fail.

Sartre insists that the connection between this personal disaster and the subsequent "collective failure of 1848" can be read by *this* public "*as an oracle,* and—through a disaster that will become manifest in and through the work as a singular universal—as the symbolization of the advent of the Second Republic, of its impotence and its crimes, of its collapse and its death, crushed under the boot" (*FI* 5:386).

We have studied his notion of the singular universal, an idea he developed in an address on Kierkegaard by that title.[43] More than symbolization or even incarnation, perhaps the most adequate mediation between biography and history in Flaubert's case would be to understand the life *and* the work as the "singular universal." This would be the boldest application thus far of Sartre's principle of totalization which has been operative throughout *The Family Idiot,* namely, that a person totalizes his or her epoch to the extent that he or she is totalized by it. This principle has been implicit in our foregoing analyses of the choice of the imaginary, objective spirit, and neurotic art. But how might totalization and the singular universal qualify Flaubert's crisis as prophetic?

THE *SENS* OF A SOCIAL WHOLE

Sartre has continued to distinguish concept from notion as well as their respective correlates, knowledge from comprehension and *signification* (signification) from *sens* (roughly, meaning). Recall that he introduced *sens* in an aesthetic context but insisted that the artwork could make present (that is, re-present) any totality, even the Cold War.[44] He now explains that objective spirit materialized in cultural artifacts, "even in literature," addresses us in *imperatives.*[45] So the reader awakens the *sens* of these sometimes contradictory commands by a totalizing movement whose origin is his personal unity: "I provoke collisions of ideas and feelings, and by lending them my time and my life, I exalt and exacerbate innumerable contradictions" (*FI* 5:46). Of course, the totalizing synthesis which the reader effects is only partial and ongoing; the congealed meaning of the artifacts calls for still other revivals.[46] But my point is that the *sens* of the objective spirit of the post-'48 bourgeoisie could be "realized" in an imaginary mode that totalized that spirit in its

essential form, namely, as misanthropy, flight from the real (specifically, from historical praxis and responsibility), and bad faith. Even the
life of the survivor at the price of the Other's death is presignified in the
drama at Pont-l'Evêque.

Sartre seems to confirm this interpretation when he writes:

> For although that memorable historical moment distantly follows the
> individual misadventure of the author, it is nonetheless a singular uni-
> versal as well. Through tens of thousands of individuals, something
> was begun in pain and blood, then broke apart, that bore general *signif-*
> *ications* even at the outset, but its *meaning* [*sens*]—even in the midst of
> generality—is a singular temporalization, a lived and plural determi-
> nation of intersubjectivity that marks the epoch at least as much as the
> epoch marks it, and that "will never be seen twice." (*FI* 5:386)[47]

It seems that the historical fall in both cases is followed by the resurrection to a world free of historicity, unencumbered by the pain and guilt of
existing: a derealized world. Sartre once described the dream as "a privileged experience which can help us to conceive what a consciousness
would be like which would have lost its being-in-the-world and which
would be, by the same token, deprived of the category of the real" (*PI*
229). It is with this understanding of the imaginary world that he refers
to aesthetic awareness as an "induced dream." The reading public under
the Second Empire, like the young artist, is in flight from a reality
marked by failure. Both are living a dreamlike existence.

One could object that our defense of the prophetic dimension of this
symbolic event deserves as much credence as prognostications from tea
leaves. In both cases, it might be argued, one is relying on generic pronouncements based on sources that have no essential relation to the predicted event. What I am suggesting is that Flaubert's "prophetic" action
becomes so only after the prefigured occurrence. This is a real case of
vaticinatio post eventum. But it does not undermine the "bond of interiority" that is discovered to have obtained between Flaubert's seizure
and the events of '48. Before that date, Gustave's crisis as an anticipation of the future social upheaval would not merit any more belief than
the configuration of leaves in a teacup. In retrospect, however, a reciprocal comprehension emerges: each illumines the other. The "prophetic" nature of the one is purely a function of its earlier status on the

time line. Had the private episode and the public event occurred simultaneously, we might have had something closer to a Kantian "sign of history," but not a Sartrean "prophecy."[48]

One might mount the defense in other terms. Given the objective possibilities and necessities that form the glue of history (Sartre's denial that chance "as popularly conceived" is operative in the spiral of personalization), the same or analogous relationships that conditioned Flaubert's "fall" "necessitated" the collective "choice" of the national bourgeoisie in flight from the harsh reality of its "truth," the awakening proletariat. It is in light of the latter that the former assumes its analogous character. But the performance succeeds only if Flaubert follows through with a demoralizing masterpiece that captivates this new generation. The opus confirms that his option for the imaginary was no mere velleity; its meteoric success reveals the oneiric avidity of its public.[49]

A Novel That is True: History and Imagination

> I would like my study to be read as a novel because it really is the story of an apprenticeship that led to the failure of an entire life. At the same time, I would like it to be read with the idea in mind that it is true, that it is a true novel. Throughout the book, Flaubert is presented the way I imagine him to have been, but since I used what I think were rigorous methods, this should also be Flaubert as he really is, as he really was. At each moment in this study I had to use my imagination.[50]
> —Sartre, *Life/Situations*

By calling *The Family Idiot* "a true novel" (*un roman vrai*), Sartre was, perhaps inadvertently, quoting Raymond Aron. The latter had argued that history of the historians was a true novel. The fictional aspect of Sartre's Flaubert study stems from his imaginatively framing hypotheses and filling the gaps between the data culled from documents, including Flaubert's own fiction. Sartre's reluctance to pursue a similar tack with regard to Robespierre, we saw, was attributed to a paucity of evidence. Any difference between this and "scientific" history-biography is primarily one of degree, that is, the size of the gaps in the evidence to be filled with imaginative construction. If his biographies are "creations," they are not fashioned out of whole cloth. And his "novel" about the family idiot has had an impact on scholars' subsequent reading of Flaubert's life and times. Its three volumes are no mere flight of fancy, a self-indulgent jeu d'esprit.[51]

But if it is a real work of fiction, a "true" novel, in what sense is *The Family Idiot* a factual account, a novel that is "true"? The answer must begin with Sartre's understanding of "truth" in a historical and dialectical context. "For us," he writes, "truth is something which becomes, it *has* and *will have* become. It is a totalization which is forever being totalized. Particular facts do not signify anything; they are neither true nor false so long as they are not related, through the mediation of various particular totalities, to the totalization in process" (*SM* 30–31). And that totalization entails the respective praxes of the agent, the historian, and the reader of the text. The questions of whether and where they coalesce raise the overarching and related questions of a "single truth for History" and of "totalization without a totalizer."

The second key to Sartre's response is found in the *Annexe* which Arlette Elkaïm-Sartre added to the second edition of the third French volume of *The Family Idiot.*[52] It consists entirely of notes Sartre had left for the unwritten fourth volume, which was to have been a reading of *Madame Bovary.* There we find him asking whether, in view of the numerous interpretations to which the novel has been subjected over the years, it makes sense to question whether Emma Bovary did or suffered such and such "in truth" (*L'Idiot* 2d ed., 3:769). Especially, he wonders whether someone writing in 1972 does not have an anthropology so different from that of 1857 that it is not possible to produce more than just another reading, without any claim to greater accuracy. His answer is relevant to the "truth" of his Flaubert study and merits quoting at length:

> I think it is the same as when a doctor validly diagnoses the disease of a historical person one hundred years later, based on symptoms recorded at the time. Will we say that he has made the correct [*véritable*] reading of the sickness? No, because there will be others in the future. But the others, if the diagnosis is *truly* made according to current science, will take the prior one into account, and will expand and transform it dialectically (via an internal relation). It is set on the road of truth.
>
> The case is more complex for a [literary] work because of the plurality of intentions, but it is the same thing: there is a reading that will place itself on the road of truth. There is the relation of the man to the work and vice versa. *In addition* there is the relation of the work to its first readers (Taine, Renan, the Empress Eugénie, Mlle. Leroyer de

Chantpie, etc.). Whence a first level is constituted that permits us to *situate* the other levels (Zola, for example). The readings are diverse but one always forgets (idealism) to interpret them in terms of the social position of the reader (class, ideology, evolution, and the like). Hence readings can be understood and objectified but in terms of this double consideration: (1) the content of the reading and (2) the social situation which explains it. There remains something more (the very thing that allows us to understand that Flaubert wrote *Madame Bovary*) that will permit creative readings. But that something more [*au delà*] merely deepens the social situation of the reader when it is a spontaneous reading. The critic must break with his own ideology in order to place himself at the level of the ideology of the time. (*L'Idiot*, 2d ed., 3:769)

That "something more" (*au delà*) beyond content and context is the historical agents' comprehension (as distinct from their knowledge) of what they are about. This is precisely dialectical action (praxis) as internalization/externalization of objective spirit. It is the moment and the locus where history and biography intersect. It is for the reader-interpreter to grasp it.

In these notes Sartre reaffirms his opposition to relativism and repeats his conviction that the only possible critique comes from the Left because it alone is able to interpret itself as well as other readings. And he announces the perspective from which his own interpretation proceeds, namely, "Marxism and freedom" (*L'Idiot* 2d ed., 3:769).

What this sketch of an answer to the question of the "truth" of his "novel" suggests is a restatement of committed biography-history as we have watched Sartre formulating it earlier.[53] The context is performative and moral. The historian or biographer does not simply describe but produces an object or oeuvre. Given the present state of humanity (the class struggle, on Sartre's account), any exploration of the life and times of a subject that ignored this "motor of history" would not be "on the road to truth"; in other words, the reading would not fit into the dialectical mesh that recognizes its relationship to previous attempts even as it builds upon them. Neither would it be subject to adjustment and correction from subsequent, better informed accounts. But the appropriate criterion is not "correspondence" to some ideal set of facts ("wie es eigentlich gewesen ist") nor abstract "coherence" with itself and other narratives. Rather, the standard is adequacy in expressing the norms of social struggle.[54]

Lest this be dismissed as socialist realism, a theory that Sartre consistently derided, what we are calling Sartre's "committed" biography and history is not a theory about the formal structure of an opus. Neither does it entail the heavy-handed moralism that earned the disdain of critics worldwide. It is a corollary to Sartre's thesis that all knowledge is committed ("the world we know is the world we make" [*BEM* 168], his version of Vico's *verum, factum*) and that good faith requires, first, that we assume responsibility for these commitments, and, second, that the value of "freedom" is ingredient in every authentic choice.[55] We have observed the play of Sartre's acknowledged Marxism in his reference to class consciousness and struggle throughout *The Family Idiot.* The "materialism" of his theory prevents him from slipping into cultural history of an idealistic sort or the subjectivism of purely psychological narrative.

But one could question Sartre's analogy with medical diagnosis and its implicit appeal to scientific progress. Is there anything equivalent in hermeneutics? Sartre, who has vehemently rejected the "bourgeois" faith in progress, could scarcely come down on the side of cumulative advance in the human sciences. And yet this is where he seems to be heading. The only way to relieve him of inconsistency is to underline his reference to the social condition of the reader of a text. This brings the discourse back to its material conditions and places in motion the Marxist "scientific" confidence in consciousness raising. What saves Sartre from what he criticizes as Marxist economism is precisely what makes his theory existentialist and not Marxist *sans phrase.* This is what we have called the "primacy of praxis" in his social theory. To paraphrase a well-known Sartrean remark: if Flaubert is a provincial bourgeois, not every provincial bourgeois is a Flaubert. It is up to existential psychoanalysis to determine the difference.

THE SARTREAN PROJECT AS PSYCHOHISTORY

Existentialism has always been a person-centered philosophy. This is equally true of its theory of history. The primacy of individual praxis as well as the progressive movement in Sartre's method integrates the social agent fully into historical causality. Or such is its intent. Given the numerous objections against his excessive individualism, it seems appropriate to examine the Flaubert study as a form of history and not simply as biography writ large. The closest precedent in the literature is the genre known as "psychohistory." How does *The Family Idiot* fit into that category? If the Sartrean method is a form of *psychohistory* (with Marxist underpinnings), how does it face the standard criticisms leveled against that approach by philosophers and professional historians?

We have described the progressive-regressive method as a hybrid of existential psychoanalysis and historical materialism. As such, it resembles what in recent decades has come to be called "psychohistory."[56] But Sartre's relation to psychohistorical method, with its commitment to the unconscious and its emphasis on the transference phenomenon, is as complex and nuanced as is his relation to Freudian psychoanalysis in general. If one accepts his "prereflective awareness," "comprehension," and "lived experience" (*le vécu*) as functional equivalents of the classical unconscious (or simply restricts the psychological component of psychohistory to forms of so-called ego psychology), then Sartre may be read as a kind of psychohistorian. Indeed, his growing sense of the decisive mediation of the family in the agent's "personalization" evidences a psychohistorical method. Even his adoption of "that truth of microphysics: the experimenter is a part of the experimental system" (*SM* 32 n) can be seen as an opening to the phenomenon of transference. But the additional historical materialist dimension separates him from the majority of psychohistorians, who are suspicious of such metanarratives. And the concept of objective spirit or "culture as practico-inert" makes Sartre less vulnerable to criticisms of individualism and psychologism than many psychohistorians.

There is an old comedy routine in which a sheriff says to his deputy: "I'll go in and you surround the house!" History is just the sort of thing one person cannot do any more than he or she can surround a house alone. History is a "collective" or "group phenomenon, using these terms in Sartre's technical sense. Hegel's "world historical figure" is a social individual, indeed with a vengeance, as is the hapless capitalist whom Marx grudgingly excuses "for relations whose creature he socially remains."[57] Recall Sartre's avowal that "an individual cannot do anything [politically revolutionary] by himself" (*ORR* 171). It is significant that Sartre has chosen famous literary figures as the subjects of his "biographies." Not only does this afford him a wealth of resource material for his analysis, but it favors his abiding concern with the relation between the real and the unreal-imaginary. More to the issue at hand, Sartre's concentration on influential figures has facilitated his account of the society they influenced and that made them famous. In other words, there is still a hint of the "great man" theory of history afoot in Sartre's approach. Not that Baudelaire, Flaubert, Mallarmé, or Genet acted *in vacuo.* Sartre's notion of dialectical praxis precludes the methodological individualism with which Aron erroneously saddled him.[58] But each subject emerges in Sartre's account as a historically significant agent. Flaubert, for example, in Sartre's opinion, was the "creator of the 'modern' novel" (*FI* 1:x). In other words, none was chosen to exemplify the average everyday, though each as the "incarnation" of objective spirit was a "concrete universal."

In the final analysis, it is the "notion" of the concrete universal and its dialectical framework that distinguishes Sartre from most psycho-historians. He is a moralist and an ontologist in his approach to history as elsewhere. What might otherwise be read as psychological facts about an individual emerge in this context as ways of interiorizing the exterior and exteriorizing the interior in a manner that renders concrete, that is, "real," such abstractions as "objective spirit" and "atomic individual."

Conclusion to Part Two:

The Biographical Illusion

O nce it became clear that *The Family Idiot* was to remain another torso, Sartre
remarked that those who had read carefully
the previous volumes could write the fourth
themselves.[1] Something similar can and
must be said of the theory of history contained in this work. The concepts of personalization and objective spirit are important
expansions of his theoretical repertoire.
Clearly, "biography" is no longer an individualistic undertaking for the existentialist.
Praxis and dialectic have ramified the notion
of situation for the postwar Sartre just as intentionality did for the prewar philosopher.
This socialization reaches its climax in what
we have called Sartre's principle of totalization: a person totalizes his or her age to the
extent that he or she is totalized by it. This is
the ontological and epistemic foundation for
that "internal relation of comprehension"
that the existentialist seeks between the
most personal item, Leconte de Lisle's monocle, for example, or the kaiser's withered
arm, and macrophenomena such as the
Louis-Philippard literary mentality or German foreign policy.

But the implicit relations are to be articulated, the points connected. Sartre believes

that a relation of mutual intelligibility between the individual and the social is possible and that he has exhibited it in the psychoanalyses that he has elaborated for Flaubert or sketched in the case of Stalin. Before I undertake a final assessment and critique of his project of an existentialist theory of history in the next two chapters, let me conclude with a review of what Sartre's theory does not claim to be, lest my criticism be directed at a phantom target.

Despite its prizing of totalization, Sartre's approach is rigorously nontotalitarian. Some critics have confused these concepts. Yet a strict and coherent picture of Sartre's dialectical nominalism emerges from his fundamental concepts of the primacy of praxis, the mediating third, the phenomenon of personalization, and the like. This has led others to misconstrue his approach as methodological individualism, as we have seen. When he writes that Marxism is "the humus of every particular thought and the horizon of all culture [in our day]" (*SM* 7), we now know that this should not be taken to mean that it cannot be surpassed, though it does imply a commitment to the dialectical framework of negation and surpassing that totalization entails. Like Foucault, Sartre recognized the acquisition of Marxist (and Freudian, for that matter) concepts and methods for our present-day discourse.[2] In fact, on several occasions Sartre speaks of his hypothesis with reference to the interpretation of Flaubert's neurosis, for example, or the socialist *sens* of History.[3]

It is this presence of the hypothetical and the categorical in Sartre's epistemology that accounts for a certain tension running through his theory. The urge for the apodictic, with its implicit appeal to the clarity of consciousness, struggles against the inertia of institutional phenomena and social causation. Sartre is clearly aware of the strain as, for example, when he warns us against the "biographical illusion, which consists in believing that a lived life can resemble a recounted life" (*WD* 81). His point seems to be that the *histoire* which we produce from the facts of a person's life and times is one way among possibly many (the "pluridimensionality of the act") of reading this life—which does not mean that all interpretations are equally true/false. Given the Sartrean ontology that grounds his progressive-regressive method, there are clear criteria for accounts in bad faith, as the protagonists in *No Exit* exemplify. And any story that failed in coherence and comprehensiveness would likewise be rejected.

When we expand our story to "totalize the epoch," we are still in the hypothetical mode. What would make it categorical would be the moral dimension of our commitment to fostering the value of freedom for humankind. Like the image in a medieval grail quest, the vision of the "city of ends" has increasingly unified and directed Sartre's dialectic. But it has not blinded him to the harsh fact of counterfinality or to the potential for abuse of freedom that history documents all too well. The historical equivalent of the biographical illusion would perhaps be the dogmatic insistence that there is only one truth to History. And it is this belief that Sartre tries, at times without success, to keep in question. I say "without success" because his major concern to relate history and morality depends on a positive answer to the query. If History fragments into histories, Sartre seems to think, authentic existence becomes all but impossible. But if the "one truth of History" is a matter of decision rather than discovery, its connection with morality becomes more evident. So too does the mediating role of poietic vision. For, as he admits early in *Critique 1,* "we are not trying to reconstruct the real history of the human race; we are trying to establish the *Truth of History*" (*CDR* 1:52). Establishing the "truth" is a poietic act.

PART THREE

It is often said in common parlance that the historian *represents* the past (instead of describing or interpreting it). The vocabulary of representation has the advantage of not being suggestive of the kind of presuppositions the other two vocabularies gave rise to. The suggestion is rather that the historian could meaningfully be compared to the painter representing a landscape, a person, and so on. The implication is, obviously, a plea for a *rapprochement* between philosophy of history and aesthetics.

—F. R. Ankersmit, *History and Tropology*

Chapter Nine
Sartre and the Poetics of History:
The Historian as Dramaturge

I f Sartre is known as a philosopher of freedom and a moralist, he may with equal justification be called a philosopher of the imagination.[2] His 1926 thesis for advanced studies dealt with the imagination as did his first philosophical book, published ten years later. But of greater significance is his *Psychology of Imagination* (1940), where he introduces his concept of the analogon and describes imaging consciousness as the locus of "possibility, negativity and lack"—features that will emerge in *Being and Nothingness* to characterize consciousness in general. It is this paradigmatic role of imaging consciousness that lends Sartre's subsequent work its aesthetic cast.

As we near the end of our reconstruction of his theory, let us summarize and synthesize the aesthetic aspects of Sartre's approach to history, the better to understand how they relate to the moral and biographical dimensions of his thought. As one who espoused the methodological premise that "man is a totality, not a collection," he could scarcely resist our attempt to "totalize" his own enterprise. Indeed, he invited it.[3]

Historia est proxima poesis et quodammodo carmen solutum.

—Quintillian[1]

The Image and the Work of Art

Given the way Sartre's philosophy of history terminates, with the centrality of the concept of struggle and the impossible reconciliation of the unavoidable concepts of fraternity and violence, it may seem odd to conclude our reconstruction of his theory by examining his philosophical psychology, especially his philosophy of art. But a basic thesis I have been defending thus far is that Sartre likens the intelligibility of history to that of an artwork because he considers the former as much the product of creative freedom as the latter. One will miss a crucial dimension of Sartre's reading of history by overlooking its psychological and aesthetic nature. And the implicit concept of what we have called "committed" history will make little sense if not placed in the context of Sartre's concomitant theory of committed literature.

Since I have treated the matter at length elsewhere,[4] let me simply sketch the elements of Sartre's theory of the imaging consciousness relevant to his reflections on the meaning of history. As he argues in *The Psychology of Imagination,* the image is not a "thing," not even a mental thing, but a form of consciousness, a way of being present to the world. The way of consciousness in general is called "intentionality" by Husserl and his followers in the phenomenological movement. Sartre never questions the claim that consciousness is characteristically other-referring, that it "intends" an object in its every act. Where he augments the Husserlian thesis is in his account of the way consciousness "intends" its objects imaginatively, as distinct from perceptively or emotively.

Sartre offers the following definition: "The image is an act that intends [literally "aims at" (*vise*)] an absent or nonexistent object in its corporeality by means of a physical or psychical content that is given not for its own sake but as an 'analogical representative' of the intended object."[5] Unlike perceiving, the imaging act intends its object "as a nothingness"; that is, it affirms or believes its objects to be nonexistent, absent, existing elsewhere or in some neutral mode that prescinds from existence entirely. Moreover, the spontaneity of imaging consciousness is contrasted with the passive syntheses of perception; and the unblinking eye of Sartrean consciousness is aware of having adopted the imaging mode of being "present-absent" to the world by "derealizing" what would be the perceptual object, were such available for perceiving. In other words, I can imagine my friend in certain circumstances while knowing that these do not in fact obtain, yet be aware too that it is my friend "in flesh and blood" and not some simulacrum that I have in mind.

Perhaps the most distinctive feature of Sartre's theory, one that he affirmed to the end of his life and that figures in his understanding of history, is his concept of the "analogical representative" or "analogon" in imaging consciousness. This may be a physical thing, like a carving or the printed letters on a page, or physiological changes, like the eye movements that serve as content for hypnagogic images. The analogon is synthesized with cognitive, emotive and, often, kinesthetic elements to yield the intended object. Indeed, we have an analogon only so long as we have the imaged object. The carving, for example, is simply a piece of polished wood until it is "derealized" into the analogue for the aesthetic object.

We have seen that the early Sartre, in particular, but the author of *The Family Idiot* as well, took the historical event for an analogon of what we commonly call "history." In other words, history, for him, is no more a concatenation of brute facts or simple events than the aesthetic object is a mere linkage of perceptual items. The synthesizing activity of consciousness is at work in both cases and, most importantly, there is a corresponding *moral* dimension to each. This is the root of Sartrean commitment in both history and art and serves as the basis for his existentialist theory of each. Its goal is freedom as value.[6]

AESTHETIC, NOT AESTHETICIST

Nietzsche writes that "only if history can endure to be transformed into a work of art" will it be able to preserve or even evoke those life instincts he so valued.[7] A similar claim can be made for Sartre's theory of history and the value of freedom it promotes. His approach carries a distinctively aesthetic quality that complements and completes the moral and epistemic aspects we have studied thus far. We have argued that what enabled him to accommodate History at the same time he began to deal with society was his subsumption of an earlier philosophy of consciousness, with its looking/looked-at model of social relations, into a philosophy of totalizing praxis. We must stress the fact that Sartrean praxis is conscious both thetically and nonthetically.[8] But "praxis," the model for which is physical labor, emphasizes the situated and dialectical nature of consciousness, while leaving open the possibility of the agent's ideological mystification. Of course, this discovery of praxis was conceptual, though promoted by extraphilosophical, especially political, considerations.[9] His interest in the philosophy of history dates at least from the late 1930s, as we have seen.

And yet if history, like every human undertaking, is a praxis, a doing, it is also for Sartre a *poiesis,* a making. Imaging consciousness plays a significant role under both descriptions. It figures in the act of totalization toward an ideal goal by fashioning the "not yet" and the "as if" of our projects. And, as empathetic, imagination sustains the progressive and regressive "decodings" of the relevant documents and monuments that yield the comprehended *sens* of a given event both for the agents themselves and for others. It is just such an imaginative reading of Flaubert's letters and literary works that enabled Sartre to uncover the artist's self-defining project as the author of *Madame Bovary.*

The model for re-presenting the totalized meaning (*sens*) of a historical movement or epoch is, as we saw, the work of art. Sartre shares with Hans-Georg Gadamer and other hermeneuticists the conviction that the past is essentially a meaningful whole and that the historian's task is to interpret rather than (causally or nomologically) explain it, after the manner of a work of art. But Sartre moves beyond hermeneutics when he appeals to "dialectical rationality" which, he claims, renders intelligible every form of praxis, and when he takes for granted at least the partial adequacy of historical materialist explanations.

In Sartre's view, art is essentially "re-presentational," though not mimetic.[10] This is worth noting because, as Ankersmit observes, "Historiography . . . is the discipline of representation *par excellence*—even more so than artistic representation" (*HT* 118). But Sartre's imaginative reconstructions of the life projects of significant artists like Genet or Flaubert render "present" the meaning (*sens*) not only of their lives but of their times. It is in this aesthetic sense that what we have called the "principle of totalization" assumes its full significance.

Similarly, the pervasiveness of the aesthetic renders more plausible Sartre's avowal that *The Family Idiot* is "a novel that is true [*un roman vrai*]" (*S* 9:123). I have suggested that the totalizing *sens* that guides Sartre's investigation is not simply "discovered," the way one stumbles over an artifact on an ancient battlefield or hits upon the solution to a problem, though it is closer to the latter than to the former. The historian "reads" this *sens* in the material the way novelists sense the moves of their protagonists once the action is underway: each stage in the advance further clarifies, and not merely adds to, its antecedents. I characterized this feature earlier as "retrospective necessity" out of respect for Sartre's own usage. But it seems more accurate to call this dialectical linkage "fittingness," an aesthetic term that unites constitutive parts into their constituted whole, not "logically" like premises to conclusion, nor mechanically as cause to (external) effect, but in terms of propriety, the "hanging together" of the events in a story or the notes in a melody.[11] In each case there is freedom and contingency; matters could have been otherwise. But, had they been so, the opus would have been essentially altered. So the "inner relation of comprehension" between private life and historical event that Sartre has been seeking since his initial reflections on the kaiser's withered arm to his interpretation of Flaubert's first seizure can be seen as one of aesthetic "fittingness." A fittingness to the facts, no doubt, and to the agent's totalizing praxis; but fittingness also to Sartre's political-moral project as committed historian.

Aron referred to historical narrative (*l'histoire-narration*) in general as "un roman vrai."[12] In fact, he once observed that "what Sartre takes for the essence of the novel—the reader experiences the feeling that the characters are acting freely and, at the same time, that their acts are never arbitrary or haphazard [*quelconques*]—constitutes the final justification of the historical narrative as well" (*IPH* 475). Sartre's "biographies" are clearly narratives in this respect, but so too is his dialectical history. It is the notion of dialectic, he believes, that saves him from determinism, which he associates with analytic Reason (see *ORR* 100).

One is reminded of Roland Barthes's appeal to the "reality effect" of the historical novel and his concomitant claim that it is the same in the writing of history.[13] Indeed, Barthes takes the nineteenth-century realist novel as the model for this comparison. Just as the careful historian mentions irrelevant details in order to suggest a vast background unmentioned but mentionable, so the realistic novelist, Flaubert, for example, describes with precision a number of nonessential facts, thereby implying a wealth of possible items as great as reality itself. Barthes's point is that the sheer gratuity of these items stands in stark contrast with the "necessity" of the story. Their essential unpredictability is the textual function of "reality" as distinct from meaning-direction (*sens*), which is intelligible and predictive in the expectations it creates. As Ankersmit observes apropos of Barthes, "the reality of the past is an *effect* caused by a tension in and between historical texts" (*HT* 140).[14] In Barthes's words: "In 'objective' history, the 'real' is never anything but an unformulated signified, sheltered behind the apparent omnipotence of the referent."[15]

The similarities and differences with Sartre's view are illuminating. On the one hand, as if describing the practico-inert, Barthes grants the text an autonomy of signification by which it communicates a morality, an ideology, a worldview unsuspected by the author or the reader.[16] But he finds the "reality effect" entirely within the text or between texts, not in any presumed relation between the text and the nontextual. To think otherwise, for Barthes, is to fall prey to the "referential illusion."[17] Clearly, Sartre's "realism" will not be satisfied by this failure to relate to the heterogeneous, the nontextual. His continued use of intentionality is motivated in large part by the desire to overcome idealism, including textual idealism. The function of the "reality effect," if we may use such a term for Sartre, is played both by his appeal to Gaston Bachelard's "coefficient of adversity" (the bald recalcitrance of the material world)[18] and by what we might call the "risk factor," namely, the agent's lively awareness of the unpredictable consequences of his or her act. But more than a purely psychological *Erlebnis* or a feature of probabilistic reasoning, the risk factor is a function of the *contingency* of reality itself, a theme that Sartre exhibited novelistically in *Nausea*.[19]

Finally, both Barthes and Sartre take the nineteenth-century realist novel as the model for historical writing. Barthes reveals this in several essays as well as in his study of the renowned French historian Jules Michelet.[20]

By drawing attention to the fittingness of the story to the guiding ideal and the constitutive role of imaging consciousness in Sartre's theory of history, I do not wish in the least to dissolve the moral message of the *Critique* in the liquor of aestheticism. Sartre was, after all, the originator of the phrase "committed literature" as well as the implacable foe of *l'art pour l'art*. But appeal to narrative history serves to underscore the kind of "truth" and "evidence" that one should expect to find in his histories. Their truth will be a function of their emancipating power to further the advent of the "reign of freedom" or the "city of ends."

Another example of "committed history" may help to clarify what I take to be this dimension of Sartre's enterprise. Apropos of the Zionist interpretation of the Holocaust, Hayden White observes: "Its truth, as a historical interpretation, consists precisely of its effectiveness in justifying a wide range of current Israeli political policies that, from the standpoint of those who articulate them, are crucial to the security and indeed the very existence of the Jewish people" (*C* 80). In Sartre's case, the evidence adduced will be primarily that which justifies dialectical (that is, totalizing) reasoning, namely, the experience of dialectical circularity and what he calls "dialectical necessity." All other evidence—for example, information regarding the prehistory and protohistory of the agents in question, structural relations such as social and economic institutions, cultural practices, "mentalities," and the like—is of use only insofar as it is relevant to the emancipatory project. Such is the praxis of the "committed historian." I hope to have confirmed this hypothesis by a detailed reading of the notes for volume 2 of the *Critique,* subtitled "The Intelligibility of History."

It is clear that Sartre labors far from the "scientific" history of those who would find in our study of the past mere instantiations of general laws, even laws of a statistical nature. Cause-effect relations have always characterized uniquely the realm of nature, for Sartre. And yet we see him seeking an intelligibility in history that exceeds simple temporal continuity. Dialectical relationships afford him this new intelligibility, but only insofar as they incorporate freedom and contingency, the two root ideas (*idées-racines*) of his life's work.[21] So his task is to relate dialectic and narrative. The *mythos* must connect individual and collective praxes, but with a necessity that respects their freedom and existential contingency. Without freedom, history's moral character is lost; without contingency, its nature as history evaporates.[22] The key factor is the concept of dialectical necessity as we saw in chapter 3.

But, I have argued, integral to Sartre's dialectic is the ideal of a socialism of abundance where nonalienating reciprocities would prevail, the fraternity of the reign of freedom. This practical *als ob* is an imaginative extrapolation from our experience in closely knit groups. Imagination obviously plays a major role in the dialectic through the projective totalization of the past. It is this paradoxical "action of the future [on the present]" (*SM* 92 n) that Sartre takes as essential to dialectical intelligibility. As the locus of possibility and ideal ends, imagination is intrinsic to any Sartrean dialectic. But it figures in several other aspects of his theory of history.

We have seen the parallel Sartre draws between understanding, a work of art and comprehending another freedom. This practical hermeneutic not only grasps the point of the other's praxis, it incorporates that awareness into the undertaking that defines its own project. This too is clearly the work of imagination.

Likewise, the concrete universals that are the goal of dialectical understanding—Flaubert, for example, as the author of *Madame Bovary,* or Stalin as the director of the five-year plans—these are "notions" that incorporate the temporally future as well as the ontologically possible, for which imagination is requisite. Though he does not use the expression "historical imagination," Sartre's appeal to the concrete or singular universal is clearly the fruit of comprehensive imaging: Genet *as . . .* , Flaubert *as . . .*

It should be clear that I am taking "aesthetic" in its broadest sense, to include not merely the "beautiful," but also what since Longinus has come to be called the "sublime." The latter category entails both imaginative and emotive consciousness in addition to its cognitive grounding. Sartre's aesthetic of history expresses an ontology that synthesizes the primacy of praxis and imaging consciousness with the politico-ethical ideal of "what could be" as critical mirror of what is.[23]

In an interesting and provocative essay, White notes the rhetorical role that history played until its conversion into an academic discipline during the last century. The price of its scientific legitimacy, he argues, was a repression of what, following Schiller, he calls the "historical sublime," namely, the delight one might feel before the spectacle of human freedom throughout history, "the uncertain anarchy of the moral world."[24] This link of the historical, the aesthetic, and the moral (political) is broken by the professional domestication of the historian, who claims to eschew the utopian, the rhetorical, and the political in his or her rage for neutrality and scientific "objectivity." White points out that this "disciplining . . . of the historical imagination" helps "constitute what can count as a specifically historical fact" (*C* 66). In effect, "historical facts are politically domesticated precisely insofar as they are effectively removed from displaying any aspect of the sublime that Schiller attributed to them in his essay of 1801" (*C* 72). But, White argues, such

facts thereby exclude a "politics of vision . . . more concerned to endow
social life with meaning than with beauty." As if to comment on Sartre's
vision of the city of ends, he adds: "In my view, the theorists of the sublime had correctly divined that whatever dignity and freedom human
beings could lay claim to could come only by way of what Freud called a
'reaction-formation' to an apperception of history's meaninglessness."
White sees Marxist "rationalism" as an obstacle to the historical sublime
much as Sartre is critical of the (social) engineer. But it is precisely Sartre's model of the artist and of creative freedoms in reciprocal interchange within a fundamentally contingent world that saves him from
White's strictures. For Sartre as for White, the role of utopian thought is
to "goad living human beings . . . to endow their lives with a meaning
for which they alone are fully responsible" (*C* 72).[25]

Reconstituting Praxis

Recall that Sartre's initial project of wedding biography to history was
to establish "an internal relation of comprehension" between the subject and his time—what we have emblemized as "the kaiser's withered
arm." Its point is to "comprehend the other's comprehension" by a dialectical move that resembles what Collingwood advocated under the title of "re-enactment" and Johan Huizinga, following Dilthey, described
as *Nacherleben*. We will better appreciate Sartre's method by comparing
it with these analogous approaches.

A practitioner of what Frederick Olafson calls "analytic hermeneutics," Collingwood claimed that "all history is the re-enactment of past
thought in the historian's own mind."[26] We imaginatively relive the
very thoughts of Caesar, for example, as he makes the fateful decision to
transgress the boundary of the Rubicon. Although such reenactment relies on all the relevant information which the informed historian can
muster, and though Collingwood is careful to distinguish the respective
"immediacies" (contexts) of Caesar's reasoning and the historian's,
what he calls their "acts of thought . . . in their mediation" (by which he
seems to mean their logical form and perhaps even their psychological
force) can be one and the same.[27] This re-enactment of Caesar's thought
is the work of what Collingwood terms "the *a priori* imagination," that
necessary piece of the "furniture of the mind" that closes the gaps in our
necessarily fragmented information about the world.[28] It functions as
the "historical imagination" when its objective is to frame a "coherent

and continuous picture" of the past.[29] He concludes that "the historian's picture of the past is thus in every detail an imaginary picture, and its necessity is at every point the necessity of the *a priori* imagination." This leads him to the further conclusion that "as works of the imagination, the historian's work and the novelist's do not differ. Where they do differ is that the historian's picture is meant to be true."[30] A novel that is true?

Much as the reader of a novel becomes engaged in the plot, the historian imaginatively reconstructs the agent's thinking, vivifying the inert data with his or her studied purposiveness. While it is imperative to gather as much of that data as possible, the hermeneutical moment arrives when one must shift from seeing to "reading" (seeing as). What distinguishes this approach from that of Sartre is its "covert flirtation" with a form of the "covering law model" of analytic historiography, as Ankersmit, Olafson, Rex Martin, and others have pointed out.[31] In other words, the analytic interpreter is not opting for understanding over explanation, as is commonly supposed, but rather is using understanding to further explanation in the manner of "what any such x would do if p." The thoughts at that moment are not Caesar's as such but those of any rational agent.[32]

Sartre, who would assign the covering law to analytical Reason, is playing in a different register. He underscores the historian's own situatedness (*SM* 32 n) as well as the "totalizing" nature of the latter's comprehension as praxis. The touchstone of lived reality, for Sartre, is the risk it entails. By reducing risk to mere ignorance that an ideal observer would not suffer, analytic reason dissolves lived reality (*le vécu*) as well. I think Sartre's chief criticism of Collingwood's account of re-enactment would be that it misses the anguish of the lived experience by focusing on antiseptic, "mediated thought."

As I suggested apropos of Barthes's reality effect, Sartre's existentialist account turns on lived experience (*le vécu*), especially in its future dimension of possibility and risk. "To have a body," he insists, "is to be in danger in the world in order to change it. This is what justifies pessimism and suppresses it at the same time. Everything may always turn out badly, but I am the being through which all good *and* bad endings come into the world. I am the being from whom *risk* is born" (*NE* 316). Appealing to a technical term that we have discussed in chapter 4, Sartre would say of Collingwood what he said of Hegel: "[His] philosophy is a

History in the sense that History is a discipline turned toward the past. Not a *historialization* in the sense that it really unveils the future dimension. For the future dimension is ignorance, risk, uncertainty, a wager" (*NE* 467). Disembodied spirit (*nous*) may follow a sequence of arguments, but it has no "history," it runs no risks.

While rejecting the expression "historical imagination," the distinguished historian Johan Huizinga defends a concept of "historical sensation" similar to what Humboldt called *Ahnung* (presentiment). In a manner that resonates both with Sartre's remarks about Michelangelo's *David* incarnating the *sens* of the Renaissance and with his description of the work of art as a generous appeal from one freedom to another, Huizinga writes:

> This not completely reducible contact with the past is an entry into an atmosphere, it is one of the many forms of reaching beyond oneself, of experiencing truth, which are given to man. . . . This contact with the past, which is accompanied by an utter conviction of genuineness and truth, can be evoked by a line from a document or a chronicle, by a print, by a few notes of an old song. It is not an element that the writer infuses in his work by using certain words. It lies beyond the book of history, not in it. The reader brings it to the writer, it is his response to the writer's call.

Though it is in the same line as our aesthetic enjoyment, religious emotion, and awe of nature, Huizinga does not want to psychologize the phenomenon of historical sensation:

> If it is this element in the understanding of history which is indicated by many historians as re-experiencing [*Nacherleben*], then it is the term that is wrong. "Re-experiencing" indicates much too definite a psychological process. One does not realize the historical sensation as a re-experiencing, but as an understanding that is closely related to the understanding of music, or rather of the world by means of music. Re-experiencing as a method of cognition assumes a more or less continuous perception constantly accompanying the labor of reading and thinking. In reality this sensation, vision, contact, *Ahnung*, is limited to moments of special intellectual clarity, moments of a sudden penetration of the spirit.

Huizinga concludes that "this historical sensation is apparently so essential that it is felt again and again as the true moment of historical cognition."[33] Still, he is quick to assure us, "it is merely one part of historical understanding." The main point of great historiography, he soberly reminds us, is to cause one "not to experience moods, but to understand contexts."[34]

If it is Sartre's existential realism, appealing to the experiences of adversity and risk and relying on intentionality, that moves him beyond Collingwood's Platonism, it is his emphasis on the performative character of historiography as reconstituting praxis that distinguishes him from Huizinga, with whose thought he has more in common. Both share a sympathy for what literary critics now call "reader response" theory, in the basic sense that understanding is "brought" to the text more than it is "found" there. Yet neither writer wants to sacrifice such "comprehension" to purely aesthetic considerations.[35] It is not a case of epistemic subjectivism or moral anarchy. In Sartre's case, the root of the problem of objective meaning lies in the basic ambiguity of the "given" and the "taken" (of what is "found" and what is "brought") in/from a situation or a text.

As we have seen, for Sartre the historian's opus, like a historical painting of Charles V, is an analogon that beckons us to reactivate the event "of flesh and blood" in its imaginative mode as "present-absent." It is not a matter of recollection, unless the event in question is one we had experienced in person. But neither is it a pure "fabrication," since its historical character requires a link with the once perceptual or, at least, the immediately experienceable (with what Collingwood calls "evidence"). The micrototalizations of events and anecdotes are ingredients in the emancipatory praxis of the macrototalization under way. Once again, Sartre's rigorous use of intentionality sustains his robust (in this case, historical) realism.

Just as the imaginative reconstitution of Charles V requires a distinctively cognitive component that extends beyond mere physical resemblance (itself problematic, given that none of us has ever seen the subject in person), and as the factual claims of the Genet biography are open to falsification within certain limits ("in that or some other way") without changing the plausibility of the narrative, so the analogon of the historical event is subject to a kind of falsification in that it might misfire by failing to promote and guide the expected/intended reconstitution. It would not enable us to invest the analogon with "presence" whereby the *sens* of the event is grasped. But this liability at the microlevel reappears in an expanded, if somewhat different, sense at the macrolevel. There its falsehood will be a function of its inappropriateness to the liberating project. In this sense, purely analytic (for example, structuralist) accounts would be inappropriate and to that extent false, whereas counterfinalities and other dialectical setbacks ("counterevidence," if you will) would be most relevant. Ankersmit seems to have something like this in mind, minus the reference to dialectical reason, when he observes: "We tend to regard a text consisting of true but irrelevant statements as 'less true' than a relevant text which contains some factual errors" (*HT* 136).

THE MORAL OF THE STORY: HISTORY AND BAD FAITH

Narrativizing discourse serves the purpose of moralizing judgments.
—Hayden White, *The Content of the Form*

We said at the outset that Sartre was a moralist. At his death, a leading Parisian newspaper announced that "France has lost its conscience." Sartre defended his extended study of Flaubert as a socialist work "in the sense that, if I succeed, it will allow us to advance in the comprehension of men from a socialist viewpoint" (*ORR* 73–74). As such, he admits, it will belong to that future culture, popular and socialist, to which he is committed, "provided there are mediations" (*ORR* 74); in other words, on the condition that the work is approached via dialectical reason. Given Sartre's view of the link between class identity and forms of reason, one's "choice" of rationality is a moral one. So too is one's corresponding "choice" of History/histories.

"Let us say that the Flaubert is a concrete application of the abstract principles that I have given in the *Critique of Dialectical Reason* to ground the intelligibility of History" (*ORR* 77). If so, it is more than an exercise in dialectical intelligibility. As a model "socialist" biography, it is a political act. But as an existentialist praxis, it is replete with moral significance. Sartre's depiction of Second Empire society is a portrait of collective bad faith. His account of Flaubert's "choice" of the imaginary, of the need to make himself *l'homme imaginaire,* of his nihilism and misanthropy, stands in condemnation of the exploitative relations that produced the public that avidly seized the baited trap of *Madame Bovary*. Biography has shifted dialectically into literary history, which in turn is subsumed in political and cultural critique—under the guiding value of concrete freedom, its structural exploitation, and its personal oppression.

Merleau-Ponty once noted perceptively that Sartre always privileges oppression over exploitation, the implication being that his Marxism could never be genuine. While this is not the place to pursue the semantics of what makes one a genuine Marxist, it is clear that Sartre's contribution to Marxist historiography is his emphasis on what I have called the "primacy of (individual) praxis" and, in the present context, its moral primacy ("It is men whom we judge and not physical forces" [*SM* 47]). The image that Sartre re-presents of the Flaubert "of flesh and blood" is colored by ethical concerns. As with his earlier accounts of industrial capitalism, racism, and colonialism, the meanness is not entirely in the system.[36] If one side of Sartre's Janus-faced freedom is hope ("you can always make something out of what you've been made into"), its other visage is moral responsibility: behind exploitative necessities lie oppressive choices. The moral of Sartrean narrative in its dialectic of the biographical and the historical is that *there is always a moral* to be drawn.

AN EXISTENTIALIST THEORY OF HISTORY

Machiavelli proposed his *Florentine Histories* as a set of lessons to be learned, specifically regarding the opposition between *fortuna* and *virtù*.[37] This was, indeed, a leading rhetorical use of history that prevailed at least until its scientific professionalization in the nineteenth century.[38] As we have just remarked, it is a defining characteristic of Sartre's theory of history as existentialist that this rhetorical use be revived. To this end existentialist moral responsibility must be preserved throughout the most tortuous workings of impersonal processes and collective endeavors. The concept of the *practico*-inert transmits the influence of previous praxes, and the genius of the mediating third is precisely to guard the responsibility of the group member in the midst of historically efficacious group activity. It is this primacy of praxis that carries into history the moral claim from Sartre's vintage existentialism that "we are without excuse."

Second, this same praxis, as "translucid" and homogeneous with group praxis, also grounds the dialectical intelligibility of concrete history. No doubt, practico-inert structures, essences, and the like are intelligible without immediate reference to praxis. But by themselves they yield the abstract, conceptual knowledge proper to analytical Reason. In the concrete social realm, that of series, groups, and institutions in inter-action, the intelligibility is dialectical and the dialectic is constituted by individual, totalizing praxes.[39]

The third feature of an existentialist theory is its respect for the speci-ficity of the social, in opposition to methodological individualism, which tends to reduce the social to the psychological. It is precisely the function of the mediating third (as a practical, constitutive relation and not just a psychological experience) to steer a middle course between methodological holism and individualism in social theory. Although the group is a synthetic enrichment of individual action and irreducible to it, the collective subject of history is nothing more than praxes in practical relation; in no way is it a superorganism (as Sartre takes Durkheim's collective consciousness to be). Again, the point of this dialectical nomi-nalism is to preserve the primacy of an (admittedly socially "enriched") organic praxis in historical understanding.

It should not be surprising, fourth, to find a concept of collective bad faith at work in Sartre's historical analyses. This extrapolation of the dividedness of human reality to the collective domain is based on the concept of "objective spirit," which, in the case of the French industrial bourgeoisie in the late 1800s, for example, masked oppressive action under the ideology of the rights of man. It is the primacy of praxis once more that enables Sartre to apply categories from his existentialist clas-sic to the analyses of nineteenth-century French social history.

Finally, the existentialist concept of committed literature is extended to committed history. Sartre's theory not merely analyzes but advocates a certain totalizing view. As we noted earlier, his continued writing of the Flaubert study in the midst of the student uprising of 1968 was justi-fied in part by the fact that this was a "socialist" approach to biography, much as Michelet's was a "republican" approach to history. If, as we have seen him insist, the historical "facts" are ambiguous, allowing for a multiplicity of readings, then the interpretation which emerges as "true" for our times is the one that gives hope and purpose to the op-pressed of the world. This, in effect, is Sartre's guide for writing histo-ries and biographies that totalize one another. The ideal which inspires these efforts is called variously the "city of ends," a "socialism of abun-dance," or simply "freedom."

Did Sartre's theory anticipate the linguistic turn that historiography was taking at the time of his death? We must admit at the outset that he has no explicit philosophy of language.[40] But by locating speech acts and language (roughly, *parole* and *langue*) in the conceptual space of "praxis" and "practico-inert" respectively, he was able to pursue the linguistic dimension of social reality in both its synchronic and diachronic aspects. His mistrust of linguocentrism never weakened his regard for the situating as well as the transgressive power of speech.[41]

The sustaining question of Sartre's theory of history, Can there be totalization without a totalizer? must find its response in the features just listed. The *sens* that the dialectical historian discovers/achieves is the actualization of an enveloping totalization, which in turn reflects the dialectical interplay of organic praxis and its practico-inert conditions. But the primacy of organic praxis, which dialectical nominalism demands, seems to exclude any larger historical unity that is neither praxis nor a relation among praxes. The experience of dialectical necessity, where the exigencies and counterfinalities of the practico-inert reveal their positive force, might be taken to support the claim that some larger logic is directing the unintended results of individual actions. Sartre's growing sense of objective possibility in his later works attests to the power of the practico-inert and the force of circumstance.[42] But he has neither the conceptual equipment nor, arguably, the need to interpret these necessities as anything more than the force of inertia (facticity) that praxis brings into play. Whether this force is unifying or disruptive, whether it advances History or retards it, though dialectically dependent on the inertial force itself (the exercise of freedom is fostered by some conditions and thwarted by others) hangs, in the final analysis, on the use or abuse of individual freedoms.

LIMITS OF COMMITTED HISTORY

Before undertaking an explicit confrontation between Sartre and Michel Foucault in my concluding chapter, let me underscore what I take to be the chief weaknesses of Sartre's philosophy of history as I have reconstructed it. Not surprisingly, these liabilities stem from his existentialist philosophy as such, intensified by its attempted synthesis with Marxist social thought. I shall focus on four categories—the ontological, the epistemic, the moral, and the aesthetic. Together, they lend Sartre's theory its unique and original character; separately, they expose its vulnerabilities.

Ontological Limits. Sartre was a philosopher of being. His masterwork, *Being and Nothingness,* begins with an all-too-brief reference to "the notion of being in general" that encompasses his famous divisions of *en-soi* and *pour-soi* (*BN* lxiii).[43] Indeed, toward the end of his life he reaffirmed that "one must either begin with being or go back to it, like Heidegger." And he insisted that this ontological approach constituted his real difference from Marxism, which did not begin with being but with a kind of being, namely, class-being (*PS* 14). Sartre's much-proclaimed ontological dualism is not the Cartesian dichotomy of consciousness/matter but is the more profound duality of spontaneity/inertia. Whether as being-for-itself or praxis, the "prodigious power of the negative" that Descartes failed to tap breaks forth in Sartre's account of freedom, meaning, action, and event.

But each of these concepts suffers from a legacy of ambiguity inherited from the spontaneity/inertia pair. As we have observed repeatedly throughout our study, it becomes impossible to determine the "given" from the "taken" in any situation. Once freedom becomes "concrete" so that it implies the freedom of others ("EH" 307–8), its circumstantial conditioning grows apace. So too in the case of meanings: they are not merely projected by consciousness on a blank noematic screen but constitute the practico-inert limits of sense-making in a given society. As action thickens into praxis, its social and historical dimension expands accordingly. Even the "pure" event of Sartre's *War Diaries* remains an abstraction until it has been "dated," that is, incorporated into the complex of givens that are put into play ("taken" up) by our projects.

Of course, Sartre would respond that this urge to divide and quantify bespeaks the very analytic prejudice he is attempting to transcend. Dialectical Reason, one must conclude, is a logic of ambiguity (in the analytic sense). By incorporating the "is/was" of temporality into its "notions," such reason respects the processive character of its subject matter. But it thereby leaves in suspense definite answers to the what and whether of our historical inquiries. Above all, it eschews any but internal critique, which strikes the outsider as dogmatic. In a sense, Sartre's criticism of Hegel has come home to roost: either we are in stasis and History is at an end, or we are in process and History eludes any but provisional and ideal forms of intelligibility. Not surprisingly, this refers the matter to epistemology.

Epistemic Problems. In the course of his Gifford Lectures, the first volume of which is devoted to the *Critique of Dialectical Reason,* Raymond Aron observes: "Sartre is scarcely troubled by epistemology and perhaps would never have examined the methodology of the social sciences nor written of a prolegomena to every future anthropology had circumstances not forced him into a dialogue with Marxism-Leninism."[44] Though perhaps an accurate assessment of Sartre's move toward heuristic dialectic at midcareer, this overlooks the epistemological concern implicit in the work of every practicing phenomenologist. And it shows no inkling of Sartre's early critique of Aron's own writing on historical objectivity that lay concealed in the *Diaries.* But Aron is correct to imply that Sartre's *ex professo* treatment of methodological questions appeared only with *Search for a Method* (1960).

The epistemic difficulties with Sartre's approach to historical intelligibility concern first of all the adequacy of the *Verstehen* model in whatever form it takes. This approach has often been criticized for its imprecision, its subjectivity, and its unavailability to public confirmation or disconfirmation. Although Sartre is careful to insist that *Verstehen* is not the exercise of some esoteric faculty—that we use our comprehension every time we deal with another human being—he shows a rather uncritical confidence in its reliability and freedom from prejudice. We have seen him adopt the Heideggerian "pre-"understanding of numerous aspects of our world, but he never bothers to defend those claims or to subject them to critical scrutiny. Given the major role of comprehension in the progressive phase of his progressive-regressive method, this is a serious weakness. To that extent, Aron is right about Sartre's epistemic insouciance.

A second difficulty concerns our knowledge of the "absolute" historical event. From the moment he discovered Husserlian phenomenology, Sartre was an intuitionist in the sense that he brought investigation to a close with an immediate grasp of the essence, which he understood as "the principle of the series" of manifestations of the object (*BN* xlvi), that is, of the thing "in flesh and blood." He never abandoned intentionality as the instrument for achieving his robust realism. For example, extending his analysis of the realist painting to our knowledge of the historical event, Sartre clearly assumes that it is the "absolute event" that is ingredient in our historical accounts. Still, that event by definition remains out of reach for perceptual knowledge (the touchstone of Sartrean realism as it was for Husserl). It seems that we must approach it as an "ideal term" of our convergent descriptions, much as Husserl dealt with the physical object. In fact, we found Sartre using the Husserlian concept of "profiles" to accommodate the "pluridimensionality" of the event to its ontological unity. As we noted at the time, this looks like a promising move. It was employed to similar advantage by Merleau-Ponty. It accounts for the singularity of the historical event and the multiplicity of its interpretations, without entrapping Sartre in the relativistic perspectivism in which Nietzsche was tangled. One and the same event can support many descriptions. But this leaves us as much in doubt about Sartre's historical realism as he was about Husserl's. For it turns in Husserl's case, at least, on a transcendental consciousness, and for Husserl and for Sartre on the primacy of perceptual consciousness, which Sartre never defends, though he has assumed it at least since *The Psychology of Imagination* (1940).

But Sartre's difficulties increase when he shifts from Husserlian contemplation toward praxis and the dialectic. The historical event, for dialectical Reason, is a moving target. Its liabilities are both ontological and epistemic as befits a dialectical phenomenon. Sartre's all-too-simple ontological account of dialectical nominalism—the claim that "there are only men and real relations between them"—leaves unclarified the nature of these relations. Are they internal and constitutive? In which case the "men" intrinsically bound together and the nominalistic individual are absorbed in the nodal points of these relations—an odd kind of nominalism. There are times when Sartre speaks in this manner. Consider the question posed in *Being and Nothingness* of whether an agent could have acted otherwise or not. Sartre responds that the question should be formulated: "Could I have done otherwise without perceptibly modifying the organic totality of the projects which I am? . . . I could have done otherwise. Agreed. But *at what price?*" (*BN* 454). In other words, the link between self-defining "project" and at least some of the individual actions that instantiate it appears to be internal. This bodes well for the specificity of social phenomena, but it threatens the consistency of Sartre's nominalism.

And yet Sartre does distinguish between "secondary possibles," which at times, he claims, resemble the Stoic "indifferents" and the "fundamental possible of the formal totality of my possibles" (*BN* 470). So it seems that at least some of these real relations are "external" and are even "constituted" by organic praxis. The latter is clearly implied by the threefold primacy of individual praxis that we have been defending. But this leaves their properly "social" dimension seriously compromised, as his critics have never failed to point out.[45]

But with the weakening of Sartre's nominalism, the spontaneity/inertia ambiguity returns with a vengeance. For the very notion of "event" displays both a permanence and a malleability insofar as it suffers a multiplicity of possible descriptions according to the interest of the narrator. And this reproduces at the epistemic level the ambiguity of the given and the taken at a most foundational site. Even appeal to perceptual immediacy will not solidify the fluidity of its concomitant interpretative moment, due to the indeterminacy of the seeing/reading distinction. And this indeterminacy may disqualify Sartre's Husserlian use of "profiles" just mentioned. For unless the perceptual primacy of the event can be safeguarded from hermeneutical infection, we slip back into a Nietzschean infinity of interpretations of interpretations, "all the way down." For it seems that no account of the "given" can be offered that does not implicitly entail appeal to its mode of givenness. And it is not clear how simple appeal to being-in-itself, absent any reference to a transcendental field, can warrant the claims Sartre makes for the "absolute" event. In other words, having abandoned the raft of the transcendental ego early in his career, Sartre may be caught in the whirlpool of relativism despite his frantic realist splashing.

The root of these problems, I believe, lies in a fatal ambiguity in Sartre's own epistemology, his simultaneous subscription to two mutually incompatible theories of knowledge, evidence, and truth. Elsewhere I have characterized these as epistemologies of praxis and of vision.[46] Without repeating the argument here, suffice it to note that the linguistic symptom of this ambiguity is his simultaneous use of phenomenological and dialectical discourses, especially in *The Family Idiot.*[47]

Moral Weaknesses. The foregoing ambiguities undermine what I have argued is Sartre's overarching concern, the moral responsibility of the historical agent. The diachronic structures of the practico-inert, with their sedimentation of synchronic praxes, witness to the prior use and abuse of individual freedom. But the category of objective spirit ("culture as practico-inert") introduces the social dimension of moral responsibility. As Sartre wrote of capitalism, "the meanness is in the system" (*CP* 138). But what he criticizes as the systems of capitalism, racism, and colonialism falls into the category of praxis-process or what, in the context of historical intelligibility in *Critique 2,* he calls "enveloping totalization." In other words, there is a moral dimension to our overarching sense-making praxes. And history, as the *narratio rerum gestarum,* can be as authentic or inauthentic as any praxis.

But what would "authentic" historiography denote? If we extrapolate from Sartre's not unproblematic use of personal "authenticity," we may conclude that it is based on the practically acknowledged truth of the human condition, namely, that individually (and now collectively) we are not substantial selves but nonsubstantial "presences to self," beings who introduce and sustain a temporalizing, totalizing "distance" or "otherness" into every relationship, including the relation to our past.[48] In history, too, "existence precedes essence." So the authentic historian would acknowledge the social and diachronic non-identity of historical action, its fundamental ambiguity, its risks, and the performative nature of his or her enterprise.[49] Authentic historiographic poiesis would unmask the violence and bad faith at work in human history, while fostering the individual and social freedom, the account of which is being written. And that requires that the enveloping totalization be assessed from the moral point of view.[50]

Here is where the difficulties arise. For the ascription of moral predicates to structures and impersonal processes (such as the economic need for a certain level of unemployment in a capitalist system) is a metaphorical use of terms from Sartre's individualist vocabulary. The "meanness" is not entirely in the system. Indeed, it is not primarily in the system, but in the choices of those who sustain it—the standard Sartrean position that we have called "the moral primacy of individual praxis." And it is at this point that his spontaneity/inertia ambiguity returns to haunt him. For he has come to allow that the practico-inert establishes objective possibilities and impossibilities: "It is history which shows some the exits and makes others cool their heels before closed doors" (*CP* 80), and the *Family Idiot* describes these as conditioning factors in our personalizing spirals. If Cromwell had had the benefit of orthoscopic surgery, if Grouchy had arrived on time, if Flaubert had lived in the era of HMOs, if Stalin had not been paranoid . . . The transcendental fact of material scarcity turns practico-inert mediation into violence, and "violence" remains the counterconcept to "fraternity," related as the unethical to the ethical in Sartre's social thought. The point is that these conditions are not simply formal but include a specific content that can be characterized as moral. In other words, if the motto of Sartrean humanism is "you can always make something out of what you've been made into," the debilitating and even enslaving character of your historical situation ("what you've been made into") is more a "given" than a "taken." The nature and degree of one's moral responsibility should be graded accordingly, a refinement that Sartre never bothers to make. Sartre's lengthy discussion of the situation of young post-Romantic writers in the age of Louis-Philippe as an "objective neurosis" and his implicit ascription of collective bad faith to the Second-Empire bourgeoisie are examples that trade on this underlying ambiguity of the given and the taken. If its roots are ontological, and its branches epistemic, its fruit is a softening of the force of Sartre's moral ascriptions.

Historical Inadequacies. Marx, with his deterministic appeal to the material conditions of life, has been criticized for applying to history Aristotle's injunction to explain the many through one. He thereby disregarded this same Aristotle's caution against seeking a degree of precision in a field of inquiry, greater than the subject matter allows. Specifically, he disregarded the Stagirite's advice not to look for mathematical intelligibility in human affairs, where we are limited to what occurs "for the most part."

Sartre's use of "material scarcity" has been subject to a similar critique. Its appeal lies in both its simplicity and its generality. He defends Marx's thesis about the predominance of "the mode of production of material life" over social, political, and intellectual life as pointing to "a factual evidence which we cannot go beyond *so long as* the transformations of social relations and technical progress have not freed man from the yoke of scarcity" (*SM* 34). What Klaus Hartmann calls "a version of the principle of the contingency (of being)," scarcity colors all history as we know it but need not apply to prehistorical peoples, if such there were, nor to all possible worlds.[51] In other words, scarcity is profoundly historical in nature and yet curiously a priori in function. One might liken it to a Foucauldian "historical a priori."

Of course, the "one size fits all" simplicity of this Sartrean principle invokes again the ambiguity of the given/taken. The very meaning of "scarcity" is both need- and desire-relative, and needs and desires are notoriously historical. Although when pressed, Sartre agrees that scarcity originally is an "objective lack" and that need is "a normal biological characteristic of the living creature," he insists that "naturally the greatest scarcity is always the one based on social oppression. . . . We create a field of scarcity around us" (*PS* 31).

Such ambiguity invites a dialectic, and Sartre is quick to oblige:

> Everything is to be explained through *need* [*le besoin*]; need is the first totalizing relation between the material being, man, and the material ensemble of which he is part. . . . Indeed, it is through need that the first negation of the negation and the first totalization appear in matter. . . . The original negation, in fact, is an initial contradiction between the organic and the inorganic. . . . As soon as need appears, surrounding matter is endowed with a passive unity, in that a developing totalization is reflected in it as a totality. . . . Already, it is in terms of the total field that need seeks possibilities of satisfaction in nature, and it is thus totalization which will reveal in the passive totality its own material being as abundance or scarcity. (*CDR* 1:80–81)[52]

So Sartre interprets the need-scarcity relationship in an explicitly dialectical manner, but the terms of the dialectic can shift. Sometimes he reads (biological) need as "natural," scarcity as negation, and praxis (work) as the negation of that negation.[53] At other times need itself is interpreted as negation of negation.[54] Similarly, he distinguishes the "formal dialectic" of scarcity, which he is analyzing in the *Critique,* from "a historical, concrete dialectic" about which he intends to be silent "since it is for historians to retrace its moments." But within the formal dialectic, he distinguishes absolute from relative scarcity, without locating the former in a biological context (*CDR* 1:153 n). He subsequently adds that "strictly speaking, scarcity is not social. Society comes after scarcity. The latter is an original phenomenon of the relation between man and Nature.[55]

When he speaks of a socialism of abundance, Sartre seems to have in mind both a political arrangement and an economic condition. But the overcoming of some scarcities—lack of time or of ideas, for example— seems incompatible with the human condition as such. Yet to conclude that human history will forever be one of violence ("interiorized scarcity") and bewitchment would likewise counter his remarks about the end of prehistory and the new, currently unimaginable philosophy of freedom that would emerge "as soon as there will exist *for everyone* a margin of *real* freedom beyond the production of life" (*SM* 34). Clearly, not all scarcities are of a piece.[56]

Finally, Sartre's Rousseauian tendency to see the darkness of human history as simply the shadow cast by material scarcity on human freedom, while in accordance with his abiding hope, is difficult to reconcile with our experience of moral evil. More than a scruple, the recalcitrance of moral evil constitutes a fatal flaw in a theory of history that aims to respect a constitutive role for moral responsibility amid structural relations and historical necessities. In the long run, mere counterfinality will not suffice to make sense of it. Sometimes one gets just what one wants, sometimes what one deserves; oftentimes they are distinctly different. It is this tragic sense of Sartrean hope and the history it fashions that make his theory a kind of failed theodicy—a secular theodicy, no doubt, but a theodicy nonetheless.[57]

Chapter Ten
History and Structure:
Sartre and Foucault

" *The Critique of Dialectical Reason* is the magnificent and pathetic attempt by a man of the nineteenth century to think the twentieth century. In that sense, Sartre is the last Hegelian and, I would even say, the last Marxist."[1] Obviously, Foucault had in mind more than the existentialist's fascination with, if not fixation on, nineteenth-century poets and novelists. For someone who would baptize his new position at the Collège de France "Chair in the History of the Systems of Thought," Foucault's term "systems" says it all. Conjoined with the word "history," it states the question with which I wish to conclude this first portion of my comparative study. If Marx found Hegel on his head and set him right-side up, Foucault took Sartre's existentialist dictum, "It is men whom we judge and not physical forces" (*SM* 47) and turned it inside out, but with structural constraint replacing physical force, Saussure subtending Hobbes and Marx.

As if to reenforce Foucault's inversion and discount the kaiser's withered arm, a contemporary philosopher of history informs us that "twentieth-century historiography prefers to see the past from a point of view different from that of the historical

Making historical analysis the discourse of the continuous and making human consciousness the original subject of all historical development and all action are the two sides of the same system of thought. In this system, time is conceived in terms of totalization and revolutions are never more than moments of consciousness.
—Foucault, *Archaeology of Knowledge*

agents themselves and this reduces the intention of analytical hermeneutics to a futile enterprise" (*HT* 99). But a major problem of this description for Foucault, as for twentieth-century historiography in general, is to determine just where what we might call this "point of view that is not one" is to be located—the Archimedean challenge. Richard Rorty suggests the sketch of the postmodern answer to this challenge when he remarks: "Edifying philosophers have to decry the very notion of having a view, while avoiding having a view about having views."[2] In other words, they simply refuse to pick up the gauntlet.

By confronting Sartre and Foucault on the question of reason in history, my concluding chapter broaches the issue of the difference between a modern and a postmodern approach to historical intelligibility and, indeed, to rationality in general. One should regard what follows as a summing up of the Sartrean brief and an initial statement of Foucault's case. I shall argue the latter at length in the next volume.

Since Foucault denominates his enterprise a "history" of systems, we encounter a difficulty similar to the one Sartre had faced of constructing a "historical, structural" anthropology. No doubt, the two approaches separate at the crossroads of history and anthropology (the latter taken in the broader, French sense of "human sciences" or *sciences de l'homme*) because it is precisely the relationship of history to *l'homme* that is at issue. The much-debated history/structure problem is really a controversy over the meaning and function of "man" in the human sciences. So, despite his protests,[3] we may ask what kind of "history" Foucault is writing to ascertain what kind of "historian" he is—the identity question. This query seems legitimate even if we take our comparative sketch to be a "diagnosis" and concede Foucault's well-known thesis that, "diagnosis does not establish the fact of our identity by the play of distinctions. It establishes that we are difference, that our reason is the difference of discourses, our history the difference of times, our selves the difference of masks. That difference, far from being the forgotten and recovered origin, is this dispersion that we are and make" (*AK* 131). For even under these stringent conditions, we can seek to determine, if only comparatively and not *in se,* the "dispersion"[4] called "Foucault" from an analysis of the histories he makes.

At the outset, we should note that there are at least three senses in which Sartre will agree that we humans are "dispersed": temporally, spatially, and what I will call "existentially" or "ontologically." Human reality is ekstatically temporal, as Heidegger insisted; unlike being-in-itself, it is not primarily "in" time but, rather, "temporalizes itself." Sartre takes seriously Bergson's critique of our tendency to spatialize our understanding of time. On the contrary, he insists that ekstatic temporality, like the consciousness that generates it, is sui generis and that human reality, in his famous paradox, "is what it is not and is not what it is."

Similarly, human reality, again as Heidegger argued, is a "being of distances" and that "inner distance" is a function of its "nihilating" or "othering" relation to the in-itself. One can sense a tension in Sartre's epistemology between the "rest" of evidence and the "motion" of Heraclitian consciousness, or, put otherwise, between the identity of phenomenological insight and the difference of temporalizing and spatializing subjectivity. Still, it is the "prodigious power of the negative," which he thought Descartes failed to exploit, that motors Sartre's dialectic (whether as consciousness or more explicitly as praxis) and renders history intelligible.

Finally, and most radically, human reality is ontologically "free because [one] is not a self but a presence-to-self" (*BN* 440; F 516). Although one could find the equivalent of Sartre's third dispersive dimension in Heidegger as well, I think it is here that the two differ profoundly. It is human reality's ontological nonself-coincidence (again, Descartes' "prodigious power of the negative") that grounds its spatial and temporal diaspora and not the reverse. And it is in this same respect that Sartre and Foucault differ as well. For it is precisely Sartre's attempt to "personalize" and "moralize" the categories, if you will, that leads him to valorize history over structure and to read Foucault as undertaking the converse. But it is Sartre's robust epistemic realism that inoculates him against the historicism so often associated with such an approach. Ironically, Foucault's idiosyncratically "structuralist" stance makes him vulnerable to just such historicist infection.[5] The issue is not consciousness versus its absence; the issue, as Rorty suggests, is the very possibility of an Archimedean point.

In what follows, I shall sketch a preliminary answer to the Archimedean challenge and the identity issue in the case of Foucault so that the contrast may secure our grasp of Sartre's existentialist theory. I intend to redress the enormous imbalance in this incipient dialogue by a close examination of Foucauldian texts in my second volume. Only then will we be in a position to undertake a full confrontation. At this initial stage, we must be content with mutual reconnaissance, preparing for that fuller exchange by reviewing each author's view of the other.

Sartre Regards Foucault: Analytic Reason as *Mauvaise Foi*

We have seen that Sartre is keenly sensitive to the problem of generational differences. On three occasions he describes the contrasting comprehension and practices of three successive generations of French industrial capitalists.[6] In an instance of the progressive/regressive method *avant la lettre,* his novella "Childhood of a Leader" depicts once again the individual's appropriation of the structural limits of interpersonal relations within the capitalist system with an eye to generational differences. And in an interview with three young Maoists, he attacks Marxist historians for writing as if the agents of history as well as their narrators were basically ageless, unaffected by the generational conflict and, more importantly, by the difference in "problematic" entailed by their different situations (cf. *ORR* 126–27). Of course, much of the argument of the final volume of *The Family Idiot* turns on the contrasting objective possibilities faced by young would-be writers of the immediate post-Romantic period in France and their older siblings.[7] So Sartre could scarcely ignore the fact that he too was both enabled and hobbled by his intellectual birth order.[8]

Foucault belonged to the next generation and when speaking of Sartre often couched the discussion in generational terms. In fact, the phenomenal success of his *The Order of Things* led the press to proclaim him Sartre's intellectual successor (see *DE* 3:671). Sartre's first recorded reference to the dauphin occurs in the context of the mounting structuralist challenge to existentialist values and principles. In an interview in the journal *L'Arc,* published shortly after *The Order of Things* made its remarkable appearance, Sartre lists Foucault among the structuralist enemies of history, who sacrifice concrete praxis to impersonal necessities and abstract forms.[9] Specifically, Sartre sees no originality in Foucault's work. From the epistemological viewpoint, he links Foucault with the latter's teacher Althusser in that both opt for the "concept" over the "notion." As we saw in chapter 5, the concept, Sartre believes, is atemporal and incapable of denoting adequately a fluid reality like history. The notion, in contrast, "can be defined as the synthetic effort to produce an idea that works itself out by means of contradictions and successive overcomings [*dépassements*] and so is homogeneous with the development of things." What he sees at work in both Foucault and Althusser is a kind of positivism, but not one of facts. Rather, betraying his suspicion of the depersonalizing nature of semiotics, Sartre calls it a "positivism of signs." "Totalities, structured wholes," he explains, "are constituted along with [*à travers*] man, and his whole function is to decipher them."[10] So, in Sartre's opinion, "Foucault is giving the public what it needed: an eclectic synthesis in which Robbe-Grillet, structuralism, linguistics, Lacan, and *Tel Quel* are used in turn to show the impossibility of a historical reflection."[11] Sartre reaffirms his high regard for structural aspects of the human sciences as exemplified by the extensive role accorded the practico-inert and impersonal processes in the *Critique*. But he reiterates his belief that structures do not answer the guiding questions of history: "If one admits, as I do, that the historical movement is a perpetual totalization and that each man at every moment is both totalizing and totalized," what is the *sens* of the totalizing praxis by which man surpasses the structures that condition him?[12] In other words, Sartre is reaffirming his humanist thesis that we can always make something out of what we have been made into, as he echoes the view commonly held at the time that Foucault was primarily a historian of science and a structuralist.

Sartre never entered into a direct confrontation with Foucault. Instead, he left it to the next generation of Sartreans to take up the cudgels. In the January issue of *Les Temps modernes* following the publication of Foucault's *Les Mots et les choses,* two essays appeared that were severely critical of Foucault's work. Sylvie Le Bon, later de Beauvoir's adopted daughter and literary heir, described Foucault as a "dispirited positivist" in an article by that title, and Michel Amiot in a more careful analysis of the text questioned the possibility of the kind of radical discontinuity among epistemes that formed the core of Foucault's thesis. A brief review of each essay will give us the gist of the controversy as well as a taste of its bitterly polemical flavor.

As its title announces, Le Bon's essay attacks the "positivism" of Foucault's archaeological method, where the "a priori" of his famous "historical a priori" greatly outweighs the historical and where "temporal unfolding is made a function of [*ramené à*] a spatial deployment."[13] In an ironic move against Foucauldian epistemes, she picks up the

Foucauldian theme that Sartre had mentioned in his *L'Arc* interview: "doxology," which reduces history to a collection of opinions (Plato's "doxa") as distinct from knowledge (Plato's "episteme"). The episteme of an epoch, she believes, is the "ahistorical totality of conditions that make history both possible and necessary as an epiphenomenon." But there is no "becoming" of the epistemes themselves, only the factical "there is" (*il y a*) of their brute existence: "a network of *positivities*."[14] So she accuses Foucault (and the tone is accusatory) of substituting the "historical a priori" as a "retrospective artifice" for the historical changes and conditionings from which, in fact, that contrivance is drawn. In other words, Foucault concocts a "system" of nonexistent relations (*entia rationis*) out of actual historical data in order to "discover" what he has in fact decided to find "beneath" the appearances (now dismissed as mere "doxa") that so concern practicing historians.[15] Foucault's goal, she insists, is to eliminate history as a discipline capable of yielding knowledge and not just opinion. He does this first by immobilizing becoming, the properly historical category, within the confines of a series of a priori limits, themselves subject to brute convulsions (epistemic events or breaks), which are "the only events properly speaking that occur in *Les Mots et les choses*." The second prong of his attack, she argues, is to metamorphose history into a set of necessary consequences of these constraining limits; in other words, to deduce works, events, and even historical individuals from a general structure. But, reflecting the Sartrean emphasis on contingency and freedom, she writes: "A history that is nothing but the carrying out of a necessity is no longer a history."[16]

If one were to counter in Foucault's defense that his intended result is not history but "histories," the Sartrean might respond that what occurs within the confines of a specific episteme is not even history in the plural but rather a series of Leibnizian rationalist implications from a shared set of epistemic conditions of possibility. In other words, the contingency so important to history "properly speaking" is banished to the confines of the respective epistemes themselves. The "a priori" may be historical but what they condition is not. Such, I believe, is the substance of her Sartrean critique.

The lead essay of the same issue of the journal is Michel Amiot's "Le Relativisme culturaliste de Michel Foucault." In far less antagonistic tone but with equal intensity, he summarizes the argument of *Les Mots et les choses* chapter by chapter and then turns to question Foucault's very method of questioning. In effect, the cultural material that Foucault has so impressively amassed, Amiot argues, gains its signification only via the interpretive grid that he has imposed on it, a criticism similar to Le Bon's. Although he admits there is something original going on here, Amiot thinks that in the final analysis Foucault has come up with "a philosophy of history that refuses to acknowledge itself as such."[17] He perceptively notes that Foucault must admit a certain unity to Western culture since his ethnologist's gaze is directed on it to the exclusion of other historical cultures. So Foucault seems to vacillate between continuity and discontinuity. But, unlike Bachelard, whose epistemic "breaks" he is imitating, Foucault is not willing to admit a progressive increase in rationality subject to unexpected redefinitions. Enlightenment "progress" is as antithetical to him as is the humanism it promotes. Perhaps Amiot's most telling criticism concerns the coexistence in our episteme of other ways of formulating knowledge (such as commentary, critique, and exegesis, not to mention mathematical deduction and linear evidential reasoning) that Foucault claims are proper to previous but now outmoded epistemes. Such observations by Amiot and others doubtless led Foucault subsequently to revise his claim that there is but one episteme for the science of a particular epoch.[18]

But Amiot thinks Sartre underestimates the distance separating Foucault from Althusser. There is room for neither Sartrean "notion" nor Althusserian "concept" in the "historicist skepticism" that pervades Foucault's philosophy of discrete epistemes. Amiot concludes with a quasi-Sartrean description of "the fundamental choice, the *a priori* from which Foucault reads the past." He finds it in the primacy that Foucault accords to language, a primacy that Amiot does not hesitate to call ideological, favoring the new posthumanist epoch whose dawn it announces.[19]

Although Foucault responded with a long personal letter to Amiot, he never entered further into the polemic. Neither did he forget it. When his friend Daniel Defert asked whether he would join the obsequies at Sartre's death, he responded: "Why should I? I don't owe him anything."[20]

A brief review of Sartre's theory of history as we have reconstructed it suffices to indicate that the two philosophers were on collision course from the outset. Even without a detailed study of Foucault's archaeologies, genealogies, and finally "problematizations," his intellectual reputation conveys a sense of his distrust of moralizing discourse and totalizing thought—the very warp and woof of Sartre's theory. "Intellectual history" was Foucault's declared enemy during the archaeological period, though it enjoyed a curious reprieve in his last two published works. And the emancipatory character of what we have called Sartre's "committed history," not to mention the progressive-regressive method itself, would indeed fall under Foucault's strictures of Marxism as existing in nineteenth-century thought like a fish in water, "unable to breath anywhere else" (*OT* 262). Again, Marx and now Sartre emerge as essentially nineteenth-century thinkers.[21]

FOUCAULT VIEWS SARTRE: THE MYTH OF HISTORY

Significantly, Foucault's first recorded reference to Sartre is to the latter's *The Psychology of Imagination*. The context is Foucault's introduction to the French translation of Ludwig Binswanger's *Dream and Existence* where he questions Sartre's thesis that the image refers to the real itself, albeit in a "derealized mode" (*DE* 1:110).[22] On the contrary, Foucault urges, it is myself, not the perceptual object, that I "derealize" in order to constitute myself as the world in which the imagined object occurs. In fact, "every act of imagination points implicitly to the dream. The dream is not a modality of the imagination," he argues, "the dream is the first condition of its possibility" (*DE* 1:110; "D" 67). In other words, image is much closer to dream than to percept. In an early display of his penchant for spatial metaphors, Foucault concludes: "The imaginary is not a mode of unreality, but very much a mode of actuality, a way of approaching presence diagonally to bring out its primordial dimensions" (*DE* 1:114; "D" 70).

Still a graduate student, the bright young Turk is making his debut by contesting a well-known thesis of one of the best known philosophers of his father's generation and using the philosopher's own example to do so. But his claim that "the dream has absolute primacy for an anthropological understanding of concrete man" (*DE* 1:118; "D" 74) implicitly undermines the primacy of perception that grounds Sartre's historical realism and the "absolute event" on which it revolves.

Although Foucault soon repudiated his early flirtation with phenomenology and existentialism, his rejection of the image as "representing" the perceptual object remained a constant in his archaeological critiques. Toward the conclusion of *The Order of Things,* he reflects: "Representation is not simply an object for the human sciences; it is, as we have just seen, the very field upon which the human sciences occur, and to their fullest extent." From which he draws the historical conclusion: "The human sciences, unlike the empirical sciences since the nineteenth century, and unlike modern thought, have been unable to find a way around the primacy of representation" (*OT* 363). It is clear that the Sartrean theory of history, read as an extension of his philosophy of imaginative re-presentation, is liable to the same criticism. Only a major "linguistification" of Sartre's method could possibly save it. But, Sartre would protest, at what price?

The same year Sartre gave his *L'Arc* interview, Foucault was interviewed by Madeline Chapsal for *La Quinzane littéraire.* Referring to him at age thirty-eight as one of the youngest philosophers of his generation, she added: "According to you, existentialism and Sartre's thought, for example, are on the way to becoming museum pieces." Without protesting the phrasing of the question and with a certain *franc-parler* that would return to haunt him, Foucault explained how, some fifteen years earlier, it began to dawn on those like himself who came of age after the Second World War that they were very far from the preceding generation, "the generation of Sartre, of Merleau-Ponty—the *Temps modernes* generation that had been our law for thinking and our model for existing." In a way that neatly summarizes and defines their respective approaches to history, Foucault continued, "We had experienced Sartre's generation as certainly courageous and generous with a passion for life, politics, existence. . . . But we have discovered something else, another passion: passion for the concept and for what I shall call 'system'" (*DE* 1:513).[23] In Foucault's view, Sartre revealed to a bourgeois world faced with the absurdity of its existence that "there was meaning [*sens*] everywhere." But Foucault underscored perceptively what we have been encountering throughout our investigation, namely, the ambiguity of Sartrean *sens:* "It was the result of a deciphering, a reading and then it was also the obscure pattern [*trame*] that unfolded in our actions despite us. For Sartre, one was both the reader and the automatic printer [*mécanographe*] of meaning: one discovered *sens* and was used [*était agi*] by it." Foucault's generation, on the contrary, learned from Lévi-Strauss and Lacan "that *sens* was probably only a kind of surface effect, a shine, a foam, and that what penetrated us deeply, preceded and sus-

tained us in time and space was *system*," which he defines as "an ensemble of relations that maintain themselves and are transformed inde-
pendently of the things they relate" (*DE* 1:514). So there you have it:
surface versus depth, appearance versus reality, froth versus substance.
Of course, on second thought, Foucault would reject such dichotomies,
especially the metaphysical ones, but even Homer nods.

Foucault tells another version of virtually the same story in his preface to the English translation of Georges Canguilhem's *The Normal and
the Pathological.* There he traces two lines of philosophical thought that
have divided French intellectual life since the 1930s: the one pursued
experience, meaning (*sens*), and the subject, while the other focused on
knowledge (*savoir*), rationality, and the concept. On the one side stood
Sartre and Merleau-Ponty; on the other, Jean Cavaillès, Bachelard, and
Canguilhem. He sees these as two ways of taking up the phenomenology that Husserl had introduced in France with his lectures later published as *Cartesian Meditations.* The former concentrated on the subject,
the latter on foundational questions of formalism and intuitionism.[24]

So anyone seeking intelligibility in the social domain, at least in the
structuralist heyday of the 1960s, is faced with a methodological choice
between system and *sens* or what, following Sartre, we may describe as
analytical concept and dialectical notion. In subsequent interviews and
in his programmatic *Archaeology of Knowledge*, Foucault will draw the
contrast in terms of multiplicity versus totalization or discursive formations as opposed to consciousness. This pattern is developed, not dis-
rupted, by his subsequent versions of these alternatives.

Foucault's second attack on Sartre was again occasioned by an interviewer's remarks following the publication of Foucault's next major
work, *The Archaeology of Knowledge.* This time it was the accusation that
Sartre had reproached Foucault and company "for neglecting and
showing contempt for history." Foucault's defense consisted of an attack on "the philosophical myth of History" propounded by philosophers who as a rule "are very ignorant of other disciplines outside their
own." Veiling his critique of Sartre with a professional generalization,
Foucault explained:

> For philosophers, History is a kind of grand and extensive continuity
> where the liberty of individuals and economic and social determina-
> tions come to be intertwined. If you touch one of these great themes—

continuity, the effective exercise of human freedom, the articulation of individual liberty with social determinations—then right away these grave gentleman begin to cry rape, and that history has been assassinated. In fact, it was some time ago that people as important as Marc Bloch, Lucien Febvre and the English historians put an end to this myth of History. They write history in a completely different mode. . . . The philosophical myth of History . . . I would be delighted if I have killed it, since that was exactly what I wanted to do. But not at all history in general. One doesn't murder history, but history for philosophy. That's what I wanted to kill. (*FL* 41)

One could scarcely be more unequivocal. Foucault is appealing to one kind of history to undermine another.

We have watched Sartre's early interest in human freedom and historical meaning grow into a full-blown theory of History that could be called "existentialist." Foucault's defense against Sartre's critique is a reversal of this sequence, an explosion of this "myth of History" in order to dismantle its component parts. What we have discovered to be the threefold primacy of praxis (ontological, epistemic, and moral) that forms the existentialist basis of Sartre's theory is systematically attacked in the name of what Foucault refers to as his "happy positivism" (*AK* 234).[25] The famous epistemic "breaks" between epistemes charted in *The Order of Things* cannot be deduced but only encountered. The professed aim of archaeology, Foucault insists, is "to free history from the grip of phenomenology," from the "transcendental narcissism" of a "constituent consciousness" that he sees supporting the thesis of historical continuity. For he believes that "if you recognize the right of a piece of empirical research, some fragment of history, to challenge the transcendental dimension, then you have conceded the main point" (*AK* 203). Ironically, one is reminded of Kierkegaard's attack on the Hegelian "system" in the name of the contingent individual: an event could occur in the future that would falsify the foregoing Hegelian dialectic. If History is understood backwards, it must be lived forwards.[26] Foucault shares with the father of existentialism this antitranscendental bias in favor of contingency.

DIAGNOSTIC: THE VIEW FROM ELSEWHERE

Perhaps the most adequate contrast between the two thinkers is the one Foucault draws between Sartrean totalization and his own philosophic method of *diagnostic*. Archaeological study, he explains, "is always in the plural" (*AK* 157). The object of analysis is the "discursive formation," defined as "the general enunciative system that governs a group of verbal performances" (*AK* 116). Foucault speaks of "mapping discursive formations" rather than recounting their descent. We are at the level of the statement (*l'énoncé*) and discursive practices, not that of actions and intentions. If the model is synchronic and "geographical," it is one of comparative geography, as Veyne recommends.[27] There is no absolute beginning (origin) nor any nonrelative place.

The comparisons in archaeological analysis are always limited and regional. Foucault's archaeologies of psychiatric discourse in *Madness and Civilization* or of medical perception in *The Birth of the Clinic*, for example, used the comparative method to establish their respective temporal limits. The archaeology of general grammar, analysis of wealth, and natural history in *The Order of Things*, on the other hand, besides contrasting these fields with other types of discourse at other periods, established an "interdiscursive configuration" among these disciplines in the classical period, what he calls a "region of interpositivity" between them, but not a *Weltanschauung* for an entire period. This last he explicitly excludes as the stuff of intellectual history (*AK* 159). As if to counter the Sartrean project at its core, Foucault summarizes:

> The horizon of archaeology . . . is a tangle of interpositivities whose limits and points of intersection cannot be fixed in a single operation. Archaeology is a comparative analysis that is not intended to reduce the diversity of discourses, and to outline the unity that must totalize them, but is intended to divide up their diversity into different figures. Archaeological comparison does not have a unifying but a diversifying effect. (*AK* 159–60)

Archaeology uncovers the play of "analogies and differences" among the rules of discursive formation. As such, it operates at a deeper level, if you will, than that of causal influence, agent, or opus. In one of his more arresting claims, in this regard, Foucault concludes: "If we question Classical thought at the level of what archaeologically made it possible, we perceive that the dissociation of the sign and resemblance in the early seventeenth century caused these new forms—probability, analysis, combination, and universal language system—to emerge, not as successive themes engendering one another or driving one another out, but as a single network of necessities. And it was this network that made possible the individuals we term Hobbes, Berkeley, Hume, or Condillac" (*OT* 63). A more direct rejection of Sartre's "primacy of praxis" could scarcely be imagined.[28]

Foucault implies that diagnostic remains "historical" precisely because of its positivist character. Like the Sartrean Other, discourses are encountered, not deduced. "Discourse," Foucault's term for a group of statements insofar as they belong to the same discursive formation,

> does not form a rhetorical or formal unity, endlessly repeatable, whose appearance or use in history might be indicated (and, if necessary explained); it is made up of a limited number of statements for which a group of conditions of existence [not of a priori possibility] can be defined. Discourse in this sense is not an ideal, timeless form that also possesses a history; the problem is not therefore to ask oneself how and why it was able to emerge and become embodied at this point of time; it is, from the beginning to the end, historical—a fragment of history, a unity and discontinuity in history itself, posing the problem of its own limits, its divisions, its transformations, the specific modes of its temporality rather than its sudden irruption in the midst of the complicities of time. (*AK* 117)

But if archaeological diagnostic is historical, it too is historical in the plural. In other words, it works at "the particular level in which history can give place to the definite types of discourse, which have their own type of historicity, and which are related to a whole set of various historicities" (*AK* 165). It exemplifies Foucault's concept of "general" as opposed to "total" history.[29]

What Foucault calls a relation of "articulation" obtains between this relatively autonomous level of discourse and the whole domain of nondiscursive practices: institutions, economic processes, and social relations. Although this relationship is problematic, and does not receive anything approaching the attention lavished on discursive practices in his archaeologies, Foucault is far from encapsulating himself in the "linguocentrism" that critics think insulates many so-called poststructuralist thinkers. But it is relevant that he refuses to consider discourse as simply the expression or symbolic projection of nondiscursive events or processes. For in *The Family Idiot* Sartre too is not satisfied with ascribing these same relations of expression and symbolization unqualifiedly to the "prophetic event"—to Flaubert's "attack" of 1844, for example, and that of which it was the prophecy, the loss of innocence by the French bourgeoisie in the massacres of June 1848 and their aftermath. But whereas Foucault's point is to preserve the relative autonomy of discursive practices and with it that of his archaeological method, Sartre's purpose is to chart the curve of temporalization in order to defend his principle of totalization and dialectical Reason itself. "In this sense," Sartre explains, "a life like Gustave's and an era like the reign of Louis-Philippe can enter into reciprocal rapport on a *real* foundation; it is enough that they are conditioned by the same factors, and that these factors totalize them and are retotalized by them in such a way that they present the *same curve,* the same profile of temporalization" (*FI* 5:407).[30]

What, in his study of clinical medicine, Foucault calls "the diacritical principle of medical observation," namely, that "the only pathological fact is a comparative fact"[31] applies to his concept of contemporary philosophy in general as a "diagnosis of the present." As he explains, "to diagnose the present is to say what the present is, and how our present is absolutely different from all that is not it, that is to say, from our past" (*FL* 38–39). When he subsequently describes the genealogical method of his *Discipline and Punish* as a "history of the present," it is this comparativist move that he has in mind.[32] If his is a history of the present, as diagnostic, it is necessarily a history of its Other.

THE ARCHIMEDEAN CHALLENGE

An all-pervasive theme in Sartrean philosophy is "the prodigious power of the negative." It is consciousness as "nihilating" (or what we might call "othering") that brings it about that "there is" a world, a world in which I am always immersed but never fully identified. But Foucault would insist that this very "there is" replaces the "I cause it to be" of humanism, specifically Sartrean humanism. Foucault asks:

> What is this anonymous system without a subject? who is it that thinks? The "ego" [*je*] has exploded (note modern literature)—it's the discovery of the "il y a." There is a *one.* In a certain way we are returning to the 17th-century viewpoint, but with this difference: rather than putting man in the place of God, [that role is assumed by] an anonymous thought, knowledge without a subject, theory without identity. (*DE* 1:515)

Of course, Sartre strenuously rejected any hint of a substantial self. And if he adamantly favored individual responsibility, he equally opposed causal relations between consciousness and the world. The point of the "il y a" for both Sartre and Husserl is more epistemic than ontological. It prescinds from the ontological claims that land one in realism or idealism, though we know Sartre's predilection for a kind of materialist realism. The "pure spontaneous upsurge" of being-for-itself, like the biblical Melchizedek "without ancestry," is the functional equivalent of Foucault's "there is." Both are brute facts, except that Foucault's is a "structural fact," if you will. But in both cases, these respective answers to our "why" are, like the rose of Angelus Silesius, themselves without "why."[33]

It is the essential situatedness of consciousness (and a fortiori of praxis) that raises Sartre's version of the Archimedean question. We saw him face it squarely in *Search for a Method* with his reference to "that truth of microphysics: the experimenter is a part of the experimental system" (*SM* 32 n). But the ambiguity that infects his epistemologies of vision and praxis affects his response to the Archimedean question as well. He wavers between a Cartesian search for the intuitive and apodictic in subjectivity and a neopragmatic commitment to time-bound categories and liberating truths. In other words, he waffles between foundationalism and its Other.

Foucault's archaeological approach to "history" makes the Archimedean problem more urgent. For it assumes an epistemic "system" as the necessary condition for sense-making in a certain society for a designated period, which the system itself serves to designate! In other words, the epistemic conditions delimit the rationality of a historical era, but that era is defined by those very conditions. This, I take it, is the gist of Amiot's criticism. The circularity is more than hermeneutic, and it leads to Chapsal's question of Foucault's own *locus standi*. He responds that *The Order of Things* attempts partially to illuminate what our contemporary "anonymous and constraining thought" may be. He admits that in order to think what he calls "the thought before thought, the system prior to every system" he was "already constrained by a system behind the system, which [he] did not know and which would withdraw to the extent that [he] discovered it or it made itself known" (*DE* 1:515). In other words, as he insists in *The Archaeology of Knowledge*, one cannot known one's own archive ("the general system of the formation and transformation of statements" [*AK* 130]) any more than one could have "knowledge" in the Kantian sense of the transcendental conditions for the possibility of such knowledge.[34]

So the Foucauldian investigator, like the Sartrean, is situated, and neither can be desituated by appeal to a transcendental Ego. A self-proclaimed neo-Kantian interviewer (Giulio Preti) poses the Archimedean question to Foucault explicitly. His response, though in the main evasive, is telling:

> In all of my work I strive . . . to avoid any reference to this transcendental as a condition of possibility for any knowledge. When I say that I strive to avoid it, I don't mean that I am sure of succeeding. My procedure at this moment is of a regressive sort, I would say; I try to assume a greater and greater detachment in order to define the historical conditions and transformations of our knowledge. I try to historicize to the utmost in order to leave as little space as possible to the transcendental. I cannot exclude the possibility that one day I will have to confront an irreducible *residuum* which will be, in fact, the transcendental. (*FL* 79)

If Sartre is ambivalent in his appeal, sometimes to the intuitive grasp of a phenomenological *eidos,* at other times to the lived experience of dialectical necessity, Foucault is even more elusive in his account of his cognitive ideal. It seems that his "diagnostic" gains credibility to the extent that it distances itself from the recent past, that is, insofar as it shows itself to be other than the rules, principles, and criteria constitutive of modernity (that it "historicizes to the utmost"). And if the archive of modernism is deeply "Historical" with a capital "H," then Foucault is committed a priori to counter such History and the humanism it both assumes and fosters. So his structuralist claims of the sixties and his Nietzschean suspicions of the seventies should be seen as tactical moves toward rendering himself "foreign" to a culture that he still bears. In the insightful judgment of Axel Honneth, Foucault is undertaking nothing less than an ethnology of his own culture![35] This is a plausible account of Foucault's approach to the question of his *locus standi,* for it accords with his claim that "we can perfectly well apprehend our own society's ethnology" (*OT* 377). Presumably, the genitive is objective; we can study the system of our own culture. Foucault's Archimedean point is located in the space between our traditional culture and its Other in the "possibility of thinking" that he exults in finding with the disappearance of "man."[36]

In sum, Foucault is reluctant to answer the Archimedean question which he conjoins with the identity question and puts to himself at the conclusion of *The Archaeology of Knowledge:* "What then is the title of your discourse? Where does it come from and from where does it derive its right to speak? How could it be legitimated? . . . In short, what are [these discourses of yours], history or philosophy?" (*AK* 205). Like Rorty's edifying philosopher, Foucault eschews transcendental viewpoints: "My discourse, far from determining the locus in which it speaks, is avoiding the ground on which it could find support." Rather than searching for underlying laws, origins, or starting points, "its task is to *make* differences: to constitute them as objects, to analyze them, and to define their concept. . . . It is continually making *differentiations,* it is a *diagnosis*" (*AK* 205–06). So, depending on how you define the terms, Foucault's archaeologies may count neither as philosophy nor as history. Their protean character would scarcely bother him.

And yet he does present them with the seriousness of a theoretical analyst armed with historical evidence and conceptual tools. His finessing of the Archimedean question, far from being a rhetorical "first strike," is a candid admission that something is missing from his enterprise. I am suggesting that his distancing himself from the modern episteme by questioning its basic presuppositions is his way of "making the difference" that enables him to view our own society "from without" while avoiding even implicit appeal to a transcendental field.

The Discourse of Man

It is perhaps here that the most important philosophical choice of our period has its roots—a choice that can be made only in the test of a future reflection. For nothing can tell us in advance upon which side the through road lies. The only thing we know at the moment, in all certainly, is that in Western culture the being of man and the being of language have never, at any time, been able to coexist and to articulate themselves one upon the other. Their incompatibility has been one of the fundamental features of our thought.

—Foucault, *The Order of Things*

As so often happens in Foucault's books (if you discount their striking opening performances), the best is saved for last: for the end of a chapter or subsection, the concluding pages of the opus. His lectures at the Collège de France were crafted similarly. It is as if the cookie dough required thorough mixing in order to be squeezed into meaningful patterns as it emerged from the tube. The concluding pages of *The Order of Things* chart the privileged position of ethnology and psychoanalysis in our present-day knowledge. As such, they invite a comparison with

Sartre's synthesis of psychoanalysis and historical materialism, the progressive-regressive method. How these two approaches to social meanings and practices intersect and diverge will place in relief these respective techniques of historical understanding as alternative forms of rationality.

No disciplines better accommodate Foucault's "ethic of the intellectual in our time"—"to take distance on oneself [*se déprendre de soi-même*]"—than psychoanalysis and ethnology. The former situates itself in the domain of the unconscious as the locus of the unrepresentable Other (specifically, death, desire, and law) that ceaselessly questions the social sciences' insuperable commitment to representation; the latter takes root in the realm of historicity, questioning "from outside" the sovereignty of Western rationality that inspired and sustains the social sciences. Because psychoanalysis "frames and defines on the outside the very possibility of representation," Foucault explains, psychologists and philosophers must dismiss it as mythology. But on closer inspection, he insists, one discovers in this trio of death, desire, and law (language), "the very forms of finitude as it is analyzed in modern thought . . . [and] the conditions of the possibility of all knowledge about man" (*OT* 375).[37] But this "discovery" cannot be theoretical under pain of succumbing to the very representations it questions. "All analytic knowledge is . . . invincibly linked with praxis. . . . That is why nothing is more alien to psychoanalysis than anything resembling a general theory of man or an anthropology" (*OT* 376).

And yet, what we have described as the Sartrean primacy of praxis, while couched in terms of a general theory of the human (anthropology), is equally distrustful of value-free knowing, "pure" reason, and a spectator consciousness. Even more than Foucault, Sartre requires a "conversion" to effect the shift from analytic to dialectical Reason. And he is proverbially opposed to a concept of human nature, to the point of claiming in the *Critique* that "all concepts forged by history, including that of man, are individualized universals" (*CDR* 1:49). But what Foucault dismisses as "the slenderness of the narrative" (*OT* 371), Sartre promotes as "the depth of the world" that dialectical accounts must plumb. It is this blurring of the distinction between reality and representation, as Jameson points out, that results in the "depthlessness" of postmodern accounts.[38] While we have insisted that Foucault is not locked in the prison house of language, there is little doubt that he holds at least trustee status when compared to Sartre, who scarcely passes through the carceral gates of the signifier/signified relationship.

What makes ethnology possible is a peculiar event, the emergence of Western *ratio,* that opens other cultures as well as its own to investigation. What protects this *ratio* from the occupational hazard of intellectual colonization is its self-critique. In the language of *The Order of Things,* "it places the particular forms of each culture . . . within the dimension in which its relations occur with each of the three great positivities (life, need and labor, and language)" (*OT* 377). And yet ethnology "avoids the representations that men in any civilization may give themselves of their life, of their needs, of the significations laid down in their language" (*OT* 378). As we have noted, this critical analysis succeeds only if one is able to perform an ethnology of one's own society—a move, we have noted, that Foucault carefully assures us is possible.

As Foucault concludes, their primary character made it inevitable that ethnology and psychoanalysis should share a profound kinship and symmetry. They both should be sciences of the unconscious, "not because they reach down to what is below consciousness in man, but because they are directed towards that which, outside man, makes it possible to know, with positive knowledge, that which is given to or eludes his consciousness" (*OT* 378). It is for this reason that Foucault can see his own project as "unearthing an autonomous domain that would be the unconscious of science, the unconscious of knowledge [*savoir*]" (*FL* 40). And it is why Honneth can characterize it as an "ethnology of his own culture." He could have called it a "psychoanalysis of his culture" as well.

Foucault once described his work as "trying to discover in the history of science and of human knowledge something that would be like its unconscious" (*FL* 39). As he explained,

> My working hypothesis is roughly this: the history of science and of knowledge [*connaissances*] doesn't simply obey the general law of reason's progress; it's not human consciousness or human reason that somehow possesses the laws of its history. Underneath what science itself knows there is something it does not know; and its history, its progress, its periods and accidents obey a certain number of laws and determinations. These laws and determinations are what I have tried to bring to light. I have tried to unearth an autonomous domain that would be the unconscious of science, the unconscious of knowledge

[*savoir*], that would have its own laws, just as the individual human unconscious has its own laws and determinations. (*FL* 39–40)

Now if all the human sciences have inherited a critical function from their Kantian forebears, theirs is primarily a self-critique: unlike the other sciences that seek to grow in precision and generality, the human sciences are "constantly demystifying themselves." That is why the problem of the unconscious is not a mere adjunct to the human sciences, but "is a problem that is ultimately coextensive with their very existence" (*OT* 364). In Foucault's view, the human sciences back into that space which psychoanalysis treats *ex professo,* namely, "that fundamental region in which the relations of representation and finitude come into play," the unconscious. He thinks that the modern legacy of Kantian man as a "transcendental-empirical doublet" is a corresponding duality of consciousness and representation on the one side and the unconscious and the unthought on the other. The basic categories of human sciences—life, labor, and language—together circumscribe the possibility of man's self-knowledge but also permit the dissociation of consciousness and representation (cf. *OT* 362). Recall the thesis of *The Order of Things* that "the human sciences . . . have been unable to find a way around the primacy of representation" (*OT* 363). But if they must speak within the element of the representable, they do so "in accordance with a conscious/unconscious dimension" (*OT* 363). Psychoanalysis "advances and leaps over representation, overflows it on the side of finitude," and "in this region where representation remains in suspense" we find a kind of threefold "foundation" for the categories of life, labor, and language respectively: death, desire, and law (see *OT* 374). Psychoanalysis thereby "frames and defines, on the outside [of the representable] the very possibility of representation" (*OT* 375). Indeed, Foucault insists that death, desire, and law are "the very forms of finitude, as it is analyzed in modern thought" (*OT* 375).[39]

Psychoanalysis and ethnology are "countersciences," not, Foucault explains, because they are less "rational" or "objective" than the others, "but because they flow in the opposite direction, . . . they lead . . . back to their epistemological basis, and . . . they ceaselessly 'unmake' that very man who is creating and re-creating his positivity in the human sciences" (*OT* 379). We know that Sartre hoped to construct a "structural, historical anthropology" that would enable us to comprehend, for example, that "singular universal" which is Flaubert the author of *Madame Bovary*. Foucault would bring into intersection, not synthetically but "at right angles," what looks like Lacanian psychoanalysis and Lévi-Straussian ethnology. As if to parody Sartre's singular universal and the progressive-regressive method that uncovers it, Foucault claims:

> The signifying chains by which the unique experience of the individual is constituted is perpendicular to the formal system on the basis of which the significations of a culture are constituted: at any given instant, the structure proper to individual experience finds a certain number of possible choices (and of excluded possibilities) in the system of the society; inversely, at each of their points of choice the social structures encounter a certain number of possible individuals (and others who are not)—just as the linear structure of language always produces a possible choice between several words or several phonemes at any given moment (but excludes all others). (*OT* 380)

In order to distinguish this intersection from any humanist enterprise, he warns that it is not "at the level of the relations between the individual and society, as has often been believed, that psychoanalysis and ethnology could be articulated one upon the other; it is not because the individual is part of his group, it is not because a culture is reflected and expressed in a more or less deviant manner in the individual, that these two forms of knowledge are neighbors" (*OT* 380).

This clearly suggests an approach to history that is more structuralist than humanist, one that accords greater import to both material and formal conditions than to individual or collective agency in any historical account. It is a case of addressing the matter at a different and more basic level rather than simply dismissing traditional approaches as being mistaken or irrelevant. At least that is how Foucault sounds in his more irenic moments. In the heat of polemics (when he is at his most brilliant), however, he seems to claim that archaeology must replace the received historiography because of the fundamental incompatibility of the being of man and the being of language. "For the entire modern *episteme*," he reflects, "was bound up with the disappearance of Discourse and its featureless reign, with the shift of language toward objectivity, and with its reappearance in multiple form." Which raises the fundamental question: "Since man was constituted at a time when language

was doomed to dispersion, will he not be dispersed when language re-
gains its unity? . . . Ought we not to admit that, since language is here
once more, man will return to that serene non-existence in which he was
formerly maintained by the imperious unity of Discourse?" Foucault
quickly assures us that, rather than affirmations, "these are at most
questions to which it is not possible to reply; they must be left in suspense, where they pose themselves, only with the knowledge that the
possibility of posing them may well open the way to a future thought"
(*OT* 386). Would not this constitute the ultimate instance of "taking distance on ourselves"—the ethic of the Foucauldian intellectual in our
time?

By Force of Reason

By linking the positivist and formalist aspect of his thought to the work
of the Frankfurt school, and by locating both in the tradition of the German Enlightenment, Foucault intends to historicize and relativize the
universalizing claims of eighteenth-century occidental Reason in the
hope that so-called liberating Reason might free itself as well. Much as
Sartre in *Search for a Method* sought to preserve a place for human agency
in Marxist thought, Foucault seeks to break the monopoly of Enlightenment Reason on rationality *überhaupt.* By stressing the singular event of
the emergence of the discipline of ethnology in the West, namely, that it
could arise "only within the historical sovereignty . . . of European
thought" [*OT* 377], he hopes to bring a triumphalist Western Reason to
recognize its limits and acknowledge its historical abuse of power (see
DE 3:433).

   In this, too, his enterprise is not unlike Sartre's. Both seek a kind of
liberation from constraining structures. Each sees "reason" as both enabling and confining. If the Foucault of the genealogies (*Discipline and
Punish* and vol. 1 of *The History of Sexuality*) is critically aware of the inevitably limiting character of any set of norms and rules, whether for
behavior or argument, Sartre is outspoken in his opposition to analytic
(that is, Enlightenment) Reason as, in our day, politically reactionary.
For neither thinker is there such a thing as value-free thought. As Sartre
put it with characteristic drama, by the time one decides to be reasonable, "the chips are [already] down." For both theorists, reason is a force
to be reckoned with.

   The major practical difference in their respective approaches lies in the *manner* in which each reckons with the force of reason. For Sartre, it seems that the adoption of dialectical Reason is as much a moral and a political as an epistemic act—requiring something like a conversion from the bad faith that averts one's eyes from exploitation and class struggle. Dialectical Reason, for Sartre, is one with human praxis. It must be recognized in our every action and put into play in our collective life. In other words, it must be promoted over those antidialectical (read "analytic") forms of reasoning that do violence to it by a tactical use of practico-inert mediation. Indeed, in the late sixties, Foucault considered Sartre to be "a philosopher in the most modern sense of the term because in the final analysis, for him, philosophy is reduced essentially to a form of political activity. For Sartre," Foucault explained, "to philosophize today is a political act. I do not believe that Sartre thinks any longer that philosophical discourse is a discourse about totality" (*DE* 1:612). If one respects Sartre's continuing concern for totalization as distinct from totality, this is probably an accurate assessment.[40]

But is not such "totalizing" thought at the same time "totalitarian"? Thinkers as diverse as Karl Popper, Hannah Arendt, Gilles Deleuze, and Jean-François Lyotard have thought so. So has Foucault.[41] The most concise response to the accusation of dialectical totalitarianism is that the same anarchistic nominalism that saves Foucault from the tyranny of the "disciplines" of social science comes to Sartre's aid against serial bureaucracy and the cult of personality in his social ontology. Sartrean individuals are ontologically and politically "*detotalized* totalities" that recognize an insuperable alterity in the midst of their most enthusiastic group activity. The highest degree of social integration possible on Sartrean terms is achieved within the spontaneous group and its more permanent avatar, the sworn group. Yet even these respect the freedom and autonomy of their members by rendering practically innocuous the ontological otherness of their constituents as individuals in what Sartre calls their "free alterity" at moments of voluntary cooperation in pursuit of a common goal. The members of the soccer team, for example, set aside their mutual animosities for the sake of the match. Whatever one may think of the adequacy of Sartre's social ontology, there can be no doubt that it is fundamentally opposed to "collectivism" of any sort.[42]

But what of the "fraternity terror" that in Sartre's account infects what is presumably the majority of social institutions? What of Sartre's rather cavalier reference to "a little bit of terror" (see *ORR* 171) binding even the sworn group against the scarcity that gives us history as we know it? Doubtless this reveals the political realism that balances whatever utopian proclivities he sometimes evidences. Still, it does leave open the thought that the difference between the violence of the social contract (to employ a contractarian discourse Sartre would resist) and the "control" by a "man on horseback" is merely one of degree.

Rhetorically, we should note that this inevitable violence plays a role not unlike that of power in Foucault's genealogical approach to social institutions: both concepts apply to free individuals, and each is accompanied by a co- or counterconcept, namely, fraternity and resistance respectively. Moreover, there is a contingent, factical dimension to the use of each term: Sartrean violence is dependent on the "transcendental fact" of material scarcity and Foucauldian power is the summation of a multiplicity of empirical instances of production, limitation, and control. Further similarities will emerge as we examine the Foucauldian term in our next volume. Still, the impersonal, structural nature of the latter in contrast with the essentially praxis-conditioned character of the former confirms the basic difference in approach to historical intelligibility on the part of each thinker.

Toward the end of his life, Sartre admitted that he had not succeeded in reconciling the two equally necessary social concepts of fraternity and violence (terror). At the same time, he allowed that his hope for the advent of socialism and ultimately for a socialism of abundance was no guarantee; that the same freedom that made libertarian socialism possible could turn against it in bad faith or seek refuge in the myriad forms of seriality, of which twentieth-century totalitarianism is the most graphic example.[43]

But Sartre's guarded optimism, at first blush, seems not that far from Foucault's neo-Stoic commitment. The latter resembles that of Camus in some respects.[44] Like Dr. Rieux in *The Plague,* Foucault continues the battle despite never-ending defeat, rolling the stone of resistance up the hill of insuperable power relations. Must one imagine Foucault happy like Camus's Sisyphus? A survey of the Foucauldian oeuvre (a term he disliked), especially in light of his final inquiries into moral "subjectivation" and "games of truth," leaves the impression that Foucault's passion was for a truth that would neither make you happy nor set you free.

In his last published interview, Sartre summarized his view of historical meaning and progress:

> I assumed that the evolution through action would be a series of failures from which something unforeseen and positive would emerge, something that was implicit in the failure but that had been overlooked by those who had hoped to succeed. That something would be a series of partial, local successes, decipherable only with difficulty by the people who were doing that work and who, moving from failure to failure, would nonetheless be achieving a certain progress. This is how I always understood history. ("LW," 403)

In his *Saint Genet*, Sartre introduced a phrase that he would repeat on several occasions: "In our day, Ethics [*la morale*] is both necessary and impossible." Could not the same be said of Sartrean History, and for the same reason? Both require a conversion that is moral as well as epistemic, but which rides dialectically on the back of fundamental socio-economic change. The very possibility of such a History and the Ethics it entails will be the implicit theme of my detailed analysis of Foucault's "mapping" of history in my second volume.

Conclusion to Volume One:

Sartre *Resartus*

Nietzsche, the gray eminence of post-modern thought, had a profound influence on the young Sartre as well.[1] Sartre's early essay, "The Legend of Truth," is clearly Nietzschean in tone.[2] Perhaps the Nietzschean concept of "contingency" forges the major link between Sartrean existentialism and what has come to be called "postmodernism." This connection is best illustrated by juxtaposing the following:

> *Anything* can happen, *anything*. . . . The essential thing is contingency. . . . To exist is simply *to be there;* those who exist let themselves be encountered, but you can never deduce anything from them. . . . They are *superfluous [de trop].* . . . Every existing thing is born without reason, prolongs itself out of weakness and dies by chance.[3]

> It seems to me that the *datum* . . . which we are dealing with, the *Begabenheit* which marks what has been called "postmodernity" to designate our time . . . is the feeling produced by the *fission* of the great discursive nuclei I mentioned at the beginning of this lecture.[4]

What Lyotard, citing Kant, calls the "sign of history" resembles Sartrean "nausea."

Each denotes a "metaphysical" experience, though the term has fallen into disrepute among postmodern writers. But the challenge faced by existentialist and postmodernist alike is to "make sense" out of a history adrift in an oceanic void. Our foregoing reconstruction of a Sartrean theory of history, though it confirms how traditional a philosopher Sartre actually is, uncovers certain theses and themes that set him at odds with modern thought: the nonself-identity of human reality, for example, the limited validity of analytic rationality, and the absence of any transcendental foothold in the cosmos. Of course, such themes betray the common debt of all three—postmoderns, existentialists, and Nietzsche himself—to an earlier, Romantic tradition. Metaphysical contingency and ontological freedom (freedom as the definition of human reality) converge in Sartrean history-biography, for "in History, too, existence precedes essence."

Reason plays a unifying role in existentialist historiography. It is historical without being historicist. It has temporalized the categories and itself in the process. So one can query with Terence: "Who guards the guards?" What unifies "reason" itself? Rationalists, both analytic and dialectical, have a ready answer. But Sartre, though clearly tempted, is not satisfied.

This is where imagination and existential choice enter the picture. Just as the resolute project gives meaning-direction (*sens*) to an individual life and the refusal to own that reality constitutes bad faith, so the unity of a history that yields "History" is the "synthetic enrichment" of common praxes creating the social and economic conditions for the emergence of "integral humanity." The value-image that guides this common project also motivates the "choice" of dialectical rationality. The resultant historiography is a tale of possible emancipation, but with this anti-Hegelian proviso: individuals or groups may abuse their freedom for the comfort of collective identities and private gain. The "march" of History is neither inevitable nor even reasonably foreseeable. But History as social value remains possible and that possibility, Sartre believes, depends on our willingness to undergo a "conversion" that is at once moral and epistemic. If the moral of Sartrean stories is that there is always a moral to the story, their epistemological lesson is the ancient one that method determines content; in other words, that one notices only what one looks for. Biography underscores the epistemic and the moral primacy of praxis. Existential history discovers this praxis in the midst of abstract social phenomena. History without biography is lifeless, biography without history is blind.

But if Sartre allows for structuralist categories in the realm of the practico-inert, he is not ready for the poststructuralist fission of unity or the dehistoricized man of which Foucault speaks (see *OT* 369). In fact, Sartrean "authenticity" serves as a gyroscope amidst our Nietzschean moral free fall. "Authentic history" is called to perform a similar function for the group. It thereby summons poststructuralist writers to address the ethical implications of their fragmenting and dispersive discourses. In the best existentialist sense of the term, Sartrean history challenges poststructuralist diagnostic mapping of discursive and nondiscursive practices to *assume responsibility for their methodological choices,* choices that identify them in their very resistance to the logic of identity.

Foucault poses the question: "*What* is this Reason that we use? What are its historical effects? What are its limits, and what are its dangers?" After uncovering the racist formulae that followed from the "rationality" of social Darwinism in the last century, he warns: "If philosophy has a function within critical thought, it is precisely to accept . . . this sort of revolving door of rationality that refers us to its necessity, to its indispensability, and at the same time, to its intrinsic dangers."[5] We now know that Sartre could only agree.

Foucault's odyssey from existential phenomenology through archaeology, genealogy, and problematization ended with reflections on the "constitution of the moral self" and lectures that traced the shift of plain-speaking (*le franc parler, parrhesia*) from a political to a personal virtue in the ancient world.[6] In other words, he too was weighing the ethical implications of his thought. Whether the charts he drew along the way map a route that Sartre could have taken or whether their respective journeys carry each thinker across a different sea is a question that calls for our second volume.

Notes

INTRODUCTION

1. Paul Veyne, *Writing History: Essay on Epistemology,* trans. Mina Moore-Rinvolucri (Middletown, CT: Wesleyan University Press, 1984), 65.

2. See Hubert Dreyfus and Paul Rabinow, *Michel Foucault: Beyond Structuralism and Hermeneutics,* 2d ed., augmented (Chicago: University of Chicago Press, 1983), 237. Although Foucault denied the similarity, what I wish to emphasize at this initial stage of my investigation is the appropriateness of the question rather than the nature of the response.

3. Michel Foucault, *Dits et écrits,* ed. Daniel Defert and François Ewald with the collaboration of Jacques Legrange, 4 vols. (Paris: Gallimard, 1994); hereafter cited as *DE* with volume and page number.

CHAPTER ONE

1. "Furthermore, History was present all around me. First, philosophically: Aron had just written his *Introduction to the Philosophy of History* and I read it. Secondly, it surrounded and gripped me like all my contemporaries, making me feel its presence." Jean-Paul Sartre, *The War Diaries of Jean-Paul Sartre,* trans. Quintin Hoare (New York: Pantheon, 1984), 185; hereafter cited as *WD* (*Les Carnets de la drôle de guerre* [Paris: Gallimard, 1983], 227). Where I employ my own translations from works available in English versions, I follow the English citation by a reference to the original, designated by "F" and the page number. Unless otherwise noted, all emphases are in the original.

A sixth *carnet,* the first in order of composition, consisting of more than one hundred and fifty pages in print, was discovered subsequent to the publication and translation of the five listed above. It is included in the new edition of *Carnets de la drôle de guerre: Septembre 1939–mars 1940* (Paris: Gallimard, 1995) but remains as yet untranslated. Though it contains little of relevance to our topic, I shall also cite the new, augmented edition when referring to the French text. Single references following the "F" are to the earlier edition of the *Carnets;* double references are to the original and the augmented editions respectively.

2. Raymond Aron, *Mémoires* (Paris: Julliard, 1983), 125. In the introduction to the English translation of several of his essays, Aron insists: "I am still convinced that the four categories of my postwar works constitute a logical, if not necessary, continuation of the basic question raised in the *Introduction to the Philosophy of History* [viz., the relation between action and history]" *Politics and History: Selected Essays by Raymond Aron,* trans.

and ed. Miriam Bernheim Conant (New York: Free Press, 1978), xix. This view is shared by his critics; for example, J.J. in a biographical essay on the occasion of Aron's death calls *Introduction* "the constitutive text for Aron's thought." *L'Express*, no. 1685 (27 October 1983), 100.

3. Raymond Aron, *Introduction to the Philosophy of History: An Essay on the Limits of Historical Objectivity,* 2d ed., rev. and trans. George J. Irwin (Boston: Beacon Press, 1961), 108; F 134; hereafter cited as *IPH.* This is a translation of *Introduction à la philosophie de l'histoire,* 2d ed. rev. (Paris: Gallimard, 1948). Though for ease of accessibility, my French references are to the Collection Tel augmented edition (Paris: Gallimard, 1981), I shall consider only those portions of the expanded work that occur in the first edition (1938), the one to which Sartre was responding.

In his lectures at the Collège de France thirty-five years later, Aron mentions his original desire to complement this text with another so as to "dissipate the impression of relativism or of skepticism" left by his two doctoral theses (Raymond Aron, *Leçons sur l'histoire* [Paris: Editions de Fallois, 1989], 30). Since my purpose is to analyze Sartre's understanding of Aron rather than determine the accuracy of that reading, I shall not devote much time to assessing the latter.

4. See *IPH* 86 ff. and esp. 111, 118–20; F 107 ff., 138, 148–49.

5. See *IPH* 72, 73, and 100; F 88, 90, and 125.

6. This remark, recorded by Gaston Fessard, who attended the defense, forms the center point of his study, *La Philosophie historique de Raymond Aron* (Paris: Julliard, 1980), 9; and see 44, 141. This volume also contains a separate bibliography of Aron's principal works in the philosophy of history.

7. One of Sartre's biographers calls Aron's *Introduction* "the first important philosophical work of its generation to have broached the problematic that will characterize existentialism: the meaning, the rationality of history." Anna Boschetti, *Sartre et "Les Temps modernes"* (Paris: Minuit, 1985), 226–27. Indeed, Aron recommends that "the historian must make his way through the diversity of works in order to come to the unity, both evident and perhaps intangible, of human existence" (*IPH* 93; F 116), which sounds very much like what Sartre is seeking at this time. But Sartre, as we shall see, finds Aron's underlying anthropology too "pluralist" and hence incapable of attaining that existential unity.

8. See *IPH* 341 and 299–300; F 429 and 378–79.

9. *Quiet Moments in a War: The Letters of Jean-Paul Sartre to Simone de Beauvoir, 1940– 1963,* ed. Simone de Beauvoir, trans. Lee Fahnestock and Norman MacAfee (New York: Scribners, 1993), 107 (letter of 12 March 1940).

10. See *IPH* 342, 347, and 365 respectively; F 432, 437, and 333.

11. "Philosophy is an inquiry concerning being and beings. Any thought that does not lead to an inquiry concerning being is not valid. . . . One must either begin with being or go back to it, like Heidegger," Sartre insisted in the opening "Interview with Jean-Paul Sartre," in *The Philosophy of Jean-Paul Sartre,* ed. Paul Arthur Schilpp (LaSalle, IL: Open Court, 1981), 14; hereafter cited as *PS.*

12. See Jean-Paul Sartre, *The Transcendence of the Ego,* trans. Forest Williams and Robert Kirkpatrick (New York: Noonday Press, 1957); hereafter cited as *TE.*

13. For a discussion of this ontology in a social context, see my *Sartre and Marxist Existentialism* (Chicago: University of Chicago Press, 1984), chaps. 1 and 2.

14. See Jean-Paul Sartre, "Intentionality: A Fundamental Idea of Husserl's Phenomenology," *Journal of the British Society for Phenomenology* 1, no. 2 (May 1970): 4–5. This essay originally appeared in January 1939.

15. "I opted for realism since my first year of philosophy," Sartre to Simone de Beauvoir in her *La Cérémonie des adieux* suivi de *Entretiens avec Jean-Paul Sartre* (Paris: Gallimard, 1981), 205.

16. This argument for metaphysical realism seems to anticipate Sartre's famous "reverse ontological argument" in *Being and Nothingness,* trans. Hazel E. Barnes (New York: Philosophical Library, 1956), 27–29; hereafter cited as *BN.*

After the war, Sartre will appeal to a "realism of temporality" in *What Is Literature?* trans. Bernard Frechtman (New York: Washington Square Press, 1966), 158 n; hereafter cited as *WL.* The expression denotes the "mediating role" of temporality in the insertion of a reader in the consciousness of a fictional character. Sartre wishes thereby to render effectively "the multidimensionality of the event." Though its dimensions are revealed via subjectivities, the event remains transcendent, that is, *other* than those revealing subjectivities. See below, chap. 4.

17. Quintin Hoare translates it by the equally awkward "be-been" (*WD* 205); F 253. See *BN* 78; F 121. The expression occurs for the first time in the same diary (*WD* 177; F 218).

18. Gilles Deleuze, *Bergsonism,* trans. Hugh Tomlinson and Barbara Habberjam (New York: Zone Books, 1991), 116. Bergson had already broached the topic in *Time and Free Will (Essai sur les données immédiates de la conscience,* 1889), but his most explicit treatment of simultaneity occurs apropos of Einsteinian relativity in *Duration and Simultaneity,* trans. Leon Jacobson (Indianapolis: Bobbs-Merrill, 1965).

19. See, e.g., Edward W. Soja, *Postmodern Geographies: The Reassertion of Space in Critical Social Theory* (London: Verso Books, 1989): "The discipline imprinted in a sequentially unfolding narrative predisposes the reader to think historically, making it difficult to see the text as a map, a geography of *simultaneous* relations and meanings that are tied together by a spatial rather than a temporal logic. My aim is to spatialize the historical narrative, to attach to *durée* an enduring critical human perspective" (1; emphasis mine).

20. John M. E. McTaggert, *The Nature of Existence,* 2 vols., (Cambridge: Cambridge University Press, 1927), vol. 2, 9–31.

21. He speaks of a "felt simultaneity" among his group of comrades at the Ecole Normale: "Because of the solidarity that united us, each of our gestures in the unity of our set would give itself as simultaneous with some other gesture of one of my comrades: that used to confer upon it a kind of necessity. I was horrified, in Berlin, to see how much the Germans enjoyed that kind of simultaneity" (*WD* 279).

Years later, when analyzing the practical identity of the group members via common action in the *Critique of Dialectical Reason,* Sartre harkens back to his early understanding of "simultaneity" but without resurrecting the term: Each other is the same and each there is here in practical identity and concern—like the teammates in a soccer match. This example of "dialectical nominalism" yields an account of collective identity and action without appeal to a collective subject (substance). See my "Mediated Reciprocity and the Genius of the Third," in *PS,* esp. 355–56.

22. Among the topics relevant to the philosophy of history that do interest him in *Being and Nothingness,* in addition to temporality, we should mention: historicity (temporality as the unique and incomparable mode of being of selfness [*BN* 158]), the phenomenon of historializing oneself (*s'historialise*) (*BN* 158), the Past (as coincidence of my ekstatic dimension and the past of the world; it is through the past that I belong to universal temporality [*BN* 208]), the infinite density of the world (*BN* 326), and prehistoric historization (*BN* 339).

23. Jean-Paul Sartre, *Search for a Method,* trans. Hazel E. Barnes (New York: Vintage Books, 1968); hereafter cited as *SM.* He does make brief reference to "comprehension" in *BN* in terms of the look, our understanding of the body, and the problem of other minds. In his *Notebooks for an Ethics,* trans. David Pellauer (Chicago: University of Chicago Press, 1992) he remarks, "to explain is to clarify by causes; to comprehend is to clarify by ends" (276); hereafter cited as *NE.* For the French, see *Cahiers pour une morale* (Paris: Gallimard, 1983); hereafter cited as *CM.*

24. For a recent restatement of this last thesis, see Volker R. Berghahn, *Imperial Germany, 1871–1914: Economy, Society, Culture, and Politics* (Providence, RI: Berghahn Books, 1994): "It was the men gathered at the Imperial Palace in Berlin who pushed Europe over the brink" (283).

25. Admittedly, his dialectical nominalism allows for a kind of collective—that is, social—subject as developed in the *Critique.* See n. 21 above and chap. 6.

26. "Human reality" is Henri Corbin's translation of Heidegger's *Dasein,* which Sartre adopts (see Martin Heidegger, *Qu'est-ce que la métaphysique? suivi d'extraits sur l'être et le temps et d'une conférence sur Hölderlin,* trans. Henri Corbin [Paris: Gallimard, 1937]). Human reality becomes the "everyman" of existentialist philosophy.

27. I trace the genesis and nature of this social ontology in my *Sartre and Marxist Existentialism,* chaps. 5 and 6.

28. Speaking of his early penchant to "overwhelm things in a hail of images," Sartre explains that "the invention of images was, fundamentally, a moral, sacred ceremony: it was the appropriation of that absolute, the thing, by that other absolute, myself" (*WD* 84). Of course, it is not a question of his supporting any two-substance ontology. Sartre's "myself" is not a thing but a "no-thing," a position he has maintained since *Transcendence of the Ego.*

29. I am presenting Aron's position as Sartre summarized it in the *War Diaries.* In fact, a lengthy comparison would find many similarities between Aron's influential volume and Sartre's subsequent reflections on history. But their alternative "anthropologies" and corresponding moral visions sharply distinguished the two former friends.

For a careful examination of the "covert debate" that Merleau-Ponty conducted with Aron on the philosophy of history during the 1940s, see Kerry H. Whiteside, "Perspectivism and Historical Objectivity: Maurice Merleau-Ponty's Covert Debate with Raymond Aron," *History and Theory* 25, no. 2 (1986): 132–51.

30. Thanking de Beauvoir for having mailed him some books, Sartre writes: "*Guillaume II* looks *enthralling*. I hope to find something concrete in it about that troubling business: the role of *one* man in a social event. I know Aron will say it's one layer of meaning among others. But even granting that, the meaning isn't simple" (de Beauvoir, ed., *Quiet Moments*, 97 [letter of 5 March 1940]).

31. The renderings of *s'historialiser* (to historialize oneself), *s'historiciser* (to historicize oneself), and *s'historiser* (to historize oneself) as well as their respective cognates are not consistent among Sartre's translators. I explain my choices in chap. 4, n. 20.

Although I discuss historialization at length in chap. 4, the following remark from *The Family Idiot,* his last major work, may serve to indicate where Sartre is heading when he adopts this terminology in the *War Diaries.* In what sounds like an attack on "structuralists," Sartre criticizes those who "have connived to suppress historialization [*historialisation*] as a dialectic of necessity and freedom in human praxis, and in the final analysis, in order to disclaim all responsibility, contested that praxis itself." Jean-Paul Sartre, *L'Idiot de la famille,* 3 vols. (Paris: Gallimard, 1971–72; vol. 3 rev. 1988), 3:429; trans. by Carol Cosman as *The Family Idiot,* 5 vols. (Chicago: University of Chicago Press, 1981–93), 5:397; hereafter cited as *IF* and *FI,* respectively, with volume and page numbers.

32. Foucault's directive in *The Archaeology of Knowledge* was to transform documents into monuments. See Michel Foucault, *The Archaeology of Knowledge,* trans. A. M. Sheridan Smith (New York: Harper Colophon Books, 1972), 7; hereafter cited as *AK.*

33. Anticipating a similar approach to his autobiography and with characteristic honesty, Sartre admits: "My own manner of being my dead eye is certainly my way of wanting to be loved through intellectual seduction" (*WD* 306).

34. In their influential *Introduction aux études historiques* (1898), Charles-Victor Langlois and Charles Seignobos had recommended that young historians of a "positivist" persuasion limit themselves to producing scholarly "monographs," leaving the reconstruction of the larger picture to older heads (see Philippe Carrard, *Poetics of the New History: French Historical Discourse from Braudel to Chartier* [Baltimore: Johns Hopkins University Press, 1992], 6).

35. "Between individuals and ensembles." Raymond Aron, *La Philosophie critique de l'histoire* (Paris: J. Vrin, 1969), 190. Originally published in 1938, this was the secondary thesis for his *doctorat d'état.*

36. In "Materialism and Revolution" he would later recommend that the concept of "situation" be exploited to build a philosophy of revolution. See Jean-Paul Sartre, *Literary and Philosophical Essays,* ed. Annette Michelson (New York: Crowell-Collier, Collier Books, 1962), 253. In fact, he will expand the concept to include the "social" situation, once his ontology allows it.

37. It is ironic that what two critics have called Aron's "most accomplished book," *Penser la guerre, Clausewitz* (Paris: Gallimard, 1976), is precisely such a blend of biography, sociopolitical history, philosophical reflection, and analysis of strategy (see Jean-Louis Missika and Dominique Wolton, "Chronologie," in the special issue on Aron of *Magazine littéraire,* no. 198 (September 1983), 21.

CHAPTER TWO

1. For loci of relevance to a theory of history in *Being and Nothingness* in addition to those listed in chap. 1, n. 22, see *BN* 158 (historicity), 267 (simultaneity), 347–49 (understanding and the document), and 557–75 (existential psychoanalysis: Flaubert).

2. I addressed these misgivings in the first two chapters of my *Sartre and Marxist Existentialism.*

3. There are 112 page references to Hegel listed in the index to the English translation of the *Notebooks,* surpassing by far the two next most frequently cited authors, Kant and Marx, with twenty-three apiece.

Pierre Verstraeten confirms this view: "Sartre's reading of Hyppolite's commentary on the *Phenomenology of Spirit* and of his translations of Hegel certainly had a decisive impact on his *Cahiers pour une morale* where Hegel's presence may be felt throughout" ("Appendix: Hegel and Sartre," in *The Cambridge Companion to Sartre,* ed. Christina Howells [Cambridge: Cambridge University Press, 1992], 353–54).

4. Alexandre Kojève, *Introduction à la lecture de Hegel: Leçons sur "La Phénoménologie de l'Esprit, "*ed. Raymond Queneau (Paris: Gallimard, 1947). Shadia B. Drury discusses the influence of these lectures rather unsympathetically in her *Alexandre Kojève: The Roots of Postmodern Politics* (New York: St. Martin's Press, 1994).

5. On three occasions Sartre cites Hyppolite's claim that "the whole must be immanent in the development of consciousness" in order to understand Hegel's basic claim that the negation of a negation can be a positivity (see *NE* 62, 164, 167).

6. The occasion was the only address Sartre ever delivered to the Société Française de Philosophie. See the English translation of this session, "Consciousness of Self and Knowledge of Self," in *Readings in Existential Phenomenology,* ed. Nathaniel Lawrence and Daniel O'Connor (Englewood Cliffs, NJ: Prentice-Hall, 1967), 113–42. Robert D. Cumming offers an excellent discussion of the Sartre-Hegel relationship in his "To Understand a Man," in *PS,* 55–85.

7. *PS,* 9. Of course, one should not ignore two other influential French Hegelian documents of the prewar period, Jean Wahl's proto-existentialist *Le Malheur de la conscience dans la philosophie de Hegel* (1929) (cited, though not by title, in *BN* 408) and the essays published in the Hegel centennial issue of the *Revue de Metaphysique et de morale* (1930). Still, neither of these is quoted in the *Notebooks.* Finally, one should mention Bruce Baugh's thesis that Sartre used a French anthology of Hegel's works in writing *Being and Nothingness,* specifically, *Morceaux choisis d'Hegel,* trans. and intro. Henri Lefebvre and N. Gutterman (Paris, 1936). This would confirm his avowal in the interview published in the Schilpp volume.

8. Consider, for example, his analyses of reciprocity (*NE* 284–90), joy (*NE* 484–85), gift giving (*NE* 368–77), generosity (*NE* 280–81, 499), "purifying reflection" (*NE* 480 ff.), and authentic love (*NE* 418, 501–8). These reflect accurately his self-assessment in the *War Diaries:* "If I leave to one side the destructive, anarchistic individualism of my nineteenth year, I see that immediately afterwards I concerned myself with a constructive morality. I have always been constructive, and *La Nausée* and *Le Mur* gave only a

false image of me, because I was obliged first to destroy" (*WD* 81–82). To be sure, at about the same time in *What Is Literature?* after arguing that, "if negativity is one aspect of freedom, constructiveness is the other," and that "literature is in essence a taking of position," Sartre had insisted that "our works should be presented to the public in a double aspect of negativity and construction" (*WL* 163, 192–93). But it was the negative aspect that captured the public's attention and, frankly, the one Sartre seemed most ready to promote.

9. François Dosse, *New History in France: The Triumph of the Annales,* trans. Peter V. Conroy, Jr. (Urbana: University of Illinois Press, 1994), 223. The journal, *Annales d'histoire économique et sociale,* founded in 1929 by Marc Bloch and Lucien Febvre, became the emblem and the leading voice of the French New Historians for the remainder of the century.

10. *WL* 158 n. These essays first appeared as articles in *Les Temps modernes* from February to July 1947.

11. See *BN* 180. Likewise in the *Notebooks* he insists: "There has to be a duality at the heart of freedom. And this duality is precisely what we are calling detotalized totality" (*NE* 332).

12. "Man is free because he is not a self but a presence-to-self" (*BN* 440; F 516). Sartre derives from Heidegger the notion that human reality (*Dasein*) is a "being of distances" (*WD* 108).

13. Contrasting Nikolay Bukharin or "our will *to be together* carried to the point of martyrdom" with Jean Genet or "our solitude carried to the point of Passion," Sartre notes: "We spent our time fleeing from the objective into the subjective and from the subjective into objectivity." But he warns, "This game of hide-and-seek will end only when we have the courage to go to the limits of ourselves in both directions at once," in other words, only when we have the courage to live authentically (Jean-Paul Sartre, *Saint Genet: Actor and Martyr,* trans. Bernard Frechtman [New York: New American Library, 1963], 599); hereafter cited as *SG.* One senses the postmodern tenor of this advice, with its rejection of dialectical sublation and emphasis on a chiasmic intensification of otherness.

14. "The historical fact experienced as a pluridimensional reality by a free consciousness is apprehended by the government as a statistical reality. Consequently it becomes inert and passive, it is a *thing* and one takes it into account as a thing: 27 per cent of the voters abstained from voting" (*NE* 75).

15. See *NE* 81.

16. Which is not to say it is totally without precedent. But its antecedents are evidence of a prior absorption of freedom into facticity (see *NE* 75 ff.)

17. "We could define the body as *the contingent form which is assumed by the necessity of my contingency"* (*BN* 309). Entry number 52 in the *Notebooks* reads: "The contingency of History = the necessity of our contingency. Existence of the body" (*NE* 41).

18. Later, in the *Critique,* Sartre will claim: "The essential discovery of Marxism is that labor, as a historical reality and as the utilization of particular tools in an already determined social and material situation, is the real foundation of the organization of

social relations. This discovery *can no longer* be questioned" (*Critique of Dialectical Reason,* vol. 1, trans. Alan Sheridan-Smith, [London: New Left Books, 1976], 1:152 n; hereafter cited as *CDR* with volume and page numbers.)

He adds in the *Notebooks* that work itself carries an ambiguous character. In order to act in the domain of the identical-exterior (that is, being-in-itself), "one must imitate the order of identity-exteriority in one's thought and in one's body." This "mechanistic" approach to reality he sees as materialistic and antidialectical. In fact, it is antidialectical precisely because it is materialistic—the argument he had mounted against the communists in his essay, "Materialism and Revolution," published the previous year (1946). It expresses "the analytical spirit of the polytechnician [like his stepfather] and the mathematician." Sartre warns that this "mechanistic thought [*la pensée-machine*] or nondialectical thinking in terms of exteriority is an important substructure of History. It acts as both *ideology* and as direct historical activity at the same time. It is the negation of the dialectic within History" (*NE* 64; F 70).

19. "All Freedom is transcended by all the other freedoms. It becomes *chance* for these others and its action becomes an object. Owing to this fact there is a *statistical* character to History" (*NE* 59).

20. Foucault will likewise seek to reintroduce the element of chance into historical analysis, though his context will no longer be that of Sartre's spontaneity-inertia dualism. I will discuss this apropos of Foucault's understanding of "event" in vol. 2.

21. Merleau-Ponty uses a similar Husserlian defense of historical objectivity in his implicit debate with Aron (see Whiteside, "Perspectivism," 142).

22. Though respecting each of the six layers or dimensions, an existentialist theory presumably would focus on original contingency and freedom.

23. Emmanuel Le Roy Ladurie, *The Territory of the Historian,* trans. Ben and Siân Reynolds (Chicago: University of Chicago Press, 1979), 285.

24. François Furet, *In the Workshop of History,* trans. Jonathan Mandelbaum (Chicago: University of Chicago Press, 1984), 10.

25. This emphasis on the importance of a philosophy of action and what later we shall call "the primacy of praxis" immediately separates Sartre from "postmodern" philosophers of history. F. R. Ankersmit, for example, states categorically: "Since it deals only with the components of historical narrative, philosophy of action can never further our insight into historical narrative." Specifically, it is the agent's unintended consequences that, according to Ankersmit, cannot be accounted for in this manner. "Von Wright's and Ricoeur's attempts to solve this problem for philosophy of action are unsuccessful," he continues. "Historical meaning is different from the agent's intention" (F. R. Ankersmit, *History and Tropology: The Rise and Fall of Metaphor* [Berkeley: University of California Press, 1994], 35; hereafter cited as *HT*).

26. Likewise in the *Notebooks* he observes that "in alienated action one acts in order to be or one acts in order to have" (*NE* 512).

27. This is how he describes "freedom" as well: "Freedom is internalization of exteriority (making *there be* these limits and that they be limits of a project) and externalization of interiority (realization of a project)" (*NE* 326). Once he fully adopts a praxis philosophy in the *Critique,* Sartre will describe subjectivity as "the moment in the objec-

tive process . . . in which exteriority is internalized" (*SM* 33 n) and dialectical praxis itself as "a passage from objective to objective through internalization." It involves "the joint necessity of 'the internalization of the external' and 'the externalization of the interior' " (*SM* 97).

28. A warning he later repeats apropos "the absolute and unsurpassable existence of the Other," where, without "a third term," to mediate me and the Other, there can be "an alignment of one of these modes of being, in its specificity, in terms of the other but not a *synthesis*" (*NE* 451–52).

29. In an interview with Pierre Verstraeten in 1965, Sartre avows with characteristic hyperbole: "[I] rarely use the notion of subjectivity except in a limiting sense such as 'this is only subjective,' . . . and the like. But for me, subjectivity does not exist; there is only internalization and exteriority" (*Situations,* 10 vols. [Paris: Gallimard, 1947–76], 9:51; hereafter cited as *S*; see William L. McBride, *Sartre's Political Theory* [Bloomington: Indiana University Press, 1991], 177, 236 n. 9).

30. In fact, he is already using "praxis" in *What Is Literature?* (1947), where he distinguishes a literature of "exis" from one of "praxis" defined as "action in history and on history; that is, as a synthesis of historical relativity and moral and metaphysical absolute, with this hostile and friendly, terrible and derisive world which it reveals to us" (*WL* 165; see below, chap. 6).

31. In the context of internalization/externalization, Sartre discusses at length the ontological, as distinct from the economic and social, conditions for oppression in history (see *NE* 325–411). That he devotes so much space to the topic indicates its growing importance for his theory. We shall recall the ontological when we treat the socioeconomic in chap. 6.

32. See below, chap. 10, n. 40.

33. On Sartre's relation to the Revolutionary People's Assembly (Rassemblement Démocratique Révolutionnaire [RDR]), which he joined in 1948, to the French Communist Party with which he labored pro and contra over the years, and to the *Gauchistes* of the late sixties and seventies, see my *"L'Imagination au pouvoir:* The Evolution of Sartre's Political and Social Thought," *Political Theory* 7, no. 2 (May 1979): 175–80, as well as Michel-Antoine Burnier, *Choice of Action,* trans. Bernard Murchland (New York: Random House, 1968).

34. See "Collective Responsibility as Socioethical Ideal" in my *Sartre and Marxist Existentialism,* 201–4. Already in the *War Diaries* he had linked acting "as if" to his thesis about radical moral responsibility in our ambiguous human condition (see *WD* 95). The moral ideal ("as if") of "fraternity" figures prominently in his last interviews with Benny Lévy (see "The Last Words of Jean-Paul Sartre: An Interview with Benny Lévy," *Dissent* 27 [Fall 1980]: 397–422; hereafter cited as "LW").

35. See *NE* 435–37. He excepts from this indeterminability "artificially and conventionally limited" situations like sports contests and also admits we can succeed in judging "certain cases of flagrant failure" (*NE* 436).

36. "Was the founding of Constantinople a success for Constantine or a failure?" Sartre asks. "That depends on where one cuts off the operation" (*NE* 436), a claim which could have been made by Aron. But recall that Sartre in the *War Diaries* had at-

tributed Aron's historical "relativism" in large measure to his lack of a concept of simultaneity. He reaffirms this concept equivalently in *Being and Nothingness* when he points out that "freedom causes a whole system of relations to be established, from the point of view of the end, between *all* in-itselfs; that is, between the *plenum* of being which is revealed then as the *world* and the being which it has to be in the midst of this *plenum* and which is revealed as *one* being, as one 'this' which it has to be" (*BN* 487).

37. Although Sartre has claimed that the good/bad faith distinction carries no moral significance in his writings, it seems clear that it does. I argue this in *Sartre and Marxist Existentialism,* chap. 3. Two recent studies of this issue are Ronald E. Santoni, *Bad Faith, Good Faith, and Authenticity in Sartre's Early Philosophy* (Philadelphia: Temple University Press, 1995) and Joseph Catalano, *Good Faith and Other Essays* (Totowa, NJ: Rowman and Littlefield, 1996).

38. For a discussion of the objective dialectic of chance and necessity in Marx and Hegel, see Alfred Schmidt, *History and Structure,* trans. Jeffrey Herf (Cambridge, MA: MIT Press, 1981) esp. 117 n. 122.

39. See the last word of the leading character of *Dirty Hands,* as he goes to his death rather than revise his story to conform with the new party line: "Unsalvageable! [*Irrécupérable!*]."

40. Speaking of the dissociation of the sign from resemblance in the early seventeenth century, Foucault remarks that there resulted "a single network of necessities." And he claims an archaeological analysis would show that "this network made possible the individuals we term Hobbes, Berkeley, Hume, or Condillac" (Michel Foucault, *The Order of Things: An Archaeology of the Human Sciences,* trans. A. Sheridan [New York: Random House Vintage Books, 1970], 63; hereafter cited as *OT*).

41. "No doubt every human action is creation, but we can consider most of them as secondary and as being reducible to two particular types: the engineer and the artist" (*NE* 537).

42. For further discussion of the analogue, see my "The Role of the Image in Sartre's Aesthetic," *The Journal of Aesthetics and Art Criticism* 33 (Summer 1975): 431–42. On "exigency," see Monica Hornyansky's essay, "Sartre and the Humanism of Spontaneity," in David Goicoechea, ed., *The Question of Humanism: Challenges and Possibilities* (Buffalo: Prometheus, 1991), 244–52, and my *Sartre and Marxist Existentialism,* 82–83.

43. See below, chap. 9.

44. More than twenty years later Sartre will contrast the "man of action" with the "pure artist" in terms of the former's dealing with a world of contingency/necessity that the latter escapes. By this time, however, he has at hand a fully developed concept of praxis and thus has more than the engineer for an alternative model of activity (see *FI* 5:170 ff.). Still, the creative artist remains for Sartre, as for Marx, the very model of the disalienated agent.

45. "Historical movement: two aspects: every idea is taken up [*reprise*] by free consciousness—every idea becomes a thing" (*NE* 13). From these cryptic remarks Sartre concludes: "The idea has two layers of objectivity: objectivity in immanence, that is, that it is not just thought and lived by me, but thought and lived by others. . . . [And

objectivity in] exteriority: that it exists for others who do not share it, [for] adversaries, neophytes, the indifferent. At this level the idea is completely a thing because it is opaque. One observes it from outside; one refuses to make the effort to enter in" (*NE* 14).

46. His thesis in "Materialism and Revolution," written at the same time as the *Notebooks*, was that the materialism of the Marxists is incompatible with historical dialectic (see Jean-Paul Sartre, *Literary and Philosophical Essays*, ed. Annette Michelson [New York: Collier Books, 1962], 198–256; hereafter cited as "MR"). For an excellent discussion of Sartre's own materialism, see Hazel E. Barnes, "Sartre as Materialist," in *PS* 661–84. On the concept of objective spirit, see below, chap. 8.

47. Sartre's use of the term "free alterity" to characterize disalienated relations among group members in the *Critique* (*CDR* 1:366) should suffice to prove the difference between alienation and otherness *sans phrase*. In other words, it would seem that at least at that moment and in that context the urge to escape freedom-limiting alterity has been satisfied.

The equivalence of alienation and objectification, as I have noted elsewhere (*Sartre and Marxist Existentialism*, 242 n. 8), is more complicated. Sartre is ambiguous on the matter, and opinions are justifiably divided. It must be admitted that he does speak of a basic, apparently ineliminable alienation both in the *Notebooks* and in the *Critique* (see, e.g., *NE* 413 and *CDR* 1:228 n). To the extent that this is coterminous with objectification, as McBride points out, it could be taken as a return from Marx to Hegel on this point (see McBride, *Sartre's Political Theory*, 130). Perhaps the most reasonable suggestion in this controversy is McBride's, namely, that we respect Sartre's attempt in the *Critique* "to distinguish between this ontological level of alienation and those more concrete, historically relative levels with which Marxism is generally concerned" (ibid. 77). Whoever would pursue this matter must take into account the role of scarcity (*la rareté*) in Sartre's understanding of alienation in its dehumanizing sense. See below, chap. 6.

48. See Thomas W. Busch, *The Power of Consciousness and the Force of Circumstances in Sartre's Philosophy* (Bloomington: University of Indiana Press, 1990), 26.

49. "Nothing can act on History without being in History and in question in History" (*NE* 45). This principle, which parallels his understanding of consciousness and his resultant opposition to psychological determinism in *Being and Nothingness*, constitutes his chief objection to historical materialism. By insisting on a one-way influence between economics and the superstructure, he insists, this theory places economics in effect *outside* history, despite its reference to the history of tools and technology. On the contrary, Sartre argues, if religion and ethics, for example, are affected by economics, the converse is equally true: "the economic is afloat in religion and ethics" (*NE* 45; F 50).

50. Jean-Paul Sartre, *The Psychology of Imagination*, trans. Bernard Frechtman (New York: Washington Square Press, 1966), 243–46; hereafter cited as *PI*.

51. See "MR" 200–217.

52. "History," he concludes, "is both the work [*oeuvre*] of humanity and its Destiny" (*NE* 107). From one point of view, Sartre argues, "it may also seem that humanity has no destiny and that destinies are merely intrahistorical since they come to each person as

to another. But my destiny is me coming to myself as an image. . . . The individual coming to himself in terms of the features of the universal, this is humanity's destiny" (*NE* 421–22). Aron had argued that "to free oneself from historicism is first of all to overcome fatalism" (*IPH* 298).

53. See below, chap. 7.

54. See "Existentialism Is a Humanism," in *Existentialism from Dostoevsky to Sartre,* ed. and intro. Walter Kaufmann (Cleveland: World Publishing, Meridian Books, 1956), 291 ff; hereafter cited as "EH." I reconstruct and analyze this argument in my *Sartre and Marxist Existentialism,* 33–41.

55. The term "open future" figures centrally in Simone de Beauvoir's elaboration on the unfinished theoretical business of Sartre's "Existentialism and Humanism" lecture of October 1945. Thus, she states as a basic thesis that "my freedom, in order to fulfill itself, requires that it emerge into an open future: it is other men who open the future to me, it is they who, setting up the world of tomorrow, define my future" (*An Ethics of Ambiguity,* trans. Bernard Frechtman [Secaucus, NJ: Citadel Press, 1948; French ed., 1947], 82).

56. See Martin Heidegger, *Sein und Zeit* (Tübingen: Max Niemeyer Verlag, 1963), 328 ff.

57. Elsewhere, Sartre describes the order of "things in the world in universal time" as one of "replacing each other without entering into any relation other than the purely external relations of succession" (*BN* 158).

58. Later in the *Notebooks* Sartre speaks of "objective temporalization" and of "given" temporality as nothing but "the noematic unification of many temporalities." But "it is *no one's* temporality," he insists, and, to the extent that my temporality is so objectified, it is alienated: "I perceive my own time on the basis of others' times" (*NE* 505).

CHAPTER THREE

1. "Nothing is further from the city of ends than the realized city of ends. This is why every historical system that *stops* the development of humanity at the phase of the self recuperating the self becomes a form of authoritarianism. This, properly speaking, is the *totalitarian idea.* Marx was correct to call what Hegel called the end of History the end of prehistory. Hence the city of ends, in realizing the human totality, because each man becomes an end for all others and all others ends for him, in fact realizes totalitarianism" (*NE* 169–70). What Sartre will later describe in the *Critique* is the formal structure of attempts, largely unsuccessful, to get *beyond* totalitarianism, that is, beyond "prehistory." But to link Sartrean totalization with totalitarianism as Lyotard and others do is to misread the *Critique.*

2. Thus Robert D. Cumming speaks of Sartre's "phenomenological dialectic" dating from his early Husserlian writings (see "To Understand a Man," in *PS* 68 ff.). Klaus Hartmann discovers a dialectical "logic of being" at work in *Being and Nothingness* that is similar to Hegel's *Science of Logic* (see Hartmann, *Sartre's Ontology* [Evanston, IL: Northwestern University Press, 1966]) as well as his essay, "Sartre's Theory of *Ensembles,*" in *PS* 631–60. For a broader-ranging study of the topic, see Gerhard Seel, *Sartres Dialektik*

(Bonn: Bouvier, 1971). In view of the foregoing, it is curious to find Sartre insisting late in his life: "At first I was a non-dialectician, and it was around 1945 that I really began to concern myself with the problem" (*PS* 18). Perhaps we should say of him what he said of Bergson, that before 1945 he was "a dialectician without knowing it" (*NE* 466).

3. "The motive force of History is freedom as negativity" (*NE* 116).

4. See below, chap. 4. Toward the end of his life he will confess: "But in all truth I still don't see clearly the real relationship between violence and fraternity" ("LW" 415).

5. Foucault argues: "From this follows a refusal of analyses couched in terms of the symbolic field or the domain of signifying structures, and a recourse to analyses in terms of the genealogy of relations of force, strategic developments, and tactics. Here I believe one's point of reference should not be to the great model of language [*langue*] and signs, but to that of war and battle. The history which bears and determines us has the form of a war rather than that of a language: relations of power not relations of meaning." As if to counter Sartre's prognosis even as he confirms his diagnosis, Foucault adds: "Neither the dialectic, as logic of contradictions, nor semiotics, as the structure of communication, can account for the intrinsic intelligibility of conflicts. 'Dialectic' is a way of evading the always open and hazardous reality of conflict by reducing it to a Hegelian skeleton, and 'semiology' is a way of avoiding its violent, bloody and lethal character by reducing it to the calm Platonic form of language and dialogue." Michel Foucault, *Power/Knowledge: Selected Interview and Other Writings, 1972–1977,* ed. Colin Gordon (New York: Pantheon Books, 1980), 114–15.

6. Sartre mentions a "nominalist dialectic" ("there is no strike, there are only strikers") at this point (*NE* 457), but is unwilling to adopt the term himself, as he will do in the *Critique.* But, by then, "real relations between men" have been added to his "nominalist" ledger, increasing its explanatory power as well as its problematic character as nominalist (see *SM* 76).

7. See the discussions of historialization in chap. 1 n. 30 and 4 n. 20.

8. See Robert Denoon Cumming's perceptive essay, "This Place of Violence, Obscurity and Witchcraft," in *Political Theory* 7, no. 2 (May 1979): 181–200.

9. Jean-Paul Sartre, *Réflexions sur la question juive* (Paris: Paul Morihien, 1946), trans. by George J. Becker as *Anti-Semite and Jew* (New York: Schocken Books, 1948), 148; hereafter cited as *AJ*. See also *NE* 316.

10. "The only authentic form of willing here consists in wanting the end to be realized by the other. And wanting here consists in engaging oneself in the operation. But not to do it oneself, rather to modify the situation so that the other can do it. Indeed, in so doing, I keep my *comprehension* since, in effect, I in no way negate the value and the end by surpassing them [as in the two previous examples of inauthentic willing], but, on the other hand, I preserve their autonomy for them in relation to me" (*NE* 279).

11. A similar claim regarding the priority of the ethical over the epistemic could be made for Sartre's use of Husserl's *epoche,* the bracketing of being, in the *Notebooks.* That the term has carried a moral as well as an epistemological significance for Sartre since he adopted it in *Transcendence of the Ego* (see *TE* 99–103) is indicative of his fundamental philosophical project.

12. Klaus Hartmann calls it "a dialectic of pairs" (*Sartres Sozialphilosophie* [Berlin: de Gruyter, 1966], 31). For a discussion of the several aspects of Sartre's dialectical Reason, see my *Sartre and Marxist Existentialism,* 84–91.

13. In his foreword to Lyotard's *The Postmodern Condition,* Fredric Jameson speaks of "the so-called crisis of representation, in which an essentially realistic epistemology, which conceives of representation as the reproduction, for subjectivity, of an objectivity that lies outside it—projects a mirror theory of knowledge and art, whose fundamental valuative categories are those of adequacy, accuracy, and Truth itself" (Jean-François Lyotard, *The Postmodern Condition,* trans. Geoff Bennington and Brian Massumi [Minneapolis: University of Minnesota Press, 1984], viii). Despite Sartre's ontological "realism" of events and consciousness (a "nonsubstantial absolute"), his epistemology does not fit easily into the mold of "mirror of nature" criticized by Rorty, Lyotard, or Foucault.

Similarly, although we are observing Sartre likening historiography to the production of a work of art, he would not subscribe to Lyotard's thematization of representation as a problem of theatricality, unless one took "re-presentation" in the sense Sartre will ascribe to "historialization," namely, the informed, empathetic comprehension of the historical agent's comprehension of his or her lived situation (see chap. 4).

Lyotard writes:

> We are used to positing the following sequence: there is the fact, then the witnesses' account, i.e., a narrative activity transforming the fact into a narrative. . . . The work proper to historical science will be to undo what is done by narration, to set out from the linguistic datum of the narrative to reach, by critical analysis (of document, text, sources), the fact that is the raw material of this production.
>
> This way of posing the problem of history poses a theatrics: outside is the fact, external to the theatrical space; on the stage is the narrative unwinding its dramatics; hidden in the wings, in the flies, under the stage, in the auditorium, is the director, the narrator, with all his machinery, the *fabbrica* of narration. The historian is supposed to undo all the machinery and machination, and restore what was excluded, having knocked down the walls of the theater. And yet it is obvious that the historian is himself no more than another director, his narrative another product, his work another narration, even if all this is assigned the index *meta- :* meta-diegesis, meta-narration, meta–narrative. History which talks about history, to be sure, but whose claim to reach this reference to the thing itself, the fact, to establish and restore it, is no less crazy, all in all rather crazier, than the power of literary fiction freely deployed in the hundreds of discourses from which is born the huge legend of, for example, the *Odyssey. (Des dispositifs pulsionnels* [Paris: Union générale d'éditions, 1973], 180–81; cited and trans. by Geoffrey Bennington, *Lyotard: Writing the Event* [New York: Columbia University Press, 1988], 10)

Although Sartre's concept of "fact" and its relation to "interpretation" has already become more nuanced than in the *War Diaries,* it will never evaporate into a mere placeholder in a language game, as Lyotard and perhaps even Foucault would have it. But when one shifts from "fact" to "event," the matter becomes more complex for both Lyotard and Foucault. I shall address that matter in volume 2.

14. See Claude Lévi-Strauss, *The Savage Mind* (Chicago: University of Chicago Press, 1966), 245–46. Raymond Aron raises the same objection in his *History and the Dialectic of Violence*, trans. Barry Cooper (Oxford: Basil Blackwell, 1975), 200. What Sartre says about "representation" in the *Notebooks* and elsewhere suggests that he has a rather uncritical understanding of the nature of language and the way that words relate to things. But his implicit semantic theory is considerably refined in *The Family Idiot*. This will constitute a major point of comparison with Foucault in volume 2.

15. See Aristotle, *Metaphysics*, 7.25.1035ᵇ35.

16. "Dialectic as a movement of reality collapses if time is not dialectic; that is, if we refuse to recognize a certain action of the future as such" (*SM* 92 n). Explaining why Marxism has to be dialectical, Sartre observes that "precisely because the present is violence and negativity, what saves it is *the action of the future*" (*NE* 167; F 175). That future is the socialist ideal of solidarity or brotherhood.

In a 1972 interview with Pierre Verstraeten, Sartre reaffirms: "I do think the future conditions the present, but you know how: as a possibility of going beyond it, not as a completed and determined reflexive term of that possibility" ("'I Am No Longer A Realist': An Interview with Jean-Paul Sartre," in *Sartre Alive*, ed. Ronald Aronson and Adrian van den Hoven [Detroit: Wayne State University Press, 1991], 98). The "realism" in the title is the political realism or *Realpolitik* with which Sartre had flirted in the 1950s.

17. Sartre dismisses Hegelian freedom as "Spinoza's necessity transferred to the temporal succession" (*NE* 464). It is absence of uncertainty, of risk, of chance, and, ultimately of moral *evil*—indications of the real for Sartre—that qualifies Hegel's dialectic and his freedom as "idealist."

Sartre once observed that, for his former teacher, the critical idealist Léon Brunschvicg, "evil and error were only false shows, fruits of separation, limitation, and finiteness" (*WL* 149). Whereas, in an early entry in his *War Diaries*, he admits: "From the onset I undoubtedly had a morality without a God—without sin, but not without evil. I shall return to this" (*WD* 70).

For Sartre's forceful statement that moral evil "can in no way be diverted, brought back, reduced, and incorporated into idealistic humanism, like the shade of which Leibnitz has written that it is necessary for the glare of daylight," see *WL* 150. His conclusion that "evil cannot be redeemed" (*WL* 151) lends the optimism of his theory of history a somber hue.

18. In the *Critique*, apocalypse is the point at which group unity emerges out of "serial" dispersion. Its paradigm is the mob fusing into a group as it storms the Bastille, 14 July 1789.

19. On Sartre's political anarchism, see my *Sartre and Marxist Existentialism*, 70, as well as "From '*Socialisme et Liberté*' to '*Pouvoir et Liberté*': Sartre and Political Existentialism," in *Phenomenology in a Pluralistic Context*, ed. William L. McBride and Calvin O. Schrag (Albany: State University of New York Press, 1983), 25–38.

20. See *The Psychology of Imagination, What Is Literature?*, various essays gathered in the ten volumes of *Situations*, as well as his "biographies" of Baudelaire, Genet, and Flaubert.

21. "Historical revolution depends on moral conversion. Utopia is when the conversion of everyone at once, which is always possible, is the least probable occurrence (because of the diversity of situations). One must therefore seek to equalize these situations to make this combination less improbable and to give History a chance of getting beyond pseudo-History" (*NE* 49).

22. See my *Sartre and Marxist Existentialism,* esp. chap. 6, "Sartre's Social Ontology: The Problem of Mediations."

23. But it would be a mistake simply to equate methodological individualism with one of its (more vulnerable) subspecies, "psychologism," as J. W. N. Watkins points out in a series of essays reprinted in *Modes of Individualism and Collectivism,* ed. John O'Neill (London: Heinemann, 1973), esp. 173 ff. On the holist/individualist distinction, see my *Sartre and Marxist Existentialism,* chap. 7.

24. "What is particularly bad in *L'Etre et le Néant* is the specifically social chapters, on the 'we,' compared to the chapters on the 'you' and 'others'" (*PS* 13).

25. "Noematic" in phenomenology denotes the object pole, the "object-as-meant," of intentional analysis. It is the "other than consciousness" that consciousness aims toward in each of its meaning-giving (noetic) acts. As such, it is "real" rather than merely mental.

26. See Edmund Husserl, *Husserliana,* vol. 14, *Zur Phänomenologie der Intersubjektivität,* pt. 2, ed. Iso Kern (The Hague: Martinus Nijhoff, 1973), 200–204, 404. See also David Carr's excellent discussion of this matter in chap. 5 of his *Time, Narrative, and History* (Bloomington: Indiana University Press, 1986).

27. See, for example, G. A. Cohen, *Karl Marx's Theory of History* (Princeton, NJ: Princeton University Press, 1978), 134–80; Allen Wood, *Karl Marx* (London: Routledge and Kegan Paul, 1981), 70 ff., 245 n. 20; John McMurtry, *The Structure of Marx's World-View* (Princeton, NJ: Princeton University Press, 1978), 54–71, 188–239; and William H. Shaw, *Marx's Theory of History* (Stanford, CA: Stanford University Press, 1978), 53–82. Richard W. Miller takes issue with what he admits is "the dominant position" in his *Analyzing Marx: Morality, Power and History* (Princeton, NJ: Princeton University Press, 1984), 188 ff.

28. See Philippe Gavi, Pierre Victor, and Jean-Paul Sartre, *On a raison de se révolter* (Paris: Gallimard, 1974), 60 ff.; hereafter cited as *ORR.*

29. See Raymond Aron, *Marxism and the Existentialists,* trans. Helen Weaver, Robert Addis, and John Weightman (New York: Harper and Row, 1969), 30.

30. One sees a theoretical basis for his later progressive-regressive method in the strict parallelism that Sartre describes in the *Notebooks* between historical materialism and psychoanalysis. The parallels follow ten points: (1) both conceive phenomena as possessing a signification that is at once itself and the expression of something other than itself; (2) both deal with phenomena that are mystifying and merely symbolically satisfying when they are taken as independent entities; (3) in each case one tries to demonstrate the superstructure as an effect of the infrastructures by means of a deciphering of what is manifest; (4) each shows a certain hesitancy about the reality of the phenomenon they are considering; (5) "in both cases there is a projection, behind the contingent series of phenomena, of an underlying offensive and defensive dialectic—especially a

defensive one"; both explain the contingency of the conscious by a strategy of the unconscious; (6) both reduce the higher to the lower, class warfare to interest and individual human activity to sexuality or the will to power. Both replace the idea of the total fact
(Marcel Mauss) by an analytic relation; (7) both share the common modern idea of a
hermeneutic which must do violence to man in order to uncover his secret; (8) both use
methods aimed more at changing the world than at knowing it; (9) "in both cases these
kinds of pragmatism are at the same time forms of skepticism"; and finally (10) there are
numerous passages from one discipline to the other. He concludes by asking: "What is
the structure of our society that provokes the appearance of this emphasis on hermeneutics?" (*NE* 434–35; F 449–50) The very idea that a social structure can "provoke" an
activity of any sort indicates the degree to which Sartre has moved toward a concept of
social conditioning, difficult to reconcile with the absolute autonomy of the individual
during his vintage existentialist days. And yet, years later, in an explicit appeal to dialectics, Sartre will distinguish being "conditioned" from being "determined"; the former
remains on the level of freedom (see *Sartre Alive*, ed. Aronson and van den Hoven, 94).
Again, it is a question of refining his notion of being-in-situation (see my *Sartre and
Marxist Existentialism*, 72–84).

CHAPTER FOUR

1. "After the war came the true experience, that of *society*." "The Itinerary of a
Thought," in Jean-Paul Sartre, *Between Existentialism and Marxism*, trans. John Mathews
(New York: William Morrow, 1974), 34; hereafter cited as *BEM*. Elsewhere he links the
experience with his mobilization in 1939. See "Self-Portrait at Seventy," in Jean-Paul
Sartre, *Life/Situations*, trans. Paul Auster and Lydia Davis (New York: Pantheon Books,
1977), 47–48; hereafter cited as *L/S*. His "official" biographer, John Gerassi, locates
Sartre's politicization at the time of the Spanish Civil War. See John Gerassi, *Jean-Paul
Sartre: Hated Conscience of His Century*, vol. I, *Protestant or Protester?* (Chicago: University
of Chicago Press, 1989), 131 ff.

2. See "LW" 397–422, as well as de Beauvoir, *La Cérémonie des adieux*, esp. 54–56,
150–51, where she insists that "this vague and soft philosophy that Victor [Benny Lévy]
attributed to Sartre did not become him at all" (151). In a footnote she claims that Aron
shares her criticism of Lévy.

3. This is not to say that I would go so far as Jeannette Colombel, who reads the
Notebooks as the authentic Sartre, revived in the Lévy interview, and his subsequent
"Marxist" writings as unfortunate but temporary lapses. See her *Jean-Paul Sartre*, 2 vols.
(Paris: Librairie générale française, le Livre de poche, 1986), 2:739 ff. For a more moder-
ate assessment of this matter, though one that I believe fails to appreciate the full value
of the *Notebooks* in Sartre's intellectual evolution, see Sonia Kruks, "Sartre's *Cahiers pour
une morale*: Failed Attempt or New Trajectory in Ethics?" *Social Text*, no. 13/14 (Win-
ter/Spring, 1986), 184–94.

4. In his sole attempt at an epistemology, the posthumously published *Truth and Existence*, he writes with characteristic drama: "In any *truth* there is an *irreparable* aspect.
Each truth is both dated and historical, and it mortgages the infinity of the future; and it
is *I* who confer this infinite existence of the 'has been' on everything that I see. . . .

Therefore, in the face of the dazzling night of Being, consciousness . . . discovers a type of pitiless being without compromises or accommodations, the absolute and irremediable necessity of being what we are—forever and beyond all changes" (Jean-Paul Sartre, *Truth and Existence*, trans. Adrian van den Hoven [Chicago: University of Chicago Press, 1992], 45–46; hereafter cited as *T*).

5. In *What Is Literature?*, Sartre speaks in favor of a realism "of temporality" as distinct from dogmatic realism, by which the author imposes on the reader "the time of [the character's] consciousness without abridgement." Presuming what he had written about the temporality of being-in-itself in *Being and Nothingness,* this realism relies, not only on the order of relationships that choice brings into play (facticity, simultaneity, or "the fibrous unity of the world"), but also on the "absolute, undated time" of the existential ekstases of project and presence-to, that is, of the future and the present. The novelist must respect these dimensions and these relationships even as he or she intervenes to order them artfully, that is, by "lying in order to tell the truth" (*WL* 158 n).

6. See Arthur C. Danto, *Narration and Knowledge* (New York: Columbia University Press, 1985), 84–87, 147; and Gilbert Ryle, *The Concept of Mind* (London: Hitchinson's University Library, 1949), 301–4.

7. See his remarkable interview with Pierre Verstraeten, "L'Ecrivain et sa langue," *S* 9:40–82.

8. In his review of Paul Veyne's *Comment on écrit l'histoire*, reprinted in the appendix of his *Introduction à la philosophie de l'histoire*, Aron seems to agree with the author: "L'histoire-narration est un roman vrai" (509). Sartre insists that his Flaubert study is "un roman vrai" (see *S* 9:123). Elsewhere Aron notes: "What Sartre takes as the essence of the novel—the reader has the feeling that the characters are acting freely and, at the same time, that their acts are never arbitrary or random—constitutes as well the final justification of the historical narrative" (*Introduction à la philosophie de l'histoire*, 475).

9. Fredric Jameson, *The Political Unconscious: Narrative as a Socially Symbolic Act* (Ithaca: Cornell University Press, 1981), 35.

10. Denis Hollier, *Politique de la prose: Jean-Paul Sartre et l'an quarante* (Paris: Gallimard, 1982), 99; trans. by Jeffrey Mehlman as *The Politics of Prose: Essay on Sartre* (Minneapolis: University of Minnesota Press, 1986), 59.

11. See below, chap. 6, where I discuss the "serial" relations between individuals in the "collective," what Sartre terms "fundamental sociality" (*CDR* 1:318), and the "pledged group," which he characterizes as "the origin of humanity" (*CDR* 1:436) and, we might add, of "history" as well. Later he will go so far as to admit: "I don't believe that an individual alone can accomplish anything" (*ORR* 171). I consider this at greater length in my *Sartre and Marxist Existentialism.*

12. Hayden White, *The Content of the Form* (Baltimore: Johns Hopkins, 1987), 24; hereafter cited as *C*. He insists that "narrativity, certainly in factual storytelling and probably in fictional storytelling as well, is intimately related to, if not a function of, the impulse to moralize reality, that is, to identify it with the social system that is the source of any morality that we can imagine." Echoing Frank Kermode (*The Sense of an Ending*), he continues, "the demand for closure in the historical story is a demand, I suggest, for

moral meaning, a demand that sequences of real events be assessed as to their significance as elements of a moral drama" (*C* 14, 21).

13. See, e.g., his series of conversations with the Maoists Philippe Gavi and Pierre
Victor (a.k.a. Benny Lévy), *ORR.* Sartre's support of direct action as counterviolence
reached its extreme in his preface to Frantz Fanon's *The Wretched of the Earth,* trans. Con-
stance Farrington (New York: Grove Press, 1968).

14. He does introduce a "literature of praxis" in preference to one of "hexis" in *What
Is Literature?* There he describes praxis as "action in history and on history; that is, as a
synthesis of historical relativity and the moral and metaphysical absolute, with this hostile and friendly, terrible and derisive world which it reveals to us" (*WL* 165–66; F 265).
"Praxis" will become the pivotal concept in his later thought. But as yet it has not figured in his social ontology.

15. See my "From '*Socialisme et Liberté,*' " 26–38. Late in life, when asked about his
acceptance of the term "libertarian socialism," Sartre replied: "It is an anarchist term,
and I keep it because I like to recall the somewhat anarchist origins of my thought." But
when pressed to say whether he would "adopt an anarchist view of history" in the series
of television programs that he was then considering producing, he responded: "Anarchist, no; but we will talk about anarchism" (*PS* 21).

16. See "LW" 397–422.

17. Jean-Paul Sartre and Michel Sicard, "Entretien: L'écriture et la publication,"
Sartre Inédit, special issue of *Obliques* (1979, nos. 18–19), 15. The interview is dated
1977–78.

18. I have added the causal connector "because of" where Sartre merely juxtaposes
two sentences. For the justification of this move, see his earlier aperçu, "my freedom
implying mutual recognition" (*NE* 470) as well as my reconstruction of his argument in
"Existentialism Is a Humanism" to that effect (see my *Sartre and Marxist Existentialism,*
33–41).

19. In a note to *Truth and Existence,* Sartre's adopted daughter, Arlette Elkaïm-Sartre,
explains: "Sartre's thesis of conversion is developed in *Notebooks for an Ethics* (471–531).
For Sartre, to state that inauthenticity is a mode of common being is to state that, in
order to escape from contingency, the primordial human project seeks perpetually to
become one with one's 'character,' one's social situation, one's possessions, etc. . . . *Accomplice reflection* is the means by which the for-itself tries to make itself in-itself-for-
itself. These attempts remain futile: I cannot convince myself in a lasting manner that I
am such and such. On the other hand, the look of the other unifies, whether I wish it or
not, the totality of my behaviors and tends to consider me as a *being.* This is the origin of
alienation, either because I do everything to identify myself with that being that the look
of the other returns to me, or because I seek to escape from it. *Pure reflection* is the conscious grasping of that fundamental failure of accomplice reflection; it is the first step
towards what Sartre calls *conversion,* or the project of calling oneself into question as
existent, instead of seeking to congeal oneself in *being* [*être*]. It is the acceptance of the fact
that the mode of being of the existent is 'diasporatic' " (*T* 83 n. 1).

20. A word about terminology. Sartre is rather consistent in distinguishing *historicité*

and its verb *s'historiciser* from *historisation* and its verb *s'historiser,* and in separating both pairs from *historialisation* and its verb *s'historialiser.* This is already evident in the *War Diaries* and in *Being and Nothingness* (for example, *BN* 158; F 205, and *BN* 339; F 405); it continues throughout the *Notebooks.*

Unfortunately, there is no uniformity among his English translators of these terms. For example, *s'historialise,* the chief troublemaker, is rendered as "historializes himself" (Quinton Hoare [*WD* 318] and Adrian van den Hoven [*T* 78]), as "historicizes itself" (Hazel Barnes [*BN* 158] and Bernard Frechtman [*WL* 80]), and as "historizes himself" (David Pellauer [*NE* 489], though he also uses "historialization" where consistency would have counseled "historization" [see *NE* 451; F 466, and *NE* 467; F 483]). Pellauer cites Corbin's coinage of *s'historialiser* (from the old French word, *historial*) to translate Heidegger's *geschehen* and Macquarrie and Robinson's creation of "to historize" to render the same German term as his reason for following Macquarrie and Robinson (see Heidegger, *Qu'est-ce que la métaphysique?,* 16, 23). For Sartre followed Corbin in this case as he did, unfortunately, when he translated *Dasein* as *realité humaine* (human reality). We know the misreading of Heidegger that resulted from the latter decision. Moreover, Paul Ricoeur, who translates Heidegger's related term *Geschichtlichkeit* as *historialité,* which McLaughlin and Pellauer(!) render "historicality," explains that two of the features of "historicality" are "the extension of time between birth and death, and the displacement of accent from the future to the past" (Ricoeur, *Time and Narrative,* trans. Kathleen McLaughlin and David Pellauer, 3 vols. [Chicago: University of Chicago Press, 1984–88], 1:61–62; trans. from Ricoeur, *Temps et récit,* 3 vols. [Paris: Editions du Seuil, 1983–85], 1:97). Though the first feature approaches Sartre's "historialization," the second clearly belongs with "historization." In other words, one should not imitate Corbin in this case either, because Sartre, though seeming to gloss Heidegger, once again has something of his own in mind.

But Pellauer's decision gives rise to further difficulties. By translating *s'historialise* as "historizes itself," he is forced to translate *s'historise* as "historicizes itself" (*NE* 38; F 43), which is not only awkward but unlikely, as becomes evident when, five lines later, he translates *historicisation* as the unexceptionable "historicization." In fact, later he translates *s'historicise* also as "historicizes himself" (*NE* 89; F 96). So this game of musical chairs has come to an end, as it seemed bound to, with two French terms trying to fit on the same English translation. Though I understand Pellauer's reasons (and we are all indebted to him for his fine translation of the *Notebooks*), I think that confusion will be minimized if we stay as close as possible to the virtually transliterated French terms. Thus I shall follow Hoare and van den Hoven in this matter. So when Sartre writes to himself cryptically: "Oppose the lived historical fact to the historical fact interpreted by the following generations" (*NE* 40), I shall read him as intending to oppose "historialization" to "historization" with its consequent "historicity."

21. Interestingly, we have the testimony of one such figure, Jean Genet, to whom Sartre devoted a major existential biography. After having read the manuscript, Genet wrote to Jean Cocteau: "You and Sartre have turned me into a monument. I am somebody else, and this somebody else must find something to say." To which Cocteau notes: "Jean has changed since the publication of Sartre's book. . . . He looks as if he

were trying at once to follow it and to escape it" (quoted by Annie Cohen-Solal, *Sartre: A Life*, trans. Anna Cancogni [New York: Pantheon Books, 1987], 317). On Sartre's account, "when Genet held in his hands the manuscript of my book about him, his first impulse was to throw it in the fire" (*L/S* 122).

Sartre was not unaware of the problem: "[Genet] was teaching French in Prague at a time he told us he was in prison; a private teacher, but still a teacher. The prison was sheer invention; he was teaching French. So he is a much more complex character than the one I showed, but I knew that" (*Sartre Alive*, ed. Aronson and van den Hoven, 93). As he repeated on several occasions, in art "one must lie to tell the truth."

22. Appeal to hermeneutics reminds one immediately of Gadamer and Ricoeur and whatever parallels might obtain between project-situation and text-context. Cf. White, "The 'reading' of an action, according to Ricoeur, resembles the reading of a text; the same kind of hermeneutic principles are required for the comprehension of both" (*C* 50).

23. For a defense of the thesis that Sartre is fundamentally a philosopher of the imagination, see my "Philosophy of Existence 2: Sartre," in *Continental Philosophy in the Twentieth Century,* Routledge History of Philosophy, vol. 8, ed. Richard Kearney (London: Routledge, 1994), 74–104.

24. In a remark that epitomizes his existentialist approach to history, Sartre assures us: "It is in historialization that the concrete absolute, and the unveiling of truth to the absolute-subject reside. The mistake," he assures us, "is in seeing an epiphenomenon of historicity there, instead of seeing historicity as the meaning conferred on my project insofar as it is no longer lived or concrete, but pure abstract in-itself" (*T* 79–90).

At the start of the same work, Sartre appeals to what we have been calling "history as fact and as value" with the lapidary remark: "Authenticity must be sought in historialization [*historialisation*]" (*T* 2). He concludes with the injunction that we "historialize ourselves against historicity" and explains that "this can be done only by clinging to the finitude of the lived experience as interiorization," thereby linking historialization and authenticity once more (*T* 80).

Finally, in his Flaubert study, in what sounds like an attack on "structuralists," Sartre criticizes those who "have connived to suppress historialization [*historialisation*] as a dialectic of necessity and freedom in human praxis, and in the final analysis, in order to disclaim all responsibility, contested that praxis itself" (*FI* 5:397; F 3:429).

25. This Heideggerian theme of choice as revelatory of Being is central to de Beauvoir's argument (see de Beauvoir, *Ethics of Ambiguity*, 23, 30, 34, 42, 70, 78). Sartre adopts it when he describes truth as the "progressive disclosure of Being" in *Truth and Existence*, 5. Composed shortly after the *Notebooks*, this posthumously published manuscript comprises Sartre's reflections on Heidegger's *On the Essence of Truth*, which had recently appeared in French translation. Significantly, though the text is in large part a phenomenology of ignorance, and as such makes a major contribution to Sartrean epistemology, it devotes considerable attention to morality and history.

26. "We shall use the expression *Circuit of selfness* [*Circuit de l'ipséité*] for the relation of the for-itself with the possible which it is, and 'world' for the totality of being in so far as it is traversed by the circuit of selfness" (*BN* 102).

27. He echoes this remark in *Truth and Existence*, linking it with the concept of the

concrete universal: "In the total historialization of the for-itself, which assumes a lived knowledge of its place in relationship to yesterday, today, and tomorrow and defines this place as an absolute, there is *the choice* of the consciousnesses to whom this truth is given in order that they may live it: this is the concrete universal of today and tomorrow. . . . I hand them my truth but as freedoms exterior to my history; these freedoms will reassume it to make of it whatever they want. In a sense, I define *our* 'end of history' within a larger history." But he is quick to warn us: "This does not mean at all that the truth I defend appears to me relative *to my age;* this has no meaning at all. It is true for me in the absolute and I give it to others as absolute. And *it is* indeed absolute. Simply, I determine the period when it will be alive" (*T* 10–12).

Rhiannon Goldthorpe points out that "both Dilthey and Sartre use the term 'epoch' in a specialized sense, seeing it as a center of concrete purposes and values, in terms of 'lived' emotions and impulses, and as a whole but finite system of dynamic connections discovered through intersubjectivity" ("Understanding the Committed Writer," in *The Cambridge Companion to Sartre,* ed. Howells, 275 n. 8).

28. One could compare this to the relationship whereby the spectator, by adopting the aesthetic attitude, "animates" the artifact into the analogon for the work of art. See above, chap. 2, and *PI* 239–40, 246–53.

29. In the inaugural editorial to *Les Temps modernes* (1945), Sartre had already voiced his intention to publish historical studies that worked on the assumption that "the age expresses itself in and by persons and that persons choose themselves in and by their age" (*S* 2:29).

30. Robert Stone and Elizabeth Bowman describe the three manuscripts as: (1) A 165-page manuscript (139-page typescript) of notes for the 1964 Rome lecture, hereafter cited as *RLN*; (2) An untitled 499-page typescript of unorganized notes labeled "Sartre's *Morale* 1964" by its owner, John Gerassi; and (3) a 225-page manuscript of notes in six titled sections, probably drafted for "*Recherches pour une Morale*"—the title of a lecture series Sartre planned to give at Cornell in April 1965 (see Stone and Bowman, "Dialectical Ethics: A First Look at Sartre's Unpublished 1964 Rome Lecture Notes," *Social Text* 13–14 [Winter/Spring 1986]: 195). Stone and Bowman consider the *Rome Lecture Notes* "by far the most finished of the three writings on dialectical ethics" and add that "Sartre edited the typescript himself with publication in mind" ("Dialectical Ethics" 196).

For discussion of the third manuscript, see their "Sartre's *Morality and History*: A First Look at the Notes for the Unpublished 1965 Cornell Lectures," in *Sartre Alive,* ed. Aronson and van den Hoven, 53–82 (where the number of pages for ms. 2 is listed as 589 and for ms. 3 as 120); and their " 'Making the Human' in Sartre's Unpublished Dialectical Ethics," in *Writing the Politics of Difference,* ed. Hugh J. Silverman (Albany: SUNY Press, 1991), 111–22. A portion of the Rome lecture has been translated as "Determinism and Freedom," in *The Writings of Jean-Paul Sartre,* ed. Michel Contat and Michel Rybalka, trans. Richard McCleary, 2 vols. (Evanston: Northwestern University Press, 1974), 2:241–52. Passages from the first manuscript, titled significantly "*Notes sur les rapports entre la morale et l'histoire,*" are cited in Francis Jeanson, *Sartre* (Paris: Desclée de Brouwer, 1966), 137–38. Because of its inaccessibility, I have not consulted the second manuscript, but quote from references to it from the essay by Verstraeten, "Impératifs et valeurs," in *Sur les écrits posthumes de Sartre,* ed. Pierre Verstraeten, Annales de l'Institute de Philosophie et de Sciences morales, 1987 (Bruxelles: Editions de l'Université de Bruxelles, 1987).

Regarding Sartre's second ethics, one should consult several of the essays gathered by Verstraeten in *Sur les écrits posthumes de Sartre.* These include Juliette Simont's "Autour des Conférences de Sartre à Cornell" as well as Verstraeten's comments on the second manuscript, "Impératifs et valeurs." And Benny Lévy's observations on this topic in his *Le Nom de l'homme* (Lagrasse: Editions Verdier, 1984) are relevant as well.

Finally, there is Thomas C. Anderson's excellent *Sartre's Two Ethics: From Authenticity to Integral Humanity* (Chicago: Open Court, 1993). This is the only book-length study to date of Sartre's first two attempts at formulating an ethics.

31. On the accessibility question, see McBride, *Sartre's Political Theory,* 212–13 n. 19. Like McBride, I am deeply indebted to Bowman and Stone for generously sharing the relevant material in their possession.

32. Note to Robert Stone, cited in Bowman and Stone, "Dialectical Ethics," 319 n. 13.

33. Sartre makes a similar claim in the collection of notes to himself (in the second manuscript): "Ethics [*la morale*] is basically the meaning/direction [*le sens*] of history— to the extent that the future is defined beyond inert norms as the unconditioned possibility of being a totality that governs its parts, [that is] inasmuch as men wish praxis to escape the practico-inert." Quoted by Pierre Verstraeten, "Impératifs et valeurs," 66.

34. On praxis and the practico-inert, see below, chap. 6. As Stone and Bowman remark, "If Sartre, in *Critique of Dialectical Reason,* traces the structures of history back to praxis of the common individual, then in the *Rome Lecture Notes* he does the same for the structures of morality. Against the post-structuralist current of our times, he places morality back in the hands of free practical agents" ("Dialectical Ethics," 211).

35. Verstraeten informs us that the second manuscript discusses the complementary but equally alienated and alienating ethics of "the imperative" and of "values" that dominate our current moral landscape. The latter is more idealist, the former more materialist, but they complement each other in what Verstraeten calls their "ontological hypocrisy" of seeming to foster freedom-autonomy when, in fact, they curtail and mystify it ("Impératifs et valeurs," 71).

36. *RLN* 100, cited by Jeanson, *Sartre,* 138.

37. The qualification "quasi"-naturalist seems called for because Anderson, for example, argues for the "naturalist" reading while Stone and Bowman resist it (in discussions at the biennial meeting of the North American Sartre Society in Chicago, 9 October 1994). Given the command both parties have of the texts in question, my thesis of the basic *ambiguity* of the ontology sustaining that debate gains in plausibility.

Anderson notes this with regard to the topic of the present chapter when he writes: "Actually, in this lecture Sartre's position on history is somewhat ambiguous. Occasionally, he speaks, as he did in the *Critique,* as if all of history is *in fact* moving toward this single goal [integral humanity]; other times he sounds as if he means only that history *should* move toward this end" (*Sartre's Two Ethics,* 123). I am arguing that this ambiguity between fact and value permeates Sartre's entire theory of history, including the *Critique.*

Now if we recall that Sartre is in the process of forming a *dialectical* ethics, then this

ambiguity may seem less a liability than an asset. Sartre implies this in his discussion
with the young Maoists a few years later. The topic is the movement from fact to value,
from social situation to revolt. He is contrasting the universal/particular as value and
antivalue respectively:

> Value and antivalue are not given like facts but like the meaning [*sens*] of facts.
> Each person must invent them, create them. . . . And this surpassing of facts and of
> false values toward true ones is the moment of freedom [*la liberté*]. Because values
> already exist. I am not at all an idealist, but values are such that one must discover
> them or invent them, and the two words mean the same. And it's this invention that
> makes us abandon the field of facts pure and simple in order to find there the con-
> tradiction of the universal and the particular that I call freedom. If you care to see
> this as a moment in a dialectical process, that's the same thing as far as I'm con-
> cerned. . . . Facts determine other facts, but can't account for revolt, that is to say,
> for the passage to value and the judgment: "That's not just!" (*ORR* 139–40)

Apropos of another issue with which we have been concerned from the outset, Sartre
reiterates a claim about rationality that we have seen taking shape in his earlier works
but which is fully formed in the *Critique,* namely that for structuralism and positivist
thought generally, there are histories but not a unified history, because the kind of rationality they employ blinds them to dialectical, totalizing praxis (see *RLN* 25).

38. Jeanson, *Sartre,* cited in Bowman and Stone, "Dialectical Ethics" 203.

39. I have not seen the second manuscript (the hundreds of pages of notes to himself
in preparation for his second ethics). But Verstraeten analyzes some one hundred pages
of this collection in his essay, "Impératifs et valeurs," 55–75. I have already cited the
second manuscript via this text, but shall not discuss the essay itself. The second manuscript does not seem to differ substantially from the other two in content.

40. Cited by Simont, "Autour des conférences de Sartre à Cornell," 45. As she para-
phrases this portion of his argument:

> Ethics [*l'ethique*] is an essential but provisional moment of every action: the mo-
> ment of invention, of positing the end as a definite nonbeing in terms of which one
> deciphers being. By realizing itself in historical action, this moment becomes [*fait*]
> the object of a circular reconditioning, and so of an immersion in history. Ethical
> action is intelligible insofar as it merely exploits a possibility given in every action,
> the unconditional possibility: it extends this possibility, gives it its greatest full-
> ness, but at the same time limits it to that, excluding from it other dimensions of
> action. That is where we find the movement of every *praxis,* namely, its being a
> totalizing undertaking that gives itself its own limits. Ethical action totalizes itself
> as unconditional possibility and limits itself to that dimension of itself. So ethics is
> not essentially an ideal type of exceptional action, but only a certain mode of devel-
> opment of the free structure of every action. ("Autour," 48).

41. Ibid., 51.

42. See his 1948 play by that title in *"No Exit" and Three Other Plays,* trans. Lionel
Abel (New York: Random House, Vintage Books, 1955).

43. Consider these passages from *The Psychology of Imagination:* "All existence as

soon as it is posited is surpassed by itself. But it must retreat *towards something*. The imaginary is in every case the 'something' concrete toward which the existent is surpassed" (*PI* 244). "All apprehension of the real as world implies a hidden surpassing towards the imaginary. . . . The imaginary thus represents the implicit meaning of the real" (*PI* 245). It is in this context that one should understand these remarks from "Existentialism Is a Humanism": "For in effect, there is not one of our acts that, in creating the man we wish to be, does not at the same time create an image of man such as we judge he ought to be" ("EH" 291; F 25); and "What is at the very heart and center of existentialism is the absolute character of the free commitment, by which every man realizes himself in realizing a type of humanity" ("EH" 304).

Elsewhere I explained this "argument" of "Existentialism Is a Humanism" as follows:

> In this first argument, therefore, it is the value-image which invests individual choice with collective import: "I create a certain image of the man that I choose; in choosing myself, I chose man" ("EH" 292; *L'Existentialisme est un humanisme* [Paris: Nagel, 1970] 27). This image, I am arguing, constitutes a general ethical ideal, not a universal principle. It serves as a moral paradigm or concrete model of how the moral person ought to choose. Accordingly, it will function in an integrative, not in a nomological, sense, unifying projects and allowing degrees of approximation. So when Sartre writes: "I am obliged at every instant to perform actions which are examples" ("EH" 393), he is not merely alluding to being-for-others as an inescapable dimension of human reality. He is also underscoring the imaginative articulation of an ideal theme occurrent in every moral choice: "That's how man ought to be!" Consider Sartre's reference to *image*, not rule, in the preceding passages. It is the indirect communication of such value-images through imaginative literature that has become the hallmark of existentialism. (Flynn, *Sartre and Marxist Existentialism,* 34)

44. See Simont, "Autour des conférences de Sartre à Cornell," 41. She explains that the source of Sartre's "ethical paradox" lies in reconciling the *historicity* of ends with the *inert permanence* of ethical action: "Ethical action, whatever may be its historically conditioned ends and whatever the institution of permanence aiming to maintain a *state* of history via the overcoming of historicity and so however much it may seem to be entirely conditioned, *is lived as unconditional*" (50).

CONCLUSION TO PART ONE

1. In fact, "commitment" (*l'engagement*) is not identical with "authenticity," though the terms are closely related. So, before pursuing the matter of committed history, we must explain that relationship. Consider these two "definitions" formulated within a year of each other: "Authenticity . . . consists in having a true and lucid consciousness of the situation, in assuming the responsibilities and risks that it involves, in accepting it in pride or humiliation, sometimes in horror and hate" (*AJ* 90). "A writer is *engagé* when he tries to be as lucidly and as completely conscious of his involvement as possible; that is to say, when he raises *engagement* for himself and for others from the level of immediate spontaneity to the level of reflection" (*WL* 49; *S* 2:124). Though both authenticity and

commitment require truth and lucidity about the nature of the existential choice being made, the former underscores the modality of the creative choice, its emotional resonances, for example, whereas the latter stresses only the practical cognition (the "knowing that is a doing") implied by commitment.

In the *Notebooks,* dating from about the same time as *What Is Literature?* Sartre works out his understanding of "a new 'authentic' way of being oneself and for oneself, which transcends the dialectic of sincerity and bad faith" (*NE* 474). In sum, it entails the "*ethical unity*" that arises from the consent to live the tension of my "diasporic being." This tensive state of *solidarity* (not "unity" or "identity") with myself and with others Sartre calls "love" (*NE* 477).

2. See Trian Stoianovich, *French Historical Method* (Ithaca, NY: Cornell University Press, 1976), esp. chap. 4, "An Impossible *Histoire globale,*" 102–33.

3. Sartre is in fact appealing to the maxims enunciated in "Existentialism Is a Humanism" that one chooses freedom in choosing anything at all and that one cannot be concretely free unless everyone is free (see "EH" 307–9). Despite their questionable status as either evident or demonstrated, these same maxims are operative in his theory of committed literature in *What Is Literature?* By the mid-1940s they are entrenched in his philosophy. For an extended discussion of these maxims and their conceptual context in Sartre's thought at the time, see my *Sartre and Marxist Existentialism,* chap. 3.

4. Etienne Barilier, *Les Petits Camarades* (Paris: Julliard/L'Age d'Homme, 1987), 9.

Chapter Five

1. On Sartre's role in establishing a noncommunist nonparty of the Left, the Rassemblement Démocratique Révolutionaire (RDR), as well as his ambivalent relationship with the French Communist Party, see Burnier, *Choice of Action,* and Mark Poster, *Existential Marxism in Postwar France: From Sartre to Althusser* (Princeton, NJ: Princeton University Press, 1975).

2. *CDR* 1:822; the quotation is taken from the preface to the combined edition of *Search for a Method* and the *Critique,* partially omitted in the English translation of *Search for a Method.*

3. Aron is likewise concerned with the very existence of a science of history. See *IPH* 10.

4. "The only theory of knowledge which can be valid today is one which is founded on that truth of microphysics: the experimenter is a part of the experimental system" (*SM* 32 n). We shall examine this claim in our discussion of the "situated" historian in chap. 7.

5. See, e.g., G. H. Von Wright, *Explanation and Understanding* (Ithaca, NY: Cornell, 1971), the collection of essays of H. G. Gadamer, Paul Ricoeur, Charles Taylor, and others in *Interpretive Social Science: A Reader,* ed. Paul Rabinow and William M. Sullivan (Berkeley and Los Angeles: University of California Press, 1979), and Danto, *Narration and Knowledge,* 206, 337–40.

6. Aron, *La Philosophie critique de l'histoire,* 175.

7. Thus, in his later work, even that sanctuary of infallible self-awareness, the prereflective *cogito,* seems vulnerable to external influence. Speaking of Flaubert's "truth-

sickness," for example, Sartre admits: "Presence to self in everyone has a basic structure of praxis. Even on the level of nonthetic consciousness, intuition is conditioned by individual history" (*FI* 1:148; F 1:141). This is a claim he would not have made in *Being and Nothingness.* See my "Praxis and Vision: Elements of a Sartrean Epistemology," *Philosophical Forum* 8 (Fall 1976): 30–31.

8. Dilthey considers it "perhaps the supreme triumph of hermeneutics . . . to understand an author better than he understood himself" (Wilhelm Dilthey, *Gesammelte Schriften,* vol. 5: *Die Geistige Welt* [Stuttgart: Teubner Verlag, 1957], 335).

9. G. E. M. Anscombe, *Intention,* 2d ed. (Ithaca: Cornell University Press, 1963), 13–14.

10. Sartre, whose use of Dilthey is increasingly evident as his pursuit of the biography-history relationship intensifies, seems to be approaching what Rudolf Makkreel calls Dilthey's concept of *reflective experience,* which "suggests a kind of intermediate standpoint in which aspects of both the introspective and transcendental approaches remain in contact with the empirical study of outer experience." As Makkreel explains, "For Dilthey, a full knowledge of psychic life has to be mediated by acts of attentive perception or 'observation' (*Beobachten*)." Rudolf A. Makkreel, *Dilthey: Philosopher of the Human Sciences* (Princeton: Princeton University Press, 1975), 210, 213, and see 251–62 on Dilthey's use of *Verstehen* and *Erlebnis.*

11. See chap. 4 above.

12. *S* 4:30. This roughly parallels his distinction made in *What Is Literature?* between "poetry" and "prose" respectively. See my "The Role of the Image in Sartre's Aesthetic," 431–42.

13. See Sartre's preface to a catalog of Rebeyrolle's paintings, "Coexistences" reprinted in *S* 9:316–25. Coincidentally, Foucault also contributed an essay, "Force of Flight," to that same catalog. This is one of several instances of the two philosophers' having discussed the same object.

14. For such identification see *S* 8:445–46, 8:449–50, 9:178. In a set of lectures delivered in Japan at about the same time he must have been composing the notes for his "dialectical ethics" (1965), Sartre argues that the literary artist writes to communicate not knowledge (*savoir*) but "the human condition in the form of an object (the work, *l'oeuvre*) such that it can be grasped in its most radical depth (being-in-the-world)." Rather than using abstract concepts that only approximate universality,

> The writer can *witness* only to his own being-in-the-world, by producing an *ambiguous object* which suggests it allusively. Thus the real relationship between reader and writer remains non-knowledge: when reading a writer's work, the reader is referred back indirectly to his own reality as a *singular universal.* He realizes himself—both because he enters into the book and does not completely enter into it—as another part of the same whole, as another view-point of the world on itself. (Jean-Paul Sartre, "A Plea for Intellectuals," *BEM* 277; *S* 8:444, emphasis mine)

He repeats what has been his thesis since *The Psychology of Imagination,* that the work of art, which "has all the characteristics of a singular universal," is the solicitation by one creative freedom to another "to grasp his own being-in-the-world as if it were the product of his freedom. . . . as if he were the world freely *incarnate.*" We saw him appeal to the artwork in the *Notebooks* for an example of nonobjectifying communication among freedoms. Now he insists that "the total unity of the *recomposed* work of art is silence— that is to say, the free incarnation, through words and beyond words, of being-in-the-world as non-knowledge folded back over a partial but universalizing knowledge" ("Plea," *BEM* 278).

15. See *S* 4:31, *PI* 139–43. Given the image as an illustration of a thought (*David* and the Renaissance, for example), Sartre argues that we are faced with the choice of either slipping into reverie or "by a creative effort" advancing toward comprehension itself. In this context Sartre speaks of the image as being "like an incarnation of nonreflective [*irréfléchie*] thought" (*PI* 143; *L'Imaginaire* [Paris: Gallimard, 1940], 216–17).

16. See *FI* 3:429; F 2:1544. For his lengthy analysis of the Rouen collegians' "comprehension" of their world, see *FI* 3:222 ff.; F 2:1331 ff.

17. "Epoch" has a quasi-technical sense for Sartre, which he articulates years later: "[Epoch] is the name I give to any historical temporalization to the extent that it produces its own boundaries" (*FI* 5:406–7; F 3:440). See above, chap. 4, n. 27.

18. "We will attempt to show . . . that Michelet's 'phantasms' and effects of style really define the conditions of the scientific speaking of the *Annales,* that they are the operators of what has recently been termed an epistemological break, of what I prefer to call a *revolution in the poetic structures of knowledge*" (Jacques Rancière, *The Names of History,* trans. Hassan Melehy [Minneapolis: University of Minnesota Press, 1994], 42; emphasis mine).

For a discussion of Michelet's relation to the *Annales* school and the paradoxical revival of romanticist historiography, see Rancière, *Names,* 42–60. For example, after noting that "Lucien Febvre hailed Michelet as the founding father of the *Annales* school," Rancière explains that "Michelet's 'romantic' excess is only the excess of the foundation, of the symbolic order that makes possible the decipherings of a more sober history" (42, 56).

19. Sartre pursues the contrast between *sens* and signification by distinguishing the quasi-Hegelian "notion" from the Kantian "concept." With "*la notion,*" one has "integrated temporality into the categories" and thereby rendered it capable of expressing the *sens* of an object (see his address to the French Philosophical Society, reprinted in "Consciousness of Self and Knowledge of Self," 131).

In an interview given several years later, Sartre avows: "Personally, I have been compelled, in order to criticize Althusser, to look again at the idea of 'notion' and to draw a series of conclusion in the process" (*BEM* 134). Already in "Materialism and Revolution" he had contrasted the "concept" of science with the "notion" of dialectic (see "MR" 209).

20. Sartre specifies a "formal homogeneity" between three forms of comprehension, namely, comprehension (1) of the group-object by nongrouped subjects; (2) of the group-subject by the nongrouped as object; and (3) of the group-praxis by each of its members as a mediation of function and objectification. Only the third, which we shall address later, surpasses the limits of the looking/looked-at model of *Being and Nothingness* and the *Notebooks.*

His point, I take it, is that we as outsiders can comprehend these three forms of comprehension; for example, that we can understand what it is like to exclude or be excluded by another group. For he admits that comprehension of another group is not easy: "the *modality* of action, its normative aspect, often eludes those who are not members" (*CDR* 1:518). Thus, what appears to outsiders as fanaticism or blindness is really the inner adhesive "fraternity-terror" of the group, a term to be discussed shortly. It is the *mediating* nature of the third form of comprehension that breaks new ground. Previously, the most Sartre could offer us in this regard was the "thousand absolute facets" of the historical age, unified in the reflection of each, but not fashioned by all (*NE* 491). In other words, the "social" was quantitatively, but not qualitatively, distinct from the "individual."

21. See Mikel Dufrenne, "La *Critique de la raison dialectique,*" reprinted in Mikel Dufrenne, *Jalons* (The Hague: Martinus Nijhoff, 1966), 162–63.

22. Georg Lukács, *History and Class Consciousness,* trans. Rodney Livingston (Cambridge, MA: MIT Press, 1971).

23. See his lengthy and ponderous "definition" of "praxis" in the *Critique:* "an organizing project which transcends material conditions towards an end and inscribes itself, through labor, in inorganic matter as a rearrangement of the practical field and a reunification of means in the light of the end" (*CDR* 1:734).

24. Deleuze adopts the mathematical concept of "multiplicity" from Riemann (and Bergson and Husserl) to characterize Foucault's statements (*énoncés*) and discursive formations because the term avoids reference either to the one or to the many—standard terms in the logic and metaphysics of identity (see Gilles Deleuze, *Foucault,* trans. Séan Hand [Minneapolis: University of Minnesota Press, 1988], 13–14). It is true that Foucault claims that "archaeological study is always in the plural" (*AK* 157) and, in his review essay of two of Deleuze's works, he agrees with Deleuze that "the problem cannot be approached through the logic of the excluded third, because it is a dispersed multiplicity" (Michel Foucault, *Language, Counter-Memory, Practice,* ed. Donald F. Bouchard [Ithaca, NY: Cornell University Press, 1977], 185). So, given Foucault's frequent appeal to the "multiplicity and dispersion" of statements and discursive formations in *The Archaeology of Knowledge,* Deleuze's adaptation of this technical term seems appropriate to Foucault's archaeological project even if the latter doesn't employ it as such.

25. See Hans-Georg Gadamer, *Truth and Method* (New York: Seabury Press, 1975), 273 ff.

26. "Thus, in its most immediate and most superficial character, the critical investigation of totalization is the very life of the investigator in so far as it reflexively criticizes itself. In abstract terms, this means that only a man who lives within a region of totalization can apprehend the bonds of interiority which unite him to the totalizing movement." In other words, the investigator must be "situated."

But how is this to happen without sacrificing that very critical perspective just called for? The investigator must reflectively appropriate his *life,* not in its particular content but in its *formal* or "structural" conditions. "If he is to be totalized by history," Sartre writes, "the important thing is that he should *re-live* [*revivre*] his membership of human ensembles *with different structures* and determine the reality of these ensembles through the bonds which constitute them and the practices which define them":

In short, if there is such a thing as the *unity of History,* the experimenter must see his own life as the Whole and the Part, as the bond between the Parts and the Whole, and as the relation between the Parts, in the dialectical movement of Unification; he must be able to leap from his individual life to History simply by the practical negation of the negation which defines his life. From this point of view, the order of the investigation becomes clear: it must be *regressive.* (*CDR* 1:52)

27. The regressive method "will set out from the immediate, that is to say from the individual fulfilling himself in his abstract (in the sense of incomplete) *praxis,* so as to rediscover . . . the structures of the various practical multiplicities and, through their contradictions and struggles, the absolute concrete: historical man" (*CDR* 1:52). Note how Sartre's earlier "absolute event" has ripened into the Hegelian "absolute concrete," which he will soon call the "singular universal." Not only has his discovery of the dialectic enabled him to "temporalize the categories," but it has allowed him to redefine the "abstract" and the "concrete" in a quasi-Hegelian manner, namely, as the incomplete or indeterminate and the fully determined respectively. This opens the door to such notions as *sens,* "incarnation," and "totalization" that ill fit a more analytic discourse. And it reaches its goal in the "singular universal," as we shall see.

In chap. 6 I shall argue for a threefold primacy of praxis in Sartre's philosophy, namely, an ontological, an epistemological, and a moral primacy. Free organic praxis alone is constitutive of social wholes, as we have seen; comprehension is based on the understanding individuals have of their own praxis; and one should be able to ascribe moral responsibility, bad faith, and the like to praxes in the midst of the most impersonal situations. These are points I have developed elsewhere in another context (see my *Sartre and Marxist Existentialism,* 104–12).

28. On the individual's life as symbol of the diachronic totalization of other individuals, see *CDR* 1:53. "Reciprocity of symbolism between a man and his era is often possible. But whatever the life and era under consideration, this reciprocity is valid only as a *rhetorical* illustration of the macrocosm by the microcosm (and vice versa), that is, as an image elaborated by an author and whose practical value resides in its convenience alone, *unless* history were *in fact condensed* in the era's *abridgment,* which a singular biography claims to be." Sartre assures us immediately in a footnote, "To be sure, it would be the same for any collective object of microsociology" (*FI* 4:398–99).

In a similar context he will speak of the *sens* of eighteenth-century German life being "incarnated" in the playing of a Bach fugue as "little more than an image." He explains: "I wanted to give an intuitive idea of the real enjoyment of a historical *meaning* [*sens*]" (*CDR* 2:296–97). In *The Psychology of Imagination,* he offers a lengthy discussion of the symbolic relation between Michelangelo's *David* and the Renaissance. He uses expressions like "by a kind of participation" (*PI* 141; F 213) and "affective *sens*" to communicate this function. Analogously, he urges that "if you visit the Berlin castle you will understand the *sens* of Bismarck's Prussia" (*PI* 140–41; F 213).

Finally, in *The Family Idiot* he refers to the work of art as the means for an imaginary totalization (*FI* 4:188, 198, 258; F 2:1962, 1971, 2033). Though these views are attributed to Flaubert, given the previous citations, they closely resemble Sartre's own.

29. Speaking in the *Notebooks* of geniuses who "transcend the given [of their situations]," Sartre remarks that even they "carry their epoch along with them like a banner" in that very transcending (*NE* 490; F 506).

30. Macrototalization resembles Merleau-Ponty's "interworld," a term Sartre adopts to designate our social field peopled by collective objects such as Gothic cathedrals and philosophical idealism (see *SM* 76). In a way that invites comparison with Foucault's analysis of statements and discursive formations in chap. 4 of *The Archaeology of Knowledge*, Sartre speaks of the "concrete materiality" of collective objects (see *SM* 78). A technical term introduced in *Critique 2*, "enveloping totalization," assumed many of the functions of "macrototalization" in *Critique 1*. See *Critique of Dialectical Reason*, vol. 2, trans. Quintin Hoare (London: Verso, 1991), hereafter cited as *CDR* 2.

31. Consider, e.g., the following: "There is, however, a Sartrean semiology; it is resolutely antilinguistic" (Hollier, *The Politics of Prose*, 59); or "Existentialist anthropos, even rid of its reference to a human nature, would remain an arrogant anthropos who would take himself as the unique source of meaning" (Jean-Marie Benoist, *La Révolution structurale* [Paris: Bernard Grasset, 1975], 11).

32. Still, Sartre does speak of Flaubert's "realism" as a "reciprocal symbolization" with regard to the social and political evolution of the petite bourgeoisie in the Second Empire (see *SM* 57 f.). Incarnation is not symbolic only.

33. Though he attributes this threefold method to the Marxist sociologist Henri Lefebvre (see *SM* 52 n), Sartre had employed the term and a form of the method before Lefebvre's work appeared; see, e.g., *PI* 234; F 345 and *BN* 460. He insists it is a valid method "in all the domains of anthropology" (*SM* 52 n).

34. Nonetheless, when asked late in his life whether he had ever abandoned phenomenology, he replied: "Never. I continue to think in those terms. I have never thought as a Marxist, not even in the *Critique de la raison dialectique*" (*PS* 24).

35. "I am using the term 'abstract' here in the sense of *incomplete*. The individual is not abstract from the point of view of his individual reality (one could say that he is the concrete itself); but only *on condition* that the ever deeper determinations which constitute him in his very existence as a historical agent and, at the same time, as a product of History, have been revealed" (*CDR* 1:52 n). On the Hegelian sense of "abstract" and "concrete" that Sartre is employing, see George Kline's essay "The Existentialist Rediscovery of Hegel and Marx," in *Phenomenology and Existentialism*, ed. Edward N. Lee and Maurice Mandelbaum (Baltimore: Johns Hopkins University Press, 1967), 125 n. 32. Though Kline accuses Sartre of "regularly confusing" the Hegelian with other uses of the distinction, the quotation just given should indicate that Sartre appreciates and employs "abstract" and "concrete" in their Hegelian senses to the extent that his dialectical nominalism will allow.

36. See Klaus Hartmann, "Sartre's Theory of *Ensembles*," in *PS* 659–60 n. 63, and Hartmann, *Sartres Sozialphilosophie*, 52–56.

37. Since Sartre probably has explanatory ultimacy in mind, this claim is reminiscent of the "self-evident intuition" that terminates a successful existential psychoanalysis (see *BN* 574).

CHAPTER SIX

1. I differ from Klaus Hartmann, who sees an improper transcendental argument at work in the *Critique* (see below, chap. 9 n. 51). Though I agree that scarcity (*la rareté*) serves as a "transcendental fact" in the *Critique,* this oxymoron functions in a manner similar to Foucault's "historical a priori." It explains, but in a hypothetical, contingent manner: it could have been otherwise, it was not always so, and it may someday cease to be the case.

2. See Sartre, *The Transcendence of the Ego.*

3. In a note to the second volume of the *Critique,* Arlette Elkaïm-Sartre observes: "This comment gives a hint that the whole investigation of the *Critique* is a long detour in order to tackle once more the problem of ethics in history, raised in 1947 in *Cahiers pour une morale*" (*CDR* 2:150 n).

4. Louis Althusser, Etienne Balibar, and Roger Establet, *Lire le capital,* 2 vols. (Paris: François Maspero, 1965), 2:98.

5. Raymond Aron, *History and the Dialectic of Violence,* trans. Barry Cooper (Oxford: Basil Blackwell, 1975), 200.

6. I discuss these matters at length in *Sartre and Marxist Existentialism,* chap. 6.

7. See, e.g., Paul Ricoeur, *Time and Narrative,* 3:119–26, where he discusses at length what earlier he called "the entire problematic of the trace" (2:200). Ricoeur admits to being inspired in this regard by Emmanuel Lévinas's seminal essay "La Trace," in Lévinas, *Humanisme de l'autre homme* (Paris: Fata Morgana, 1972), 62–70. Jacques Derrida develops "la trace" in a deconstructive mode in his *"Speech and Phenomena" and Other Essays on Husserl's Theory of Signs,* trans. David B. Allison (Evanston, IL: Northwestern University Press, 1973). By the time we reach Derridian pyrotechnics, however, the Sartrean "practico-inert" looks rather flat-footed—or commonsensical.

8. "Exigency is *always* both man as a practical agent and matter as a worked product in an indivisible symbiosis" (*CDR* 1:191). This is the term Sartre favors to describe the relation between a free, situated agent and his or her situation. Again, the ambiguity of the given and the taken reappears in this "indivisible symbiosis."

9. Sartre's account of "objective class spirit" in terms of the circulation of significations, makes the triad of incarnation, presentification, and *sens,* which we shall examine in chap. 7, seem more than merely symbolic.

10. "Serial praxis" denotes "the praxis of an individual in so far as he is a member of the series and the praxis of the series as a whole or as totalized via individuals" (*CDR* 1:266; F 316). I discuss this seldom-remarked form in my *Sartre and Marxist Existentialism,* 105. Its existence at this seemingly impotent stage confirms what I have been calling "the primacy of praxis" in Sartre's social philosophy.

11. In his notes for the unfinished second volume of the *Critique,* Sartre writes: "Totalization is never completed (otherwise: totality). Let us clearly understand, moreover, that abundance or the end of pre-history change [*sic*] nothing here: a dialectical relationship is involved" (*CDR* 2:448).

12. Again, his rather ponderous definition of "praxis" is "an organizing project which transcends material conditions towards an end and inscribes itself, through labor,

in inorganic matter as a rearrangement of the practical field and a reunification of means in the light of the end" (*CDR* 1:734). One sees here the anatomy of his basic dialectic of internalization/externalization.

13. Joseph S. Catalano, *A Commentary on Jean-Paul Sartre's Critique of Dialectical Reason: Volume I: Theory of Practical Ensembles* (Chicago: University of Chicago Press, 1986), 263.

14. See my *Sartre and Marxist Existentialism,* 105–12.

15. "I think that an individual in the group, even if he is a little bit terrorized [!], is still better than an individual alone and thinking separation. I do not believe that an individual alone can do anything" (*ORR* 171).

16. Normally, one would think the converse to be the case, namely, that need precedes scarcity. Sartre is willing to admit this in the "natural" or "biological" sense. But in the *Critique,* as he explains, scarcity "is always a fact of social oppression" (*PS* 31). His account of the need-scarcity relationship in the Schilpp volume, frankly, looks inconsistent.

17. "Each proletariat [e.g., French, German, and English] derives its constituted violence . . . not only from the real conditions of production and from the structures proper to the worker, but also *from its own History*" (*CDR* 1:797 n).

18. This "placeholder" concept of the historical agent is not limited to (present-day) structuralists. Collingwood held a similar position according to Jack W. Meiland, *Scepticism and Historical Knowledge* (New York: Random House, 1963), 76–77.

19. See his interview in *PS* 30.

20. It seems that phenomenological *eide* or essences are being historicized in the Sartrean dialectic just as the categories are being temporalized. In his only address to the French Philosophical Society (1947), Sartre summarized his epistemological project of reconciling Husserl's nondialectical consciousness with Hegel's dialectical thought by recommending such a temporalizing of essences (see below, chap. 7).

But in the second volume of the *Critique,* drafted in 1958 though never published in his lifetime, Sartre seems to have modified his irenic position between Husserl and Hegel. Attempting to stress "the singularity of human praxis" by showing that "the inner cohesion of action is ensured by bonds of immanence," he offers an example from "the sphere of knowledge":

> We may note that praxis has forged *its idea of unity by unifying*; and that this very idea—as a schema regulating all human activity—is the equivalence between disintegration of the organic by the inorganic, and integration of the latter into a form engendered by the former. Nothing shows this better than the unity of Platonic "forms," or that which philosophers still often attribute to geometrical entities. . . . The rationalism of essences requires the act to be the unity that the object imposes on itself of its own accord: the synthesis it realizes of its multiplicities of inertia. Moreover, there is no man to *make* this act, and thought is only the place where this form is actualized as unity of the diverse (and without the effective presence of diversity). Seen in this way, this activity of the inert . . . *is not intelligible.* It is not a matter here of denying that unities can be produced in the Universe (the living organism is one such); but of stressing how this common conception attri-

butes to the object in the form of a cohesive force, that which is the extended result of human action. This conception thus conceals an underlying recourse to *the unity that produces itself:* in other words, *organic unity.* (*CDR* 2:343–44)

Allowance made for the mathematical referent of his example, this is a striking example of Sartre's "dialectical" nominalism in action. It is not uncongenial to Foucault's anti-Platonism.

21. We should keep in mind the specific "rationalities" of the collective and the institution when we discuss the "logic" of subgroup conflict in chap. 8.

22. Sartre uses these terms to describe a worker who seeks an abortion because her wages will not support another child as "executing a sentence" leveled on her by the Malthusian policies of bourgeois industrial society (see *CDR* 1:782–83). In his study of Sartre's theory of history, Andrew Dobson sees an analogous "sentence," in Sartre's mind, necessitating the advent of a Stalin in the struggling Soviet revolution in the 1930s (see Dobson, *Jean-Paul Sartre and the Politics of Reason: A Theory of History* [Cambridge: Cambridge University Press, 1993], 111).

23. On the relation between reconstituting praxis and Collingwood's concept of historical reenactment, see below, chap. 8 n. 29.

24. Sartre is unequivocal in his warning: "The abstract point of view of *critique* can obviously *never* be that of the sociologist or the ethnographer. It is not that we are denying or ignoring the concrete distinctions (the only ones) which they establish: it is simply that we are at a level of abstraction at which they have no place. In order to connect with them, one would need the set of mediations which transform *a critique* into a *logic* and which, by specification and dialectical concretization, redescend from logic to the real problems, that is to say, to the level at which real History, through the inversion which is to be expected of this abstract quest, becomes the developing totalization which carries, occasions, and justifies the partial totalization of critical intellectuals" (*CDR* 1:482 n).

25. Clifford Geertz, *Local Knowledge: Further Essays in Interpretive Anthropology* (New York: Basic Books, 1983), 58.

26. Referring to Flaubert's "truth-sickness," Sartre admits: "Presence to self for each of us possesses a rudimentary structure of praxis. . . . At the very level of nonthetic consciousness intuition is conditioned by individual history" (*FI* 1:141; F 1:148).

27. Fernand Braudel, *The Mediterranean and the Mediterranean World in the Age of Philip II,* trans. Siân Reynolds (London: Collins, 1972), 1239; cited by Sartre, *CDR* 1:169.

28. See "EH" 307 and my discussion of the "universal freedom conditional" in *Sartre and Marxist Existentialism,* 33–41.

29. This is a sophisticated echo of his remark in the *War Diaries* that "there's no revolution without dictatorship. For want of having *first* been dictators, the leaders of the Commune lost their way" (*WD* 332).

30. See his early contrast between analytic and "synthetic" reason in his *Anti-Semite and Jew* (71), which anticipates his later distinction between analytic and dialectical reason.

31. See, for example, William Dray, *Laws and Explanation in History* (Oxford: Oxford University Press, 1957), 158–69.

CHAPTER SEVEN

1. C. Wright Mills, *The Sociological Imagination* (Oxford: Oxford University Press, 1959), 143.

2. This is Walter Biemel's translation of Heidegger's *die Gewesenheit* and *die Vergangenheit* respectively (see his *Le Concept du Monde chez Heidegger* [Paris: Vrin, 1950], 126). The latter is a kind of tomb into which previous presents have fallen, the "ontic" past. The former is the kind of past we say is still with us, Heidegger's "ontological" past. Sartre was familiar with this work and cited it in *CDR* 1:181 n. 56. In fact, he seems to distinguish the living and the dead past as *sens* and signification respectively (see *CDR* 2:402). We shall observe the critical import of the latter contrast for his theory in the present chapter.

Though Sartre sometimes employed Heidegger's ontic/ontological distinction, especially in *Being and Nothingness,* his focus, unlike Heidegger's, remained steadily on the human in the doublet "human being," a fact Heidegger noted critically in his famous *Letter on Humanism.* Consequently, Sartre's existential masterwork proved to be more available to ethicists than to theologians, whereas the opposite was true of *Being and Time.*

3. See, e.g., *SM* 157.

4. To appreciate how far Sartre's development of dialectical mediation has brought him from the social sterility of *Being and Nothingness,* compare his account of two men fighting one another in the earlier work. There their unity was imposed *ab extra* by the objectifying gaze of the Other (see *BN* 418).

5. The "impossibility of living" emerges as the nonnegotiable, the ultimate in social dealings for Sartre both as theoretician (see *CDR* 2:120) and as political polemicist (see *BEM* 125 and *L/S* 167).

6. "The scarcity lived in interiority by the organ is the inorganic producing itself as a negative determination of the organism. And this *lacuna*—inasmuch as the whole organism is modified by it—is *the materiality of the action,* its reality and its foundation, its substance, and its urgency. Through the need, the individual—whoever he may be, and however gratuitous his act may be—acts upon pain of death, directly or indirectly, for himself or for others" (*CDR* 2:290).

7. Aristotle, *Physics,* 188a–91a.

8. It also suggests another point of comparison with Foucault, whose *Birth of the Clinic* waxed poetic as well as epistemic about "the life/disease/death trinity": "Nineteenth-century medicine was haunted by that absolute eye that cadaverizes life and rediscovers in the corpse the frail, broken nervure of life" (Michel Foucault, *The Birth of the Clinic: An Archaeology of Medical Perception,* trans. A. M. Sheridan Smith [New York: Vintage Books, 1973], 164, 166.

9. Ultimately, however, *historical* density or depth is a function of diachronic totalization (see *CDR* 2:107–8). Still, such totalizing praxis cannot ignore the "density of the world" (see chap. 6). By now we are accustomed to this perduring ambiguity of the given and the taken in the Sartrean situation. In *Critique 2,* praxis-process unites the discussion from a vertical dimension as "enveloping totalization," which we shall discuss shortly.

10. The possibility of an ultimate envelopment, the "totalization without a total-izer," is the problem of the meaning of History as a whole. Whether this ensnares us in the famous paradox of logical types will have to be faced in our concluding chapter.

11. "The positivist historian has distorted History and made comprehension impos-sible, whenever he has shown the organized forces' project determining 'the masses,' or 'public opinion,' or any category of individuals or groupings, in the same way that a physical factor can condition the variations of a 'natural process.' He has suppressed any possibility of totalization, by suppressing one of the essential moments of historical praxis and remaining blind to the following obvious fact: inasmuch as History studies *the action of action upon action,* the milieu in which any given praxis may create any other in accordance with strict predictions is necessarily that of retotalization. From this stand-point, conflict and the stages of every struggle are comprehensible: these reciprocal retotalizations of each opposing praxis by the other, when they are themselves re-totalized, likewise constitute a contradictory milieu where each action creates the other as its practical nullification" (*CDR* 2:161).

12. Sartre, "Consciousness of Self and Knowledge of Self," 136.

13. See "MR" 209, where he contrasts the concepts of science from the "notion" of dialectic.

14. "Jean-Paul Sartre Répond," *L'Arc* 30 (1966): 94.

15. This is my translation of *totalisation d'enveloppment,* which Quintin Hoare renders "totalization-of-envelopment" in *Critique 2.* With the exception of this term, whenever I offer a translation other than that given in the published English version, I cite the corre-sponding page in the French original by "F."

16. See, e.g., "Colonialism Is a System" (*S* 5:24–45). I discuss this in my *Sartre and Marxist Existentialism,* 57–64. The close relation, if not identification, of enveloping to-talization and praxis-process is evident in this mutual association with "system" (see chap. 6 above). It comes to the fore in a passage like the following from *The Family Idiot:*

> The man of hatred is not the product solely of these infrastructural relations caught in their entirely relative immobility; these relations had to become exacerbated in the context of a singular history, and that history—*praxis-process*—had to produce an *event* through them and against them. . . . The situation is the same for histori-cal man [as for Pascalian man]: just like the creature of God, in the *Pensées,* he is the totalizing and totalized expression of defined structures in a society defined by its mode of production and by the institutions resulting from it; and at the same time he is an irreversible event that bears in it the mark of all prior events. Pascal con-cluded that man is not *thinkable;* he envisaged him only as the object of an impos-sible intellection. It is characteristic of dialectical reason, by contrast, to understand this man-event as someone who endures history and at the same time makes it. (*FI* 5:315).

17. Obviously, Sartre, being what James Collins called a "postulatory atheist," is not constructing a theodicy in the usual sense of a theory of history that would reconcile the fact of evil with the goodness of the Creator. But his theory of history in effect is an

extended attempt to render intelligible, if not to "justify," the violence that permeates human history as we know it. If "my original fall," for Sartre, "is the existence of the Other" (*BN* 263), the role of Prince of Darkness in his version of this primordial drama must be awarded to material scarcity, which renders the human condition lupine. Relating Sartre's theory of History to the tradition which it totalizes, we might call it an "atheodicy." See below, chap. 9.

18. But if there is merely a "family resemblance" between these uses of the term, one emerges as the "head" of the family: "Enveloping totalization, inasmuch as it is implied and aimed at by all the partial totalizations, is praxis itself inasmuch as it engenders the corporeity that sustains and deviates it, and inasmuch as it attempts at every moment to dissolve its own exteriority into immanence." As Sartre explains: "This latter point does not just presuppose that praxis is objectified, sustained and limited by its objectification in the inert, in the shape of process. It further implies that the incarnation of envelopment is realized at all levels of the practical process as a mediation and as a dissolution of the practico-inert (or as its utilization). As we reject any idealist interpretation, however, it goes without saying that this dissolving mediation is carried out by men" (*CDR* 2:232).

19. "So what was the enveloping totalization during the Stalin phase of socialist construction? It was Stalin, if you like, but inasmuch as he was *made* and sustained by the praxis of all, as the sovereign uniqueness that was to integrate its structures and contain its exteriority" (*CDR* 2:233). This is a version of what we have been calling Sartre's "principle of totalization," to the effect that "a man totalized his epoch to the exact degree that he is totalized by it" (see chap. 5). It is most fully elaborated in *The Family Idiot* (see *FI* 5:394). "Enveloping totalization" underscores the aspects of inertia, passivity, and exteriority ingredient in the totalizing relationship.

Sartre places his understanding of Stalinist praxis in the context of enveloping totalization as dialectical circularity in the following:

> The movement of circularity allows one . . . to pass continuously from *being* (as sustained and produced by the act) to *the act* (as expressing its being by the very transcendence that preserves as it negates it). And it is precisely this perpetual passage—in the temporal spiral—from the being of the act to the act of being, from the practical signification of destiny to the destiny of praxis; it is the impossibility of considering for an instant the structured ensemble as a passive object, without rediscovering the group or groups as organizing themselves for and through the undertaking; it is the impossibility of totalizing the results of action, without being referred back by these very results to *their* results at the heart of the practical temporalization—sedimentations, deposits, concretions, strata, deviations; it is that perpetual necessity to climb to the apex of sovereignty, only to descend again to the base: it is all of these which constitute at once the mode of knowledge appropriate to the enveloping totalization and the type of objective reality that defines it. (*CDR* 2:244)

20. "Every incarnation is tied in two ways to the historical ensemble: on the one hand, in fact, it realizes in itself the latter's condensation; on the other hand, it refers back

in a decompressive blossoming to the ensemble of practical significations which determine it in its belonging to the social and historical field" (*CDR* 2:188).

21. See my "The Role of the Image in Sartre's Aesthetic," 431–42.

22. "From this viewpoint, it can be said that *the meaning* [*sens*] of praxis-process is
everywhere within it, in so far as a limited temporalization is incarnated in its interior. It
is thus that the *meaning* [*sens*] of the *ancien régime* . . . , of the minor German courts, of
Protestantism in the early eighteenth century, of the clash between 'reason' and 'tradition,' as well as of the social hierarchy and the status of the artist, etc., is *temporally repro-
duced* in our ears by the playing of a Bach fugue on the harpsichord. Through this
retemporalization—an incarnation of Bach's life itself—the conceptual ensemble we have
just described is reincarnated as an ongoing process-praxis *through our time*. And in so far
as—without knowing the piece played or even perhaps ever having heard many Bach
compositions—we *recognize* that the work belongs to the baroque eighteenth century,
this movement of the incipient century is 'presentified' as the transcendent *meaning* of
the fugue: a *finite* synthesis of an *object* (*the* fugue, with its laws, its structures, etc.) and of
a praxis (the performance—equivalent for the listener to creation) containing the totality of that historical movement between the two end limits of its actualization"
(*CDR* 2:296).

23. "There can be no ontological or logical difference between totalization and incarnation, except that—precisely because it is concrete and real—totalization operates
only through the limitations it imposes. In other words, every *internal* totalization (enveloped by the overall totalization) is effected by the praxis-process of incarnation; or,
conversely, every practical and concrete reality has no positive content other than the
totalized ensemble of all ongoing totalizations." He adds that even the enveloping totalization, if it is shown to be possible, "is—albeit in a different way—*incarnated likewise*"
(*CDR* 2:33 and n). "Incarnation" is used in a non-aesthetic sense in *Critique 1* as well,
whereas "totalizing envelopment" is proper to *Critique 2*.

24. Sartre had already implied as much in *Being and Nothingness* apropos of language .
There the context was his adaptation of the Hegelian distinction between truth and reality as the abstract and the concrete respectively: language is the "truth" of dialect, dialect
the "reality" of language, and "the reality of the dialect is the *free* act of designation by
which I choose myself as designating" (*BN* 516). Again, the primacy of praxis, *avant la
lettre.* By the time he writes *Search for a Method,* this is an established thesis: "every word
is the whole of language" (*SM* 172), which he then extends beyond the realm of language: "each praxis uses the whole of culture" (*CDR* 1:55).

25. See Jean-Paul Sartre, "Intentionality: A Fundamental Idea of Husserl's Phenomenology," *Journal of the British Society for Phenomenology* 1, no. 2 (May 1970): 4–5.

26. See chap. 5 n. 35.

27. "The signifier *is* the signified, always, and consequently there is a certain intimate relationship of being between the signified, which signification lacks, and the signifier, which is at the same time signified by its signification" (*S* 9:50–51).

A certain sign of Sartre's sensitivity to the structuralist movement in full force at the
time is his occasional replay of his argument in a semiotic register. Toward the conclu-

sion of *Search for a Method,* for example, he observes: "In a certain philosophy today, it is the fashion to reserve the function of *signifying* for institutions (taken in the broadest sense) and to reduce the individual (save in exceptional cases) or the concrete group to the role of the *signified.*" After granting the partial truth in such claims, he reaffirms the primacy of praxis by insisting that people "can appear as signified *only by making themselves signifying;* that is, by trying to objectify themselves *through* the attitudes and the roles which society imposes upon them." He then reiterates an underlying theme of his later writings: "Here again men *make history* on the basis of prior conditions." From this he draws a conclusion that situates his work in the history of philosophy: "The Hegel-Kierkegaard conflict finds its solution in the fact that man is neither signified nor signifying but *at once* (like Hegel's absolute subject but in a different sense) both the signified-signifying and the signifying-signified" (*SM* 165–66 n).

28. "So *the enveloping totalization is incarnated by every singularity, and every singularity defines itself simultaneously as an incarnation and an enveloped totalization.* Yet there is nothing irrational here: neither Gestaltism nor any of those ambiguous, vague forms that strive to reestablish a hyper-organism, in one shape or another. These enveloped totalizations incarnate the enveloping totalization for the sole reason that individuals as practical organisms are totalizing projects, and there is nothing else to totalize—in a society integrated by a sovereign individual [e.g., Stalin]—except the enveloping totalization itself. The latter totalizes them (by concerted and co-ordinated actions and by the exigencies of the practico-inert, as well as by the determination in interiority of each person by everybody and everything) inasmuch as it produces them. They retotalize it, inasmuch as it is through the practical transcendence of the interiorized factors that they make themselves its products. But this retotalization *enriches* it with the concrete ensemble of particular circumstances and goals. So the enveloping totalization is found in every enveloped totalization as its *signification:* i.e., as its integration into everything" (*CDR* 2:263, emphasis mine).

But Sartre is quick to warn us that "it should not be thought, however, that the signification of envelopment is to the enveloped incarnation as the abstract is to the concrete. In a praxis whose sovereign is an individual, the signification of envelopment is itself . . . individuated: i.e., the practical unity of action is also the indissoluble organic synthesis represented by a man; and for this reason the totalizing totalization *likewise* defines itself by contingency, by concrete facticity, by the limits and riches of the singular" (*CDR* 2:263).

29. Roland Barthes, *The Rustle of Language,* trans. Richard Howard (Berkeley and Los Angeles: University of California Press, 1989), 146.

30. See *CDR* 2:343–65; earlier in *Critique 2* he explains: "This operation is knowledge, precisely in so far as it discovers the real *such as it is* (and not such as it might manifest itself through categories and principles). It is an *invention,* in so far as the complex category of *unity* (as organic-inorganic, and as a mediation by the agent) is a category *of Doing* in the absolute sense of the term. . . . To know is to create, since knowledge is a determination of Being based upon the practical category of unity. *De facto,* the unity of human experience is in fact a practical unification of the multiplicities

interior to the field. Conversely, to create is to know, since it involves producing (through inert synthesis) beings wholly extraneous to man as a biological individual, whose exigencies—as a reexteriorization of practical interiority—will have to be learned . . . on the basis of a unification 'in progress': i.e., another synthetic, inert being in the process of being manufactured" (*CDR* 2:261–62). The thrust of Sartre's "pragmatist" reflections on these pages seems to be that the source of all unity is the unifying nature of constituent, organic praxis—another application of his principle of the primacy of praxis.

31. "For it is not what objectivity demands, but what *these* given men determine, on the basis of exigencies which they have grasped through *their intellectual tools*. It remains the case, of course, that the object itself corresponds, in its very texture, to the structures of the contemporary agents. But this does not imply that you can avoid a certain *inequality* between exigency (of the object, for *these* given men in *this* given historical context) and the response (of this collegial group, which has sought to eliminate any personal equation, but has merely suppressed singular differentiations while preserving the common singularity of structures and pledged inertias)" (*CDR* 2:208 n).

From the factical side, Sartre designates this aperture "*the opening of History*" (*CDR* 2:84). Elsewhere, he calls it "freedom" (see *BEM* 35).

32. We recognize here an implicit appeal to his concept of "historialization" (see chap. 4 above). On the distinction between history and sociology, see *CDR* 2:134, 139, 161, 242, 286. In general, Sartre contrasts them respectively as the dialectic and the positivist, the interior and the exterior, the sovereign praxis and the practico-inert, the unique incarnation and the "model society" (*CDR* 2:286), the common undertaking and the society-object (*CDR* 2:242), comprehension and intellection (*CDR* 2:161), the situated and the nonsituated (*CDR* 2:139), and generally as *sens* and signification.

33. "The signification of a history is not its *meaning* [*sens*]." In fact, historical meaning is a function of what is lived in *interiority* and in *need*: it is a "totalization under way." If it ignores or discounts its basis in human need, such meaning will be partial (though, pace Hegel, never false) because it expresses only a partial conception of man (*CDR* 2:402–3).

34. Sartre clarified for his young Maoist friends his view on historical necessity and contingency as follows: "I tried to show the contingency of things [in *Nausea*]. By that I mean that they are not completely explainable by determinism or necessity. Beyond the explanations, there remains the fact that they exist without reason and disappear by chance."

He then admits that he believes in historical materialism "to the extent that it explains certain forms of human behavior," but not in dialectical materialism, which tends to extend a kind of dialectical necessity from nature to humans. This latter project, he insists, is bound to fail "because the necessity in things is only partial and because reality foils the project from every side." He concludes: "In general, man as long as he has existed has tried to know and dominate the world by reason. But he has succeeded only partially because of contingency" (*ORR* 78).

35. I shall pursue this topic in volume 2 of my study. Sketches of the argument appear in the following essays: "Truth and Subjectivation in the Later Foucault," *The Jour-*

nal of Philosophy 82, no. 10 (October 1985): 531–40; "Foucault and the Career of the Historical Event," in *At the Nexus of Philosophy and History*, ed. Bernard P. Dauenhauer (Athens, GA: University of Georgia Press, 1987), 178–200; and "Foucault and Historical Nominalism," in *Phenomenology and Beyond: The Self and Its Language*, ed. Harold A. Durfee and David F. T. Rodier (Dordrecht: Kluwer Academic Publishers, 1989), 134–47.

36. See *L'Impossible Prison*, ed. Michelle Perrot (Paris: Editions du Seuil, 1980), 46. Ironically, Foucault is closer to Aron than to Sartre in this matter.

37. Veyne, *Writing History*, 156. This is a translation of *Comment on écrit l'histoire* (Paris: Editions du Seuil, 1971). Unfortunately, it omits the important essay on Foucault as historian, "Foucault révolutionne l'histoire," that accompanied the abridged edition of that same work (Collection Points, 1978).

38. In *Search for a Method*, he corrects a "weak" Marxist epistemology with the following observation: "The only theory of knowledge which can be valid today is one which is founded on that truth of microphysics: the experimenter is part of the experimental system." This is not to deny the essential role of reflection in the critical process. Rather, it accepts reflection as a point of departure "only if it throws us back immediately among things and men, in the world." In other words, we cannot seek immunity from relativism among transcendental views or "detached" theory. He relates this situatedness of the experimenter to committed knowledge when he adds: "the *revelation* of a situation is effected in and through the *praxis* which changes it" (*SM* 32 n). One must abandon the ideal of grasping the concrete situation "in itself."

39. See chap. 2 above, where he speaks of the "whole" of an event being grasped from a particular perspective. Husserl, Max Scheler, and other classical phenomenologists had provided the basis for such a claim in writings which Sartre had studied during his year in Berlin.

40. See chap. 1 above.

41. Sartre credits this ongoing unity with making possible "comparative sociology and comparative history," presumably on the traditional metaphysical thesis that you cannot compare any multiplicity without a prior unity as its condition (*CDR* 2:300). This is particularly relevant to Veyne's recommendation (which Foucault seems to follow) that we adopt the comparatist methods of geographers to replace the totalizing approach of historians inspired by Hegel (see Veyne, *Writing History*, 284–85). Again, Foucault is being more radically anti-Platonic than Sartre, for he rejects any underlying unity.

42. Because of near blindness in his final years, he did undertake a collaborative *livre à deux* with Benny Lévy, which was to be an "ethics of the 'we' " that purportedly would overturn much of what he had written in his earlier works (see Sartre's interview with Michel Sicard, "L'écriture et la publication," in *Obliques*, nos. 18–19 [October 1979: 15]). Thus far the tapes of this oral composition have not been made public. But if and when they do appear, they will constitute a hermeneutical nightmare (see McBridge, *Sartre's Political Theory*, 202–8).

43. Thus Ronald Aronson claims that "a totalization without a totalizer is inaccessible to Sartre's thought *on principle*" (Ronald Aronson, *Sartre's Second Critique* [Chicago: University of Chicago Press, 1987], 235).

44. "There can be no pre-established schema imposed on individual developments, neither in someone's head, nor in an intelligible heaven; if the dialectic exists, it is because certain regions of materiality are *structured* in such a way that it cannot not exist. In other words, the dialectical movement is not some powerful unitary force revealing itself behind History like the will of God. It is first and foremost a *resultant*; it is not the dialectic which forces historical men to live their history in terrible contradictions; it is men, as they are, dominated by scarcity and necessity, and confronting one another in circumstances which History or economics can inventory, but which only dialectical reason can explain. Before it can be a *motive force,* contradiction is a result" (*CDR* 1:37).

45. As he warns us early in the *Critique,* "thus our task cannot *in any way* be to reconstruct real History in its development, any more than it can consist in a concrete study of forms of production or of the groups studied by the sociologist and the ethnographer. Our problem is *critical*" (*CDR* 1:40). He repeats this disavowal of traditional historical purposes on several occasions in the text.

46. "Dialectical necessity is by definition *different* from the necessity of analytical Reason" (*CDR* 1:40).

47. "We must show how it is possible for [dialectical Reason] to be both a *resultant,* though not a passive average, and a *totalizing force,* though not a transcendent fate, and how it can continually bring about the unity of dispersive profusion and integration" (*CDR* 1:36).

CHAPTER EIGHT

1. "You already know from *The Words* that I read Flaubert in my childhood. I read him again more closely in the Ecole normale, and I remember going back to *Sentimental Education* in the thirties. . . . The moment when I truly confronted Flaubert was during the Occupation, when I read the correspondence in four volumes edited by Charpentier. . . . After some reflection, I said to myself in 1943 that I would certainly write a book on Flaubert some day. In fact, I announced this in *Being and Nothingness,* at the end of the chapter on existential psychoanalysis" (*L/S* 109–10).

2. An analyst friend with whom Sartre once considered undergoing analysis observed: "One day the history of Sartre's thirty-year-long relationship with psychoanalysis, an ambiguous mixture of *equally* deep attraction and repulsion, will have to be written and perhaps his work reinterpreted in the light of it" (J. B. Pontalis, *BEM* 220). A few hints in that direction may be found in Sylvie Le Bon's edition of Sartre's *La Transcendence de l'Ego* (Paris: J. Vrin, 1972). She points out that, beginning with the Baudelaire biography (1947), Sartre "Would abandon the notion of explanation for that of *dialectical comprehension,* which must necessarily operate in terms of an individual's past, education, and character (80–81 n. 74).

Sartre's ill-fated script for the John Huston film, later published as *The Freud Scenario* (Chicago: University of Chicago Press, 1985), affords us another example of his marriage of psychoanalysis and history—again, a fiction that is true. Of it, Sartre admitted, "It led me to rethink my ideas about the unconscious" (*L/S* 72).

For an excellent examination of Sartre's relation to the Freudian psychoanalytic tradition as well as positive suggestions for a Sartrean clinical practice, see Betty Cannon,

Sartre and Psychoanalysis: An Existentialist Challenge to Clinical Metatheory (Lawrence, KS: University Press of Kansas, 1991).

3. See *BN* 53. Actually, it is the "mythology of the unconscious" that Sartre rejects. By this he means that constellation of concepts such as "repression," "censorship," and "drive," which exhibit contradictory properties in psychoanalytic discourse. Sometimes they are conceived mechanistically as efficient causes according to the famous "hydraulic model" of the psyche; at other times they function teleologically (see *BEM* 37–38). Since his early essay on the emotions, Sartre has insisted on the intentional character of all psychic phenomena. In his Flaubert study, he expands this claim to include a certain intentional structure proper to the lived body as well. Flaubert's "autosuggestion" and "somatization" of ideas, e.g., exemplify this thesis adopted from Merleau-Ponty.

4. Limiting ourselves to *Being and Nothingness,* e.g., we find Sartre appealing to a pre-ontological comprehension of being (17), of nonbeing (7), of the futility of "sincerity" (63), of the criteria of truth (156), of the experience of the Other (251), of human reality (561), of the human person (568), and of one's fundamental project (570).

5. See *FI* 5:514–30.

6. "Which is to say that I no longer [*sic*] believe in certain forms of the unconscious even though Lacan's conception of the unconscious is more interesting. . . . I want to give the idea of a whole whose surface is completely conscious, while the rest is opaque to this consciousness and, without being part of the unconscious, is hidden from you. When I show how Flaubert did not know himself and how at the same time he understood himself admirably, I am indicating what I call lived experience [*le vécu*]—that is to say, life aware of itself, without implying any thetic knowledge or consciousness. This notion of lived experience is a tool I use, but one which I have not yet theorized." Interview, "On *The Idiot of the Family,*" in *L/S* 127–28; *s* 10:110.

I prefer to translate *le vécu* as "lived experience" (the common translation of Dilthey's technical term *Erlebnis*) rather than as "experience" *sans phrase*. Although Sartre was critical of any "purely subjective *Erlebnis*" (*BN* 420), the point of the participle "lived" in the English translation is to prevent its being taken in a merely psychological sense.

7. On this aspect of his thought, see Robert Harvey's *Search for a Father: Sartre, Paternity, and the Question of Ethics* (Ann Arbor: University of Michigan Press, 1992).

8. "Inertia, laziness, inner torments, lethargies—we encounter these features from one end of his existence to the other. Taken together they define a strategy that we shall meet again later under the name of passive activity, a kind of nervous weakness in the depths of his physical organism that makes surrender *easier*" (*FI* 1:35).

9. "For the deep wound that *they* have inflicted—this vertigo, this disgust with life, this impossibility of undertaking anything, this difficulty denying and affirming which bars his way into the universe of discourse—must be called, I believe, his *passive constitution*" (*FI* 1:37).

10. *Vers le concret* was the title of an important book by Jean Wahl that captured the spirit of Sartre and his friends in the thirties (see *SM* 19). It might aptly summarize Sartre's philosophical and literary project, especially in his lifelong struggle with the metaphysical and epistemological idealism of his professors.

11. "[Flaubert] moves from *Saint Anthony* to *Madame Bovary*. He wants to do a *novel*.

. . . The novel had become *a* literary genre since the 18th century. In the 19th century it is *the* literary genre. So Flaubert can call himself a writer [*écrivain*] and be only a novelist [*romancier*] (something that would not have been possible in the 18th century). Meanwhile, the novel = the art of prose in the 19th century. It is in those terms that he conceives of style in the novel. And when he writes: prose is young, he means: the novel is young" (Jean-Paul Sartre, *L'Idiot de la famille,* 2d ed., enl. [Paris: Gallimard, 1988], vol. 3, 793; hereafter cited as *L'Idiot* 2d ed., with volume and page numbers).

Sartre rejects the distinction which the *Tel Quel* group, following Roland Barthes, made between *écrivain* (writer) and *écrivant* (the one who is writing) (see *S* 9:45–46).

12. This intentional structure of our psychic life, including our feelings and emotions, has been a constant in Sartre's writings since *The Emotions: Outline of a Theory* (trans. Bernard Frechtman [New York: Philosophical Library, 1947]), originally published in 1939 as part of an unfinished study in phenomenological psychology to be entitled "The Psyche." This early work lays the theoretical foundation for Sartre's analyses of Flaubert's "somatization" of ideas: "In the case of emotions, it is the body directed by consciousness which changes its relations with the world in order that the world change its qualities. If emotion is a game, it is a game we believe in" (44). In *The Family Idiot* Sartre contrasts the passive activity of the pseudo agent with the active passivity of the organism. "Autosuggestion" is the result of their encounter (see *FI* 3:621). Of autosuggestion he writes: "What one began by wanting one suddenly takes on as something suffered" (*FI* 4:40). In earlier works, Sartre had cited the example of a child frightening itself by the faces it makes in a mirror. Now autosuggestion reveals to Flaubert "the frightening power of his body" (*FI* 4:22).

13. This is Flaubert's self-assessment in a letter of 15 August 1846 (see *FI* 3:61 n).

14. Sully Prudhomme records having heard Flaubert remark: "When someone tells me about a base action or knavery, it gives me as much pleasure as if they were giving me money" (quoted in *FI* 5:293).

15. This is Sartre's view of the matter. But, as Hazel Barnes remarks: "Unfortunately, Sartre seems to have erred in attributing this [family] origin to Gustave Flaubert's ambivalent attitude to religious belief. Bruneau and Levin have both pointed out that the evidence shows Madame Flaubert to have been a nonbeliever like her husband, and Sartre does not claim to have uncovered new documentary information. If he drew from a real-life situation, I am afraid it was his own. He has given us a comparable description of his early life [in *The Words*]" (Hazel E. Barnes, *Sartre and Flaubert* [Chicago: University of Chicago Press, 1981], 51–52.

16. It is in two characters from his stories—Dr. Larivière, the renowned physician in *Madame Bovary,* and Dr. Mathurin of his youthful *Les Funérailles du docteur Mathurin*—that Flaubert incarnates and mocks his father's Voltairean skepticism and scientism; see *FI* 1:440 ff.

17. It is worth noting that Sartre claims otherwise in an interview with Contat and Rybalka: "In his correspondence [Flaubert] is just as open as if he were lying on the analyst's couch—unlike George Sand, for example, who constantly hides herself in her correspondence" (*L/S* 125). The difference is reconciled when we realize that the "insincere" first-person accounts occur in Flaubert's early autobiographical stories.

18. For the credo of this tradition, see Emile Durkheim's *The Rules of Sociological Method,* trans. Sarah A. Solovay and John H. Mueller, 8th ed. (New York: Free Press, 1966). The rise and fall of the French school of sociology is the theme of essays collected by Charles E. Lemert in *French Sociology: Rupture and Renewal Since 1968* (Columbia University Press, 1981).

19. "I found in about 1939 that I had assimilated many things from Hegel, though I didn't know his work well. I did not really come into contact with Hegel until after the war, with Hippolyte's translation and commentary" (*L/S* 127).

20. Merleau-Ponty, whose influence on the evolution of Sartre's social thought is only beginning to be appreciated, sets the agenda when he attempts to bring the Cartesian subject out of ontological and epistemic isolation:

> If the subject were taken not as a constituting but as an instituting subject, it might be understood that the subject does not exist instantaneously and that the other person does not exist simply as a negative of myself. . . . Thus the instituted subject exists between others and myself, between me and myself, like a hinge, the consequence and the guarantee of our belonging to a common world.
>
> Thus what we understand by the concept of institution are those events in experience which endow it with durable dimensions, in relation to which a whole series of other experiences will acquire meaning, will form an intelligible series or a history—or again those events which sediment in me a meaning, not just as survivals or residues, but as the invitation to a sequel, the necessity of a future. (*Themes from the Lectures at the Collège de France, 1952–1960,* trans. John O'Neill [Evanston: Northwestern University Press, 1970], 40–41)

21. Several years earlier, in the *Notebooks for an Ethics,* he had conflated these definitions by describing "Spirit" as "the World as already thought by Others, insofar as this thought submerges me and insofar as I surpass it" (*NE* 429). This in turn is an elaboration of his category of "techniques for appropriating the world," introduced in *Being and Nothingness* (see *BN* 512 ff.).

22. On Foucault's use of "archive" and the discipline, "archaeology," that studies it, see his "On the Archaeology of the Sciences," *Theoretical Practice* 3–4 (Autumn 1971): 108–27. This is an abridged translation of "Réponse au Cercle d'épistémologie," *Cahiers pour l'analyse* 9: *Génélogie des sciences* (Summer 1968): 9–40. Of course, the locus classicus is Foucault's *The Archaeology of Knowledge.*

The essential difference between Sartrean "objective spirit" in this semantic sense and Foucauldian "archive" is that the former relies on the cognate concepts of "intentionality" and "comprehension"—fundamental to Sartre's existential-moral project and the humanism on which it rests. Foucault rejects both "intentionality" and the subjectivity it seems to imply. We shall determine the full weight of this difference in the next volume of our study. But the "positivity" of "objective spirit" in the sense of its factical nature (it is encountered, not deducible a priori) and its availability for immediate scrutiny is shared by both thinkers.

23. The first of these occurs in *The Communists and Peace* (trans. Martha H. Fletcher [New York: George Braziller, 1968], 148 ff., hereafter cited as *CP*); it is more fully devel-

oped in the *Critique* (1:758 ff.) and it is extended, mutatis mutandis, to the provincial bourgeois in *The Family Idiot* (*FI* 2:357 ff., 3:340 ff.).

24. Already in the *Notebooks* Sartre speaks of the *objective bad faith* of the "kind" slave owner: "You are generous within the limits of the institution and the rule. . . . In reality your generosity is vitiated, you are, if not subjectively, at least objectively in bad faith. You intended to uphold the regime by humanizing it and in humanizing it you render it more unacceptable" (*NE* 572).

25. See Karl R. Popper, *Objective Knowledge: An Evolutionary Approach* (Oxford: Clarendon Press, 1972), chap. 4, "On the Theory of Objective Mind," 153–90.

Popper's "third world" of ideas in themselves is close to Sartre's objective spirit in being more than a mere psychological *Erlebnis*. Popper calls it "the world . . . of *ideas in the objective sense;* it is the world of possible objects of thought: the world of theories in themselves, and their logical relations; of arguments in themselves; and of problem situations in themselves" (154). This world also resembles objective spirit in being man-made rather than transcendent and timeless. Finally, both terms denote a reality that is autonomous; that is, each refers to the locus of what we have called "objective possi-bility" in Sartre's dialectical discourse, and each is "discovered" rather than created by individuals, though their effects in the practical arena are mediated by human agents (Sartre's primacy of praxis). When characterizing the ontological status of the entities in the third world, Popper might well have used Sartre's category of the practico-inert to keep his ontology from floating off into a Stoic, if not a Platonic, idealism.

But Sartre's Husserlian proclivities, especially his abiding conviction that conscious-ness and praxis are intentional, separate him from Popper and distinguish his objective spirit from the latter's third world. This comes to the fore in their respective understand-ings of "understanding" (hermeneutics) and in Sartre's project of existential histo-riography as what we have called "reconstituting praxis" (see below, chap. 9 n. 26).

26. In fact, Sartre offers a description of objective spirit in the literary realm that is worthy of Foucault in his positivist moments: "The objective Spirit of an age [in the realm of writing] is at once the sum of works published during a specific period and the multiplicity of totalizations effected by contemporary readers" (*FI* 5:47).

27. Referring to his method of psychoanalyzing family conditioning for historical roles, Sartre remarks: "Robespierre could be taken as an example, for instance. But it would be impossible to pursue such a study of him, because there are no materials for doing so. What would be necessary to know is what was the encounter of the revolution which created the Committee of Public Safety, and the son of Monsieur and Madame Robespierre of Arras" (*BEM* 44).

28. This is one of the theses of my *Sartre and Marxist Existentialism*. There I have ar-gued that Sartre's is a decidedly revisionist Marxism or what would now be termed "neo-Marxism."

While insisting that the essential aspects of Marxism are still valid, Sartre admitted to Michel Contat in 1975: "We must develop a way of thinking which takes Marxism into account in order to go beyond it, to reject it and take it up again, to absorb it. That is the condition for arriving at true socialism" (*L/S* 61).

One could continue this Odyssey by citing his final interview with Michel Rybalka and others (1975) where he is less dialectical in his assessment of his relation to Marxism: "That was my mistake [to have claimed that existentialism was only an enclave of Marxism]. It cannot be an enclave, because of my idea of freedom, and therefore it is ultimately a separate philosophy. I do not at all think that ultimately this philosophy [in the *Critique*] is Marxist. It cannot ignore Marxism; it is linked to it, just as some philosophies are linked to others without, however, being contained by them. But now I do not consider it at all a Marxist philosophy" (*PS* 20).

29. The case of their contemporary, Leconte de Lisle, is problematic. As Sartre remarks: "He is perceived [by the reader of 1850] as seriously deficient, as practicing art-neurosis without being neurotic himself" (*FI* 3:372). And further: "He does what he must, but *without believing in it;* inevitably the reader doesn't believe in it either" (*FI* 5:381). Though appreciated in the Third Republic, Sartre finds it significant that, unlike Flaubert, Leconte de Lisle was not read during the Empire.

30. On the threefold failure (*échec*) of the artist, the man, and work, that neurotic art demanded, see *FI* 5:130–82, 619. Flaubert recognized the victory of reality (praxis) over the imaginary in the billeting of Prussian officers in his home after Sedan.

31. See Friedrich Nietzsche, *The Will to Power,* trans. Walter Kaufmann and R. J. Hollingdale (New York: Vintage Books, 1967), notes collected under the title "European Nihilism," 9–82.

32. Of course, Sartre has discussed rebellion among the students in young Gustave's school as a "psychodrama" of the historical events in the adult world (see *FI* 3:222 ff.). And the decisive "fall" of that winter's evening in 1844 certainly renders Flaubert "*l'homme événement.*" But these occurrences are of mainly biographical import until the events of 1848, of which they are a preview (and in the case of the "fall," more than a preview), confer on them their full historical meaning.

33. Ever since his *War Diaries* Sartre has referred to this historical facticity and to "Pascalian man, that nonconceptualizable become-being [*être-devenu*] who has a history and not an essence" (*FI* 3:47 n; *F* 2:1152).

34. "In June 1848, the veils were torn away: the bourgeoisie was tainted in its class reality by a crime: it lost its universality in order to define itself in a divided society by relations of power [*force*] with the other classes" (*FI* 5:370 n; *F* 3:401 n).

35. "The *black* literature of the 1850s is exactly suited to the ruling classes because in the meantime they have been *blackened* by the history they made; the reader demands that his reading allow him to become unrealized through the imaginary appeasement of his hatred. . . . The reader assigns a precise function to literature-neurosis, which is to put him in possession of his hatred without naming it, to allow him to enjoy it in imagination without departing from a fierce objectivity" (*FI* 5:307).

36. Sartre had long maintained a historical approach to interclass relations in France, "temporalizing" the abstract sociological (structuralist) analyses of Marxists and others. As early as 1952 he was arguing: "The French proletariat is a historical reality whose singularity was made manifest in recent years by a certain attitude; I do not go looking for the key to this attitude in the universal movement of societies, but in the movement

of French society; that is to say, in the history of France" (*CP* 135). This work had originally appeared as a series of articles in *Les Temps modernes,* beginning July 1952.

37. "We can claim with certainty that we never dealt with [Flaubert] from the outside, purely as the object of conceptual knowledge: everything we know about him he
experienced and said. This book would make no sense if its purpose were not—at least
in the first sections—to stay constantly on the level at which the internalization of the
external is transformed into the externalization of the internal. Indeed, while enumerat-
ing objective conditions and organizing them, our primary aim is to show how these
conditions were maintained and surpassed toward objectivization by the subjective moment, that irreducible element. On this assumption, we must acknowledge that Flaubert
is not mistaken about his illness" (*FI* 4:19). That is, he too considered the attack at Pont-
l'Evêque a turning point in his life.

38. After noting how the Flaubert studies by Victor Brombert and Jonathan Culler
have tended to confirm most, though certainly not all, of Sartre's factual claims, Hazel
Barnes writes with characteristic balance: "It seems only reasonable to conclude that
whatever judgment may finally prevail, *The Family Idiot* will direct the course of Flaubert
studies for a long time to come" (Barnes, *Sartre and Flaubert,* 406).

39. In fact, Sartre's notion of totalization seems more apt for constructing a "history
of the present" than does Foucault's famous genealogy (see Michel Foucault, *Discipline
and Punish,* trans. Alan Sheridan [New York: Pantheon Books, 1977], 31).

40. Recalling how psychoanalysis unites both objective structures (material conditions) "to the action upon our adult life of the childhood we never wholly surpass,"
Sartre concludes: "Henceforth it becomes impossible to connect *Madame Bovary* directly
to the political-social structure and to the evolution of the petite bourgeoisie," as Marxist
theorists would do; "the book will have to be referred back to contemporary reality
insofar as it was lived by Flaubert through his childhood." He admits the need for dialectical mediation if we are to grasp the "organic bond of interiority" between author,
work, and epoch that we are seeking:

> There results from this a certain discrepancy, to be sure; there is a sort of *hysteresis*
> on the part of the work in relation to the very period in which it appears; this is
> because it must unite within itself a number of contemporary significations and
> certain others which express a state recent but already surpassed by society. This
> *hysteresis,* always neglected by the Marxists, accounts in turn for the veritable social
> reality in which *contemporary* events, products, and acts are characterized by the
> extraordinary diversity of their temporal depth. There will come a moment at
> which Flaubert will appear to be *in advance* of his period (at the time of *Madame
> Bovary*) because he is *behind it,* because his book, in disguised form, expresses to a
> generation disgusted with romanticism the post-romantic despairs of a student of
> 1830. The objective meaning of the book . . . is the result of a compromise be-
> tween what this new generation of readers claims in terms of its own history and
> what the author can offer to it from his own; that is, it realizes the paradoxical
> union of two past moments of this intellectual petite bourgeoisie (1830 and 1845).
> (*SM* 64)

41. The *Trois Contes* were written after 1870 but never published in Flaubert's life-time, and *Bouvard et Pécuchet* was deemed a failure. Many critics have an opposing view of Flaubert's last works. For example, see Dominick LaCapra, *A Preface to Sartre* (Ithaca, NY: Cornell University Press, 1978), 207. As we have seen, Flaubert considered the event at Pont-l'Evêque to have divided his life in two.

42. *November,* conceived in the winter of 1840–41 and abandoned several times, was completed on 25 October 1842. Sartre remarks that "the initial project was to write an autobiographical novel in the first person that would evoke the author's adventure with Eulalie Foucault" (*FI* 3:591). In fact, another voice sounds toward the end to finish the novel, declaring "The manuscript breaks off here, but I knew its author" and recounting his death. This emergence of Flaubert's double, in Sartre's view, is a prolepsis of the incident at Pont-l'Evêque, fourteen months before the attack, that made Gustave "feel *the same* and *other*" (*FI* 3:600).

43. See "Kierkegaard: The Singular Universal," *BEM* 141–69. E.g., "Kierkegaard was perhaps the first to show that the universal enters History as a singular, in so far as the singular institutes itself in it as a universal. In this novel form of historiality [*historialité*] we encounter paradox once again: here it acquires the unsurpassable [*indépassable*] appearance of ambiguity" (*BEM* 163; *S* 9:182). But, directing an objection toward Kierkegaard that others would later raise against himself, Sartre adds:

> Kierkegaard demonstrated his historiality [*historialité*] but failed to find History. Pitting himself against Hegel, he occupied himself over-exclusively with transmit-ting his instituted contingency to the human adventure and, because of this, he neglected *praxis,* which is rationality. At a stroke, he denatured *knowledge,* forget-ting that the world we know is the world we make. Anchorage is a fortuitous event, but the possibility and rational meaning of this chance is given by *general structures of envelopment* which found it and which are themselves the universaliza-tion of singular adventures by the materiality in which they are inscribed. (*BEM* 168; *S* 9:189–90)

The ideal, Sartre argues and subsequently exhibits, is the mixture of Kierkegaard and Marx, the very union that Raymond Aron held to be impossible.

44. See chap. 5 above.

45. Michel de Certeau, explaining three traits common to the genus of historiogra-phy, remarks that "the story which speaks in the name of the real is injunctive. It 'signi-fies' in the way a command is issued." His point is that historians, newscasters, and other "ministers of current events" make these "facts" speak in order to command in their name (*Heterologies: Discourse on the Other,* trans. Brian Massumi [Minneapolis: University of Minnesota Press, 1986], 206).

46. "Every enterprise, even one brought to a triumphant conclusion, remains a *fail-ure,* that is to say an incompletion to be completed. It lives on because it is open" (*BEM* 168). If this is true of life, it is especially true of art, whose interpretive nature is open-ended.

47. For Sartre's identification of singular universal with *sens,* see my "The Role of the Image in Sartre's Aesthetic," 441 n. 44 as well as *S* 8:445–46, 8:449–50, 9:178.

48. Kant uses the expression "sign of history" (*Geschichtszeichen*) in part 5 of the *Conflict of the Philosophy Faculty with the Faculty of Law* (Immanuel Kant, *The Conflict of the Faculties,* trans. and intro. Mary J. Gregor [New York: Abaris Books, 1979]). It encompasses all three temporal dimensions, being a *signum* at once *"rememorativum, demonstrativum, [et] prognostikon"* (151).

See Jean-François Lyotard's discussion of this topic in his "The Sign of History," in *The Differend: Phrases in Dispute,* trans. George Van Den Abbeele (Minneapolis: University of Minnesota Press, 1988), 151–81, and "The Sign of History," trans. Geoff Bennington in *Post-Structuralism and the Question of History,* ed. Derek Attridge, Geoff Bennington, and Robert Young (Cambridge: Cambridge University Press, 1987), 162–80.

49. "Failure will therefore be oracular if the readers of the Second Empire read into it their own political and social history and see it dissolve in an eternity forever begun anew" (*FI* 5:387). That is, it is the readers' *response* that makes it oracular in fact.

50. In an interview published two years earlier, Sartre elaborated this claim in response to the question of why he had stopped writing novels:

> Writing on Flaubert is enough for me by way of fiction—it might indeed be called a novel. Only I would like people to say that it was a true novel. I try to achieve a certain level of comprehension of Flaubert by means of hypotheses. Thus I use fiction—guided and controlled, but nonetheless fiction—to explore why, let us say, Flaubert wrote one thing on the 15th March and the exact opposite on the 21st March, to the same correspondent, without worrying about the contradiction. My hypotheses are in this sense a sort of invention of the personage. (*BEM* 49)

51. In this respect, Sartre's Flaubert study follows a trail blazed by Roland Barthes (*Michelet* [Paris: Editions du Seuil, 1954]) and broadened by Hayden White (*Metahistory* [Baltimore: Johns Hopkins University Press, 1973]). Of this last, F. R. Ankersmit writes: "It was part of White's enterprise to read the great texts of nineteenth-century historians as if they were novels—something no theorist [except perhaps Barthes] had ever done before" (*HT* 7). But Sartre is reading a nineteenth-century novelist as if he were a historian and is doing so in a text that is itself both factual and imaginative: a novel that is true.

52. See note 11, above.

53. "The real work of the committed writer is, as I said before, to reveal, demonstrate, demystify, and dissolve myths and fetishes in a critical acid bath" (*BEM* 29).

54. "I consider this work [*The Family Idiot*] a socialist piece in the sense that, if I succeed [in finishing it], it should contribute to the comprehension of men from a socialist viewpoint" (*ORR* 73–74).

55. These arguments have been reconstructed by many authors. See, e.g., David Detmer's *Freedom as a Value* (LaSalle, IL: Open Court, 1986), or my *Sartre and Marxist Existentialism,* 33–41.

56. See, e.g., Peter Lowenberg, *Decoding the Past: The Psychohistorical Approach* (New York: Alfred A. Knopf, 1983). For a critique of this approach, see Jacques Barzun's *Clio*

and the Doctors (Chicago: University of Chicago Press, 1974). Sartre is not liable to the common objections leveled against psychohistory, namely, psychologism and the "genetic fallacy," because his progressive-regressive method avoids, first, reductionism by appeal to the "multidimensionality of the act" and second, simplistic post hoc arguments and the blurring of formal distinctions among the disciplines by respecting the irreducibly "structural" and historial dimensions of his investigation.

57. Karl Marx, *Capital: A Critique of Political Economy,* trans. S. Moore, E. Aveling, and E. Untermann (Chicago: Charles H. Kerr, 1906–9), 15.

58. "In analytical language, the *Critique* tends toward the following objective: *to establish ontologically the foundations of methodological individualism*" (Aron, *History and the Dialectic of Violence,* 200; emphasis his). In an earlier work, which recorded Aron's initial view of the *Critique,* he insisted that "a follower of Kierkegaard cannot at the same time be a follower of Marx" (Aron, *Marxism and the Existentialists,* 30). Elsewhere I have argued that Aron is mistaken about Sartre's methodological individualism and that the latter's "dialectical nominalism" is a *via media* between individualism and holism in the social sciences; see my *Sartre and Marxist Existentialism,* 126 ff.

CONCLUSION TO PART TWO

1. "Someone else could write the fourth on the basis of the three I have written" (*L/S* 20). The fourth was to have been a close reading of *Madame Bovary* as concrete universal. Occasionally he spoke of a fifth volume that was to treat the remainder of Flaubert's life and work (see his interview with Michel Sicard in *Obliques* nos. 18–19 [1979], 26).

2. For Foucault's view of Marx and Freud as "initiators of discursive practices," see "What is an Author?" in Foucault, *Language, Counter–memory, Practice,* 131–36. Unlike an "author," who is presumed to be the originating source of a book or a theory, Marx and Freud produced "not only their own work, but the possibility and the rules of formation of other texts." To drive the point home, Foucault insists elsewhere: "As far as I'm concerned, Marx [the "author"] doesn't exist" (*Power/Knowledge,* 76).

3. See, e.g., *FI* 1:46, 3:56, 4:8–9, 5:32, 5:340; *CDR* 1:37, 1:66 respectively.

CHAPTER NINE

1. "History comes closest to poetry and is, so to speak, a poem in prose," quoted by Ankersmit, *HT* 107.

2. For an elaboration of the thesis of Sartre as philosopher of the imagination, see my "Philosophy of Existence 2: Sartre," in *Continental Philosophy in the Twentieth Century,* ed. Kearney, 74–104.

3. "Let [the critic] do [on me] something of what I did on Flaubert. I do not claim to have done justice to him entirely, but I hope to have found some directions, some themes" (interview, *PS* 49).

4. See my "The Role of the Image in Sartre's Aesthetic," 431–42.

5. Jean-Paul Sartre, *L'Imaginaire* (Paris: Gallimard, 1940), 45 see *PI,* 25. All translations from this work are my own.

6. For a fine development of this thesis, see David J. Detmer's *Freedom as Value.*

7. Friedrich Nietzsche, "On the Uses and Disadvantages of History for Life," in *Untimely Meditations,* trans. R. J. Hollingdale (Cambridge: Cambridge University Press, 1983), 95.

8. Arguing for an existentialist contribution to an anemic Marxist epistemology, Sartre asks, "But what are we to call this situated negativity, as a moment of *praxis* and as a pure relation to things themselves, if not exactly 'consciousness'?" Defending the role of biographical considerations in historical materialism, he continues:

> The truth is that subjectivity is neither everything nor nothing; it represents a moment in the objective process (that in which externality is internalized), and this moment is perpetually eliminated only to be perpetually reborn. Now, each of these ephemeral moments . . . is lived as a *point of departure* by the subject of history. "Class consciousness" is not the simple lived contradiction which objectively characterizes the class considered; it is that contradiction already surpassed by *praxis* and thereby preserved and denied all at once. But it is precisely this revealing negativity, this distance within immediate proximity, which simultaneously constitutes what existentialism calls "consciousness *of* the object" and "non-thetic self-consciousness." (*SM* 33 n)

9. For a lengthy defense of the political motivation behind Sartre's theory of history, see Dobson, *Jean-Paul Sartre and the Politics of Reason.* I am subscribing to a somewhat similar thesis under the rubric of "committed history."

10. See my "The Role of the Image in Sartre's Aesthetics," 435–38.

11. In the words of a well-known philosopher of art, "Truth and its aesthetic counterpart amount to appropriateness under different names" (Nelson Goodman, *Languages of Art* [Indianapolis: Bobbs-Merrill, 1985], 264).

12. *IPH* 509; see also *Magazine littéraire,* no. 198 (September 1983): 37.

13. Roland Barthes, "The Discourse of History" and "The Reality Effect," in his *Rustle of Language,* 127–48.

14. Since it appears that the origin of the details, which Barthes calls "notations," lies in their contrast with the main outline of the story, not in an extratextual relationship between a description in the text and a state of affairs in the past, Ankersmit asks whether we might better speak of a reality "illusion" instead of a reality "effect." He sees the key in the difference between a Fregian and a Saussurian theory of signs. In the Fregian context, Barthes's position should be called a reality illusion, because it never escapes the prison house of language, so to speak. But "a peculiarity of the Saussurian theory of signs generally adhered to by French philosophers (and especially as interpreted by Barthes) is that it does not differentiate between language and reality as far as the reference of the sign is concerned" (*HT* 141).

15. Barthes, *The Rustle of Language,* 139.

16. See Barthes, "Mythology Today," in *The Rustle of Language,* 65–68.

17. Barthes, *The Rustle of Language,* 132, 139 n.

18. As he becomes more historical and dialectical, Sartre discounts Bachelard's "coefficient of adversity" as denoting the mere opacity of a thing in favor of the practical necessity of necessary *means* to projected ends: "One *experiences* necessity in action. . . .

[Necessity] appears in and through the *real* absence of the necessary link whose necessity is indicated by the impossibility of carrying out the operation, which is objective and subjectively felt at the same time. . . . It is nonbeing that reveals the *lack* of the indispensable means. Yet it is being that announces to us the required qualities for the means to be utilizable" (*NE* 97–98).

19. In the case of Barthes, the question of idealism is more complicated than we can pursue here. After noting that "the interesting thing about Barthes's theory is that it does in fact project the reality of the past as an external reality in spite of its textual origin," Ankersmit suggests that "the realist in the Barthesian sense can probably reconcile himself with the definition of realism given by Putnam: 'A realist (with respect to a given theory of discourse) holds that 1) the sentences of that theory are true or false; and 2) that what makes them true or false is something external—that is to say, it is not (in general) our sense data, actual or potential, or the structure of our minds, or our language, etc." (*HT* 159 and n. 91).

20. Thus Barthes asks: "Does [historical] narration differ, in fact, by some specific feature, by an indubitable pertinence, from imaginary narration as we find it in the epic, the novel, the drama?" And he finally concludes: "By its very structure . . . historical discourse is essentially an ideological elaboration or, to be more specific, an *imaginary* elaboration, if it is true that the image-repertoire is the language by which the speaker (or 'writer') of a discourse (a purely linguistic entity) 'fills' the subject of the speech-act (a psychological or ideological entity)" ("The Discourse of History," in *The Rustle of Language*, 127, 138). His analysis of the "reality effect" in Flaubert and in Michelet attests to this connection between history and the nineteenth-century novel.

Ankersmit, assessing this "connection between the writing of history and the (nineteenth-century) realistic novel suggested by Barthes," admits that "historical reality is not a datum but a *convention* created by the reality effect." But he points out the lingering ambiguity of Barthes's appeal to the "reality effect": "Is it a generalization about realistic novels and historical studies? Is it concerned with the psychological and rhetorical effect of texts on the reader that are constructed in a certain way? Or is it both of these things? (*HT* 142, 145, 147).

21. See Sartre's interview with Michel Sicard toward the end of his life (*Obliques*, nos. 18–19 [1979]: 21) as well as *ORR*, 78, 100–101.

22. "For an event to be historical it must always have an infinite future owing to the infinity of possible interpretations. It has its depth in freedom, that is, in an unmade future" (*NE* 23). Criticizing Hegel's dialectic of History, Sartre concludes: "Its freedom is Spinoza's necessity transferred to the temporal succession" (*NE* 464).

23. In his so-called second ethics, Sartre seems to argue in the opposite direction. There he describes "subman" (our present premoral condition) in order to catch some glimmer of a vision of "integral humanity" (*l'homme intégral*), his ethical ideal (see *RLN* 51 ff.). In fact, he claims that "history as norm," that is, as "pure future, is always veiled, even to the exploited and oppressed, by the institutional whole and the alienated ethics maintained by the dominant classes and inculcated among the disfavored classes since childhood" (*RLN* 63). Both history and integral man have yet to be realized (*à faire*). Indeed, integral man-to-be-realized is "the vectorial meaning [*sens*] of history" (*RLN*

95). And since "only a world without oppression can give us integral man," the link between ethics, history, and socioeconomic revolution is clear (*RLN* 96).

But I believe the inversion of the human and the subhuman is only apparent. We could not recognize the substandard as such, if we did not have some inkling of the standard itself. But what I am calling an "inkling" is not knowledge properly speaking. Sartre insists that the "pure future" is neither knowable nor *prévisible* (*RLN* 16). Yet he admits that integral man, if not knowable, is "graspable as *orientation* by a being who defines himself by praxis, that is, by the incomplete, alienated man that we are" (*RLN* 65). Such practical orientation corresponds to the kind of hermeneutic pretheoretical "understanding" to which Sartre appeals in his other works. Each serves to illuminate the other, subman and integral man, as do perception and imagination in the dialectical interaction as we have come to expect form Sartre.

24. Friedrich von Schiller, "On the Sublime," in *C,* 69.

25. In a series of discussions with two French "Maoists" between 1972 and 1974, Sartre approvingly describes the "antihierarchical and libertarian . . . hope that, in [his] opinion, is presently a great revolutionary force [in France], namely, the idea that one can really achieve something. . . . As soon as you have hope," he explains, "you can ask people to do things they would not have done simply out of self-sacrifice. They will do it for you because they think it is going to succeed" (*ORR* 188).

26. R. G. Collingwood, *The Idea of History* (Oxford: Oxford University Press, 1980), 215.

27. Ibid., 301. I say "perhaps even their psychological force" because Collingwood, who distinguishes the "historical a priori" operative here from mere memory or recollection, must have *more than simple logical form* in mind when he claims that "the same thought" is re-enacted by the historian and by Caesar. It does not help that he clouds the issue by appealing to examples of philosophical argument (Plato) and scientific deduction (Archimedes and Euclid) to illustrate his case. For one can readily allow that such "argument" is outside the flow of time (and thus outside of history?) without concluding that the very act of arguing is not a datable event. The decisive consideration, it seems to me, should be whether Caesar was convinced by "the same argument" that we now find adequate for the action he undertook. There is something Platonic about Collingwood's claim that the distinction between the immediate and the mediate in his sense is relevant to re-enactment. The hermeneuticists have attempted to resolve this issue without such metaphysical presuppositions, though clearly they make assumptions of their own.

Earlier, we contrasted Sartre and Popper on their respective notions of "objective spirit" and "third world" respectively. But we remarked that they differ most markedly in the matters of understanding and reconstituting praxis (see chap. 8 n. 25). Since the matter involves Collingwood as well, this is the time to support that claim.

Popper sees understanding primarily as the analysis of third-world situations such as conflicts, comparisons, and analogies. It is not the "reading" of other minds, though one could describe it as the reading of their thoughts and to that extent historical understanding resembles Collingwood's re-enactment which also claims to put us in touch with the thoughts of historical agents, in fact, with their very acts of thinking, as we have just seen. But both Popperian understanding and Collingwood's re-enactment differ from

Sartre's reconstituting praxis in their fundamentally *intellectualist* bent. Though Popper allows for the role of emotional overtones in expressing and coloring understanding, he ultimately is concerned with arguments and problem-solving in an "objective problem situation" (*Objective Knowledge,* 167)—an expression that reminds one of Dewey. While admitting that "no creative action can ever be fully explained," Popper insists: "nevertheless, we can try conjecturally, to give an idealized reconstruction of the *problem situation* in which the agent found himself, and to that extent make the action 'understandable' " (*Objective Knowledge,* 179).

Popper's criticism of Collingwood's "Method of Subjective Re-enactment" focuses on the latter's "psychological way of putting things, [which] is by no means merely a matter of formulation" (*Objective Knowledge,* 187). Whereas Collingwood's method essentially demands "the historian's mental re-enactment, mental repetition of the original experience," Popper regards the psychological process of re-enactment as inessential. He insists: *"What I regard as essential is not the re-enactment but the situational analysis."* "Thus," he continues, "the historian's central metaproblem is: what were the decisive elements in the [historical agent's] problem situation? To the extent to which the historian succeeds in solving this metaproblem, he *understands* the historical situation" (*Objective Knowledge,* 188; emphasis his).

It is not my intention to study Popper's or Collingwood's positions, much less the latter's evolution, any further. For an excellent survey and analysis of both authors, one that links Collingwood's epistemology with his metaphysical monistic theory of mind, see Peter Skagestad, *Making Sense of History: The Philosophies of Popper and Collingwood* (Oslo: Universitetsforlaget, 1975).

28. Collingwood, *Idea of History,* 241. Besides the historical imagination, Collingwood refers to the artistic and the perceptual functions of a priori imagination as well (see 242).

29. Ibid., 245.

30. Ibid., 245, 246. Specifically, the historian and novelist differ in the decisive role that evidence plays in the work of the former.

31. "These later phases of analytical hermeneutics could even be seen as open or covert flirtations with the CLM [Covering Law Model]. . . . The present state of affairs in the debate should be seen as a movement toward a convergence or synthesis of the CLM and analytical hermeneutics rather than as the victory of the latter over the former" (*HT* 54). See also F. A. Olafson, "Hermeneutics: 'Analytical' and 'Dialectical,' " *History and Theory, Beiheft* 25 (1986): 28–42.

Martin concludes his study with the avowal: "I have tried in the argument of this book to bring the science of human nature and historicism and, more particularly, the 'covering law' and *verstehen* positions together on a middle ground. My aim has been to find what is of value in each and, by taking account of their positive elements, to develop a mediating position between them" (Rex Martin, *Historical Explanation: Re-enactment and Practical Inference* [Ithaca, NY: Cornell University Press, 1977], 252). What I have said in the previous section about aesthetic "fittingness" comes closer to what he calls "individualized [if not generic] assertions of appropriateness" (see Martin, *Historical Explanation,* 146–57).

32. "Many of the weaknesses of analytical hermeneutics can be traced back to its original sin of mixing the questions suggested by the hermeneutic vocabulary with the explanatory ideal of the [covering law] vocabulary" (*HT* 98).

33. Johan Huizinga, *Men and Ideas: History, the Middle Ages, the Renaissance,* trans. James S. Holmes and Hans van Marle (New York: Meridian Books, 1959), 54.

34. Ibid., 55.

35. In Sartre's case, the matter is rather more complex. Compare the following pronouncements:

> We can with absolute certainty find the answer to the question whether someone is pursuing history or literature by testing the intellectual preoccupation from which he works. If the all-predominating need for "genuineness," the deeply sincere desire to find out how a certain thing "really happened," is lacking as such, he is not pursuing history. (Huizenga, *Men and Ideas,* 43)

> A voice declares publically: "You are a thief." The child is ten years old. That was how it happened, in that or some other way. In all probability, there were offenses and then punishment, solemn oaths and relapses. It does not matter. The important thing is that Genet lived and has not stopped reliving this period of his life as if it had lasted only an instant. (*SG* 17)

36. "The meanness is in the system," Sartre once wrote apropos of capitalism, "one must not see a national characteristic in it, but the collective situation which our lords have made for us" (*CP* 138)—yet another example of the primacy of praxis.

37. See Niccolo Machiavelli, *Florentine Histories,* trans. Laura F. Banfield and Harvey C. Mansfield, Jr. (Princeton, NJ: Princeton University Press, 1988), "Translators' Introduction," vii–xv.

38. See *C* 59–68, as well as Hayden White and Frank E. Manuel, "Rhetoric and History," in *Theories of History: Papers of the Clark Library Seminar,* ed. Peter Reill (Los Angeles, 1978), 1–25.

39. The concrete social reality, of course, is a mix of praxis and practico-inert mediation: "Any social field is constituted, very largely, by structured ensembles of groupings which are always both praxis and practico-inert, although either of these characteristics may constantly tend to cancel itself out; only experience can indicate the internal relation of the structures in a definite group and as a definite moment of its interior dialectic" (*CDR* 1:254).

40. "I think that a philosophy of language could be drawn out of my philosophy, but there is no philosophy of language that could be imposed upon it" (interview, *PS* 17). For an interesting initial attempt at such an extraction, see the unpublished dissertation by Kenneth L. Anderson, "Freedom, Meaning, and the Other: Toward Reconstructing a Sartrean Theory of Language," Emory University, 1991.

41. On several occasions he cited (from Stendhal's *The Charterhouse of Parma*) Mosca's apprehension regarding Fabrice and La Sanseverina: "If the word 'love' is pronounced between them, I am lost." On this occasion, Sartre invokes both praxis and the practico-inert when he continues: "Through this expression the collectivity affirms its right of surveillance over the most purely subjective intimacy, socializing the rather

foolhardy tenderness the young aunt and her nephew feel for one another" (*FI* 2:128). These words could have been uttered by Foucault!

Consider the following remarks on the power of language: "Alongside false knowledge, ideologies that impose themselves on the worker—ideologies of his class, of the middle or ruling class—are introduced or reintroduced into him in the form of recipes explicitly presented as a verbal exposé or a related set of determinations of discourse that would illuminate his condition and offer him the means to tolerate it" (*FI* 5:37).

"Thus the general categories of the culture, the particular systems, and the language which expresses them are already the objectification of a class, the reflection of conflicts, latent or declared, and the particular manifestation of alienation. The world is outside; language and culture are not inside the individual like stamps registered by his nervous system. It is the individual who is inside culture and inside language; that is, inside a special section of the field of instruments" (*SM* 113).

42. See my *Sartre and Marxist Existentialism*, 72–84, as well as Thomas W. Busch, *The Power of Consciousness and the Force of Circumstance in Sartre's Philosophy*.

43. Near the midpoint of the work he promises, "At the end of this book we shall even be able to consider this articulation of the For-itself in relation to the In-itself as the perpetually moving outline of a quasi-totality which we can call *Being*" (*BN* 216). Under the rubric "Metaphysical implications" he gestures toward filling this promise by referring to "Being (as a general category belonging to all existents)" divided into "two incommunicable regions, in each one of which the notion of Being must be taken in an original and unique sense" (*BN* 617). He then faces the obvious question of what there is in common between them and concludes: "an internal relation." Which raises the objection that it is this totality which should be given the name "being" or "reality" (*BN* 621). Finally, Sartre leaves it to metaphysics, as distinct from ontology, to deal with this matter.

Sartre adopts a specifically Heideggerian discourse of "unveiling" and "revealing Being" in the immediate postwar years. This is most notable in the posthumously published *Truth and Existence* (see 17 ff., 74 ff.) and *Notebooks* (see 482–513), but already occurs in *What Is Literature?* Consider the following: "Each of our perceptions is accompanied by the consciousness that human reality is 'unveiling' [*dévoilante*], that is, it is through human reality that 'there is' being, or, to put it differently, that man is the means by which things are manifested" (*WL* 23; *S* 2:89).

44. Aron, *History and the Dialectic of Violence*, 19.

45. See, for example, Ron Aronson, *Jean-Paul Sartre* (New York: New Left Books, 1980), 11, 285 ff. Istvan Mészaros speaks of a "characteristically Sartrean" conflation of the individual and the collective subject (see his *The Work of Sartre*, vol. 1, *Search for Freedom* [Atlantic Highlands, NJ: Humanities Press, 1979], 144).

46. See my "Praxis and Vision: Elements of a Sartrean Epistemology," 21–43.

47. The phenomenological method predominated in *Being and Nothingness* whereas the dialectical took precedence in the *Critique*. But as Robert D. Cumming has pointed out, the dialectic was not absent from *Being and Nothingness* (see his "To Understand a Man," in *PS* 63–66), and Sartre himself gives us a "translation" of dialectical terms into the those of *Being and Nothingness* in the *Critique* (see *CDR* 1:227 n). The progressive-

regressive method, of course, is an amalgam, if not a synthesis, of dialectic and phenomenology.

48. I say "beings who" because of Sartre's adoption of the Heideggerian term *Jemeinichkeit,* rendered *moïté* or "myness," into our fundamental relation to the world. There is no reason to believe he abandoned this "prepersonal" aspect of our relationship when his attention shifted from consciousness to praxis. In fact, his long analysis of Flaubert's "spirals of personalization" in *The Family Idiot* confirms this view.

49. "If each human being is a risk, humanity as a whole is a risk. The risk of no longer existing, the risk of indefinitely stagnating in one aspect of its history" (*NE* 467). Authentic history will acknowledge this truth. Indeed, "authenticity lies on the side of the risk" (*NE* 294).

50. For a fine defense of the moral significance of Sartrean authenticity, see Ronald E. Santoni, *Bad Faith, Good Faith, and Authenticity in Sartre's Early Philosophy* (Philadelphia: Temple University Press, 1995), 89–109.

51. See Klaus Hartmann, *Sartres Sozialphilosophie,* 1:93. He concludes: "Thus scarcity appears along with praxis and reciprocity as a genuine principle of understanding [in the *Critique*]" (1:91). But he acknowledges the problematic nature of such a "principle" that remains "suspended between *historical fact* and *anthropological-foundational fact*" (1:93). Hartmann's larger thesis is that both Marx and Sartre are committing a "transcendental fallacy, namely, that of mistaking abstractions of dialectical principiation for existent determinants" (see *PS* 651).

52. He adds that "organic functioning, need and praxis are strictly linked in a dialectical manner; dialectical time came into being, in fact, with the organism; for the living being can survive only by renewing itself. . . . The cyclical process—which characterizes both biological time and that of primitive societies—is interrupted *externally* by the environment, simply because the contingent and inescapable fact of scarcity disrupts exchanges. . . . The only real difference between primitive synthetic temporality and the time of elementary praxis lies in the material environment which, by not containing what the organism needs, transforms the totality as future reality into *possibility*" (*CDR* 1:82–83).

53. "Thus, in so far as body is function, function is need and need praxis, one can say that *human labor,* the original praxis by which man produces and reproduces his life, is *entirely* dialectical: its possibility and its permanent necessity rest upon the relation of interiority which unites the organism with the environment and upon the deep contradiction between the inorganic and organic orders, both of which are present in everyone" (*CDR* 1:90).

But Sartre warns us: "I do not claim to have revealed the historically primary moment of the dialectic: I have merely tried to show that our most everyday experience, which is surely labor, considered at the most abstract level, that is as the action of an isolated individual, immediately reveals the dialectical character of action" (*CDR* 1:91). So part of the ambiguity that has plagued his social thought is attributable to the fact that there are several dialectics operative in the *Critique,* one of which is that of the "abstract" and the "concrete" in the Hegelian sense of less and more fully "determined."

54. "There is no question of denying the fundamental priority of need; on the con-

trary, we mention it last to indicate that it sums up in itself all the existential structures. In its full development, need is a transcendence and a negativity (negation of negation inasmuch as it is produced as a lack seeking to be denied), hence a *surpassing-toward* (a rudimentary pro-ject)" (*SM* 171 n).

As in the previous note, what might seem like dialectical equivalency (in this case, of need and praxis) could more plausibly be seen as another example of Sartrean loose usage—the kind of thing that gives "dialectic" a bad name.

55. When asked toward the end of his life whether need could be related to scarcity as the natural to the social, Sartre replied; "Need is natural, but that does not mean that the object of our desire is there. Scarcity is social to the extent that the desired object is scarce for a given society. But strictly speaking, scarcity is not social. Society comes after scarcity. The latter is an original phenomenon of the relation between man and Nature. Nature does not sufficiently contain the objects that man demands in order that man's life should not include either work, which is struggle against scarcity, or combat" (*PS* 32).

56. Nor is Sartre's "utopian" vision conceived as immediately attainable. Late in his life, in answer to the question whether he saw a possible end to scarcity, he remarked: "Not at the moment." When then asked about the "socialism" he had been speaking about earlier, he responded: "It would not lead to the disappearance of scarcity. However, it is obvious that at that point ways of dealing with scarcity would be sought and found" (*PS* 32).

57. For an excellent study of the *Critique* as a transformation of radical evil from the human agent (in *BN* and *No Exit*, e.g.) to matter, specifically, to material scarcity, see Dina Dreyfus, "Jean-Paul Sartre et le mal radical," *Mercure de France* 341 (January 1961): 154–67. For a curious but telling discussion between Sartre and Pierre Verstraeten concerning freedom, contingency, and "grace," see the interview, "I Am No Longer a Realist," in *Sartre Alive*, ed. Aronson and van den Hoven, esp. 84–91.

CHAPTER TEN

1. Foucault, interview with C. Bonnefoy, 1966 (*DE* 1:541–41).

2. Richard Rorty, *Philosophy and the Mirror of Nature* (Princeton, NJ: Princeton University Press, 1979), 371.

3. "Do not ask me who I am and do not ask me to remain the same: leave it to our bureaucrats and our police to see that our papers are in order" (*AK* 17).

4. On our historicity and "the radical dispersion [in us] that provides a foundation for all other histories," see Michel Foucault, *The Order of Things* (New York: Random House Vintage Books, 1970), 370; hereafter cited as *OT*. This is a translation of *Les Mots et les choses* (Paris: Gallimard, 1966). Although the flux of change and temporality has grounded the dispersion of identities in Western thought at least since Heraclitus, Heidegger, inspired by Kierkegaard, ascribed a *unifying* function to what he called "ekstatic temporality" that Sartre assumed under the rubric of fundamental "project." In partial response to this "existentialist" move, the dispersive function is being reintroduced by Foucault's "spatializing" thought. Of course, none of these philosophers denies the dispersive power of time *sans phrase*.

5. For a defense of the claim that "postmodernism is a radicalization of historism," see *HT* 223 ff.

6. See chap. 8 n. 23. He raises the generational issue a fourth time in his unpublished *Rome Lecture Notes*.

7. See "The Literary Situation of the Postromantic Apprentice Author," *FI* 5:57–410.

8. This fact comes home in many of his interviews toward the end of his life.

9. "What Foucault offers us is . . . [not an archaeology but] a geology: the series of successive levels that form our 'ground.' . . . But Foucault doesn't tell us what would be the most interesting, namely, how each thought is constructed from these conditions or how men move from one thought to another. For that he would have to allow praxis and thus history to intervene, and that's precisely what he refuses to do. To be sure, his perspective remains historical. He distinguishes epochs, a before and an after. But he replaces the movie with the magic lantern, movement with a succession of immobilities." "Jean-Paul Sartre répond," *L'Arc* 30 (1966):87.

Once, when asked to define structuralism, Foucault answered coolly: "You must ask Sartre who the structuralists are, since he thinks that Lévi-Strauss, Althusser, Dumézil, Lacan and me constitute a coherent group, a group constituting some kind of unity that we ourselves don't perceive" ("Foucault Responds to Sartre," in *Foucault Live (Interviews, 1966–84),* trans. John Johnston, ed. Sylvère Lotringer [New York: Semiotext(e), 1989], 39; hereafter cited as *FL*).

10. "Sartre répond," 94.

11. Ibid., 87–88.

12. Ibid., 95.

13. Sylvie Le Bon, "Un Positivist désespéré: Michel Foucault," *Les Temps modernes,* no. 248 (January 1967):1304.

14. Ibid., 1302.

15. Ibid., 1314–15.

16. Ibid., 1316–18.

17. Michel Amiot, "Le Relativisme culturaliste de Michel Foucault," *Les Temps modernes,* no. 248 (January 1967): 1291.

18. Compare *OT* 168 (there is only one episteme per period) with *AK* 159 where he claims that historical disciplines and textual criticism, e.g., presume a quite different system of relations from those of general grammar, analysis of wealth, and natural history, with overlap of their interdiscursive networks only at certain points. In his foreword to the English edition of *OT,* Foucault insists that he is presenting a "strictly regional study" (x).

19. Amiot, *"Le Relativisme,"* 1297–98.

20. Daniel Defert, "Lettre à Claude Lanzmann," in the two-volume, triple issue of *Les Temps modernes* 531–33 (October–December 1990), 2:1201. In fact, after working together on behalf of several political causes, Foucault admitted: "My generation is getting close to Sartre" (*DE* 2:301). And when asked whether his criticism of the "universal intellectual" [the bourgeois thinker who tells workers what is good for them] was directed at Sartre, he responded: "It was not my intention to criticize Sartre. It was rather Zola who is the typical case. He did not write *Germinal* as a miner" (*DE* 3:531). But one

doubts whether Zola was in people's minds when they read Foucault's original remarks, or that Foucault could have believed he would be. (For the record, Foucault did walk in Sartre's immense funeral cortege.)

21. In a victory of the practical over the theoretical, however, Sartre and Foucault came to appreciate and respect each other's political commitments.

22. Aside from his book-length studies, all references to Foucault will be taken from what is doubtless now the definitive source, the four-volume collection *Dits et écrits* (*DE*; see introduction, n. 3). For the English translation by Forest Williams of Foucault's introduction, see Michel Foucault and Ludwig Binswanger, "Dream, Imagination, and Existence," *Review of Existential Psychology and Psychiatry* 19, no. 1 (1984–85): 29–78, hereafter cited as "*D.*"

23. For a similar claim, see his subsequent interview with J.-P. Elkabbach, "Foucault répond à Sartre," *La Quinzaine littéraire* 46 (1–15 March 1968): 20–22, English trans. in *FL* 35–43.

24. See *DE* 3:430; English trans. by Carolyn Fawcett, *On the Normal and the Pathological* (Boston: D. Reidel, 1978), ix–xx. In a slightly modified later version of the same essay, Foucault adds Alexandre Koyré to the formalist side and admits that an analogous opposition could be traced to nineteenth-century thought (see *DE* 4:763).

25. Actually, Foucault's remark was: "If, by substituting the analysis of rarity for the search for totalities, the description of relations of exteriority for the theme of the transcendental foundation, the analysis of accumulations for the quest of the origin, one is a positivist, then I am quite happy to be one" (*AK* 125), an obvious illusion to Sylvie Le Bon's characterization of him in *Les Temps modernes* as "un positiviste désespéré."

26. Søren Kierkegaard, *Journals,* ed. Alexander Dru (New York: Harper Torchbooks, 1958), entry for 17 May 1843.

27. Veyne, *Writing History,* 284–86.

28. For a direct critique of the primacy accorded the subject in philosophy from Descartes to Sartre, see Foucault's interview with Moriaki Watanabe, "La scène de la philosophie" (*DE* 3:571–95, esp. 590).

29. Using the term "articulation" to denote the relation between the discursive and the nondiscursive, Foucault explains: "The archaeological description of discourses is deployed in the dimension of a general history; it seeks to discover that whole domain of institutions, economic processes, and social relations on which a discursive formation can be articulated; it tries to show how the autonomy of discourse and its specificity nevertheless do not give it the status of pure ideality and total historical independence; what it wishes to uncover is the particular level in which history can give place to definite types of discourse, which have their own type of historicity, and which are related to a whole set of various historicities" (*AK* 164–65; see 9–10).

30. Sartre admits that "reciprocity of symbolism" between a person and his era is often possible. But, he cautions, "whatever the life and era under consideration, this reciprocity is valid only as a *rhetorical* illustration of the macrocosm by the microcosm (and vice versa) . . . *unless* history were *in fact condensed* in the era's *abridgment,* which a singular biography claims to be. . . . I am prepared to say that the life of Leconte de Lisle *rhetorically* symbolizes the history of French society, from the Three Glorious Days to

the coup d'état, and that it really does express the historical moment that is made manifest by the events of the February days, the June days, and then 2 December 1852." Sartre offers a semiotic rationale for this reciprocal symbolization: Leconte de Lisle is "*on every level* (infrastructures, mores, dietary regimen, fashions in clothing, etc.) a *signified-signifier*" (*FI* 5:398–99).

But Sartre insists that such "synchronous symbolization . . . is *real* but superficial and in a way *false* (in the sense that Spinoza defines the false idea as an idea that is true but incomplete) because, considering it in itself and without another temporal determination, it does not seem *evolved*." But if what he calls Flaubert's "*expressive* bond" to this same history "is *real* in its diachronic form, it must be understood that the collective past and that of Flaubert the individual are indistinguishable and that an identical future grasped as an inevitable destiny illuminates an identical present on the basis of an identical *original* curse" (*FI* 5:400). Leconte comes on the scene too late for his pessimism to be anything but expressive of the times; in no way could it be taken as "prophetic" in Sartre's use of that term.

So though Sartre does apply the terms "expression" and "symbolization" to the prophetic event, he is usually careful to distinguish this "diachronic" use from the synchronic one that is semiotic and merely rhetorical. He argues that "the *real* incarnation of the macrocosm in a microcosm is based not on the fact that both are finite (which would be a fortuitous coincidence) but on the rigorous dialectical conditioning of the two finitudes *by each other* across the medium of the practico-inert" (*FI* 1:401).

31. Foucault, *Birth of the Clinic,* 134.

32. Michel Foucault, *Discipline and Punish: The Birth of the Prison,* trans. Alan Sheridan (New York: Pantheon Books, 1977), 31.

33. "The rose is without why; it blooms because it blooms / It cares not for itself; asks not if it's seen" (Angelus Silesius, cited by John D. Caputo, *The Mystical Element in Heidegger's Thought* [Athens: Ohio University Press, 1978], 9).

34. "It is obvious that the archive of a society, a culture, or a civilization cannot be described exhaustively; or even, no doubt, the archive of a whole period. On the other hand, it is not possible for us to describe our own archive, since it is from within these rules that we speak, since it is that which gives to what we can say—and to itself, the object of our discourse—its modes of appearance, its forms of existence and coexistence, its system of accumulation, historicity, and disappearance" (*AK* 130).

35. See Axel Honneth, *The Critique of Power: Reflective Stages in a Critical Social Theory,* trans. Kenneth Baynes (Cambridge: MIT Press, 1991), 146. This accords with Foucault's occasional reference to the success of "linguistics, logic and ethnology" in uncovering the *structural unconscious* of our culture (e.g., *FL* 80).

36. "It is no longer possible to think in our day other than in the void left by man's disappearance. For this void does not create a deficiency; it does not constitute a lacuna that must be filled. It is nothing more, and nothing less, than the unfolding of a space in which it is once more possible to think" (*OT* 342).

37. Sartre characteristically links "finite history" with the realization of personal mortality *in the context* of one's situatedness between previous and subsequent generations:

The cyclical structure of history ("man is the son of man") makes comprehensible its continuity and the discontinuity of the sequences it totalizes; and as that structure is tied to birth and death, it is clear that the relative finitude of historical series is based on the absolute finitude of historical agents. Conversely, the finitude and singularity of an *epoch* (that is the name I give to any historical temporalization to the extent that it produces its own boundaries) rebound in turn on the agent, who is defined *not only* by general characteristics (the mode of production, relations of production, class, groups and subgroups, etc.) but also in his singularity as a certain moment of a greater but singular temporalization. Thus the diachronic finitude of an individual is particularized by the finitude of the social projects that include him and—by enlarging to constrict the field of his possibilities, therefore his options—give him his destiny as *finite* man with his particular alienations. In this sense, a life like Gustave's and an epoch like the reign of Louis-Philippe can enter into reciprocal rapport on a *real* foundation; it is enough that they are conditioned by the same factors, and that these factors totalize them and are retotalized by them in such a way that they present the *same curve*, the same profile of temporalization. Both must also, of course, be oriented toward the same goal on the basis of the same "prior circumstances," the same obstacles, the same intentions. (*FI* 5:406–407)

38. Address to meeting of the Sartre Society of North America, DePaul University, Chicago, 8 October 1994. See Fredric Jameson, *Postmodernism, or The Cultural Logic of Late Capitalism* (Durham, NC: Duke University Press, 1990).

39. "Death never appears as such; it is strictly *unpresentable*—it is the unpresentable itself, if that expression can have any meaning: *The death drive works in silence; the whole commotion of life emanates from Eros*" (Philippe Lacoue-Labarthe, *The Subject of Philosophy*, trans. Thomas Trezise et al. [Minneapolis: University of Minnesota Press, 1993], 112; emphasis his).

40. When asked late in life whether he thought syntheses exist, Sartre replied: "Yes, partial syntheses, in any case. I demonstrated that in the *Critique*." And when pressed whether he would then reject an absolute synthesis, he reaffirmed his established position:

Absolute, yes. But a synthesis of an historical period, for example, no. Our time is its own synthesis with itself. That is what I would have explained in the second volume of the *Critique*. Certainly one must go beyond the type of synthesis that was available to me in the first volume in order to arrive at syntheses touching oneself and others. For example, we can, at every moment, each one of us, make syntheses. . . . But these syntheses are not at all on the same level as the synthesis of the whole, and one person alone can never accomplish that. . . . Only individuals can take several individuals to make a group but not the totality since they would have to place themselves within it. It is necessary to look for another way of conceiving these latter syntheses. This is what I tried to do when I was working on the second volume of the *Critique*, but it was not finished. (*PS* 19)

41. As David Hoy has remarked, "Foucault resists this totalizing or, as he sometimes says, 'totalitarian' thinking" (David Couzens Hoy, "Power, Repression, Progress," in *Foucault: A Critical Reader*, ed. David Cozens Hoy [Oxford: Basil Blackwell, 1986],

142). For an example of his critique of "totalitarian theories" such as Marxism and psychoanalysis, see Foucault, *Power/Knowledge,* 80–81.

Fredric Jameson reaches the heart of the matter when he observes: "The deeper political motivation of the 'war on totality' lies . . . in a fear of Utopia that turns out to be none other than our old friend *1984,* such that a Utopian and revolutionary politics, correctly associated with totalization and a certain 'concept' of totality, is to be eschewed because it leads fatally to the Terror: a notion at least as old as Edmund Burke" (*Postmodernism,* 401).

42. Manfred Frank has a Sartrean ideal in mind, among other things, when he contrasts the Habermasian consensus model of social interaction with a more "organic" model that respects individuals in their individuality. He contends that "a universal consensus tends to subsume its participants as particular elements and to treat them as indistinguishable." Such "interchangeability" is the mark of social alienation in the *Critique.* Distinguishing the particular from the individual, Frank favors a society "as a community of free and single individuals (*singuliers*), whose communicative acts would bear the *telos* of mutual understanding and agreement, but without this *telos* forcing them into a general conformism." Though he doesn't use the expression, "dialectical nominalism" would aptly capture this ideal (Manfred Frank, "Two Centuries of Philosophical Critique of Reason," in *Reason and Its Other: Rationality in Modern German Philosophy and Culture,* ed. Dieter Freundlieb and Wayne Hudson [Providence, RI: Berg Publishers, 1993], 82, 84).

43. See "LW" 414–15, 422. In his interview for the Schilpp volume of essays on his thought, Sartre's optimism regarding the overcoming of material scarcity and hence of violence was even more guarded. He acknowledges that "[socialism] would not lead to the disappearance of scarcity. However, it is obvious that at that point ways of dealing with scarcity would be sought and found" (*PS* 32).

44. See Foucault's "Afterword (1983)" in *Beyond Structuralism and Hermeneutics,* ed. Dreyfus and Rabinow, 237.

Conclusion to Volume One

1. "Sartre scarcely read Marx in his youth; his basic thought, the radical heterogeneity of the in-itself and the for-itself, was formed very early, upon reading Nietzsche or as a spontaneous expression of his personality" (Aron, *History and the Dialectic of Violence,* 150).

2. See *The Writings of Jean-Paul Sartre,* ed. Contat and Rybalka, vol. 2, *Selected Prose,* 37–52.

3. Jean-Paul Sartre, *Nausea,* trans. Lloyd Alexander (New York: New Directions, 1964), 77, 131–33.

4. Jean François Lyotard, "The Sign of History," trans. Geoff Bennington in *Post-Structuralism and the Question of History,* ed. Attridge et al., 178.

5. Michel Foucault, "Space, Knowledge, and Power," in *The Foucault Reader,* ed. Paul Rabinow (New York: Pantheon Books, 1984), 249.

6. See my "Foucault as Parrhesiast: His Last Course at the Collège de France (1984)," in *The Final Foucault,* ed. James Bernauer and David Rasmussen (Cambridge: MIT Press, 1988), 102–18.

Index